Wordpress Web Application Development

Third Edition

Build rapid web applications with cutting-edge technologies using WordPress

Rakhitha Nimesh Ratnayake

BIRMINGHAM - MUMBAI

Wordpress Web Application Development

Third Edition

First published: November 2013

Second edition: May 2015

Third edition: May 2017

Production reference: 1260517

Published by Packt Publishing Ltd.
Livery Place
35 Livery Street
Birmingham
B3 2PB, UK.

ISBN 978-1-78712-680-0

www.packtpub.com

Credits

Author
Rakhitha Nimesh Ratnayake

Reviewer
Alex Bachuk

Commissioning Editor
Smeet Thakkar

Acquisition Editor
Reshma Raman

Content Development Editor
Sreeja Nair

Technical Editor
Rutuja Vaze

Copy Editor
Safis Editing

Project Coordinator
Sheejal Shah

Proofreader
Safis Editing

Indexer
Francy Puthiry

Graphics
Jason Monteiro

Production Coordinator
Shraddha Falebhai

About the Author

Rakhitha Nimesh Ratnayake is a freelance web developer, writer, and open source enthusiast. He has over 7 years of experience in developing WordPress applications and plugins. He develops premium WordPress plugins for individual clients and the CodeCanyon marketplace. User Profiles Made Easy and WP Private Content Plus are the most popular plugins developed by him. Rakhitha is the creator of, where he shares his latest WordPress plugins. He is also a regular contributor to a number of popular websites, such as 1st webdesigner, the Tuts+ network, and the SitePoint network. *Building Impressive Presentations with impress.js* was his first book, which was published by Packt Publishing. He is also the author of the first and second editions of *WordPress Web Application Development*. In his spare time, he likes to watch cricket and spend time with his family.

I would like to thank my loving wife, Dulari, my parents, and my wife's parents for the help and encouragement provided throughout this book.

I would also like to thank Packt Publishing, especially Senior Acquisition Editor, Reshma Raman, for inviting me to write this book, Content Development Editor, Sreeja Nair, and the reviewers for providing honest feedback to improve this book.

Finally, I would like to thank you for reading my book and being one of the most important people who helped me make this book a success.

About the Reviewer

Alex Bachuk is a web developer with over 9 years of experience, especially in custom JavaScript and WordPress web applications. Alex has been working with WordPress since Version 2.5 and has worked on projects ranging from a single-page website to interactive web applications and social platforms.

These days, Alex mostly works on Node.js and React.js applications. He is the founder of the `EcmaStack.com` agency and founder of a timesheet and invoicing application, `www.timebooklet.com`.

Alex organizes and talks at WordPress, Meteor.js, and GraphQL meetups in New York City. In his free time, he likes to spend time with his family and travel the world.

www.PacktPub.com

For support files and downloads related to your book, please visit www.PacktPub.com.

Did you know that Packt offers eBook versions of every book published, with PDF and ePub files available? You can upgrade to the eBook version at www.PacktPub.com and as a print book customer, you are entitled to a discount on the eBook copy. Get in touch with us at service@packtpub.com for more details.

At www.PacktPub.com, you can also read a collection of free technical articles, sign up for a range of free newsletters and receive exclusive discounts and offers on Packt books and eBooks.

https://www.packtpub.com/mapt

Get the most in-demand software skills with Mapt. Mapt gives you full access to all Packt books and video courses, as well as industry-leading tools to help you plan your personal development and advance your career.

Why subscribe?

- Fully searchable across every book published by Packt
- Copy and paste, print, and bookmark content
- On demand and accessible via a web browser

Customer Feedback

Thanks for purchasing this Packt book. At Packt, quality is at the heart of our editorial process. To help us improve, please leave us an honest review on this book's Amazon page at https://www.amazon.com/dp/1787283739.

If you'd like to join our team of regular reviewers, you can e-mail us at customerreviews@packtpub.com. We award our regular reviewers with free eBooks

Table of Contents

Preface   1

Chapter 1: WordPress as a Web Application Framework   9

  WordPress as a CMS   10

  WordPress as a web application framework   11

    The MVC versus event-driven architecture   11

  Simplifying development with built-in features   12

    User management   12

    Media management   13

    Template management   13

    Database management   13

    Routing   13

    XML-RPC API   13

    REST API   14

    Caching   14

    Scheduling   14

    Plugins and widgets   15

    Themes   15

    Actions and filters   15

    The admin dashboard   15

  Identifying the components of WordPress   16

    The role of WordPress themes   16

    Structure of a WordPress page layout   17

    Customizing the application layout   17

    The role of the admin dashboard   18

      The admin dashboard   18

      Posts and pages   18

      Users   18

      Appearance   19

      Settings   19

    The role of plugins   19

    The role of widgets   19

  A development plan for the forum management application   22

    Application goals and target audience   22

    Planning the application   23

    User roles of the application   23

Planning application features and functions	24
Understanding limitations and sticking to guidelines	25
Building a question-answer interface	27
Prerequisites for building a question-answer interface	27
Creating questions	28
Customizing the comments template	33
Changing the status of answers	35
Saving the status of answers	39
Generating a question list	42
Enhancing features of the questions plugin	45
Customizing the design of questions	45
Categorizing questions	46
Approving and rejecting questions	46
Adding star rating to answers	46
Summary	47
Chapter 2: Implementing Membership Roles, Permissions, and Features	49
Introduction to user management	50
Preparing the plugin	50
Getting started with user roles	53
Creating application user roles	53
The best action for adding user roles	54
Knowing the default roles of WordPress	56
Choosing between default and custom roles	57
Scenario 1	57
Scenario 2	57
Removing existing user roles	58
Understanding user capabilities	58
Creating your first capability	59
Understanding default capabilities	59
Registering application users	61
Implementing frontend registration	61
Shortcode implementation	62
Pros and cons of using shortcodes	62
Page template implementation	63
Pros and cons of page templates	63
Custom template implementation	64
Building a simple router for a user module	64
Creating the routing rules	64
Adding query variables	65
Flushing the rewriting rules	66

Controlling access to your functions 68
The advantages of using the do_action function 69
Creating custom templates 71
Designing the registration form 71
Planning the registration process 73
Handling registration form submission 74
Exploring the registration success path 78
Automatically logging in the user after registration 81
Activating system users 82
Creating a login form in the frontend 83
Handling login form submission 86
Checking whether we implemented the process properly 88
Essential user management features for web applications 89
Frontend login and registration 90
Custom profile fields 90
Private data 90
Search and member list 91
Frontend profile 91
Implementing user management features with popular plugins 92
BuddyPress 92
User Profiles Made Easy 94
User Role Editor 96
Time to practice 96
Summary 97
Chapter 3: Planning and Customizing the Core Database 99
Understanding the WordPress database 100
Exploring the role of existing tables 100
User-related tables 101
Post-related tables 101
Term-related tables 103
Other tables 104
Adapting existing tables in web applications 105
User-related tables 106
Post-related tables 106
Scenario 1 – an online shopping cart 106
Scenario 2 – a hotel reservation system 107
Scenario 3 – a project management application 107
Term-related tables 108
Other tables 108
Extending the database with custom tables 109

Planning the forum application tables	110
Types of table in web applications	110
Creating custom tables	111
Querying the database	113
Querying the existing tables	114
Inserting records	114
Updating records	114
Deleting records	115
Selecting records	115
Querying the custom tables	115
Working with posts	116
Extending the WP_Query class for applications	117
Introduction to WordPress query classes	118
The WP_User_Query class	118
The WP_Comment_Query class	119
Other query classes	120
Limitations and considerations	120
Transaction support	120
Post revisions	121
How do you know whether to enable or disable revisions?	121
Autosaving	122
Using meta tables	122
Summary	123
Chapter 4: Building Blocks of Web Applications	125
Introduction to custom content types	126
The role of custom post types in web applications	126
Planning custom post types for an application	126
Forums	127
Topics	128
Implementing custom post types for a forum application	129
Implementing the custom post type settings	131
Creating forum and topic classes	131
Assigning permissions to forums and topics	137
Creating custom taxonomies for topic categories and topic tags	138
Assigning permissions to the topic tags	142
Introduction to custom fields with meta boxes	144
What is a template engine?	147
Building a simple custom template loader	148
Creating your first template	150
Comparing the template loader and template engine	153
Persisting custom field data	153

Customizing custom post type messages	158
Introduction to post type templates	161
Creating and using a post type template	161
Introducing custom post type relationships	163
Pods framework for custom content types	166
Should you choose Pods for web development?	170
Implementing custom post type features with popular plugins	172
Custom Post Type UI	172
Toolset Types	172
Time to practice	173
Summary	174
Chapter 5: Implementing Application Content Restrictions	175
Introduction to content restrictions	176
Practical usage of content restrictions	176
The role of membership in content restrictions	177
Understanding restriction levels	178
User roles-based restrictions	178
User groups-based restrictions	178
Membership plans-based restrictions	179
Unique password-based restrictions	179
Implementing content restrictions in posts/pages	180
Shortcode-based restrictions	180
Individual post/page restrictions	183
Creating a meta box for topic restrictions	184
Saving topic restriction settings	186
Verifying individual post/page restrictions	188
Site lockdown	190
Enabling restrictions on WordPress core features	193
Restrictions on posts	193
Restrictions on searches	193
Restrictions on menus	194
Restrictions on widgets	195
Restrictions on archives	195
Supplementary content restriction types and techniques	196
Restrictions on custom generated content	197
Attachment protection	197
Social Locker	198
E-mail subscription	198
Private page	199

Useful plugins for content restrictions	199
Restrict Content	199
WP Private Content Plus	200
Membership 2	200
Time to practice	201
Summary	201
Chapter 6: Developing Pluggable Modules	**203**
A brief introduction to WordPress plugins	204
Understanding the WordPress plugin architecture	204
WordPress plugins for web development	205
Creating reusable libraries with plugins	206
Planning the template loader plugin	206
Using the template loader plugin	208
Handling plugin dependencies	210
Extensible plugins	213
Extending plugins with WordPress core actions and filters	213
Creating the extensible file uploader plugin	214
Converting file fields with jQuery	216
Integrating the media uploader to buttons	218
Extending the file uploader plugin	220
Customizing the allowed file types	220
Saving and loading topic files	223
Extending plugins with custom actions and filters	224
Pluggable plugins	227
Tips for using pluggable functions	231
Tips for developing extendable plugins	232
Time to practice	232
Summary	233
Chapter 7: Customizing the Dashboard for Powerful Backends	**235**
Understanding the admin dashboard	235
Customizing the admin toolbar	236
Removing the admin toolbar	237
Managing the admin toolbar items	238
Customizing the main navigation menu	241
Creating new menu items	243
Adding features with custom pages	243
Building options pages	244
Creating a custom layout for options pages	245
Building an application options panel	247
Using the WordPress options API	250
Using feature-packed admin list tables	252

Working with default admin list tables	253
The post list	253
Creating custom actions for custom posts	254
Creating custom filters for custom post types	255
Creating custom post status links	257
Displaying custom list columns	259
The user list	260
The comments list	261
Building extended lists	262
Using the admin list table for forum topics	263
Step 1 – defining the custom class	263
Step 2 – defining the instance variables	263
Step 3 – creating the initial configurations	264
Step 4 – implementing the custom column handlers	264
Step 5 – implementing the column default handlers	265
Step 6 – displaying the checkbox for records	265
Step 7 – listing the available custom columns	266
Step 8 – defining the sortable columns of list	266
Step 9 – creating a list of bulk actions	267
Step 10 – retrieving the list data	267
Step 11 – adding a custom list as a menu page	268
Step 12 – displaying the generated list	268
Managing the subscribe and unsubcribe status	271
Adding content restrictions to admin list tables	272
An awesome visual presentation for admin screens	273
Using existing themes	273
Using plugin-based third-party admin themes	274
Creating your own admin theme	276
The responsive nature of the admin dashboard	279
Supplementary admin dashboard features	280
Dashboard widgets	280
Screen options menu	281
Help menu	281
User language control	282
Time for action	283
Summary	284
Chapter 8: Adjusting Theme for Amazing Frontends	285
An introduction to the WordPress application frontend	286
A basic file structure of the WordPress theme	286
Understanding the template execution hierarchy	287
The template execution process of web application frameworks	290
Web application layout creation techniques	291

Shortcodes and page templates	291
Custom templates with custom routing	292
Using pure PHP templates	292
The WordPress way of using templates	293
Direct template inclusion	293
Theme versus plugin-based templates	294
Are you planning to create an application-specific theme?	295
Building the forum application home page	295
Building the forum list using shortcode	296
Widgetizing home page	298
What is a widget?	298
Widgetizing application layouts	299
Creating widgets	301
Designing a home page template	306
Generating the application frontend menu	309
Creating a navigation menu	309
Saving menu item restrictions	313
Displaying user-specific menus on the frontend	314
Managing options and widgets with customizer	316
Adding custom options to the theme customizer	317
Handling widgets in the theme customizer	319
Creating pluggable templates	321
Extending the home page template with action hooks	322
Customizing widgets to enable extendable locations	322
Planning action hooks for layouts	325
Managing custom CSS with live preview	327
Responsive previews in theme customizer	328
Time for action	330
Summary	330
Chapter 9: Enhancing the Power of Open Source Libraries and Plugins	331
Why choose open source libraries?	332
Open source libraries inside the WordPress core	332
Open source JavaScript libraries in the WordPress core	333
What is Backbone.js?	334
Understanding the importance of code structuring	335
Integrating Backbone.js and Underscore.js	336
Creating a forum user profile page with Backbone.js	337
Structuring with Backbone.js and Underscore.js	341
Displaying the topics list on page load	343
Creating new topics from the frontend	347
Integrating events to Backbone.js views	349

Validating and creating new models for the server	350
Creating new models in the server	351
Using PHPMailer for custom e-mail sending	354
Usage of PHPMailer within the WordPress core	355
Creating a custom version of a pluggable wp_mail function	355
Loading PHPMailer inside plugins and creating custom functions	355
Implementing user authentication with OpenAuth	359
Configuring login strategies	361
Implementing LinkedIn account authentication	363
Verifying a LinkedIn account and generating a response	364
Building a LinkedIn app	366
The process of requesting the strategies	369
Initializing the library	369
Authenticating users to our application	371
Using third-party libraries and plugins	376
Using open source plugins for web development	376
Using plugins for checking security of other plugins	377
Time for action	377
Summary	378
Chapter 10: Listening to Third-Party Applications	381
Introduction to APIs	382
The advantages of having an API	382
The WordPress XML-RPC API for web applications	383
Building the API client	384
Creating a custom API	388
Integrating API user authentication	390
Integrating API access tokens	392
Providing the API documentation	398
WordPress REST API for web applications	399
Introduction to WordPress REST API endpoints	400
Testing GET requests	402
Testing POST requests	402
Disabling REST API	404
Custom content types with REST API	404
Managing custom routes and endpoints	406
Creating custom routes and endpoints for forum topics	407
Creating custom routes and endpoints for custom table data	408
Building the REST API client	411
REST API client in the same site	411
REST API client from external site	414
REST API authentication and access tokens	415

Time for action	418
Summary	418

Chapter 11: Integrating and Finalizing the Forum Management Application — 419

Integrating and structuring the forum application	420
Integrating the template loader into a user manager	420
Working with the restructured application	421
Building the forum page	421
Displaying forum details	424
Creating new forum topics	426
Displaying forum topics	428
Joining users to forums	432
Restricting topic creation to forum members	437
Building forum topic page	437
Creating forum topic replies	438
Handling forum topic replies	439
Understanding other forum features	441
Updating a user profile with additional fields	442
Updating the values of the profile fields	444
Scheduling subscriber notifications	446
Notifying subscribers through e-mails	448
Time for action	451
Final thoughts	452
Summary	452

Chapter 12: Supplementary Modules for Web Development — 453

Internationalization	454
Introduction to WordPress translation support	454
The translation functions in WordPress	455
Creating plugin translations	455
Creating the POT file using Eazy Po	455
Creating and editing translations with PoEdit	458
Loading language files	460
Changing the WordPress language	460
Working with media grid and image editor	462
Introduction to the post editor	463
Using the WordPress editor	464
Keyboard shortcuts	465
Editor item locations	465
Highlighting broken links	465
Video embedding	466

Lesser-known WordPress features 466
  Caching 466
  Transients 468
  Testing 468
  Security 469
  Performance 470
    P3 - Plugin Performance Profiler plugin 472
    Query monitor plugin 473
    GTmetrix for WordPress 475
Managing application scripts and styles 477
  Conditionally loading script and styles 478
  Inline script loading 479
Version control 480
E-commerce 481
  Creating products with WooCommerce 483
Migrating WordPress applications 485
Importing and exporting application content 487
Introduction to multisite 487
Time for action 488
Summary 489
Chapter 13: Configurations, Tools, and Resources 491
Configuring and setting up WordPress 491
  Step 1– downloading WordPress 491
  Step 2 – creating the application folder 492
  Step 3 – configuring the application URL 492
    Creating a virtual host 492
    Using a localhost 493
  Step 4 – installing WordPress 493
  Step 5 – setting up permalinks 497
  Step 6 – downloading the Responsive theme 498
  Step 7– activating the Responsive theme 499
  Step 8 – activating the plugin 499
  Step 9 – using the application 499
Open source libraries and plugins 499
Online resources and tutorials 500
Index 501

Preface

The rise of WordPress-powered websites is one of the standout trends in the modern web development world. WordPress has taken over 25% of all the websites in the world. The power of the plugin-based architecture and the flexibility of the built-in features offered by WordPress has made developers use this framework for advanced web development. The official plugin directory contains over forty thousand plugins, covering most of the areas required in application development. Therefore, WordPress becomes one of the top solutions for rapid application development with existing plugins. This book will act as a comprehensive resource for building web applications with this amazing framework.

WordPress Web Application Development is a practical guide focused on incorporating and extending the core WordPress features into typical web application development. This book is structured toward building a complete web application from scratch. With this book, you will learn to use and extend WordPress core features to build a forum management application with the latest trending technologies.

This book follows a example-based approach while discussing each WordPress core modules, for pushing the limits of WordPress to create web applications beyond your imagination.

It begins by exploring the role of existing WordPress core features and discussing the reasons for choosing WordPress for web application development. As we move on, more focus will be put into adapting WordPress features into web applications with the help of an informal use-case-based model for discussing the most prominent built-in features. Along with core features, you will also learn the integration of new features into existing features through plugins. While striving for web development with WordPress, you will also learn about the integration of popular client-side technologies, such as Backbone.js, Underscore, jQuery, and server-side technologies and techniques such as template engines and OpenAuth integration.

After reading this book, you will possess the ability to develop powerful web applications rapidly within limited time frames with the crucial advantage of benefiting low-budget and time-critical projects.

What this book covers

Chapter 1, *WordPress As a Web Application Framework,* walks you through the existing modules and techniques to identify their usage in web applications. Identification of WordPress features beyond the conventional CMS and planning the forum management application are the highlights of this chapter.

Chapter 2, *Implementing Membership Roles, Permissions, and Features,* covers the built-in user management features and user permission concepts. Beginning the development of forum management application, implementing basic user management features such as login, registration and introduction to the MVC process through custom routing are the highlights of this chapter.

Chapter 3, *Planning and Customizing Core Database,* serves as an extensive guide for understanding the core database structure and the role of custom database tables in web applications. Database querying with built-in functions, creating custom tables, and identifying the limitations in core database tables are the highlights of this chapter.

Chapter 4, *Building Blocks of Web Applications,* explores the possibilities of using custom post types to extend WordPress posts beyond its conventional usage. Managing custom post types, loading custom templates and learn to speed up development process with existing custom post type plugins are the highlights of this chapter.

Chapter 5, *Implementing Application Content Restrictions,* focuses on identifying the different user types in applications and the possibilities of providing different content permissions based on those user types. Applying content restrictions to WordPress core features, implementing basic content restriction techniques, and innovating new content restriction strategies are the highlights of this chapter.

Chapter 6, *Developing Pluggable Modules,* introduces the techniques of creating highly reusable and extensible plugins to enhance the flexibility of web applications. Developing various flexible plugins, handling plugin dependencies, and the use of WordPress actions and filters in applications are the highlight of this chapter.

Chapter 7, *Customizing Dashboard for Powerful Backends,* walks you through the process of customizing the WordPress admin panel for adding new features as well as changing existing features and design. Building flexible data lists with WordPress admin tables, designing an admin panel with various different techniques, and understanding useful admin section settings are the highlights of this chapter.

Chapter 8, *Adjusting Theme for Amazing Frontends,* dives into the techniques of designing amazing layouts, thereby opening them for future extension. Widgetizing layouts and building reusable templates are the highlights of this chapter.

Chapter 9, *Enhancing the Power of Open Source Libraries and Plugins*, explores the use of the latest trending open source technologies and libraries within and outside WordPress core . Integrating open authentication in to your web application, structuring the application at the client side, and identify the proper usage of open source plugins in application development, are the highlights of this chapter.

Chapter 10, *Listening to Third-party Applications*, demonstrates how to use WordPress XML-RPC API and REST API to create custom API's for your web application. Building a simple XML-RPC API, identifying support for REST in WordPress core and building custom REST API's are highlights of this chapter.

Chapter 11, *Integrating and Finalizing Forum Management Application*, guides you through the integration of modules and adds new features to the existing modules, while refactoring the code developed throughout this book. Identifying the use of proper theme templates and completing the features developed throughout the previous chapters are the highlights of this chapter

Chapter 12, *Supplementary Modules for Web Development*, introduces the advanced application features such as E-commerce, multisite, and the non-functional WordPress features that defines the quality of a web applications. Introduction to important concepts in application development, such as internationalization, caching, security, performance, version control, site migration, and testing are the highlight of this chapter.

Appendix, *Configurations, Tools, and Resources*, provides an application setup guide with necessary links to download the plugins and libraries used throughout the book.

What you need for this book

Technically, you need a computer, browser, and an Internet connection with the following working environment:

- The Apache web server
- PHP Version 5.4 or higher
- WordPress Version 4.7.2
- MySQL Version 5.6 or higher

Once you have the preceding environment, you can download the Responsive theme from http://wordpress.org/themes/responsiveand activate it from the Themes section. Finally, you can activate the plugin developed for this book to get things started.

Refer to Appendix A, *Configurations, Tools, and Resources*, for the application setup guide, required software, and plugins.

Who this book is for

This book is intended for WordPress developers or designers, who know how to create a basic CMS site and looking for ways to learn the complex web application development in a reusable, maintainable, and modular way. Also, this book is quite useful for non-technical users who want to develop advanced applications by incorporating existing plugins. Basic knowledge of WordPress theme and plugin development is expected, although it's not a must for experienced PHP developers to go through this book.

Conventions

In this book, you will find a number of text styles that distinguish between different kinds of information. Here are some examples of these styles and an explanation of their meaning.

Code words in text, database table names, folder names, filenames, file extensions, pathnames, dummy URLs, user input, and Twitter handles are shown as follows: "We can set additional parameters to the search query using `$query->set` function and restrict the search features to limited posts."

A block of code is set as follows:

```
add_action('pre_get_posts', 'search_restrictions');
function search_restrictions($query) {
  if($query->is_search && $query->is_main_query() && !is_admin()){
   $search_blocked_ids = array('24','100');
   $search_allowed_types = array('wpwaf_topic','wpwaf_forum');
   $query->set('post__not_in', $search_blocked_ids );
   $query->set('post_type', $search_allowed_types );
  }
  return $query;
}
```

When we wish to draw your attention to a particular part of a code block, the relevant lines or items are set in bold:

```
add_action('pre_get_posts', 'search_restrictions');
function search_restrictions($query) {
  if($query->is_search && $query->is_main_query() && !is_admin()){
   $search_blocked_ids = array('24','100');
   $search_allowed_types = array('wpwaf_topic','wpwaf_forum');
   $query->set('post__not_in', $search_blocked_ids );
   $query->set('post_type', $search_allowed_types );
  }
  return $query;
}
```

Any command-line input or output is written as follows:

```
select option_value from wp_users where option_name='wp_user_roles'
```

New terms and **important words** are shown in bold. Words that you see on the screen, for example, in menus or dialog boxes, appear in the text like this: "Clicking the **Next** button moves you to the next screen."

Warnings or important notes appear in a box like this.

Tips and tricks appear like this.

Reader feedback

Feedback from our readers is always welcome. Let us know what you think about this book-what you liked or disliked. Reader feedback is important for us as it helps us develop titles that you will really get the most out of.

To send us general feedback, simply e-mail feedback@packtpub.com, and mention the book's title in the subject of your message.

If there is a topic that you have expertise in and you are interested in either writing or contributing to a book, see our author guide at www.packtpub.com/authors.

Customer support

Now that you are the proud owner of a Packt book, we have a number of things to help you to get the most from your purchase.

Downloading the example code

You can download the example code files for this book from your account at http://www.packtpub.com. If you purchased this book elsewhere, you can visit http://www.packtpub.com/support and register to have the files e-mailed directly to you.

You can download the code files by following these steps:

1. Log in or register to our website using your e-mail address and password.
2. Hover the mouse pointer on the **SUPPORT** tab at the top.
3. Click on **Code Downloads & Errata**.
4. Enter the name of the book in the **Search** box.
5. Select the book for which you're looking to download the code files.
6. Choose from the drop-down menu where you purchased this book from.
7. Click on **Code Download**.

Once the file is downloaded, please make sure that you unzip or extract the folder using the latest version of:

- WinRAR / 7-Zip for Windows
- Zipeg / iZip / UnRarX for Mac
- 7-Zip / PeaZip for Linux

The code bundle for the book is also hosted on GitHub at `https://github.com/PacktPubl ishing/Wordpress-Web-Application-Development-Third-Edition`. We also have other code bundles from our rich catalog of books and videos available at `https://github.com/P acktPublishing/`. Check them out!

Errata

Although we have taken every care to ensure the accuracy of our content, mistakes do happen. If you find a mistake in one of our books-maybe a mistake in the text or the code-we would be grateful if you could report this to us. By doing so, you can save other readers from frustration and help us improve subsequent versions of this book. If you find any errata, please report them by visiting `http://www.packtpub.com/submit-errata`, selecting your book, clicking on the **Errata Submission Form** link, and entering the details of your errata. Once your errata are verified, your submission will be accepted and the errata will be uploaded to our website or added to any list of existing errata under the Errata section of that title.

To view the previously submitted errata, go to `https://www.packtpub.com/books/conten t/support`and enter the name of the book in the search field. The required information will appear under the **Errata** section.

Piracy

Piracy of copyrighted material on the Internet is an ongoing problem across all media. At Packt, we take the protection of our copyright and licenses very seriously. If you come across any illegal copies of our works in any form on the Internet, please provide us with the location address or website name immediately so that we can pursue a remedy.

Please contact us at `copyright@packtpub.com` with a link to the suspected pirated material.

We appreciate your help in protecting our authors and our ability to bring you valuable content.

Questions

If you have a problem with any aspect of this book, you can contact us at `questions@packtpub.com`, and we will do our best to address the problem.

1
WordPress as a Web Application Framework

In recent years, WordPress has matured from the most popular blogging platform to the most popular content management system. Thousands of developers around the world are making a living from WordPress design and development. As more and more people are interested in using WordPress, the dream of using this amazing framework for web application development is becoming possible.

The future seems bright as WordPress has already got dozens of built-in features, which can be easily adapted to web application development using slight modifications. Since you are already reading this book, you have to be someone who is really excited to see how WordPress fits into web application development. Throughout this book, we will learn how we can inject the best practices of web development into the WordPress framework to build web applications using a rapid process.

Basically, this book will be important for developers from two different perspectives. On the one hand, beginner to intermediate level WordPress developers can get knowledge of cutting-edge web development technologies and techniques to build complex applications. On the other hand, web development experts who are already familiar with popular PHP frameworks can learn WordPress for rapid application development. So, let's get started!

In this chapter, we will cover the following topics:

- WordPress as a CMS
- WordPress as a web application framework
- Simplifying development with built-in features
- Identifying the components of WordPress
- Making a development plan for forum management application

- Understanding limitations and sticking with guidelines
- Building a question-answer interface
- Enhancing features of the questions plugin

In order to work with this book, you should be familiar with WordPress themes, plugins, and its overall process. Developers who are experienced in PHP frameworks can work with this book while using the reference sources to learn WordPress. By the end of this chapter, you will have the ability to make the decision to choose WordPress for web development.

WordPress as a CMS

Way back in 2003, WordPress released its first version as a simple blogging platform and it continued to improve until it became the most popular blogging tool. Later, it continued to improve as a **CMS** (**Content Management System**) and now has a reputation for being the most popular CMS for over five years. These days, everyone sees WordPress as a CMS rather than just a blogging tool.

Now the question is, where will it go next?

Recent versions of WordPress have included popular web development libraries such as `Backbone.js` and `Underscore.js` and developers are building different types of applications with WordPress. Also, the most recent introduction of the REST API is a major indication that WordPress is moving towards the direction of building web applications. The combination of the REST API and modern JavaScript frameworks will enable developers to build complex web applications with WordPress.

Before we consider the application development aspects of WordPress, it's ideal to figure out the reasons for it being such a popular CMS. The following are some of the reasons behind the success of WordPress as a CMS:

1. The plugin-based architecture for adding independent features and the existence of over 40,000 open source plugins
2. The ability to create unlimited free websites at www.wordpress.com and use the basic WordPress features
3. A super simple and easy-to-access administration interface
4. A fast learning curve and comprehensive documentation for beginners
5. A rapid development process involving themes and plugins
6. An active development community with awesome support
7. The flexibility in building websites with its themes, plugins, widgets, and hooks

8. The availability of large premium theme and plugin marketplaces for developers to sell advanced plugin/themes and users to build advanced sites with those premium plugins/themes without needing a developer

These reasons prove why WordPress is the top CMS for website development. However, experienced developers who work with full stack web applications don't believe that WordPress has a future in web application development. While it's up for debate, we'll see what WordPress has to offer for web development.

Once you complete reading this book, you will be able to decide whether WordPress has a future in web applications. I have been working with full stack frameworks for several years, and I certainly believe in the future of WordPress for web development.

WordPress as a web application framework

In practice, the decision to choose a development framework depends on the complexity of your application. Developers will tend to go for frameworks in most scenarios. It's important to figure out why we go with frameworks for web development. Here's a list of possible reasons why frameworks become a priority in web application development:

- Frameworks provide stable foundations for building custom functionalities
- Usually, stable frameworks have a large development community with an active support
- They have built-in features to address the common aspects of application development, such as routing, language support, form validation, user management, and more
- They have a large amount of utility functions to address repetitive tasks

Full stack development frameworks such as **Zend**, **CodeIgniter**, and **CakePHP** adhere to the points mentioned in the preceding section, which in turn becomes the framework of choice for most developers. However, we have to keep in mind that WordPress is an application where we build applications on top of existing features. On the other hand, traditional frameworks are foundations used for building applications such as WordPress. Now, let's take a look at how WordPress fits into the boots of the web application framework.

The MVC versus event-driven architecture

A vast majority of web development frameworks are built to work with MVC architecture, where an application is separated into independent layers called models, views, and controllers. In MVC, we have a clear understanding of what goes where and when each of the layers will be integrated in the process.

So, the first thing most developers will look at is the availability of MVC in WordPress. Unfortunately, WordPress is not built on top of the MVC architecture. This is one of the main reasons why developers refuse to choose it as a development framework. Even though it is not MVC, we can create custom execution processes to make it work like an MVC application. Also, we can find frameworks such as **WP MVC**, which can be used to take advantage of both WordPress's native functionality and its vast plugin library and all of the many advantages of an MVC framework. Unlike other frameworks, it won't have the full capabilities of MVC. However, the unavailability of MVC architecture doesn't mean that we cannot develop quality applications with WordPress. There are many other ways to separate concerns in WordPress applications.

On the other hand WordPress, relies on a procedural event-driven architecture with its action hooks and filters system. Once a user makes a request, these actions will get executed in a certain order to provide the response to the user. You can find the complete execution procedure at `http://codex.wordpress.org/Plugin_API/Action_Reference`.

In the event-driven architecture, both model and controller code gets scattered throughout the theme and plugin files. In the upcoming chapters, we will look at how we can separate these concerns with the event-driven architecture, in order to develop maintainable applications.

Simplifying development with built-in features

As we discussed in the previous section, the quality of a framework depends on its core features. The better the quality of the core, the better it will be for developing quality and maintainable applications. It's surprising to see the availability of a number of WordPress features directly related to web development, even though it is meant to create websites.

Let's get a brief introduction to the WordPress core features to see how they fit into web application development.

User management

Built-in user management features are quite advanced in order to cater to the most common requirements of any web application. Its user roles and capability handling make it much easier to control the access to specific areas of your application. We can separate users into multiple levels using roles and then use capabilities to define the permitted functionality for each user level. Most full stack frameworks don't have built-in user management features, and hence this can be considered as an advantage of using WordPress.

Media management

File uploading and managing is a common and time consuming task in web applications. Media uploader, which comes built-in with WordPress, can be effectively used to automate the file-related tasks without writing much source code. A super-simple interface makes it so easy for application users to handle file-related tasks.

Template management

WordPress offers a simple template management system for its themes. It is not as complex or fully featured as a typical template engine. However, it offers a wide range of capabilities from a CMS development perspective, which we can extend to suit web applications.

Database management

In most scenarios, we will be using the existing database table structure for our application development. WordPress database management functionalities offer a quick and easy way of working with existing tables with its own style of functions. Unlike other frameworks, WordPress provides a built-in database structure, and hence most of the functionalities can be used to directly work with these tables without writing custom SQL queries.

Routing

Comprehensive support for routing is provided through permalinks. WordPress makes it simple to change the default routing and choose your own routing, in order to build search engine-friendly URLs.

XML-RPC API

Building an API is essential for allowing third-party access to our application. WordPress provides a built-in API for accessing CMS-related functionality through its XML-RPC interface. Also, developers are allowed to create custom API functions through plugins, making it highly flexible for complex applications.

REST API

The REST API makes it possible to give third-party access to the application data, similar to XML-RPC API. This API uses easy to understand HTTP requests and JSON format, making it easier to communicate with WordPress applications. JavaScript is becoming the modern trend in developing applications. So, the availability of JSON in the REST API will allow external users to access and manipulate WordPress data within their JavaScript-based applications.

Caching

Caching in WordPress can be categorized into two sections called **persistent** and **nonpersistent** caching. Nonpersistent caching is provided by the WordPress cache object while persistent caching is provided through its Transient API. Caching techniques in WordPress are simple compared to other frameworks, but it's powerful enough to cater for complex web applications.

Scheduling

As developers, you might have worked with cron jobs for executing certain tasks at specified intervals. WordPress offers the same scheduling functionality through built-in functions, similar to a cron job. However, WordPress cron execution is slightly different from normal cron jobs. In WordPress, cron won't be executed unless someone visits the site. Typically, it's used for scheduling future posts. However, it can be extended to cater complex scheduling functionality.

Plugins and widgets

The power of WordPress comes from its plugin mechanism, which allows us to dynamically add or remove functionality without interrupting other parts of the application. Widgets can be considered as a part of the plugin architecture and will be discussed in detail further in this chapter.

Themes

The design of a WordPress site comes through the theme. This site offers many built-in template files to cater to the default functionality. Themes can be easily extended for custom functionality. Also, the design of the site can be changed instantly by switching to a compatible theme.

Actions and filters

Actions and filters are part of the WordPress hook system. Actions are events that occur during a request. We can use WordPress actions to execute certain functionalities after a specific event is completed. On the other hand, filters are functions that are used to filter, modify, and return data. Flexibility is one of the key reasons for the higher popularity of WordPress compared to other CMSs. WordPress has its own way of extending functionality of custom features as well as core features through actions and filters. These actions and filters allow developers to build advanced applications and plugins, which can be easily extended with minor code changes. As a WordPress developer, it's a must to know the perfect use of these actions and filters in order to build highly-flexible systems.

The admin dashboard

WordPress offers a fully-featured backend for administrators as well as normal users. These interfaces can be easily customized to adapt to custom applications. All the application-related lists, settings, and data can be handled through the admin section.

The overall collection of features provided by WordPress can be effectively used to match the core functionalities provided by full stack PHP frameworks.

Identifying the components of WordPress

WordPress comes up with a set of prebuilt components, which are intended to provide different features and functionality for an application. A flexible theme and powerful admin features act as the core of WordPress websites, while plugins and widgets extend the core with application-specific features. As a CMS, we all have a pretty good understanding of how these components fit into a WordPress website.

Here our goal is to develop web applications with WordPress, and hence it is important to identify the functionality of these components from the perspective of web applications. So, we will look at each of the following components, how they fit into web applications, and how we can take advantage of them to create flexible applications through a rapid development process:

- The role of WordPress themes
- The role of admin dashboard
- The role of plugins
- The role of widgets

The role of WordPress themes

Most of us are used to seeing WordPress as a CMS. In its default view, a theme is a collection of files used to skin your web application layouts. In web applications, it's recommended to separate different components into layers such as models, views, and controllers. WordPress doesn't adhere to the MVC architecture. However, we can easily visualize themes or templates as the presentation layer of WordPress.

In simple terms, views should contain the HTML needed to generate the layout and all the data it needs should be passed to the views. WordPress is built to create content management systems, and hence it doesn't focus on separating views from its business logic. Themes contain views, also known as template files, as a mix of both HTML code and PHP logic. As web application developers, we need to alter the behavior of existing themes in order to limit the logic inside templates and use plugins to parse the necessary model data to views.

Structure of a WordPress page layout

Typically, posts or pages created in WordPress consist of five common sections. Most of these components will be common across all the pages in the website. In web applications, we also separate the common layout content into separate views to be included inside other views. It's important for us to focus on how we can adapt the layout into web application-specific structure. Let's visualize the common layout of WordPress using the following image:

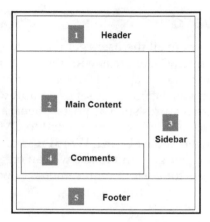

Having looked at the structure, it's obvious that the **Header**, **Footer**, and the **Main Content** areas are mandatory even for web applications. However, the **Footer** and **Comments** section will play a less important role in web applications, compared to web pages. The **Sidebar** is important in web applications, even though it won't be used with the same meaning. It can be quite useful as a dynamic widget area.

Customizing the application layout

Web applications can be categorized as **projects** and **products**. A project is something we develop to target the specific requirements of a client. On the other hand, a product is an application created based on the common set of requirements for a wide range of users. Therefore, customizations will be required on layouts of your product based on different clients.

WordPress themes make it simple to customize the layout and features using child themes. We can make the necessary modifications in the child theme while keeping the core layout in the parent theme. This will prevent any code duplications in customizing layouts. Also, the ability to switch themes is a powerful feature that eases the layout customization.

The role of the admin dashboard

The administration interface of an application plays one of the most important roles behind the scenes. WordPress offers one of the most powerful and easy-to-access admin areas among other competitive frameworks. Most of you should be familiar with using the admin area for CMS functionalities. However, we will have to understand how each component in the admin area suits the development of web applications.

The admin dashboard

The dashboard is the location where all the users get redirected, once logged into the admin area. Usually, it contains dynamic widget areas with the most important data of your application. The dashboard can play a major role in web applications, compared to blogging or CMS functionality. The dashboard contains a set of default widgets that are mainly focused on the main WordPress features such as posts, pages, and comments. In web applications, we can remove the existing widgets related to CMS and add application-specific widgets to create a powerful dashboard. WordPress offers a well-defined API to create custom admin dashboard widgets and hence we can create a very powerful dashboard using custom widgets for custom requirements in web applications.

Posts and pages

Posts in WordPress are built for creating content such as articles and tutorials. In web applications, posts will be the most important section to create different types of data. Often, we will choose custom post types instead of normal posts for building advanced data creation sections. On the other hand, pages are typically used to provide the static content of the site. Usually, we have static pages such as About Us, Contact Us, Services, and so on.

Users

User management is a must-use section for any kind of web application. User roles, capabilities, and profiles will be managed in this section by the authorized users.

Appearance

Themes and application configurations will be managed in this section. Widgets and theme options will be the important sections related to web applications. Generally, widgets are used in the sidebars of WordPress sites to display information such as recent members, comments, posts, and so on. However, in web applications, widgets can play a much bigger role as we can use widgets to split the main template into multiple sections. Also, these types of widgetized areas become handy in applications where the majority of features are implemented with AJAX.

The theme options panel can be used as the general settings panel of web applications where we define the settings related to templates and generic site-specific configurations.

Settings

This section involves general application settings. Most of the prebuilt items in this section are suited for blogs and websites. We can customize this section to add new configuration areas related to our plugins, used in web application development.

There are some other sections, such as links, pages, and comments, which will not be used frequently in complex web application development. The ability to add new sections is one of the key reasons for its flexibility.

The role of plugins

Under normal circumstances, WordPress developers use functions that involve application logic scattered across theme files and plugins. Some developers even change the core files of WordPress, which is considered a very bad practice. In web applications, we need to be much more organized.

In *The role of WordPress themes* section, we discussed the purpose of having a theme for web applications. Plugins will be and should be used to provide the main logic and content of your application. The plugins architecture is a powerful way to add or remove features without affecting the core. Also, we have the ability to separate independent modules into their own plugins, making it easier to maintain. On top of this, plugins have the ability to extend other plugins. Since there are over 40,000 free plugins and a large number of premium plugins, sometimes you don't have to develop anything for WordPress applications. You can just use a number of plugins and integrate them properly to build advanced applications.

The role of widgets

The official documentation of WordPress refers to widgets as a component that adds content and features to your sidebar. From a typical blogging or CMS user's perspective, it's a completely valid statement. Actually, the widgets offer more in web applications by going beyond the content that populates sidebars. Modern WordPress themes provide a wide range of built-in widgets for advanced functionality, making it much more easier to build applications. The following screenshot shows a typical widgetized sidebar of a website:

We can use dynamic widgetized areas to include complex components as widgets, making it easy to add or remove features without changing source code. The following screenshot shows a sample dynamic widgetized area. We can use the same technique for developing applications with WordPress:

Throughout these sections, we have covered the main components of WordPress and how they fit into the actual web application development. Now we have a good understanding of the components, we can plan our application developed throughout this book.

A development plan for the forum management application

Typically, a WordPress book consists of several chapters, each of them containing different practical examples to suit each section. In this book, our main goal is to learn how we can build full stack web applications using built-in WordPress features. Therefore, I thought of building a complete application, explaining each and every aspect of web development.

Throughout this book, we will develop an online forum management system for creating public forums or managing a support forum for a specific product or service. This application can be considered as a mini version of a powerful forum system like **bbPress**. We will be starting the development of this application from Chapter 2, *Implementing Membership Roles, Permissions, and Features*.

Planning is a crucial task in web development, through which we will save a lot of time and avoid potential risks in the long run. First, we need to get a basic idea about the goal of the application, its features and functionalities, and the structure of components to see how it fits into WordPress.

Application goals and target audience

Anyone who is using the Internet on a day-to-day basis knows the importance of online discussion boards, also known as **forums**. These forums allow us to participate in a large community and discuss common matters, either related to a specific subject or a product. The application developed throughout this book is intended to provide a simple and flexible forum management application using a WordPress plugin with the goals of:

- Learning to develop a forum application
- Learning to use features of various online forums
- Learning to manage a forum for your product or service

This application will be targeted towards all the people who have participated in an online forum or used a support system of a product they purchased. I believe that both output of this application and the contents of the book will be ideal for PHP developers who want to jump into WordPress application development.

Planning the application

Basically, our application consists of both frontend and backend, which is common to most web applications. In the frontend, both registered and unregistered users will have different functionalities based on their user roles. The following image shows the structure of our application home page:

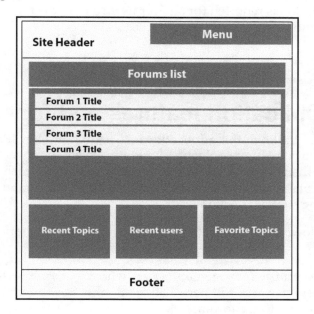

The backend will be developed by customizing the built-in admin features of WordPress. Existing and new functionalities of the admin area will be customized based on the user role permissions.

User roles of the application

The application consists of four user roles, including the built-in admin role. User roles and their respective functionalities are explained in the following section:

- **Admin**: Users of this role manage the application configurations, settings, and capabilities of the users.
- **Moderator**: Users of this role manage the forums and topics. These users can create topics, manage topic statuses, and provide admin level feedback in case of a support forum.

- **Premium Members**: These users gain access to the forums by purchasing a package or subscription. These users will have premium forum features and access to all content without restrictions.
- **Free Members**: These are normal registered users who want to access the forums. These users will have limited access to content and forum features.

 Registration is required for all four user roles in the forum management application.

Planning application features and functions

Our main intention for building this application is to learn how WordPress can be adapted to advanced web application development. Therefore, we will be considering various small requirements, rather than covering all aspects of a similar system. Each of the functionalities will be focused on explaining various modules in web applications and the approach of WordPress in building similar functionality.

Let's consider the following list of functions, which we will be developing throughout this book:

- **Forum user profile management**: Users who register for forums will have a profile where they can edit personal details and view their forum topic details without going into the forum.
- **Forums and Topics management**: The application provides the ability to create forums and topics under these forums. Admin staff will be responsible for creating and closing forum tickets while users will have the ability to create their own tickets.
- **Frontend login and registration**: Typically, web applications contain the login and registration in the frontend, whereas WordPress provides it in the admin area. Therefore, custom implementation of login and registration will be implemented in the application frontend with the support of social login.
- **Manage forum topic permissions**: Various features will be developed to provide restrictions to forum and topic features for different user levels.
- **Joining a Forum**: Users will have features to join a forum and admins will have features to approve/reject user requests.
- **Settings panel**: A comprehensive settings panel will be developed for administrators to configure general application settings from the backend.

- **REST API**: A large number of popular web applications come up with a fully functional API to allow access to third-party applications. In this application, we will be developing a simple API to access the developer details and activities from external sources.

- **Notification service**: A simple notification service will be developed to manage e-mail notifications on new topics in forums and responses to subscribed topics in forums.

- **Responsive design**: With the increase of mobile devices for Internet browsing, more and more applications are converting their apps to suit various devices. So, we will be targeting different devices for a fully responsive design from the beginning of the development process.

- **Third-party libraries**: Throughout the book, we will be creating functionalities such as OpenAuth login, RSS feed generation, and template management to understand the use of third-party libraries in WordPress.

While these are our main functionalities, we will also develop small features and components on top of them to explain the major aspects of web development.

If you are still not convinced, you can take a look at the various types of WordPress powered web applications at `http://www.innovativephp.com/demo/packt/wordpress_ap plications`.

Understanding limitations and sticking to guidelines

As with every framework, WordPress has its limitations in developing web applications. Developers need to understand the limitations before deciding to choose the framework for application development.

In this section, we will learn the limitations while building simple guidelines for choosing WordPress for web development. Let's get started!

- **Lack of support for MVC**: We talked about the architecture of WordPress and its support for MVC in one of the earlier sections. As a developer, you need to figure out ways to work with WordPress in order to suit web applications. If you are someone who cannot work without MVC, WordPress may not be the best solution for your application.

- **Database migration**: If you are well experienced in web development, you will have a pretty good idea about the importance of choosing databases considering the possibilities of migrating to another one in later stages. This can be a limitation in WordPress as it's built to work with MySQL databases. Using it with another database will be quite difficult, if not impossible. So, if you need the database to be migrated to some other database, WordPress will not be the best solution.

- **Security**: This is one of the most important aspects of application development. WordPress is open source and many sites uses free plugins without proper security and code checks. Therefore, when proper security measures are not implemented, potential hackers and programs can identify the vulnerabilities and generate security threats. Many people tend to think WordPress is insecure due to such reasons.

- **Performance**: The performance of your application is something we get to experience in the later stages of the project when we go into a live environment. It's important to plan ahead on performance considerations as they can come through internal and external reasons. WordPress has a built-in database structure and we will use it in most of the projects. It's designed to suit CMS functionality, and sticking with the same tables for different types of projects will not provide the optimized table structure. Therefore, performance might be a limitation for critical applications interacting with millions of records each day, unless you optimize your caching, indexing, and other database optimization strategies.

- **Architecture**: WordPress runs on an event-driven architecture, packed with features. Often developers misuse the hooks without proper planning, affecting the performance of the application. So, you have to be responsible in planning the database and necessary hooks in order to avoid performance overheads.

- **Regular Updates**: WordPress has a very active community involving its development for new features and fixing the issues in existing features. Once a new version of the core is released, plugin developers will also update their plugins to be compatible with the latest version. Hence, you need to perform additional tasks to update the core, themes, and plugins, which can be a limitation when you don't have a proper maintenance team.

- **Object Oriented Development**: Experienced web developers will always look for object-oriented frameworks for development. WordPress started its coding with procedural architecture and is now moving rapidly toward object-oriented architecture. So, there will be a mix of both procedural and object-oriented code. WordPress also uses a hook-based architecture to provide functionality for both procedural and object-oriented codes. Developers who are familiar with other PHP frameworks might find it difficult to come to terms with the mix of procedural and object-oriented code as well as the hook-based architecture. So, you have to decide whether you are comfortable with its existing coding styles.

If you are a developer or designer who thinks these limitations could cause major concerns for your projects, WordPress may not be the right solution for you.

Building a question-answer interface

Throughout the previous sections, we learned the basics of web application frameworks while looking at how WordPress fits into web development. By now, you should be able to visualize the potential of WordPress for application development and how it can change your career as a developer. Being human, we always prefer a practical approach to learning new things over the more conventional theoretical approach.

So, I will complete this chapter by converting default WordPress functionality into a simple question-answer interface, such as Stack Overflow, to give you a glimpse of what we will develop throughout this book.

Prerequisites for building a question-answer interface

We will be using version 4.7.2 as the latest stable version; this is available at the time of writing this book. I suggest that you set up a fresh WordPress installation for this book, if you haven't already done so.

Also, we will be using the Twenty Seventeen theme, which is available with default WordPress installation. Make sure that you activate the Twenty Seventeen theme in your WordPress installation.

First, we have to create an outline containing the list of tasks to be implemented for this scenario:

- Create questions using the admin section of WordPress
- Allow users to answer questions using comments
- Allow question creators to mark each answer as correct or incorrect
- Highlight the correct answers of each question
- Customize the question list to include a number of answers and number of correct answers

Now, it's time to get things started.

Creating questions

The goal of this application is to let people submit questions and get answers from various experts in the same field. First off, we need to create a method to add questions and answers. By default, WordPress allows us to create posts and submit comments to the posts. In this scenario, a post can be considered as the question and comments can be considered as the answers. Therefore, we have the capability of directly using normal post creation for building this interface.

However, I would like to choose a slightly different approach by using the custom post types plugin, which you can find at `http://codex.wordpress.org/Post_Types#Custom_Post_Types`, in order to keep the default functionality of posts and let the new functionality be implemented separately without affecting the existing ones. We will create a plugin to implement the necessary tasks for our application:

1. First off, create a folder called `wpwa-questions` inside the `/wp-content/plugins` folder and add a new file called `wpwa-questions.php`.
2. Next, we need to add the block comment to define our file as a plugin:

```
/*
Plugin Name: WPWA Questions
Plugin URI: -
Description: Question and Answer Interface using WordPress
Custom Post Types and Comments
Version: 1.0
Author: Rakhitha Nimesh
Author URI: http://www.wpexpertdeveloper.com/
License: GPLv2 or later
Text Domain: wpwa-questions
*/
```

3. Having created the main plugin file, we can now create the structure of our plugin with the necessary settings as shown in the following code section:

```
if( !class_exists( 'WPWA_Questions' ) ) {
  class WPWA_Questions{
    private static $instance;
    public static function instance() {

      if ( ! isset( self::$instance ) && ! ( self::$instance
instanceof WPWA_Questions ) ) {
        self::$instance = new WPWA_Questions();
        self::$instance->setup_constants();
        self::$instance->includes();

  add_action('admin_enqueue_scripts',array(self::$instance,'load_admin_scri
pts'),9);

  add_action('wp_enqueue_scripts',array(self::$instance,'load_scripts'),9);

      }
      return self::$instance;
    }
    public function setup_constants() {
      if ( ! defined( 'WPWA_VERSION' ) ) {
        define( 'WPWA_VERSION', '1.0' );
      }
      if ( ! defined( 'WPWA_PLUGIN_DIR' ) ) {
        define('WPWA_PLUGIN_DIR', plugin_dir_path( __FILE__ )
);
      }
      if ( ! defined( 'WPWA_PLUGIN_URL' ) ) {
        define( 'WPWA_PLUGIN_URL', plugin_dir_url( __FILE__ )
);
      }
    }
    public function load_scripts(){ }
    public function load_admin_scripts(){ }
    private function includes() { }
    public function load_textdomain() { }
  }
}
```

4. First, we create a class called `WPWA_Questions` as the main class of the question-answer plugin. Then we define a variable to hold the instance of the class and use the instance function to generate an object from this class. This static function and the private instance variables make sure that we only have one instance of our plugin class. We have also included the necessary function calls and filters in this function.

5. These functions are used to handle the most basic requirements of any WordPress plugin. Since they are common to all plugins, we keep these functions inside the main file. Let's look at the functionality of these functions:

   - `setup_constants`: This function is used to define the constants of the application such as version, plugin directory path, and plugin directory URL
   - `load_scripts`: This function is used to load all the plugin specific scripts and styles on the frontend of the application
   - `load_admin_scripts`: This function is used to load all the plugin specific scripts and styles on the backend of the application
   - `includes`: This function is used to load all the other files of the plugin
   - `load_text_domain`: This function is used to configure the language settings of the plugin

6. Next, we initialize the plugin by calling the following code after the class definition:

```
function WPWA_Questions() {
    global $wpwa;
    $wpwa = WPWA_Questions::instance();
}
WPWA_Questions();
```

7. Having created the main plugin file, we can move into creating a custom post type called `wpwa-question` using the following code snippet. Include this code snippet in your `WPWA_Questions` class file of the plugin:

```
public function register_wp_questions() {
    $labels = array(
    'name' => __( 'Questions', 'wpwa_questions' ),
    'singular_name' => __( 'Question',
    'wpwa_questions'),
```

```
      'add_new' => __( 'Add New', 'wpwa_questions'),
      'add_new_item' => __( 'Add New Question',
   'wpwa_questions'),
      'edit_item' => __( 'Edit Questions',
   'wpwa_questions'),
      'new_item' => __( 'New Question',
   'wpwa_questions'),
      'view_item' => __( 'View Question',
   'wpwa_questions'),
      'search_items' => __( 'Search Questions',
   'wpwa_questions'),
      'not_found' => __( 'No Questions found',
   'wpwa_questions'),
      'not_found_in_trash' => __( 'No Questions found in
   Trash', 'wpwa_questions'),
      'parent_item_colon' => __( 'Parent Question:',
   'wpwa_questions'),
      'menu_name' => __( 'Questions', 'wpwa_questions'),
      );
      $args = array(
      'labels' => $labels,
      'hierarchical' => true,
      'description' => __( 'Questions and Answers',
   'wpwa_questions'),
      'supports' => array( 'title', 'editor',
   'comments' ),
      'public' => true,
      'show_ui' => true,
      'show_in_menu' => true,
      'show_in_nav_menus' => true,
      'publicly_queryable' => true,
      'exclude_from_search' => false,
      'has_archive' => true,
      'query_var' => true,
      'can_export' => true,
      'rewrite' => true,
      'capability_type' => 'post'
      );
   register_post_type( 'wpwa_question', $args );
   }
```

This is the most basic and default code for custom post type creation, and I assume that you are familiar with the syntax. We have enabled title, editor, and comments in the support section of the configuration. These fields will act as the roles of question title, question description, and answers. Other configurations contain the default values and hence explanations will be omitted. If you are not familiar, make sure to have a look at documentation on custom post creation at `http://codex.wordpress.org/Function_Refere`
`nce/register_post_type`.

Beginner to intermediate level developers and designers tend to include the logic inside the `functions.php` file in the theme. This is considered a bad practice as it becomes extremely difficult to maintain because your application becomes larger. So, we will be using plugins to add functionality throughout this book and the drawbacks of the `functions.php` technique will be discussed in later chapters.

8. Then, you have to add the following code inside the instance function of `WPWA_Questions` class to initialize the custom post type creation code:

```
add_action('init',
array(self::$instance,'register_wp_questions'));
```

9. Once the code is included, you will get a new section on the admin area for creating questions. This section will be similar to the posts section inside the WordPress admin. Add a few questions and insert some comments using different users before we move into the next stage.

Before we go into the development of questions and answers, we need to make some configurations so that our plugin works without any issues. Let's look at the configuration process:

1. First, we have to look at the comment-related settings inside **Discussion Settings** in the WordPress **Settings** section. Here, you can find a setting called **Before a comment appears**.
2. Disable both checkboxes so that users can answer and get their answers displayed without the approval process. Depending on the complexity of application, you can decide whether to enable these checkboxes and change the implementation.

3. The second setting we have to change is the **Permalinks**. Once we create a new custom post type and view it in a browser, it will redirect you to a `404 page not found` page. Therefore, we have to go to the **Permalinks** section of WordPress **Settings** and update the **Permalinks** using the **Save Changes** button. This won't change the **Permalinks**. However, this will flush the rewrite rules so that we can use the new custom post type without 404 errors.

Now, we can start working with the answer-related features.

Customizing the comments template

Usually, the comments section is designed to show the comments of a normal post.

While using comments for custom features such as answers, we need to customize the existing template and use our own designs by performing the following steps:

1. So, open the `comments.php` file inside the **Twenty Seventeen** theme.
2. Navigate through the code and you will find a code section similar to the following one:

```
wp_list_comments( array(
    'avatar_size' => 100,
    'style'       => 'ol',
    'short_ping'  => true,
    'reply_text'  => twentyseventeen_get_svg( array( 'icon' => 'mail-
reply' ) ) . __( 'Reply', 'twentyseventeen' ),
    ) );
```

3. We need to modify this section of code to suit the requirements of the answers list. The simplest method is to edit the `comments.php` file of the theme and add the custom code changes. However, modifying core theme or plugin files is considered a bad practice since you lose the custom changes on theme or plugin updates. So, we have to provide this template within our plugin to make sure that we can update the theme when needed.

4. Let's copy the `comments.php` file from the Twenty Seventeen theme to the root of our plugin folder. WordPress will use the `wp_list_comments` function inside the `comments.php` file to show the list of answers for each question. We need to modify the answers list in order to include the answer status button. So, we will change the previous implementation to the following in the `comments.php` file we added inside our plugin:

```php
<?php
    global $wpwa;

    if(get_post_type( $post ) == "wpwa_question"){

wp_list_comments(array('avatar_size' => 100 , 'type' => 'comment',
'callback' => array($wpwa, 'comment_list')));

    }else{
        wp_list_comments( array(
            'avatar_size' => 100,
            'style'       => 'ol',
            'short_ping'  => true,
            'reply_text'  => twentyseventeen_get_svg( array( 'icon' =>
'mail-reply' ) ) . __( 'Reply', 'twentyseventeen' ),
        ) );
    }
?>
```

5. Here, we will include a conditional check for the post type in order to choose the correct answer list generation function. When the post type is `wpwa_question`, we call the `wp_list_comments` function with the callback parameter defined as `comment_list`, which will be the custom function for generating the answers list.

 Arguments of the `wp_list_comments` function can be either an array or string. Here, we have preferred array-based arguments over string-based arguments.

6. We have a custom `comments.php` file inside the plugin. However, WordPress is not aware of the existence of this file and hence will load the original `comments.php` file within the theme. So, we have to include our custom template by adding the following filter code to instance the function:

```
add_filter('comments_template',
array(self::$instance,'load_comments_template'));
```

7. Finally, we have to implement the `load_comments_template` function inside the main class of the plugin to use our comments template from the `plugins` folder:

```
public function load_comments_template($template){
   return WPWA_PLUGIN_DIR.'comments.php';
}
```

In the next section, we will be completing the customization of the comments template by adding answer statuses and allowing users to change the statuses.

Changing the status of answers

Once the users provide their answers, the creator of the question should be able to mark them as correct or incorrect answers. So, we will implement a button for each answer to mark the status. Only the creator of the questions will be able to mark the answers. Once the button is clicked, an AJAX request will be made to store the status of the answer in the database.

Implementation of the `comment_list` function goes inside the main class of `wpwa-questions.php` file of our plugin. This function contains lengthy code, which is not necessary for our explanations. Hence, I'll be explaining the important sections of the code. It's ideal to work with the full code for the `comment_list` function from the source code folder:

```
function comment_list( $comment, $args, $depth ) {
   global $post;
   $GLOBALS['comment'] = $comment;

   $current_user = wp_get_current_user();
   $author_id = $post->post_author;
   $show_answer_status = false;

   if ( is_user_logged_in() && $current_user->ID == $author_id ){
      $show_answer_status = true;
```

```
      }
      $comment_id = get_comment_ID();
      $answer_status = get_comment_meta( $comment_id,
   "_wpwa_answer_status", true );

      // Rest of the Code
   }
```

The `comment_list` function is used as the callback function of the comments list, and hence it will contain three parameters by default. Remember that the button for marking the answer status should be only visible to the creator of the question.

In order to change the status of answers, follow these steps:

1. First, we will get the current logged-in user from the `wp_get_current_user` function. Also, we can get the creator of the question using the global `$post` object.

2. Next, we will check whether the logged-in user created the question. If so, we will set `show_answer_status` to true. Also, we have to retrieve the status of the current answer by passing the `comment_id` and `_wpwa_answer_status` keys to the `get_comment_meta` function.

3. Then, we will have to include the common code for generating a comments list with the necessary condition checks.

4. Open the `wpwa-questions.php` file of the plugin and go through the rest of the `comment_list` function to get an idea of how the comments loop works.

5. Next, we have to highlight the correct answers of each question and I'll be using an image as the highlighter. In the source code, we use the following code after the header tag to show the correct answer highlighter:

```php
<?php
  // Display image of a tick for correct answers
  if ( $answer_status ) {
    echo "<div class='tick'><img src='".plugins_url(
  'img/tick.png', __FILE__ )."' alt='Answer Status'
/></div>";
  }
?>
```

6. In the source code, you will see a `<div>` element with the class reply for creating the comment reply link. We will need to insert our answer button status code right after this, as shown in the following code:

```
<div>
  <?php
  // Display the button for authors to make the answer as correct
or incorrect
    if ( $show_answer_status ) {
      $question_status = '';
      $question_status_text = '';
      if ( $answer_status ) {
        $question_status = 'invalid';
        question_status_text = __('Mark as
  Incorrect','wpwa_questions');
      } else {
        $question_status = 'valid';
        $question_status_text = __('Mark as
  Correct','wpwa_questions');
      }
  ?>
    <input type="button" value="<?php echo
  $question_status_text; ?>"  class="answer-status
  answer_status-<?php echo $comment_id; ?>"
    data-ques-status="<?php echo $question_status; ?>" />
    <input type="hidden" value="<?php echo $comment_id; ?>"
  class="hcomment" />
    <?php
    }
    ?>
</div>
```

7. If the `show_answer_status` variable is set to true, we get the comment ID, which will be our answer ID, using the `get_comment_ID` function. Then, we will get the status of answer as true or false using the `_wpwa_answer_status` key from the `wp_commentmeta` table.

8. Based on the returned value, we will define buttons for either **Mark as Incorrect** or **Mark as Correct**. Also, we will specify some CSS classes and HTML5 data attributes to be used later with jQuery.

9. Finally, we keep the `comment_id` in a hidden variable called `hcomment`.

10. Once you include the code, the button will be displayed for the author of the question, as shown in the following screen:

11. Next, we need to implement the AJAX request for marking the status of the answer as true or false.

Before this, we need to see how we can include our scripts and styles into WordPress plugins. We added empty functions to include the scripts and styles while preparing the structure of this plugin. Here is the code for including custom scripts and styles for our plugin inside the `load_scripts` function we created earlier. Copy the following code into the `load_scripts` function of the `wpwa-questions.php` file of your plugin:

```
public function load_scripts() {
  wp_enqueue_script( 'jquery' );
  wp_register_script( 'wpwa-questions', plugins_url(
  'js/questions.js', __FILE__ ), array('jquery'), '1.0', TRUE );
  wp_enqueue_script( 'wpwa-questions' );
  wp_register_style( 'wpwa-questions-css', plugins_url(
  'css/questions.css', __FILE__ ) );
  wp_enqueue_style( 'wpwa-questions-css' );
  $config_array = array(
    'ajaxURL' => admin_url( 'admin-ajax.php' ),
    'ajaxNonce' => wp_create_nonce( 'ques-nonce' )
  );
  wp_localize_script( 'wpwa-questions', 'wpwaconf', $config_array
  );
}
```

WordPress comes with an action hook built-in called `wp_enqueue_scripts` for adding JavaScript and CSS files. The `wp_enqueue_script` action is used to include script files into the page while the `wp_register_script` action is used to add custom files. Since jQuery is built-in to WordPress, we can just use the `wp_enqueue_script` action to include jQuery into the page. We also have a custom JavaScript file called `questions.js`, which will contain the functions for our application.

Inside JavaScript files, we cannot access the PHP variables directly. WordPress provides a function called `wp_localize_script` to pass PHP variables into script files. The first parameter contains the handle of the script for binding data, which will be `wp_questions` in this scenario. The second parameter is the variable name to be used inside JavaScript files to access these values. The third and final parameters will be the configuration array with the values.

Then, we can include our `questions.css` file using the `wp_register_style` and `wp_enqueue_style` functions, which will be similar to JavaScript, file inclusion syntax, we discussed previously. Now, everything is set up properly to create the AJAX request.

Saving the status of answers

Once the author clicks the button, the status has to be saved to the database as true or false depending on the current status of the answer. Let's go through the jQuery code located inside the `questions.js` file for making the AJAX request to the server:

```
jQuery(document).ready(function($) {
  $(".answer-status").click( function() {
    $(body).on("click", ".answer-status" , function() {

      var answer_button = $(this);
      var answer_status  = $(this).attr("data-ques-status");
      // Get the ID of the clicked answer using hidden field
      var comment_id = $(this).parent().find(".hcomment").val();
      var data = {
      "comment_id":comment_id,
      "status": answer_status
    };

  $.post( wpwaconf.ajaxURL, {
    action:"mark_answer_status",
    nonce:wpwaconf.ajaxNonce,
    data : data,
  }, function( data ) {
    if("success" == data.status){
      if("valid" == answer_status){
        answer_buttonval("Mark as Incorrect");
        answer_button.attr("
data-ques-status","invalid");
      }else{
        answer_button.val("Mark as Correct");
        answer_button.attr("
data-ques-status","valid");
      }
    }
  }, "json");
  });
});
```

Let's understand the implementation of saving the answer status. This code snippet executes every time a user clicks the button to change the status. We get the current status of the answer by using the `data-ques-status` attribute of the button. Next, we get the ID of the answer using the hidden field with `hcomment` as the CSS class. Then, we send the data through an AJAX request to the `mark_answer_status` action.

Once the AJAX response is received, we display the new status of the answer and update the data attribute of the button with the new status.

 The important thing to note here is that we have used the configuration settings assigned in the previous section, using the wpwaconf variable. Once a server returns the response with success status, the button will be updated to contain the new status and display text.

The next step of this process is to implement the server-side code for handling the AJAX request. First, we need to define AJAX handler functions using the WordPress add_action function. Since only logged-in users are permitted to mark the status, we don't need to implement the add_action function for wp_ajax_nopriv_{action}. Let's add the AJAX action to the instance function of the main class of the plugin:

```
add_action('wp_ajax_mark_answer_status',
array(self::$instance,'mark_answer_status'));
```

Then, we need to add the mark_answer_status function inside the main class. Implementation of the mark_answer_status function is given in the following code:

```
function mark_answer_status() {
    $data = isset( $_POST['data'] ) ? $_POST['data'] : array();
  $comment_id     = isset( $data["comment_id"] ) ?
absint($data["comment_id"]) : 0;
  $answer_status  = isset( $data["status"] ) ? $data["status"] :
0;
    // Mark answers in correct status to incorrect
    // or incorrect status to correct
    if ("valid" == $answer_status) {
      update_comment_meta( $comment_id, "_wpwa_answer_status", 1 );
    } else {
    update_comment_meta( $comment_id, "_wpwa_answer_status", 0 );
    }
    echo json_encode( array("status" => "success") );
    exit;
      }
```

We can get the necessary data from the $_POST array and use it to mark the status of the answer using the update_comment_meta function. This example contains the most basic implementation of the data saving process. In real applications, we need to implement necessary validations and error handling.

Now, the author who asked the question has the ability to mark answers as correct or incorrect. So, we have implemented a nice and simple interface for creating a question-answer site with WordPress. The final task of the process will be the implementation of the questions list.

Generating a question list

Usually, WordPress uses the `archive.php` file of the theme for generating post lists of any type. We can use a file called `archive-{post type}.php` for creating different layouts for different post types. Here, we will create a customized layout for our questions. The simplest solution is to copy the archive file and create a new file called `archive-{post type}.php` inside the theme. However, it's not the ideal way to create a custom template due to the reasons we discussed while creating the `comments.php` file. So, we have to use a plugin specific template and override the default behavior of the archive file. Refer to the following steps:

1. Make a copy of the existing `archive.php` file of the TwentySeventeen theme, copy it to the root folder of the plugin, and rename it `questions-list-template.php`. Here, you will find the following code section:

   ```
   get_template_part( 'template-parts/post/content', get_post_format()
   );
   ```

2. The TwentySeventeen theme uses a separate template for generating the content of each post type. We have to replace this with our own template inside the plugin. The `get_template_part` function is only used to load the theme specific template. So, we can't use it to load a template file from a plugin. The solution is to include the template file using the following code:

   ```
   require WPWA_PLUGIN_DIR . 'content.php';
   ```

3. Next, we have to create the content template by copying the `content.php` file of the theme from the `template-parts/post/content` folder to the root folder of our plugin.

4. Finally, we need to consider the implementation of the `content.php` file. In the questions list, only the question title will be displayed, and therefore, we don't need the content of the post. So, we have to either remove or comment the `the_excerpt` and `the_content` functions of the template. We can comment the following line within this template:

   ```
   the_content( sprintf(
   ```

```
__( 'Continue reading<span class="screen-reader-text"> "%s"</span>',
    'twentyseventeen' ), get_the_title()
        ) );
```

5. Then, we will create our own metadata by adding the following code to the `<div>` element with the `entry-content` class:

```
<div class="answer_controls"><?php
comments_popup_link(__('No Answers &darr;', 'twentyseventeen '),
    __('1 Answer &darr;', 'responsive'), __('% Answers &darr;',
'twentyseventeen')); ?>
    </div>
    <div class="answer_controls">
    <?php wpwa_get_correct_answers(get_the_ID()); ?>
    </div>
    <div class="answer_controls">
    <?php echo   get_the_date(); ?>
    </div>
    <div style="clear: both"></div>
```

> The first container will make use of the existing `comments_popup_link` function to get the number of answers given for the questions.

6. Then, we need to display the number of correct answers of each question. The custom function called `get_correct_answers` is created to get the correct answers. The following code contains the implementation of the `get_correct_answers` function inside the main class of the plugin:

```
function get_correct_answers( $post_id ) {
   $args = array(
      'post_id'   => $post_id,
      'status'    => 'approve',
      'meta_key'  => '_wpwa_answer_status',
      'meta_value'=> 1,
   );
   // Get number of correct answers for given question
   $comments = get_comments( $args );
   printf(__('<cite class="fn">%s</cite> correct answers'),
 count( $comments ) );
}
```

> We can set the array of arguments to include the conditions to retrieve the approved answers of each post, which contains the correct answers. The number of results generated from the `get_comments` function will be returned as correct answers.

We have completed the code for displaying the questions list. However, you will still see a list similar to the default posts list. The reason for that is we created a custom template and WordPress is not aware of its existence. So, the default template file is loaded instead of our custom template.

7. We need to override the existing archive template of WordPress by adding the following action to the instance function of the main plugin class:

```
add_filter( 'archive_template',
array(self::$instance,'questions_list_template' ));
```

8. Here, we have the implementation of the questions_list_template function inside the main class of the plugin:

```
public function questions_list_template($template){
  global $post;

  if ( is_post_type_archive ( 'wpwa_question' ) ) {
    $template = WPWA_PLUGIN_DIR . '/questions-list-template.php';
  }
  return $template;
}
```

This function overrides the archive template when the questions list is displayed and keeps the default template for posts lists or any other custom post type lists.

Now, you should have a question list similar to the following screenshot:

Throughout this section, we looked at how we can convert the existing functionalities of WordPress for building a simple question-answer interface. We took the quick and dirty path for this implementation by mixing HTML and PHP code inside both, themes and plugins.

 I suggest that you go through the `Chapter 1`, *WordPress as a Web Application Framework*, `source code` folder and try this implementation on your own test server. This demonstration was created to show the flexibility of WordPress. Some of you might not understand the whole implementation. Don't worry, as we will develop a web application from scratch using a detailed explanation in the following chapters.

Enhancing features of the questions plugin

In the previous sections, we illustrated how to quickly adapt WordPress into different kinds of implementations by customizing its core features. However, I had to limit the functionality to the most basic level in order to keep this chapter short and interesting for beginners. If you are willing to improve it, you can try other new features of such an application. Here, we will be looking at some of the enhancements to this plugin and how we can use core WordPress features to implement them.

Customizing the design of questions

This is one of the major requirements in such an application. Here, we have a very basic layout and it's difficult to know whether this is a question or just a normal post. Consider the following screenshot for a well-designed question interface:

Remember that we customized the comments list for adding new options. Similarly, we can customize the design of questions to create an interface such as the previous screenshot by using a separate template file for the questions custom post type. We have to create a file called `single-wpwa_question.php` and change the design and functionality as we want.

Categorizing questions

Categories allow us to filter the results and limit them to a certain extent. It's an essential feature in the question-answer application so that users can directly view questions related to their topic instead of browsing all the questions. WordPress provides categories by default. However, these categories are mainly intended for posts. Therefore, we have to use custom taxonomies to create categories for custom post types such as questions. More details about taxonomies will be discussed in the following chapters.

Approving and rejecting questions

Currently, our application can post questions without any approval process. However, this is not the ideal implementation as it can create a lot of spam questions. In a well-built application, there should be a feature to approve/reject questions when needed. This feature can be easily built with WordPress admin lists. We have a list of questions in the backend, and we can use the **Bulk Actions** dropdown on top to add custom actions and implement this feature.

Adding star rating to answers

The author who asked the question can mark the answers as correct or incorrect. However, there can be scenarios where answers are not marked as correct are more suitable than answers marked as correct. Therefore, we can introduce star rating features to answers so that the public can rate the answers. The person who looks for the answer can consider the rating before choosing answers. Implementation of this requirement is similar to the functionality of the **Mark as Correct** button. We have to get a JS plugin for star rating and integrate to the interface through the `comment_list` function. Then we can use AJAX to mark the status of answers.

We have looked at some of the possible enhancements to such an application. You can think of many more such functionalities and implement them in your own version.

In the following chapters, we'll see the limitations in this approach in complex web applications and how we can organize things better to write quality and maintainable code.

Summary

Our main goal was to find how WordPress fits into web application development. We started this chapter by identifying the CMS functionalities of WordPress. We explored the features and functionalities of popular full stack frameworks and compared them with the existing functionalities of WordPress.

Then, we looked at the existing components and features of WordPress and how each of those components fits into a real-world web application. We also planned the forum management application requirements and identified the limitations in using WordPress for web applications.

Finally, we converted the default interface into a question-answer interface in a rapid process using existing functionalities, without interrupting the default behavior of WordPress and themes.

By now, you should be able to decide whether to choose WordPress for your web application, visualize how your requirements fit into the components of WordPress, and identify and minimize the limitations.

In the next chapter, we will start developing the forum management application with the user management. Before we go there, I suggest that you research the user management features of other frameworks and look at your previous projects to identify the functionalities.

2
Implementing Membership Roles, Permissions, and Features

The success of any web application or website depends heavily on its user base. There are plenty of great web applications that go unnoticed by many people due to the lack of user interaction. As developers, it's our responsibility to build a simple and interactive user management process, as visitors decide whether to stay on or leave a website by looking at the complexity of initial tasks such as registration and login.

In this chapter, we will be mainly concentrating on adapting existing user management functionalities into typical web applications. In order to accomplish our goal, we will execute some tasks outside the box to bring user management features from the WordPress core to WordPress themes.

While striving to build a better user experience, we will also take a look at some advanced aspects of web application development, such as routing, controlling, and custom templating.

In this chapter, we will cover the following topics:

- Introducing user management
- Understanding user roles and capabilities
- Creating a simple MVC-like process
- Implementing registration on the frontend
- Implementing login on the frontend
- Time to practice with exercises

Before we get started, I suggest that you skip ahead to `Appendix`, *Configurations, Tools, and Resources* and configure the WordPress environment and setup required for this book. I assume that you are familiar with the default user management features and necessary coding techniques in WordPress. So, let's get started!

Introduction to user management

Usually, popular PHP development frameworks such as **Zend**, **CakePHP**, **CodeIgniter**, and **Laravel** don't provide a built-in user module. Developers tend to build their own user management modules and use them across many projects of the same framework. WordPress offers a built-in user management system to cater to common user management tasks found in web applications. Such things include the following:

- Managing user roles and capabilities
- A built-in user registration functionality
- A built-in user login functionality
- A built-in forgot password functionality

Developers are likely to encounter these tasks in almost all web applications. In most cases, these features and functions can be effectively used without significant changes in the code. However, web applications are much more advanced and hence we might need various customizations on these existing features. It's important to explore the possibility of extending these functions in order to be compatible with advanced application requirements. In the following sections, we will learn how to extend these common functionalities to suit various scenarios.

Preparing the plugin

As developers, we have the option to build a complete application with standalone plugins or use various independent plugins to cater to specific modules. Generally, many developers tend to use a bunch of existing plugins without developing their own. The main reason behind using other plugins is that developers want to save time and cost when developing WordPress websites. However, in most scenarios, this process is not ideal for complex web application development. I recommend that you select fewer plugins and improve them with additional functionality or develop everything from scratch.

Throughout this book, we will be integrating all the independent modules into a standalone plugin. We will create a specific plugin for our forum management application. So, let's get started by creating a new folder called `wpwa-forum`, inside the `/wp-content/plugins` folder.

Then, create a PHP file inside the folder and save it as `wpwa-forum.php`. Now, it's time to add the plugin definition, as shown in the following code:

```php
<?php
/*
     Plugin Name: WPWAF Forum
     Plugin URI : -
     Description: Forum Management application for WordPress Web
Application Development 3rd Edition
     Version    : 1.0
     Author     : Rakhitha Nimesh
     Author URI: http://www.wpexpertdeveloper.com/
*/
```

In the previous chapter, we created a plugin with a specific initial structure. We will be using the same coding structure for the forum plugin. Let's look at the basic structure of the `wpwa-forum.php` file using the following code:

```php
if( !class_exists( 'WPWAF_Forum' ) ) {
  class WPWAF_Forum{
    private static $instance;

    public static function instance() {

        if ( ! isset( self::$instance ) && ! ( self::$instance instanceof
WPWAF_Forum ) ) {
            self::$instance = new WPWAF_Forum();
            self::$instance->setup_constants();
            self::$instance->includes();

            add_action(
'admin_enqueue_scripts',array(self::$instance,'load_admin_scripts'),9);
            add_action(
'wp_enqueue_scripts',array(self::$instance,'load_scripts'),9);

            // Class object intialization
        }
        return self::$instance;
    }

    public function setup_constants() {
      if ( ! defined( 'WPWAF_VERSION' ) ) {
```

```
            define( 'WPWAF_VERSION', '1.0' );
        }
        if ( ! defined( 'WPWAF_PLUGIN_DIR' ) ) {
            define( 'WPWAF_PLUGIN_DIR', plugin_dir_path( __FILE__ ) );
        }
        if ( ! defined( 'WPWAF_PLUGIN_URL' ) ) {
            define( 'WPWAF_PLUGIN_URL', plugin_dir_url( __FILE__ ) );
        }
    }

    public function load_scripts(){ }
    public function load_admin_scripts(){ }
    private function includes() { }
    public function load_textdomain() {}
  }
}
```

Once the class is defined, we can initialize the class using the following code as we did previously in the question-answer plugin:

```
function WPWAF_Forum() {
    global $wpwaf;
    $wpwaf = WPWAF_Forum::instance();
}
WPWAF_Forum();
```

The important aspect of this structure is the use of the singleton design pattern which creates only one instance of the main class and returns it every time we need it. Let's look at the Wikipedia definition of the **singleton pattern**:

> *Singleton pattern is a software design pattern that restricts the instantiation of a class to one object. This is useful when exactly one object is needed to coordinate actions across the system.*

We can develop plugins without the singleton pattern. In such methods, you need to make sure that you don't initialize the main object multiple times, which results in execution of the same action hook multiple times. There are many plugins with this issue and it's extremely difficult to identify the conflicts since the actions are called multiple times. Using this structure will prevent accidental initialization of unnecessary classes.

Getting started with user roles

In simple terms, user roles define the types of users in a system. WordPress offers built-in functions for working with every aspect of user roles. In this section, we will look at how we can manage these tasks by implementing the user roles for our application. We can create a new user role by calling the `add_role` function. The following code illustrates the basic form of user role creation:

```
$result = add_role( 'role_name', 'Display Name', array(
    'read' => true,
    'edit_posts' => true,
    'delete_posts' => false
) );
```

The first parameter takes the role name, which is a unique key to identify the role. The second parameter will be the display name, which will be shown in the admin area. The final parameter will take the necessary capabilities of the user role. You can find out more about existing user roles at `http://codex.wordpress.org/Roles_and_Capabilities`. In this scenario, `read`, `edit_posts`, and `delete_posts` will be the capabilities while `true` and `false` are used to enable and disable status.

Creating application user roles

As planned earlier, we will need three types of user roles for our application to handle: moderators, premium members, and free members. So, we can update our plugin by adding a specific function to create the user roles, as shown in the following code:

```
public function add_application_user_roles() {
    add_role( 'wpwaf_premium_member', __('Premium Member','wpwaf'),
array( 'read' => true ) );
    add_role( 'wpwaf_free_member', __('Free Member','wpwaf'), array(
'read' => true ) );
    add_role( 'wpwaf_moderator', __('Moderator','wpwaf'), array(
'read' => true ) );
  }
```

Application user roles are created with the default capability of `read`, used by all the user roles in WordPress. Integration of this function to our main plugin will be explained in the next few sections.

You can use normal words such as member and moderator for the custom user roles created in the plugins. However, these role keys may also be used in other popular plugins for different purposes. If we use two plugins with same user role intended for different features, there will be a conflict. Therefore, it's better to add a prefix and make your user roles unique, to avoid conflicts and be compatible with popular plugins.

The best action for adding user roles

The user roles discussed in the previous section will be saved in the database as settings. Therefore, only a single call to this function is required throughout the life cycle of an application. We have two options for implementing this functionality. Application installation and plugin activation are the most suitable places to call these kinds of functions to eliminate duplicate executions:

- **Application installation**: WordPress provides a well-defined step-by-step installation process. Similarly, every application or plugin needs an installation process. Once installation is completed, these files are not accessible again. Therefore, plugin installation is the ideal place to create user roles.
- **Plugin activation**: WordPress plugin activation hooks let us execute certain functionality on plugin activation. This is also a one-time process in a plugin. However, we can deactivate and reactivate the plugin multiple times. So, this functionality gets executed multiple times and hence we have to check whether it's already been executed. If this is not checked, all the changes made after the activation will be reset to default values. So, plugin activation is the second-best option for this type of functionality.

Here, we will be using plugin activation to add and remove application user roles since we don't have an application installation feature at this stage.

First, we need to identify where we can add the activation-related functionality. Basically, these are configurations of the forum application. Therefore, we need to create a new class called WPWAF_Config_Manager inside a new folder called classes, in our main plugin. Next, we have to initialize an object from this class inside the instance function of the WPWAF_Forum class using the following code:

```
self::$instance->config_manager  = new WPWAF_Config_Manager();
```

Then we need to include the class file inside the includes function of the `WPWAF_Forum` class using the following code:

```
require_once WPWAF_PLUGIN_DIR . 'classes/class-wpwaf-config-
manager.php';
```

Now we can include the activation hook inside the `instance` function, as shown in the following code:

```
register_activation_hook( __FILE__, array( self::$instance-
>config_manager , 'activation_handler' ) );
```

The `activation_handler` function of the `WPWAF_Config_Manager` class will be responsible for handling all functionality related to forum plugin activation. Let's look at the `add_application_user_roles` function inside the `config` class, as shown in the following code:

```
class WPWAF_Config_Manager{
    public function activation_handler(){
        $this->add_application_user_roles();
    }

    public function add_application_user_roles(){
        add_role( 'wpwaf_premium_member', __('Premium Member','wpwaf'),
array( 'read' => true ) );
        add_role( 'wpwaf_free_member', __('Free Member','wpwaf'),
array( 'read' => true ) );
        add_role( 'wpwaf_moderator', __('Moderator','wpwaf'), array(
'read' => true ) );
    }
}
```

The `register_activation_hook` function will be called when the plugin is activated and hence avoids duplicate calls to the database.

> A good rule of thumb is to prevent the inclusion of such settings inside the `init` action as it will get executed in each request, making unnecessary performance overheads.

You might have noticed that all three user roles of the application are created with the read capability. WordPress is built to create websites and hence most of the default capabilities will be related to CMS features. In web applications, we need custom capabilities more often than not. Therefore, we can keep the basic read capability and add new custom capabilities as we move on. All the users will get a very basic admin area containing a dashboard and profile information, as shown in the following screenshot:

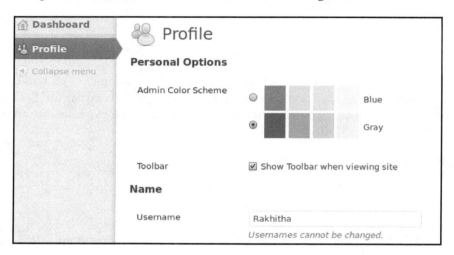

Knowing the default roles of WordPress

WordPress comes with six built-in user roles, including superadmin which will not be displayed on the user creation screen by default. As a developer, it's important to know the functionality of each of these types of roles in order to use them in web applications. First, we'll take a look at the default user roles and their functionality:

- **Superadmin**: A superadmin has administration permission in WordPress multisite implementation
- **Admin**: An admin has permission to all administration activities inside a single site
- **Editor**: An editor can create, publish, and manage posts, including the posts of other users
- **Author**: An author can create and publish their own posts
- **Contributor**: A contributor can create posts, but cannot publish on their own
- **Subscriber**: A subscriber can read posts and manage their profile

As you can see, most of the existing user types are used for blogging and content management functionality. Therefore, we might need to create our own user roles for web applications, apart from the default superadmin and admin user roles.

Choosing between default and custom roles

This is an interesting question that doesn't have a correct answer. Choosing between these two types of roles naturally comes with experience. First, you need to figure out how these built-in roles relate to your application. Let's consider two scenarios to help demonstrate the practical usage of these user roles.

Scenario 1

Usually, the roles such an editor, author, and contributor are mainly focused on publishing and managing blog posts. If you are developing an online shopping cart, these roles will not have any relation to the roles of such applications.

Scenario 2

Now, think of a scenario where we have a job posting site with three access levels called admin, companies, and individuals. Here, individuals can create job posts, while approvals are given by an admin. So, they are similar to contributors. Companies can create and publish their own job posts, similar to authors. An admin can play the role of an editor or admin in the default system.

Even though we can match certain aspects of our forum application roles with the existing roles, we will work with custom roles to keep things simple and clear. All application users will be created as custom roles with read capability by default and the necessary capabilities will be added as we move on.

It doesn't matter whether you choose existing ones or new ones as long as you are comfortable and the roles have a specific meaning within your application. If we choose custom roles, it's not necessary to keep the unused default roles. Let's see how we can remove roles when necessary.

Removing existing user roles

We should have the ability to remove existing or custom user roles when necessary. WordPress offers the `remove_role` function for deleting both custom and existing user roles. In this case, we want to get rid of existing user roles. Also, there can be situations where you use a plugin with specific user roles and suddenly you want to disable the functionality of the plugin. In both cases, we need to remove the user roles from the database. Let's create a function that removes the unnecessary user roles from the system. Add the following function to the `WPWAF_Config_Manager`class, as illustrated in the following code:

```
public function remove_application_user_roles(){
  remove_role( 'author' );
  remove_role( 'editor' );
  remove_role( 'contributor' );
  remove_role( 'subscriber' );
}
```

As mentioned earlier, the `remove_role` function involves database operations and hence it's wise to use it with the `register_activation_hook` function. So we can call this function from the `activation_handler` function of the `WPWAF_Config_Manager` class as it's responsible for handling all activation-related features.

> This code will remove the existing roles and you can't get them back without importing them again to the database. So I recommend you only add the code on a test site or just comment the code.

In this section, we looked at how user roles work in WordPress. Now, we need to see how we can associate capabilities with these user roles.

Understanding user capabilities

Capabilities can be considered as tasks which users are permitted to perform inside the application. A single user role can perform many capabilities, while a single capability can be performed by many user roles. Typically, we use the term "access control" for handling capabilities in web applications. Let's see how capabilities work inside WordPress.

Creating your first capability

Capabilities are always associated with user roles and hence we cannot create new capabilities without providing a user role. Let's look at the following code for associating custom capabilities with our member user roles created earlier in the *Creating application user roles* section:

```
public function add_application_user_capabilities(){
    $role = get_role( 'wpwaf_premium_member' );
    $role->add_cap( 'follow_forum_activities' );

    $role = get_role( 'wpwaf_free_member' );
    $role->add_cap( 'follow_forum_activities' );
}
```

First, we need to retrieve the user role as an object using the `get_role` function. Then, we can associate new or existing capability using the `add_cap` function. We need to continue this process for each user role until we assign all the capabilities to the necessary user levels. This function also needs to be executed inside the activation hook. Therefore, we can call this function from the `activation_handler` function of the `WPWAF_Config_Manager` class, as shown in the following code:

```
public function activation_handler(){
    $this->add_application_user_roles();
    $this->remove_application_user_roles();
    $this->add_application_user_capabilities();
}
```

Now, we have user role and capabilities related configurations in activation handler of the plugin.

Understanding default capabilities

You can find over 50 built-in capabilities in the WordPress default database. Most of these capabilities are focused on providing permissions related to website or blog creation. Therefore, it's a must to create our own capabilities in developing web applications. If you are curious to learn, you can look at the `wp_user_roles` option inside the `wp_options` table for all the available user roles and their capabilities. You can use any MySQL GUI client or `phpMyAdmin` application to execute the following query to view the default user role data. Take a look at the following code:

```
select option_value from wp_users where option_name='wp_user_roles'
```

You should see a serialized array like the following one:

```
a:10:{s:13:"administrator";a:2:{s:4:"name";s:13:"Administrator";s:
12:"capabilities";a:67:{s:13:"switch_themes";b:1;s:11:"edit_theme"
;b:1;s:16:"activate_plugins";b:1;s:12:"edit_plugins";b:1;s:10:"edi
t_users";b:1;s:10:"edit_files";b:1;s:14:"manage_options";b:1;s:17:
"moderate_comments";b:1;s:17:"manage_categories";b:1;s:12:"manage_
links";b:1;s:12
```

A part of the value contained in the `wp_user_roles` row is displayed in the preceding code. It's quite confusing and not practical to understand the capabilities of each user role by looking at this serialized array. Therefore, we can take advantage of an existing WordPress plugin to view and manage user roles and capabilities.

There are plenty of great and free plugins for managing user roles and permissions. My favorite is the `Members` plugin by Justin Tadlock, as it's quite clean and simple. You can grab a copy of this plugin at `http://wordpress.org/plugins/members/`.

Let's see how capabilities are displayed for the free member role in our application using the following screenshot of the plugin:

All the capabilities which are assigned to a specific user role will be ticked by default. As expected, the `follow_forum_activities` capability added in the previous section is successfully assigned to the free and premium member user roles.

So far, we have learned how to use WordPress roles and capabilities in the context of web applications. We will be updating the capabilities while creating new functionalities in the following chapters. Next, we will see how user registration works in WordPress.

Registering application users

An administration panel is built into the WordPress framework, allowing us to log in through the admin screen. Therefore, we have a registration area which can be used to add new users by providing a username and e-mail. In web applications, registration can become complex, compared to the simple registration process in WordPress. Let's consider some typical requirements of the web application registration process in comparison with WordPress:

- **User-friendly interface**: An application can have different types of user roles. Until registration is completed, everyone is treated as a normal application user with the ability to view public content. Typically, users are used to seeing fancy registration forms inside the main site rather than a completely different login area such as with WordPress. Therefore, we need to explore the possibilities of adding WordPress registration to the frontend.
- **Requesting detailed information**: Most web applications will have at least four or five fields in the user registration form for grabbing detailed information about the user. Therefore, we need to look at the possibility of adding new fields to the existing WordPress registration form.
- **Activating user accounts**: In some applications, you will be asked to verify and activate your account after successful registration. WordPress doesn't offer this feature by default. Hence, we need to see how we can extend the current process to include user activation.

These are the most common requirements of the registration process in web applications. Complex applications may come with more requirements in this process. Therefore, we need to extend the WordPress registration process, in order to cater to various requirements. In the next section, we will address the issues mentioned here by creating a WordPress registration from the frontend.

Implementing frontend registration

Fortunately, we can make use of the existing functionalities to implement registration from the frontend. We can use a regular HTTP request or AJAX-based technique to implement this feature. In this book, I will focus on using normal HTTP POST requests instead of using AJAX. Our first task is to create the registration form in the frontend.

There are various ways to implement such forms in the frontend. Let's look at some of the possibilities as described in the following section:

- Shortcode implementation
- Page template implementation
- Custom template implementation

Now, let's look at the implementation of each of these techniques.

Shortcode implementation

Shortcodes are the quickest way to add dynamic content to your pages. In this situation, we need to create a page for registration. Therefore, we need to create a shortcode that generates the registration form.

> We can add shortcodes to our application by including them inside functions.php file of the theme or within any custom plugin. I recommend adding these shortcodes in a custom plugin since you will loos the additional code in functions.php file on theme updates.

Let's take a look at the shortcode that displays our registration form, as shown in the following code:

```
add_shortcode( "register_form", "display_register_form" );
functiondisplay_register_form(){
  $html = "HTML for registration form";
  return $html;
}
```

Then, you can add the shortcode inside the created page using the following code snippet to display the registration form:

```
[register_form]
```

Pros and cons of using shortcodes

The following are the pros and cons of using shortcodes:

- Shortcodes are easy to implement in any part of your application
- It's hard to manage the template code assigned using the PHP variables
- There is a possibility of the shortcode getting deleted from the page by mistake

Page template implementation

Page templates are a widely used technique in modern WordPress themes. We can create a page template to embed the registration form. Consider the following code for a sample page template:

```
/*
* Template Name :  Registration
*/
HTML code for registration form
```

Next, we have to copy the template inside the theme folder. Finally, we can create a page and assign the page template to display the registration form. Now, let's look at the pros and cons of this technique.

Pros and cons of page templates

The following are the pros and cons of page templates:

- A page template is more stable than a shortcode.
- Generally, page templates are used as layout templates rather than rendering separate components like dynamic forms. The full-width page, two-column page, and left-sidebar page are some common implementations of page templates.
- A template is managed separately from logic, without using PHP variables.
- The page templates depend on the theme and need to be updated on theme switching.

Custom template implementation

Experienced web application developers will always look to separate business logic from view templates. This will be the perfect technique for such people. In this technique, we will create our own independent templates by intercepting the WordPress default routing process. An implementation of this technique starts from the next section on routing.

Building a simple router for a user module

Routing is one of the important aspects in advanced application development. We need to figure out ways of building custom routes for specific functionalities. In this scenario, we will create a custom router to handle all the user-related functionalities of our application.

Let's list the requirements for building a router:

- All the user-related functionalities should go through a custom URL, such as `http://www.example.com/user`
- Registration should be implemented at `http://www.example.com/user/register`
- Login should be implemented at `http://www.example.com/user/login`
- Activation should be implemented at `http://www.example.com/user/activate`

 Make sure to set up your permalinks structure to post names for the examples in this book. If you prefer a different permalinks structure, you will have to update the URLs and routing rules accordingly.

As you can see, the user section is common for all the functionalities. The second URL segment changes dynamically based on the functionality. In MVC terms, the user acts as the controller and the next URL segment (register, login, and activate) acts as the action. Now, let's see how we can implement a custom router for the given requirements.

Creating the routing rules

There are various ways and action hooks used to create custom rewrite rules. We will choose the `init` action to define our custom routes for the user section, as shown in the following code:

```
public function manage_user_routes() {
  add_rewrite_rule( '^user/([^/]+)/?',
  'index.php?control_action=$matches[1]', 'top' );
}
```

We can call this function through the `init` action. Let's add the action call the constructor of the `WPWAF_Config_Manager` class, as shown in the following code:

```
class WPWAF_Config_Manager{
  public function __construct(){
    add_action( 'init', array( $this, 'manage_user_routes' ) );
  }
}
```

Based on the discussed requirements, all the URLs for the user section will follow the `/user/custom action` pattern. Therefore, we will define the regular expression for matching all the routes in the user section. Redirection is made to the `index.php` file with a query variable called `control_action`. This variable will contain the URL segment after the `/user` segment. The third parameter of the `add_rewrite_rule` function will decide whether to check this rewrite rule before the existing rules or after them. The value of `top` will give a higher precedence, while the value of `bottom` will give a lower precedence.

We need to complete two other tasks to get these rewriting rules to take effect:

- Add query variables to the WordPress `query_vars`
- Flush the rewriting rules

Adding query variables

WordPress doesn't allow you to use any type of variable in the query string. It will check for query variables within the existing list and all other variables will be ignored. Whenever we want to use a new query variable, make sure to add it to the existing list. First, we need to update our constructor with the following filter to customize query variables:

```
add_filter( 'query_vars', array( $this, 'manage_user_routes_query_vars' ) );
```

This filter on `query_vars` will allow us to customize the list of existing variables by adding or removing entries from an array. Now, consider the implementation to add a new query variable:

```
public function manage_user_routes_query_vars( $query_vars ) {
  $query_vars[] = 'control_action';
  return $query_vars;
}
```

As this is a filter, the existing `query_vars` variable will be passed as an array. We will modify the array by adding a new query variable called `control_action` and return the list. Now, we have the ability to access this variable from the URL.

Flushing the rewriting rules

Once rewrite rules are modified, it's a must to flush the rules in order to prevent 404 page generation. Flushing existing rules is a time-consuming task which impacts the performance of the application and hence should be avoided in repetitive actions such as `init`. It's recommended that you perform such tasks in plugin activation or installation as we did earlier in user roles and capabilities. So, let's implement the function for flushing rewrite rules on plugin activation:

```
public function flush_application_rewrite_rules() {
    flush_rewrite_rules();
}
```

As usual, we need to update the `activation_handler` function to include the call to the `flush_application_rewrite_rules` function using the following line of code:

```
$this->flush_application_rewrite_rules();
```

Now, go to the admin panel, deactivate the plugin, and activate the plugin again. Then, go to the URL `http://www.example.com/user/login` and check whether it works. Unfortunately, you will still get the 404 error for the request.

You might be wondering what went wrong. Let's go back and think about the process in order to understand the issue. We flushed the rules on plugin activation. So, the new rules should persist successfully. However, we will define the rules on the `init` action, which is only executed after the plugin is activated. Therefore, new rules will not be available at the time of flushing.

Consider the updated version of the `flush_application_rewrite_rules` function for a quick fix to our problem:

```
public function flush_application_rewrite_rules() {
    $this->manage_user_routes();
    flush_rewrite_rules();
}
```

We call the `manage_user_routes` function on plugin activation, followed by the call to `flush_rewrite_rules`. So, the new rules are generated before flushing is executed. Now, follow the previous process once again; you won't get a 404 page since all the rules have taken effect.

 You can get 404 errors due to the modification in rewriting rules and not flushing it properly. In such situations, go to the **Permalinks** section on the **Settings** page and click on the **Save Changes** button to flush the rewrite rules manually.

Now we are ready with our routing rules for user functionalities. It's important to know the existing routing rules of your application. Even though we can have a look at the routing rules from the database, it's difficult to decode the serialized array, as we encountered in the previous section.

So, I recommend that you use the free plugin called `Rewrite Rules Inspector`. This plugin has not been updated for recent WordPress versions. However, I haven't found any better or simpler plugin for this functionality. You can grab a copy at `http://wordpress.or g/plugins/rewrite-rules-inspector/`. Once installed, this plugin allows you to view all the existing routing rules, as well as offering a button to flush the rules, as shown in the following screenshot:

Let's identify the columns listed in the screenshot:

- **Rule**: This column shows the rule used to match the URL. So, in the first row we try to match URL's that contain *user/{any word}*.
- **Rewrite**: This column shows how matched rules are passed into WordPress as dynamic parameters.
- **Source:** This column shows whether its a default rewriting rules related to WordPress core features like posts, categories, tags or whether it's a custom rule.

Controlling access to your functions

We have a custom router which handles the URLs of the user section of our application. Next, we need a controller to handle the requests and generate the template for the user. This works similar to the controllers in the MVC pattern.

Even though we have changed the default routing, WordPress will look for an existing template to be sent back to the user. Therefore, we need to intercept this process and create our own templates. WordPress offers an action hook called `template_redirect` for intercepting requests. So, let's implement our frontend controller based on `template_redirect`. First, we need to update the constructor of the `WPWAF_Config_Manager` class with the `template_redirect` action, as shown in the following code:

```
add_action( 'template_redirect', array( $this, 'front_controller' ) );
```

Now, let's take a look at the implementation of the `front_controller` function using the following code:

```
public function front_controller() {
  global $wp_query, $wpwaf;
  $control_action = isset ( $wp_query-
>query_vars['control_action'] ) ? $wp_query-
>query_vars['control_action'] : ''; ;
    switch ( $control_action ) {
    case 'register':
      do_action( 'wpwaf_before_registeration_form' );
      $wpwaf->registration->display_registration_form();
      break;
  }
}
```

We will be handling custom routes based on the value of the `control_action` query variable assigned in the previous section. The value of this variable can be grabbed through the global `query_vars` array of the `$wp_query` object. Then, we can use a simple switch statement to handle the controlling based on the action.

The first action to consider will be to register as we are in the registration process. Once the `control_action` query variable is matched with registration, we execute an action and a function call to `display_registration_form`.

You might be confused about the location of this function and how it was executed. Basically, we need a separate class to handle the registration-related functionality. So we need to create a new class called `WPWAF_Registration` inside the `classes` folder and create an object inside the `instance` function of the `WPWAF_Forum` class using the following code:

```
self::$instance->registration    = new WPWAF_Registration();
```

Then we need to also include this file inside the `includes` function of the `WPWAF_Forum` class with similar code to that used for the `WPWAF_Config_Manager` class. Next, we can add an empty function called `display_registration_form` to the `WPWAF_Registration` class. Finally, we need to identify how this function was called inside our controller.

We structured our main class based on the singleton pattern. So, only one object will be initialized and it will be responsible for handling all the system calls. We created a global object called `$wpwaf` in our main forum class. We can call other class functions using the global object. First, we need to add it as a global object to our `front_controller` function. Then we can call the registration object on top of the global `$wpwaf` object. Finally, we call the `display_registration_form` function on top of both of those objects as follows:

```
$wpwaf->registration->display_registration_form();
```

You might be confused about why we use `do_action` in this scenario. These actions allow us to customize and extend the registration form display in different scenarios without modifying the core code. Let's discuss `do_action` in more detail in the next section.

The advantages of using the do_action function

WordPress action hooks define specific points in the execution process, where we can develop custom functions to modify existing behavior. In this scenario, we are calling the `wpwaf_before_registration_form` function within the class using `do_action`.

Unlike websites or blogs, web applications need to be extendable with future requirements. Think of a situation where we have to restrict the registration form to users from certain countries or provide different registration forms based on certain conditions. In a normal application, we will have to change the core application code to implement such features. Changing a working component is considered a bad practice in application development. Let's see why it's considered a bad practice by looking at the definition of the open/closed principle on Wikipedia:

> *"Open/closed principle states "software entities (classes, modules, functions, and so on) should be open for extension, but closed for modification"; that is, such an entity can allow its behavior to be modified without altering its source code. This is especially valuable in a production environment, where changes to the source code may necessitate code reviews, unit tests, and other such procedures to qualify it for use in a product: the code obeying the principle doesn't change when it is extended, and therefore, needs no such effort."*

WordPress action hooks come to our rescue in this scenario. We can define an `action` for the registration template using the `add_action` function, as shown in the following code:

```
add_action( 'wpwaf_before_registration_form ', array( $this,
'custom_registration_form' ) );
```

Now you can implement this action multiple times using different functions. In this scenario, `custom_registration_form` can be used to display a new registration form. Inside this function, we can add a new template, as shown in the following code:

```
public function custom_registration_form(){
   if ( !is_user_logged_in() ) {
      include WPWAF_PLUGIN_DIR . 'templates/custom-register-
template.php';
      exit;
   }
}
```

Now the `custom_registration_form` function is executed before the primary function. So, we can remove the primary registration template and override it with our own template. Also, we can use this function to check the user's country and redirect the user to a different page when the user is not allowed to access the registration form. With this technique, we have the capability of adding new functionalities as well as changing existing functionalities without affecting the already written code.

We have implemented a simple controller which can be quite effective in developing web application functionalities. In the following sections, we will continue the process of implementing registration on the frontend with custom templates.

Creating custom templates

Themes provide a default set of templates to cater to the existing behavior of WordPress. Here, we are trying to implement a custom template system to suit web applications. So, our first option is to include the template files directly inside the theme. Personally, I don't like this option due to two possible reasons:

- Whenever we switch the theme, we have to move the custom template files to a new theme. So, our templates become theme-dependent.
- In general, all existing templates are related to CMS functionality. Mixing custom templates with the existing ones becomes hard to manage.

As a solution to these concerns, we will implement the custom templates inside the plugin. First, create a folder inside the current plugin folder and name it `templates` to get things started.

Designing the registration form

We need to design a custom form for frontend registration containing the default header and footer. The whole content area will be used for the registration and the default sidebar will be omitted for this screen. Create a PHP file called `register-template.php` inside the `templates` folder with the following code:

```php
<?php global $wpwaf_registration_params;
    if(is_array($wpwaf_registration_params)){
        extract($wpwaf_registration_params);
    }
    get_header(); ?>
<div class='wpwaf-registration-form-header' ><?php echo
__('Register New Account','wpwaf'); ?></div>
    <div id='wpwaf-registration-errors'>
        <?php
        if( isset($wpwaf_registration_params['errors']) &&
count($wpwaf_registration_params['errors']) > 0) {
            foreach ( $wpwaf_registration_params['errors'] as $error ) {
                echo '<p class="wpwaf_frm_error">' . $error . '</p>';
            }
        }
        ?>
</div>
HTML Code for Form
</div>
<?php get_footer(); ?>
```

We can include the default header and footer using the `get_header` and `get_footer` functions, respectively. After the header, we will include a display area for the error messages generated in registration. More about the errors and usage of `$wpwaf_registration_params` will be discussed later in this section. Then, we have the HTML form, as shown in the following code:

```
<form id='wpwaf-registration-form' method='post' action='<?php echo
get_site_url() . '/user/register'; ?>'>
  <ul>
    <li>
      <label class='wpwaf_frm_label'><?php echo
__('Username','wpwaf'); ?></label>
      <input class='wpwaf_frm_field' type='text'
id='wpwaf_user' name='wpwaf_user' value='' />
    </li>
    <li>
      <label class='wpwaf_frm_label'><?php echo __('E-
mail','wpwaf'); ?></label>
      <input class='wpwaf_frm_field' type='text'
id='wpwaf_email' name='wpwaf_email' value='' />
    </li>
    <li>
      <label class='wpwaf_frm_label'><?php echo __('User
Type','wpwaf'); ?></label>
      <select class='wpwaf_frm_field' name='wpwaf_user_type'>
        <option value='wpwaf_premium_member'><?php echo __('Premium
Member','wpwaf'); ?></option>
        <option value='wpwaf_free_member'><?php echo __('Free
Member','wpwaf'); ?></option>
      </select>
    </li>
    <li>
      <label class='wpwaf_frm_label' for=''> </label>
      <input type='submit' name='wpwaf_reg_submit' value='<?php echo
__('Register','wpwaf'); ?>' />
    </li>
  </ul>
</form>
```

As you can see, the `form` action is set to a custom route called `user/register` to be handled through the front controller. Also, we have added an extra field called `user type` to choose the preferred user type on registration.

You might have noticed that we used `wpwaf` as the prefix for form element names and element IDs, as well as CSS classes. Even though it's not a must to use a prefix, it can be highly effective when working with multiple third-party plugins. A unique plugin-specific prefix avoids or limits conflicts with other plugins and themes.

We will get a screen similar to the following one, once we access the `/user/register` link in the browser:

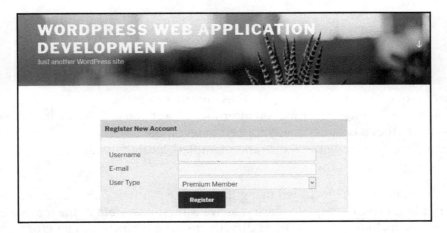

Once the form is submitted, we have to create the user based on the application requirements.

Planning the registration process

In this application, we have opted to build a complex registration process in order to understand the typical requirements of web applications. So, it's better to plan it upfront before moving into the implementation. Let's build a list of requirements for registration:

- The user should be able to register as any of the given user roles
- If the user registers as a free member, the activation code needs to be generated and sent to the user
- If the user registers as a premium member, the user will be redirected to a separate page for payments, and notification will not be sent until the user completes the payment

- The default notification on successful registration needs to be customized to include the activation link
- Users should activate their account by clicking the link

So, let's begin the task of registering users by displaying the registration form inside the WPWAF_Registration class as given in the following code:

```
public function display_registration_form(){
  global $wpwaf_registration_params;
  if ( !is_user_logged_in() ) {
    include WPWAF_PLUGIN_DIR . 'templates/register-template.php';
    exit;
  }
}
```

Once the user requests /user/register, the controller calls the display_registration_form function after the do_action call. In the initial request, we need to check whether a user is already logged in using the is_user_logged_in function. If not, we can directly include the registration template located inside the templates folder to display the registration form.

WordPress templates can be included using the get_template_part function. However, it doesn't work like a typical template library, as we cannot pass data to the template. In this technique, we are including the template directly inside the function. Therefore, we have to use a global variable to pass and access the data between the class and the template.

Handling registration form submission

Once the user fills in the data and clicks the **Submit** button, we have to execute quite a few tasks in order to register a user in the WordPress database. Let's figure out the main tasks for registering a user:

- Validating form data
- Registering the user details
- Creating and saving the activation code
- Sending e-mail notifications with an activate link or redirecting the user for payments based on the selected user type

We will be using a separate function called `register_user` to handle form submission. Validating user data is one of the main tasks in form submission handling. So, let's define the `register_user` function using the `init` action inside the class constructer, as shown in the following code:

```
class WPWAF_Registration{
  public function __construct(){
    add_action( 'init', array( $this, 'register_user' ) );
  }
}
```

Now let's take a look at the implementation of the `register_user` function inside the `WPWAF_Registration` class:

```
public function register_user(){
  global $wpwaf_registration_params,$wpwaf_login_params;
  ......
  if ($_POST['wpwaf_reg_submit'] ) {
    $errors = array();
    $user_login = ( isset ( $_POST['wpwaf_user'] ) ?
$_POST['wpwaf_user'] : '' );
    $user_email = ( isset ( $_POST['wpwaf_email'] ) ?
$_POST['wpwaf_email'] : '' );
    $user_type  = ( isset ( $_POST['wpwaf_user_type'] ) ?
$_POST['wpwaf_user_type'] : '' );

    if ( empty( $user_login ) )
      array_push( $errors, __('Please enter a username.','wpwaf')
);

    if ( empty( $user_email ) )
      array_push( $errors, __('Please enter e-mail.','wpwaf') );

     if ( empty( $user_type ) )
       array_push( $errors, __('Please enter user type.','wpwaf')
);
    // Saving user details
    // Including the template
  }
```

The following steps are to be performed:

1. First, we will check whether the request is made as POST.
2. Then, we get the form data from the POST array.
3. Finally, we will check the passed values for empty conditions and push the error messages to the $errors variable created at the beginning of this function.

Now, we can move into more advanced validations inside the `register_user` function, as shown in the following code:

```
$sanitized_user_login = sanitize_user( $user_login );

if ( !empty($user_email) && !is_email( $user_email ) )
  array_push( $errors, __('Please enter valid email.','wpwaf'));
elseif ( email_exists( $user_email ) )
  array_push( $errors, __('User with this email already
registered.','wpwaf'));

if ( empty( $sanitized_user_login ) || !validate_username(
$user_login ) )
  array_push( $errors,  __('Invalid username.','wpwaf') );
elseif ( username_exists( $sanitized_user_login ) )
  array_push( $errors, __('Username already exists.','wpwaf') );
```

The steps to perform are as follows:

1. First, we will use the existing `sanitize_user` function and remove unsafe characters from the username.
2. Then, we will make validations on the e-mail to check whether it's valid and its existence status in the system. Both the `email_exists` and `username_exists` functions check for the existence of an `email` and `username` from the database. Once all the validations are completed, the errors array will be either empty or filled with error messages.

 In this scenario, we choose to go with the most essential validations for the registration form. You can add more advanced validation in your implementations in order to minimize potential security threats.

Next, we need to pass the registration form data and errors to the registration form template. In the beginning of this function, we added a global variable called `$wpwaf_registration_params` to keep data for templates. So we can assign the errors and data to this variable, as shown in the following code:

```
$wpwaf_registration_params['errors'] = $errors;
$wpwaf_registration_params['user_login'] = $user_login;
$wpwaf_registration_params['user_email'] = $user_email;
$wpwaf_registration_params['user_type'] = $user_type;
```

We added `$wpwaf_registration_params` as a global variable in the start of this section while creating the registration template. If we get validation errors in the form, we can directly print the contents of the `error` array on top of the form using the `$wpwaf_registration_params` variable as shown in the registration template. Here is a preview of our registration screen with generated error messages:

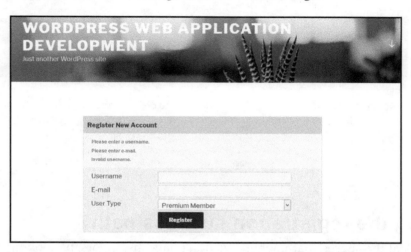

Also, it's important to repopulate the form values once errors are generated. We have passed the user-submitted data to the template using the `$wpwaf_registration_params` variable. Therefore, we can directly access the `POST` variables inside the template to echo the values, as shown in the updated registration form:

```
<form id='wpwaf-registration-form' method='post' action='<?php echo
get_site_url() . '/user/register'; ?>'>
   <ul>
     <li>
       <label class='wpwaf_frm_label'><?php echo
__('Username','wpwaf'); ?></label>
       <input class='wpwaf_frm_field' type='text' id='wpwaf_user'
name='wpwaf_user' value='<?php echo isset( $user_login ) ?
$user_login : ''; ?>'  />
     </li>
     <li>
       <label class='wpwaf_frm_label'><?php echo __('E-
mail','wpwaf'); ?></label>
       <input class='wpwaf_frm_field' type='text' id='wpwaf_email'
name='wpwaf_email' value='<?php echo isset( $user_email ) ?
$user_email : ''; ?>' />
     </li>
     <li>
```

```html
      <label class='wpwaf_frm_label'><?php echo __('User
Type','wpwaf'); ?></label>
      <select class='wpwaf_frm_field' name='wpwaf_user_type'>
        <option <?php echo (isset( $user_type ) && $user_type ==
'wpwaf_premium_member') ? 'selected' : ''; ?>
value='wpwaf_premium_member'><?php echo __('Premium Member','wpwaf');
?></option>
        <option <?php echo (isset( $user_type ) && $user_type ==
'wpwaf_free_member') ? 'selected' : ''; ?> value='wpwaf_free_member'>
<?php echo __('Free Member','wpwaf'); ?></option>
      </select>
    </li>
    <li>
      <label class='wpwaf_frm_label' for=''> </label>
      <input type='submit' name='wpwaf_reg_submit' value='<?php echo
__('Register','wpwaf'); ?>' />
    </li>
  </ul>
</form>
```

Exploring the registration success path

Now let's look at the success path, where we don't have any errors, by looking at the remaining sections of the `register_user` function:

```php
if ( empty( $errors ) ) {
  $user_pass  = wp_generate_password();
  $user_id    = wp_insert_user( array('user_login' =>
$sanitized_user_login,
    'user_email' => $user_email,
    'role' => $user_type,
    'user_pass' => $user_pass)
  );
  if ( !$user_id ) {
    array_push( $errors, __('Registration failed.','wpwaf') );
    $wpwaf_registration_params['errors'] = $errors;
  } else {
    $activation_code = $this->random_string();
    update_user_meta( $user_id, 'wpwaf_activation_code',
$activation_code );
    update_user_meta( $user_id, 'wpwaf_activation_status', 'inactive'
    );

    if($user_type == 'wpwaf_premium_member'){
      update_user_meta( $user_id, 'wpwaf_payment_status', 'inactive' );
      // Redirect User to Payment page with User Details
    }else{
```

```
            update_user_meta($user_id,'wpwaf_payment_status','active' );
            wpwaf_send_user_notification ( $user_id, $user_pass,
$activation_code );
            $wpwaf_login_params['success_message'] = __('Registration
completed successfully. Please check your email for activation
link.','wpwaf');

        }
    }
    if ( !is_user_logged_in() ) {
        include WPWAF_PLUGIN_DIR . 'templates/login-template.php';
        exit;
    }
}
```

We can generate the default password using the wp_generate_password function. Then, we can use the wp_insert_user function with respective parameters generated from the form to save the user in the database.

> The wp_insert_user function will be used to update the current user or add new users to the application. Make sure you are not logged in while executing this function; otherwise, your admin will suddenly change into another user type after using this function.

If the system fails to save the user, we can create a registration fail message and assign it to the $errors variable as we did earlier. Once the registration is successful, we will have to work with two separate paths for our member roles.

If the user is registered as a premium member, we set the initial wpwaf_payment_status as inactive and redirect the user to the payments screen. The payments screen and submission are not handled at this stage in the book.

If the user is registered as a free member, we set the initial wpwaf_payment_status as active and generate a random string as the activation code. You can use any function here to generate a random string.

Then, we update the user with an activation code and set the activation status as inactive for the moment. Finally, we have to send an e-mail containing the registration details. By default, this e-mail is sent by the wp_new_user_notification function inside the WordPress core. Here, we are going to use our own email function to include the custom content and make it flexible for our needs. So we have to add a new file called functions.php inside the forum plugin root folder and include this file inside the includes function of the WPWAF_Forum class.

Now we can add the custom `email` sending function to the `functions.php` file, as shown in the following code:

```
function wpwaf_send_user_notification ($user_id, $plaintext_pass = '',
$activate_code = '') {
  $user = new WP_User($user_id);
  $user_login = stripslashes($user->user_login);
  $user_email = stripslashes($user->user_email);

  $message = sprintf(__('New user registration on %s:','wpwaf'),
get_option('blogname')) . '\r\n\r\n';
  $message .= sprintf(__('Username: %s','wpwaf'), $user_login) .
'\r\n\r\n';
  $message .= sprintf(__('E-mail: %s','wpwaf'), $user_email) .
'\r\n';

  @wp_mail(get_option('admin_email'), sprintf(__('[%s] New User
Registration','wpwaf'), get_option('blogname')), $message);

  if (empty($plaintext_pass))
    return;

  $act_link = site_url() . "/user/activate/?
wpwaf_activation_code=$activate_code";

  $message = __('Hi there,','wpwaf') . '\r\n\r\n';
  $message .= sprintf(__('Welcome to %s! Please activate your
account using the link:','wpwa'), get_option('blogname')) .
'\r\n\r\n';
  $message .= sprintf(__('<a href="%s">%s</a>','wpwaf'), $act_link,
$act_link) . '\r\n';
  $message .= sprintf(__('Username: %s','wpwaf'), $user_login) .
'\r\n';
  $message .= sprintf(__('Password: %s','wpwaf'), $plaintext_pass)
. '\r\n\r\n';

  wp_mail($user_email, sprintf(__('[%s] Your username and
password','wpwa'), get_option('blogname')), $message);

}
```

The first part of this function, up to the first `wp_mail` execution, prepares the e-mail to be sent to the administrator with the username and e-mail of the user. The next part contains the e-mail sending functionality for the registered user. The e-mail sent to the user needs to be customized to include the activation link. Therefore, we take the activation parameter passed to the function add it to the predefined activation link. Next, we send the e-mail with the username, password, and activation link.

That's about all we need to change from the original function. Finally, we set the success message to be passed into the login screen.

Now, let's move back to the `register_user` function. Once the notification is sent, the registration process is completed and the user will be redirected to the login screen. Once the user has the e-mail in their inbox, they can use the activation link to activate the account.

Automatically logging in the user after registration

In general, most web applications uses e-mail confirmations before allowing users to log in to the system. However, there can be certain scenarios where we need to automatically authenticate the user into the application. A social network sign-in is a great example for such a scenario. When using social network logins, the system checks whether the user is already registered. If not, the application automatically registers the user and authenticates them. We can easily modify our code to implement an automatic login after registration. Consider the following code:

```
if ( !is_user_logged_in() ) {
  wp_set_auth_cookie($user_id, false, is_ssl());
  include WPWAF_PLUGIN_DIR . 'templates/login-template.php';
  exit;
}
```

The registration code is updated to use the `wp_set_auth_cookie` function. Once it's used, the user authentication cookie will be created and hence the user will be considered as automatically signed in. Then, we will redirect to the login page as usual. Since the user is already logged in using the authentication cookie, they will be redirected back to the home page with access to the backend. This is an easy way of automatically authenticating users into WordPress.

Activating system users

Once the user clicks on the activation link, redirection will be made to the /user/activate URL of the application. So, we need to modify our controller with a new case for activation, as shown in the following code:

```
case 'activate':
  do_action( 'wpwaf_before_activate_user' );
  $wpwaf->registration->activate_user();
  do_action( 'wpwaf_after_activate_user' );
  break;
```

Here, we have two actions, one before the activation function and one after the activation function. These actions can be used to alter the activation process as we did with displaying the registration form. We can use the wpwa_before_activate_user action to check certain conditions on the activation URL and then allow/deny the user to activate the account. Similarly, we can use the wpwa_after_activate_user action when we need to add additional parameters to the user in the database on successful activation.

Now let's move on to the main part of completing user activation. We have to add a new function called activate_user to the WPWAF_Registration class. Let's look at the implementation of the activate_user function:

```
public function activate_user() {
    $activation_code = isset( $_GET['wpwaf_activation_code'] ) ?
  sanitize_text_field($_GET['wpwaf_activation_code']) : '';
    $message = '';

    $user_query = new WP_User_Query(  array(
            'meta_key' => 'wpwaf_activation_code',
            'meta_value' => $activation_code ));
    $users = $user_query->get_results();

    if ( !empty($users) ) {
      $user_id = $users[0]->ID;
      update_user_meta( $user_id, 'wpwa_activation_status', 'active'
);
      $message = __('Account activated successfully.','wpwaf');
    } else {
      $message = __('Invalid Activation Code','wpwaf');
    }

    include WPWAF_PLUGIN_DIR . 'templates/info-template.php';
    exit;
  }
```

We will get the activation code from the link and query the database to find a matching entry. If no records are found, we set the message as activation failed, or else we can update the activation status of the matching user to activate the account. Upon activation, the user will be given a message using the `info-template.php` template, which consists of a very basic template like the following one:

```php
<?php get_header(); ?>
<div id='wpwaf_custom_panel'>
    <div id='wpwaf_info_message'>
        <?php echo $message; ?>
    </div>
</div>
<?php get_footer(); ?>
```

Once the user visits the activation page on the `/user/activation` URL, information will be given to the user, as illustrated in the following screenshot:

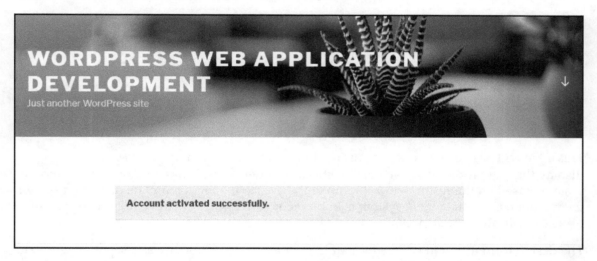

We have successfully created and activated a new user. The final task of this process is to authenticate and log the user into the system. Let's see how we can create the login functionality.

Creating a login form in the frontend

The frontend login can be found in many WordPress websites, including small blogs. Usually, we place the login form in the sidebar of the website. In web applications, user interfaces are more complex and different compared to normal websites.

Hence, we will implement a full-page login screen as we did with registration. First, we need to update our controller with another case for login, as shown in the following code:

```
switch ( $control_action ) {
  // Other cases
  case 'login':
    do_action( 'wpwaf_before_login_form' );
    $wpwaf->login->display_login_form();
    break;
}
```

We have used a new class called `login` to call this function. So we need to create a new class called `WPWAF_Login` inside the `classes` folder and do the object creation and file inclusion inside the `WPWAF_Forum` class as we did in previous occurrences. Once it's completed, we can add the `display_login_form` function to the new class using the following code:

```
public function display_login_form(){
  global $wpwaf_login_params;
  if ( !is_user_logged_in() ) {
    include WPWAF_PLUGIN_DIR . 'templates/login-template.php';
  } else {
    wp_redirect( home_url() );
  }
  exit;
}
```

This code will be executed once the user enters `/user/login` in the browser URL to display the login form. First, we need to check whether the user has already logged into the system. Based on the result, we will redirect the user to the login template or home page for the moment. Once the whole system is implemented, we will be redirecting the logged-in users to their own admin area.

The design form for login will be located in the `templates` directory as a separate template called `login-template.php`. Here is the implementation of the login form design with the necessary error messages:

```
<?php global $wpwaf_login_params;
    if(is_array($wpwaf_login_params)){
      extract($wpwaf_login_params);
    }
    get_header(); ?>
<div id='wpwaf_custom_panel'>
  <div class='wpwaf-login-form-header' ><?php echo
__('Login','wpwaf'); ?></div>
    <div id='wpwaf-login-errors'>
```

```php
<?php

    if ( isset($wpwaf_login_params['errors']) &&
count($wpwaf_login_params['errors']) > 0) {
        foreach ( $wpwaf_login_params['errors'] as $error ) {
            echo '<p class="wpwaf_frm_error">'.$error .'</p>';
        }
    }


    if( isset( $wpwaf_login_params['success_message'] ) &&
$wpwaf_login_params['success_message'] != ""){
        echo '<p class="wpwaf_frm_success">' .
$wpwaf_login_params['success_message'] . '</p>';
    }

    ?>
    </div>
    <form method='post' action='<?php echo site_url(); ?>/user/login'
id='wpwaf_login_form' name='wpwaf_login_form'>
        <ul>
        <li>
            <label class='wpwaf_frm_label' for='username'><?php echo
__('Username','wpwaf'); ?></label>
            <input class='wpwaf_frm_field' type='text'
name='wpwaf_username' value='<?php echo isset( $username ) ?
$username : ''; ?>' />
        </li>
        <li>
            <label class='wpwaf_frm_label' for='password'><?php echo
__('Password','wpwaf'); ?></label>
            <input class='wpwaf_frm_field' type='password'
name='wpwaf_password' value="" />
        </li>
        <li>
            <label class='wpwaf_frm_label' > </label>
            <input  type='submit'  name='wpwaf_login_submit' value='<?
php echo __('Login','wpwaf'); ?>' />
        </li>
        </ul>
    </form>
</div>
<?php get_footer(); ?>
```

Similar to the registration template, we have a header, error messages, the HTML form, and the footer in this template. We have to point the action of this form to /user/login. The remaining code is self-explanatory and hence I am not going to make detailed explanations.

You can take a look at the preview of our login screen in the following screenshot:

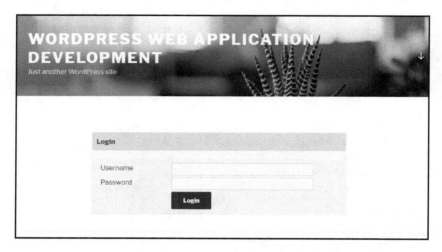

Next, we need to implement the form submission handler for the login functionality. Before this, we need to update the constructor of the WPWAF_Login class with the following code to define another custom action for login:

```
add_action( 'init', array( $this, 'login_user' ) );
```

In the next section, we will be looking at the code for the login_user function and the login submission process.

Handling login form submission

We have defined a function call on the init action to call the login_user function. This function is responsible for handling the login form submission and authenticating the users into the application. Let's take a look at the form submission handling part of the login_user function:

```
public function login_user() {
    global $wpwaf_login_params;
    $errors = array();

    if ( $_POST['wpwaf_login_submit'] ) {
        $username = isset ( $_POST['wpwaf_username'] ) ?
$_POST['wpwaf_username'] : '';
        $password = isset ( $_POST['wpwaf_password'] ) ?
$_POST['wpwaf_password'] : '';
```

```
        if ( empty( $username ) )
          array_push( $errors, __('Please enter a username.','wpwaf')
);

          if ( empty( $password ) )
          array_push( $errors, __('Please enter password.','wpwaf') );

        if(count($errors) > 0){
          include WPWAF_PLUGIN_DIR . 'templates/login-template.php';
          exit;
        }

        $credentials = array();
        $credentials['user_login']      = $username;
        $credentials['user_login']      = sanitize_user(
$credentials['user_login'] );
        $credentials['user_password']   = $password;
        $credentials['remember']        = false;
        // Rest of the code
      }
    }
```

As usual, we need to validate the post data and generate the necessary errors to be shown in the frontend. Once validations are successfully completed, we assign all the form data to an array after sanitizing the values. The username and password are contained in the credentials array with the user_login and user_password keys. The remember key defines whether to remember the password or not. Since we don't have a remember checkbox in our form, it will be set to false. Next, we need to execute the WordPress login function in order to log the user into the system, as shown in the following code:

```
$user = wp_signon( $credentials, false );
if ( is_wp_error( $user ) ){
  array_push( $errors, $user->get_error_message() );
  $wpwaf_login_params['errors'] = $errors;
}else{
  wp_redirect( home_url() );
  exit;
}
```

WordPress handles user authentication through the wp_signon function. We have to pass all the credentials generated in the previous code with an additional second parameter of true or false to define whether to use a secure cookie. We can set it to false for this example. The wp_signon function will return an object of the WP_User or the WP_Error class based on the result.

Internally, this function sets an authentication cookie. Users will not be logged in if it is not set. If you are using any other process for authenticating users, you have to set this authentication cookie manually.

Once a user is successfully authenticated, a redirection will be made to the home page of the site. Now we should have the ability to authenticate users from the login form in the frontend.

Checking whether we implemented the process properly

Take a moment to think carefully about our requirements and try to figure out what we have missed.

Actually, we didn't check the activation status on login. Therefore, any user will be able to log into the system without activating their account. Now, let's fix this issue by intercepting the authentication process with another built-in action called `authenticate`. First, we have to add the `authenticate` action to the constructor of the `WPWAF_Login` class, as shown in the following code:

```
add_filter( 'authenticate', array( $this, 'authenticate_user' ),30,
3 );
```

Next, we can look at the implementation of this function, as shown in the following code:

```
public function authenticate_user( $user, $username, $password ) {
   if(! empty($username) && !is_wp_error($user)){
     $user = get_user_by('login', $username );
     if (!in_array( 'administrator', (array) $user->roles ) ) {
       $active_status = '';
       $active_status = get_user_meta( $user->data->ID,
'wpwa_activation_status', true );
       if ( 'inactive' == $active_status ) {
         $user = new WP_Error( 'denied', __('<strong>ERROR</strong>:
Please activate your account.','wpwaf'
   ) );
       }
     }
   }
   return $user;
 }
```

This function will be called in the `authentication` action by passing the `user`, `username`, and `password` variables as default parameters. All the user types of our application need to be activated, except for the administrator accounts. Therefore, we check the roles of the authenticated user to figure out whether they are admin. Then, we can check the activation status of other user types before authenticating. If an authenticated user is in inactive status, we can return the `WP_Error` object and prevent authentication from being successful.

 This filter is also executed when the user logs out of the application. Therefore, we need to consider the following validation to prevent any errors in the logout process:

```
if(! empty($username) && !is_wp_error($user))
```

Now we have a simple and useful user registration and login system, ready to be implemented in the frontend of web applications. Make sure to check login- and registration-related plugins from the official repository to gain knowledge of complex requirements in real-world scenarios.

Essential user management features for web applications

As discussed throughout this chapter, **user management** is one of the most important tasks in web application development. Only limited types of applications can be built without needing user management. So we discussed some of the core user management features available in WordPress and we will be exploring more built-in user features in upcoming chapters.

The built-in user management features of WordPress focus more on the administrative side. There are very limited user management features for the user in the frontend of the application. Therefore, often we need to develop additional user management features for the frontend or use custom plugins that provide such features. In this section, we will be discussing some of the most important and commonly used user management features, as follows:

- Frontend login and registration
- Custom profile fields
- Private data
- Search and member list
- Frontend profile

Let's get started.

Frontend login and registration

This is one of the most important aspects of user management as it's the gateway for building the user base of your application. Therefore, we discussed this feature and the frontend implementation in the previous sections.

Custom profile fields

Once a user creates an account, they will have access to their WordPress profile on the backend. The default user profile includes basic built-in fields commonly used to identify the user. However, web applications often require advanced field and field types to capture data related to different user roles. For example, the profile of a doctor will have additional fields related to medical data, and the profile of a web developer will have additional fields related to projects and skills. Since WordPress doesn't provide features for additional fields by default, we have to implement this with custom coding or use a user management plugin that offers custom field management features.

We can capture the basic profile details of users with the support of basic HTML field types such as text, radio buttons, checkboxes, drop-down menus, text areas, passwords, and files. We have to use custom field types in situations where we can't capture the advanced user data with these basic field types. There are many plugins that offer advanced custom field types such as videos, date pickers, numeric ranges, and galleries. Planning application user fields and identifying field types to capture these details is essential in building a successful application.

Private data

The profile fields offered by WordPress are common to every user type. So the existing user roles and custom user roles will have the same set of fields inside the profile. In general, we have different user roles in web applications with different access levels. So the custom fields required for doctors are not the same as the custom fields needed for web developers.

Let's consider the user roles in our forum application. We have two user roles, called free members and premium members. Premium members pay a fee for the application and hence they should have premium features compared to the free members. In such scenarios, we provide a basic set of profile fields for free members and an advanced set of custom fields for premium members. So we need to keep these custom fields private for different user types. Also, some users may want to keep their profile data private from other users and only visible to administrators.

In general, web applications that use custom profile fields require advanced field management features for keeping data private and making them accessible by certain user levels with required permissions. There are many plugins that offer such features and hence it's wise to use them in web applications, unless you have time to create your own.

Search and member list

The application search is another crucial feature of an application. Users need to find information as quickly as possible and hence search features play a vital role in the success of an application. The WordPress built-in frontend search feature is very powerful and easily extendable through custom filters. However, it doesn't search users or user data as it's not a common feature in a normal website. We need to find a way to implement user searching when working in web applications where users play a major role. Applications such as forums, social networks, freelancing sites, and job management are great examples where we need advanced user searching features. Here, we are also discussing the frontend member list as it's something that goes together with search feature to display the results.

In such web applications, we have to look for a custom solution or plugin that offers frontend search and member list features. These features should include user custom field searching, custom search filters, restricting searching to certain fields, and paginated member lists.

Frontend profile

This feature is not required in all web applications. However, it's the most important feature in applications such as forums, social networks, freelancing sites, and job management. The WordPress backend profile is very basic and not user-friendly. Also, it requires your users to navigate away from the frontend of the website to view the profile. In these types of applications, it's a must to have a fully featured frontend profile with user-friendly design to match your application design.

We use the backend profile mainly to manage users' personal data. Web applications extend user profiles by including additional features inside the profiles, such as orders, purchases, projects, albums, activities, posts, and form submissions. Generally, these types of data are managed in separate tabs inside the profile. Social networks such as Facebook are a great example for identifying the need of an advanced profile with various tabs. We can use third-party plugins or create our own frontend profiles to suit the custom requirements of our web applications.

Implementing user management features with popular plugins

In the previous section, we discussed the need for custom user-related functionality in managing large web applications. We can use our own code to create all of the mentioned features to suit web applications. However, implementing these features from scratch is a highly time-consuming task requiring perfect planning. So we need to consider the type of application and the requirements before deciding to implement these features from scratch.

Usually, it's a wise decision to use an existing plugin-based solution in such scenarios, unless user management is the core feature of your application and existing solutions are not capable of handling your application requirements. We can find dozens of free and premium user management plugins by professional developers to manage the user-related tasks of your application. In the next section, we will be looking at three such plugins among the dozens available online.

BuddyPress

`BuddyPress` is one of the most popular plugins in the WordPress plugin directory. It is used to build applications with a user community and interactions between the users. A social network is the type of application where BuddyPress can be used to its maximum potential with all the built-in features. You can also use BuddyPress for applications such as team management, professional profile management, and help desk systems.

Let's have a look at some of the key features of BuddyPress:

- Frontend login and registration
- Frontend profiles
- Activity streams
- User groups
- User messaging
- Friend connections
- User notifications

These are the main components of BuddyPress. However, you can find many other user-management-related features in the hundreds of BuddyPress add-on plugins available in the WordPress plugin directory. Let's take a look at the default BuddyPress user profile with all the mentioned features in the following screenshot:

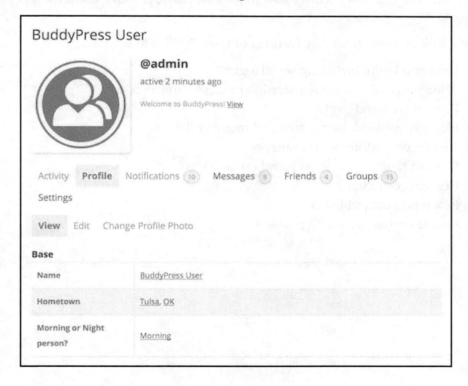

`BuddyPress` is used by over 200,000 active sites and you can use it to power your web applications. It's open source and you can modify it as you need with the support of a large group of community members. Since it's an open source solution and focuses mainly on the functionality, the frontend designs are not eye-catching for web applications. In scenarios where you need a great design, you can use a well-designed custom BuddyPress theme or custom user management plugin that offers well-designed interfaces. You can download `BuddyPress` from `https://wordpress.org/plugins/buddypress/`.

User Profiles Made Easy

User Profiles Made Easy is a premium plugin built for providing amazing user profiles and user management features for your application. Mainly, you can use this plugin to manage advanced registration processes and advanced user profiles in your applications. This plugin offers all the features we discussed in the *Essential user management features for web applications* section.

Let's have a look at some of the key features of User Profiles Made Easy:

- Frontend login, including social login
- Wide range of custom registration processes in frontend
- Elegant frontend profiles
- Flexible frontend user search and member list
- Advanced custom fields manager
- Custom field permissions based on user level
- Content restrictions
- Frontend post publisher
- Enable custom info with profile tabs

Apart from these main components, you can also use the add-ons to build applications such as social networks and portfolio management systems with this plugin. Let's take a look at the default user profile with custom tabs and all the mentioned features in the following screenshot:

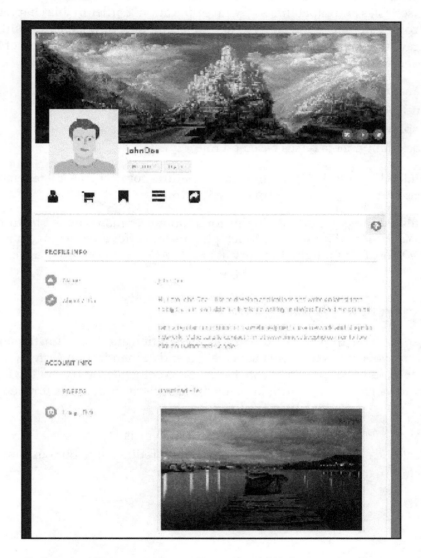

I can recommend this plugin for applications as it's a fully featured solution and I am part of its development team. You can get User Profiles Made Easy from `https://goo.gl/8G1BUh`.

User Role Editor

The User Role Editor plugin focuses on the administrative aspects of users compared to the frontend features we discussed in the previous two plugins. This plugin is intended to manage the user roles and capabilities of your application. Earlier in this chapter, we created user roles manually and used the Members plugin to view capabilities. This is also a similar plugin with many more additional features. Let's have a look at some of the key features of User Role Editor:

- Manage user roles and assign capabilities
- Block admin menu items by role
- Display widgets based on selected roles
- Block admin meta boxes based on role

You can download User Role Editor and test its features for user role management from https://wordpress.org/plugins/user-role-editor/.

We have discussed three important plugins for adding user management features to your applications. You can find hundreds of such plugins that offer a wide range of user-related features in the WordPress plugin directory at https://wordpress.org/plugins/.

Time to practice

In this chapter, we have implemented a simple registration and login functionality from the frontend. Before we have a complete user creation and authentication system, there are plenty of other tasks to be completed. So, I would recommend you try out the following tasks in order to be comfortable with implementing such functionalities for web applications:

- Create a frontend functionality for lost passwords
- Block the default WordPress login page and redirect it to our custom page
- Include extra fields in the registration form

Summary

In this chapter, we have explored the basics of user roles and capabilities related to web application development. We were able to choose the user roles for our application considering the various possibilities provided by WordPress.

Next, we learned how to create custom routes in order to achieve an MVC-like process using the frontend controller and custom template system.

Finally, we looked at how we can customize the built-in registration and login process in the frontend to cater to advanced requirements in web application development.

By now, you should be capable of defining user roles and capabilities to match your application, creating custom routers for common modules, implementing custom controllers with custom template systems, and customizing the existing user registration and authentication process.

In the next chapter, we will look at how we can adapt the existing database of WordPress into web applications, while planning the database for a forum management application. Stay tuned for another exciting chapter.

3

Planning and Customizing the Core Database

In the previous chapter, we looked at user management and permission related features of WordPress, while implementing basic user creation features. We can now move into one of the most important aspects of an application.

Generally, a database acts as the primary location from which your web application data will be accessible from frontend interfaces or third-party systems. Planning and designing the database should be one of the highest priority tasks in the initial stages of a project. As developers, we have the opportunity to design the database from scratch in many web applications. WordPress comes with a pre-structured database, and therefore the task of planning the table structure and adapting to existing tables becomes much more complex than everyone thinks. Throughout this chapter, we will focus on the basics of planning and accessing databases for web applications. This chapter contains important content for the rest of the book and is theoretical compared to other chapters.

In this chapter, we will cover the following topics:

- Understanding the WordPress database
- Exploring the role of existing tables
- Adapting existing tables in web applications
- Extending the database with custom tables
- Planning forum application tables
- Querying the database
- Limitations and considerations

Understanding the WordPress database

Typical full stack web development frameworks don't come with a predefined database structure. Instead, these frameworks focus on the core foundation of an application while allowing the developers to focus on the application-specific features. On the other hand, WordPress provides a preplanned database structure with a fixed set of tables. WordPress is built to function as a content management system, and therefore it can be classified as a product rather than a pure development framework. The WordPress core database is designed to power the generic functionalities of a CMS. Therefore, it's our responsibility to use our skills to make it work as an application development framework.

The WordPress database is intended to work with MySQL, and therefore we need to have a MySQL database set up before installing WordPress. On successful installation, WordPress will create 11 database tables to cater for the core functionality with the default MySQL table engine.

 MyISAM was used as the default MySQL table engine prior to version 5.5.5, and this has been changed to InnoDB from version 5.5 onwards.

WordPress' core features will always be limited to these 11 tables, and it's quite surprising to see the flexibility of building a wide range of applications with such a limited number of tables. Both WordPress and framework developers need to have a thorough understanding of the existing tables in order to use them in web applications.

Exploring the role of existing tables

Assuming that most of you are existing WordPress developers, you will have a solid understanding of an existing database table structure. However, I suggest that you continue with this section, as web applications can present a different perspective on using these tables. Based on the functionality, we will categorize the existing tables into four sections, as follows:

- User-related tables
- Post-related tables
- Term-related tables
- Other tables

Let's look at how each table fits into these categories, and look at their roles in web applications.

User-related tables

This category consists of two tables that contain the user-related information of your application. Let's take a look at the relationship between user-related tables before moving onto the explanation:

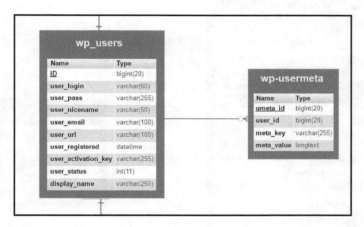

The two tables shown in the preceding diagram are as follows:

- `wp_users`: All the registered users will be stored in this table with their basic details, such as name, e-mail, username, and password.
- `wp-usermeta`: This table is used to store additional information about the users as key-value pairs. User roles and capabilities can be considered as the most important user-specific data of this table. Also, we have the freedom to add any user-related information as new key-value pairs.

 Throughout this chapter, we'll be referring to WordPress tables with the default prefix of `wp_`. You can change the prefix through the installation process or by manually changing the `wp-config.php` file in the root directory.

Post-related tables

This section consists of two tables that contain website posts and page-related information. Let's take a look at the relationship between post-related tables before moving onto the explanation:

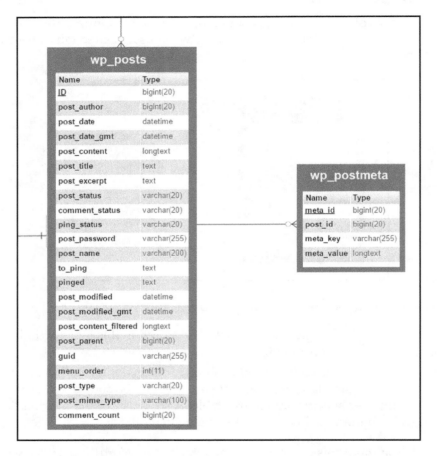

The tables shown in the diagram are as follows:

- `wp_posts`: This table contains all the posts and pages of your website with details such as post name, author, content, status, and post type.
- `wp_postmeta`: This table contains all the additional details for each post as key-value pairs. By default, it will contain details such as page template, attachments, and edit locks. Also, we can store any post-related information as new key-value pairs.

Term-related tables

WordPress terms can be simply described as categories and tags. This section consists of three tables for post category and tag-related information. Let's take a look at the relationships between term-related tables:

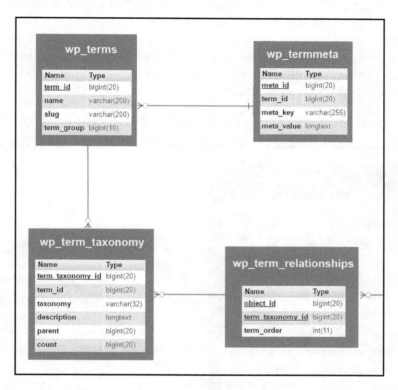

The three tables shown in the diagram are as follows:

- `wp_terms`: This table contains master data for all new categories and tags, including custom taxonomies.
- `wp_term_taxonomy`: This table is used to define the type of terms and the number of posts or pages available for each term. Basically, all the terms will be categorized as category, post-tags, or any other custom term created through plugins.
- `wp_term_relationships`: This table is used to associate all the terms with their respective posts.
- `wp_termmeta`: This table is used to add additional meta values related to taxonomies like categories and tags.

Other tables

I have categorized the remaining four tables together in this section as they play a less important role, or act independently in web applications:

- `wp_comments`: This table contains the user feedback for posts and pages. Comment-specific details such as author, e-mail, content, and status are saved in this table.
- `wp_commentmeta`: This table contains additional details about each comment. By default, this table will not contain much data as we are not associating advanced comment types in typical situations.

The following screen previews the relationship between comment-related tables:

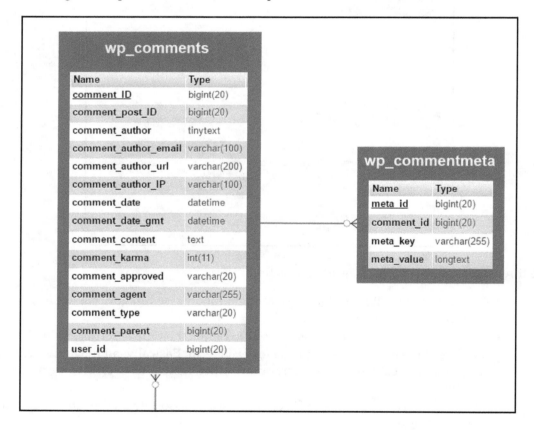

The tables shown in the diagram are as follows:

- `wp_links`: This table contains the necessary internal or external links. This feature is rarely used in content management systems.
- `wp_options`: This table acts as the one and only independent table in the database. In general, it is used to save application-specific settings that don't often change.

 You can take a look at WordPress' complete entity relationship diagram at `https://codex.wordpress.org/images/9/97/WP3.8-ERD.png`

Now you should have a clear idea of the role of existing tables and the reasons for their existence from a CMS perspective. Most importantly, our goal is to figure out how these tables work in advanced web applications, and the next section will focus solely on the web application perspective.

Adapting existing tables in web applications

Unlike CMSes, web applications have the possibility of scaling infinitely as they become popular and stable. Such systems can contain hundreds of database tables to cater to various requirements. Here, we are trying to build such applications using this popular CMS framework. Therefore, we need to figure out which features we can build using existing tables and which features need their own table structures.

We should be trying to maximize the use of existing tables in every possible scenario to get the most out of WordPress. Built-in database access functions are optimized to work directly with existing tables, allowing us to minimize the time for implementation. On the other hand, we need to write custom queries from scratch to work with newly created tables. Let's find out the possible ways of adapting the existing tables using the four categories we discussed in the previous section.

User-related tables

In web applications, the user table plays the same role as in a normal CMS. Therefore, we don't have to worry about changing the default functionality. Any other user-related functionalities should be associated with the `wp_usermeta` table. Let's recall the user activation feature we implemented in `Chapter 2`, *Implementing Membership Roles, Permissions, and Features*. We had an additional requirement for activating users before login. We made use of the new `wp_usermeta` field called `wpwa_activate_status` to build this functionality. Now, open your database explorer and take a look at the fields of the `wp_users` table. You will find a column called `user_activation_key` with no value. This field could have easily been used for the activation functionality. Table columns such as `user_activation_key` and `user_status` are used by WordPress to provide core functionality. There is every chance that other plugin developers are using these fields with a different meaning and thus creating the potential for lost data and conflicts.

 It's a good rule of thumb to use metatables or custom tables for advanced functionalities with your own unique keys by using a prefix, instead of relying on the existing columns of core tables.

Therefore, we choose the `wp_usermeta` table to keep the activation status of all users. Other plugin developers can also implement similar functionalities with unique keys inside the `wp_usermeta` table. In short, the `wp_usermata` table can be used effectively to create advanced user-related functionalities in web applications as long as it doesn't involve one-to-many relationships. It's possible to use multiple metafields with the same name; however, most developers prefer the use of custom tables for features that require multiple data rows to be associated with a single user, because it allows additional flexibility in data filtering.

Post-related tables

Usually, the `wp_posts` and `wp_postmeta` tables will act as the main data storage tables for a web application. With the introduction of custom posts, we have the ability to match most of our application data in these two tables. In web applications, we can go beyond normal posts by creating various custom post types. Let's take a look at a few practical scenarios for identifying the role of `wp_posts` and `wp_postmeta` tables.

Scenario 1 – an online shopping cart

Assume that we are building an online shopping cart application to sell books. In this scenario, books can be matched to a custom post type that will be saved in the `wp_posts` table. We can match the post title to book title, post content to book description, and post type to book. Then, all the other book-related information, such as price, author, pages, and dimensions, can be stored in the `wp_postmeta` table with the associated book from the `wp_posts` table.

Scenario 2 – a hotel reservation system

In this scenario, we need to provide the ability to book hotel rooms through the system. We can use a custom post type called rooms to keep the details of various types of room inside the `wp_posts` table. All the additional room-specific data, such as room type, check-in and check-out dates, and number of people, can be created using additional fields in the `wp_postmeta` table.

Scenario 3 – a project management application

Let's consider a much more advanced scenario in creating a relationship between post types. Assume that we have been assigned to build a project management application with WordPress. We can match projects to a custom post type. Project-specific details such as project manager, duration, and cost will be stored in the `wp_postmeta` table. It's not ideal to use the `wp_postmeta` table to store project tasks since each project contains multiple tasks, and a single project task can contain its own attributes and values. Therefore, we create another custom post type to store project tasks, and all the task-related data is stored inside the `wp_postmeta` table. Finally, we can associate projects with tasks using taxonomies or a separate custom table.

So far, we have discussed three completely different scenarios in real-world applications, and we were able to match all the requirements with custom post types. Now, you should understand the importance of these two tables in web application development. In the next chapter, we will continue our exploration of custom post types and the use of the `wp_posts` and `wp_postmeta` tables.

Term-related tables

Even though they're not as important as posts, terms play a vital part in supporting post functionalities. Let's see how we can effectively use terms in the previous three scenarios:

- **Scenario 1**: In the book store, we can use terms to store book categories or book types, such as ebooks, Kindle editions, and printed books
- **Scenario 2**: In the hotel reservation system, we can use terms to select services and facilities required for rooms
- **Scenario 3**: In the project management system, we can use terms to define the complexity of a given task

It's important to keep in mind that multiple terms can be associated with a single post. Therefore, it's not wise to use terms for a feature such as project status.

Other tables

In this section, we will discuss the practical usage of the `wp_comments`, `wp_comment_meta`, and `wp_options` tables. The `wp_links` table is skipped on purpose as we don't generally need it in web application development.

The link manager is hidden by default for new WordPress installations since version 3.5, proving that links are not considered a major aspect in WordPress.

Comments might not indicate a significant value with their default usage. However, we can certainly think of many ways of incorporating comments into web applications. In the previous section, we talked about custom post types. So, what about custom comment types? We can definitely implement custom comment types in web applications. The only difference is that custom post types are defined in the posts table, while custom comment types will have to be handled manually, as they're not currently supported in WordPress.

Let's recall the example in Chapter 1, *WordPress as a Web Application Framework*, where we created the question and answer interface using posts and comments. Answers were considered as a custom comment type. Similarly, we can match things such as bids in auctions, reviews in books, and ratings for movies as custom comment types to be stored in the `wp_comment_meta` table. Since the column called `comment_type` is not available, we have to use a meta key called `wpwa_comment_type` to filter different comments from each other.

Finally, we will take a look at the `wp_options` table for system-wide configurations. By default, this table is populated with the settings to run the website. WordPress theme settings will also be stored in this table. In web applications, we will definitely have a considerable number of plugins, so we can use this table to store all the settings of our plugins.

 Most of the existing WordPress plugins use a single field to store all the settings as a serialized array. It's considered a good practice that improves performance because of the limited number of table records.

Up until this point, we have explored the role of existing tables and how we can adapt them in real-world web applications. A complex web application will always come up with requirements for pushing the boundaries of these tables. In such cases, we have no option other than going with custom tables, so we will be looking at the importance of custom tables and their usage in the following section.

Extending the database with custom tables

A default WordPress database can be extended by any number of custom tables to suit our project's requirements. The only thing we have to consider is the creation of custom tables over existing ones. There are two major reasons for creating custom tables:

- **Difficulty of matching data to existing tables**: In the previous section, we considered real application requirements and matched the data to existing tables. Unfortunately, it's not practical in every scenario. Consider a system where the user purchases books from a shopping cart. We need to keep all the payment and order details for tracking purposes, and these records act as transactions in the system. There is no way that we can find a compatible table for this kind of requirement. Such requirements will be implemented using a collection of custom tables.

- **Increased data volume**: As I mentioned earlier, the posts table plays a major role in web applications. When it comes to large-scale applications with a sizeable amount of data, it's not recommended to keep all the data in a posts table. Let's assume that we are building a product catalog that creates millions of orders. Storing order details in the posts table as a custom post type is not the ideal implementation. In such circumstances, the posts table will go out of control due to the large dataset. The same theory applies to the existing metatables as well. In these cases, it's wise to separate different datasets into their own tables to improve performance and keep things manageable.

Planning the forum application tables

The forum management system developed throughout this book will make use of existing tables in every possible scenario. However, it's hard to imagine even an average web application without using custom tables, so here we will identify the possible custom tables for our system. You might need to revisit the planning section in the *Development plan for forum management application* section of Chapter 1, *WordPress as a Web Application Framework*, in order to remind yourself of the system requirements. We planned to create a functionality to allow free and premium members to subscribe to follow topic activities in the system. Let's discuss the requirement in detail to identify the potential tables we'll need.

Forum users will be able to create their own topics and respond to topics of other users. It's important to receive notifications on the topics, since users can't log into the forum and check topics regularly, so users will be allowed to subscribe to the topics they are interested in and get notifications when updates are available on those topics.

This is a very simple and practical scenario for identifying the use of custom tables. We can easily scale this up to be compatible with complex systems. Forum members are stored as users of the system. Therefore, we only have a choice of the wp_usermeta table for additional features. It's highly impractical to keep topic updates in the wp_usermeta table, so we need to create our first custom table, which we will call topic_subscriptions, to implement this feature.

Types of table in web applications

Database tables of web applications can be roughly categorized into three sections, as follows:

- **Master tables**: These tables contain predefined or configuration data for the application, which rarely gets changed. The options table can be considered as a perfect example of this type of table in the WordPress context.
- **Application data tables**: These tables contain the highly dynamic core application data. Posts and users can be considered as good examples of this type of table in the WordPress context.
- **Transaction tables**: These tables contain the highest volume of data in any application. Records in these tables rarely get changed, but new records will be added at an increasing speed. It's difficult to find good examples of this type of table in the WordPress context.

Based on these categories, we can clearly see that the `topic_subscriptions` table falls into the transaction table category. Next, we need to allow the members to add topics to a favorites list, so we need another transaction table, which we will call `favorite_member_topics`. We can assume that most of the transaction tables will need their own custom tables. For now, we will stick with these two tables and additional custom tables will be added in later chapters when needed.

Creating custom tables

In typical circumstances, we create the database tables manually before moving onto the implementation. With the WordPress plugin-based architecture, it's certain that we might need to create custom tables using plugins in the later stages of the projects. Creating custom tables through plugins involves certain predefined procedures recommended by WordPress. Since table creation is a one-time task, we can implement the process on plugin activation or installation. This process is similar to the user role creation process in Chapter 2, *Implementing Membership Roles, Permissions, and Features*.

We will be using activation-based table creation in this book. However, you can try the installation-based table creation to cater to advanced scenarios. We will add the database table creation functionality into the `wpwa-forum` plugin we created in Chapter 2, *Implementing Membership Roles, Permissions, and Features*. So, let's get started by creating a new function called `create_custom_tables` inside the `class-wpwaf-config-manager.php` file:

```php
<?php
    public function create_custom_tables() {
            // Creating Database Tables
    }
?>
```

Now we can implement the `create_custom_tables` function to create the tables we need for our application. Basically, we can execute direct SQL queries using the `$wpdb->query` function to create all the tables we need. WordPress recommends using a built-in function called `dbDelta` to create custom tables. This function is located in a file outside the default process, and hence, we need to load it manually within our plugins. Let's create the two tables for our application using the `dbDelta` function:

```php
public function create_custom_tables() {
   global $wpdb;
   require_once( ABSPATH . 'wp-admin/includes/upgrade.php' );
   $topic_subscriptions_table = $wpdb->prefix.'topic_subscriptions';
   if($wpdb->get_var("show tables like '$topic_subscriptions_table'") !=
```

```
$topic_subscriptions_table) {

        $sql = "CREATE TABLE $topic_subscriptions_table (
                id mediumint(9) NOT NULL AUTO_INCREMENT,
                time datetime DEFAULT '0000-00-00 00:00:00' NOT NULL,
                user_id mediumint(9) NOT NULL,
                topic_id  mediumint(9) NOT NULL,
                UNIQUE KEY id (id)
              );";
        dbDelta( $sql );
    }
    // favorite_member_topics table will be created in a similar manner
}
```

Firstly, we have to include the `upgrade.php` file to make use of the `dbDelta` function. The next most important thing is to use the prefix for database tables. By default, WordPress creates a prefix called `wp_` for all the tables. It's important to use the existing prefix to maintain consistency and avoid issues in multi-site scenarios. Next, we have to check the existence of a database table using the `show tables` query. Finally, you can define your table creation query and use the `dBDelta` function to implement it on the database.

 Check out the guidelines for creating a table creation query at `http://codex.wordpress.org/Creating_Tables_with_Plugins`, as the dbDelta function can be tricky in certain scenarios.

We have the function for creating custom tables for our application. This function needs to be executed through the plugin activation hook. In Chapter 2, *Implementing Membership Roles, Permissions, and Features*, we executed all activation-related function calls inside the `activation_handler` function of the `WPWAF_Config_Manager` class. So, we can use the same function to execute the custom table creation function as follows:

```
public function activation_handler(){
    $this->add_application_user_roles();
    $this->remove_application_user_roles();
    $this->add_application_user_capabilities();
    $this->flush_application_rewrite_rules();
    $this->create_custom_tables();
}
```

We created the custom tables using the `dbDelta` function inside the plugin activation. WordPress recommends the `dbDelta` function rather than direct SQL queries for table creation since it examines the current table structure, compares it to the desired table structure, and makes the necessary modifications without breaking the existing database tables. Apart from table creation, we can execute quite a few database-related tasks on plugin activation such as altering tables, populating initial data to custom tables, and upgrading the plugin tables.

We looked at the necessity of custom tables for web applications. Even though custom tables offer you more flexibility within WordPress, there will be a considerable number of limitations, as listed here:

- Custom tables are hard to manage in WordPress upgrades.
- WordPress default backups will not include custom tables.
- There are no built-in functions for the accessing database. All the queries, filtering, and validation needs to be done from scratch using the existing `$wpdb` variable.
- User interfaces for displaying these tables' data need to be created from scratch.

Therefore, you should avoid creating custom tables in all possible circumstances, unless they would be advantageous in the context of your application.

> The WordPress **PODS** framework works very well at managing custom post types with custom tables. You can have look at the source code at `http://wordpress.org/plugins/pods/` to learn the use of custom tables.

A detailed exploration of the PODS framework will be provided in the next chapter, `Chapter 4`, *Building Blocks of Web Applications*.

Querying the database

As with most frameworks, WordPress provides a built-in interface for interacting with the database. Most of the database operations will be handled by the `wpdb` class located inside the `wp-includes` directory. The `wpdb` class will be available inside your plugins and themes as a global variable and provides access to all the tables inside the WordPress database, including custom tables.

Using the `wpdb` class for CRUD operations is straightforward with its built-in methods. A complete guide for using the `wpdb` class can be found at `http://codex.wordpress.org/Class_Reference/wpdb`.

Querying the existing tables

WordPress provides well-optimized built-in methods for accessing the existing database tables. Therefore, accessing these tables becomes straightforward. Let's see how basic **Create, Read, Update, Delete (CRUD)** operations are executed on existing tables.

Inserting records

All the existing tables contain a prebuilt insert method for creating new records. The following list illustrates a few of the built-in insert functions:

- `wp_insert_post`: This creates a new post or page in the `wp_posts` table. If this is used on an existing post, it will update the existing record.
- `add_option`: This creates a new option in the `wp_options` table, if it doesn't already exist.
- `wp_insert_comment`: This creates a new comment in the `wp_comments` table.

Updating records

All the existing tables contain a prebuilt update method for updating existing records. The following list illustrates a few of the built-in update functions:

- `update_post_meta`: This creates or updates additional details about posts in the `wp_postmeta` table
- `wp_update_term`: This updates existing terms in the `wp_terms` table
- `update_user_meta`: This updates user meta details in the `wp_usermeta` table based on the user ID

Deleting records

We have similar methods for deleting records in each of the existing tables as we have for updating records. The following list illustrates a few of the built-in delete functions:

- delete_post_meta: This deletes custom fields using the specified key in the wp_postmeta table
- wp_delete_post: This removes existing posts, pages, or attachments from the wp_posts table
- delete_user_meta: This removes the metadata matching criteria from a user from the wp_usermeta table

Selecting records

As usual, there is a set of built-in functions for selecting records from the existing tables. The following list contains a few of the data selecting functions:

- get_posts: This retrieves the posts as an array from the wp_posts table based on the passed arguments. Also, we can use the WP_Query class with the necessary arguments to get the post list from the OOP method.
- get_option: This retrieves the option value of the given key from the wp_options table.
- get_users: This retrieves a list of users as an array from the wp_user table.

Most of the database operations on exiting tables can be executed using these built-in functions. Therefore, use of the $wpdb class is not necessary in most occasions, unless queries become complex and difficult to handle using direct functions.

Querying the custom tables

Basically, there are no built-in methods for accessing custom tables using direct functions, so it's a must to use the wpdb class for handling custom tables. Let's take a look at some of the functions provided by the wpdb class:

- $wpdb->get_results("select query"): This can be used to select a set of records from any database table.
- $wpdb->query('query'): This can be used to execute any custom query. This is typically used to update and delete statements instead of select statements, as it only provides the affected rows count as the result.

- `$wpdb->get_row('query')`: This can be used to retrieve a single row from the database as an object, an associative array, or as a numerically indexed array.

A complete list of the `wpdb` class functions can be accessed at `http://codex.wordpress.or g/Class_Reference/wpdb`. When executing these functions, we have to make sure that we include the necessary filtering and validations, as these are not built to directly work with existing tables. For example, consider the following query for the proper usage of these functions with the necessary filtering:

```
$wpdb->query(
  $wpdb->prepare("SELECT FROM $wpdb->postmeta
    WHERE post_id = %d AND meta_key = %s",
    1, 'book_title'
  )
);
```

Here, we are filtering the user input values through the `prepare` function for illegal operations and illegal characters. Similarly, you have to use functions such as `escape` and `escape_by_ref` to secure direct SQL queries.

Data validation is an important aspect of keeping the consistency of the database. WordPress offers the `prepare` function for formatting SQL queries from possible threats. Usually, developers use the `prepare` function with direct queries, including variables, instead of using placeholders and value parameters. It's a must to use placeholders and value parameters to get the intended outcome of the `prepare` function. Therefore, WordPress version 3.5 and higher enforces a minimum of two arguments to prevent developers from misusing the `prepare` function.

Working with posts

WordPress posts act as the main module in web application development as well as content management systems. Therefore, WordPress comes up with a separate class called `WP_Query` for interacting with posts and pages. You can find more details about the use of `WP_Query` at `http://codex.wordpress.org/Class_Reference/WP_Query`.

So far, we've looked at procedural database access functions using global objects. Web application developers are much more familiar with object-oriented coding. The `WP_Query` class is a good choice for such developers when querying the database. Let's see the default usage of `WP_Query` using the following code:

```
$args = array(
  'post_type' => 'topics',
  'meta_query' => array(
    array(
      'status' => '',
      'value' => 'Resolved'
    )
  )
);
$query = new WP_Query($args);
```

First, we need to add all the filtering conditions to an array. The `WP_Query` class allows us to include conditions on multiple tables, such as categories, tags, and postmeta. This technique allows us to create highly complex queries without worrying about the SQL code. The advantage of `WP_Query` comes with its ability to create subclasses that cater to project-specific requirements. In the next section, we will learn how to extend the `WP_Query` class to create custom database access interfaces.

Extending the WP_Query class for applications

The default `WP_Query` class works similarly for every type of custom post type. In web applications, we can have different custom post types with different meanings. For example, members can create topics inside our forum application. Each topic will have a status associated with it. There is no point retrieving those topics without those additional details. Now, let's look at the default way of retrieving topics with `WP_Query` using the following code:

```
$args = array(
  'post_type' => 'topics',
  'meta_query' => array(
    array(
      'key' => 'status'
    )
  )
);
$query = new WP_Query( $args );
```

This query works perfectly in retrieving topics from the database. However, each time we have to pass the status key in order to join it when retrieving topics. Since this is a topic-specific requirement, we can create a custom class to extend `WP_Query` and avoid repetitive argument passing, as it's common to all the topics-related queries. Let's implement the extended `WP_Query` class:

```
class WPWA_Topics_Query extends WP_Query {
    function __construct( $args = array() ) {
        $args = wp_parse_args( $args, array(
          'post_type' => 'topics',
          'meta_query' => array(
            array(
              'key' => 'status'
            )
          )
        ) );
        parent::__construct( $args );
    }
}
```

Now all the common conditions are abstracted inside the `WPWA_Topics_Query` class, so we don't have to pass the conditions every time we want topics. The preceding example illustrates a basic form of object inheritance. Additionally, we can use post filters to combine custom tables with topics. Now, we can access topics using the following code without passing any arguments:

```
$query = new WPWAF_Topics_Query();
```

The `WP_Query` class will play a vital part in our forum application development. In the following chapters, we will explore how it can be extended in several ways using advanced post filters provided by WordPress. Until then, you can check out the available post filters at http://codex.wordpress.org/Plugin_API/Filter_Reference#WP_Query_Filters.

Introduction to WordPress query classes

WordPress provides a set of classes that query the database in an object-oriented manner. These classes make it easier to access and understand the queries, compared to procedural functions. In the previous section, we discussed one of the query classes, `WP_Query`, in more detail. This class is the most frequently used one among all the query classes. In this section, we will explore the functionality of the remaining query classes.

The WP_User_Query class

The WP_User_Query class is used to query user-related data from the WordPress database. Basically, this class uses the wp_users and the wp_usermeta tables for its queries. This is the second-most-used class after WP_Query. Let's take a look at the basic usage of this class in the following code:

```
$user_query = new WP_User_Query( array( 'role' => 'Administrator'
  ) );
if ( ! empty( $user_query->results ) ) {
  foreach ( $user_query->results as $user ) {
    // display user details
  }
}
```

The WP_User_Query class takes an array of arguments for filtering users based on various criteria. In this scenario, we have filtered users with an administrator role. The following are some of the filtering methods that we can use with the WP_User_Query class:

- Get users by role
- Get users from a certain blog in multisite scenarios
- Get users based on a keyword search
- Get users with a specific custom field and field value from the wp_usermeta table

 More details about the use of the WP_User_Query class are provided at ht tp://codex.wordpress.org/Class_Reference/WP_User_Query.

The WP_Comment_Query class

The WP_Comment_Query class works with the wp_comments and wp_commentmeta tables for retrieving WordPress post comments-related data. This class is used in some of the themes to provide custom comments-related features. However, this is less frequently used compared to the WP_Query and the WP_User_Query classes. The following code shows the default usage of this class:

```
$comments_query = new WP_Comment_Query;
$comments = $comments_query->query( $args );
if ( $comments ) {
```

```
        foreach ( $comments as $comment ) {
          // display commnets
        }
      }
```

You can use this class to retrieve comments from a specific user, specific posts, comments with a certain status, and many other parameters.

 A complete guide to using this class can be accessed at http://codex.wor dpress.org/Class_Reference/WP_Comment_Query.

Other query classes

Apart from these main query classes, there are several other query classes in WordPress. Most of these classes are not needed or used frequently by developers. However, these classes are widely used within the WordPress core and work with the main query classes. The following are some of the other query classes available in WordPress:

- WP_Meta_Query: This class is used to generate the necessary SQL for meta-related queries
- WP_Tax_Query: This is a container class for multiple taxonomy queries
- WP_Date_Query: This class is used to generate the MySQL WHERE clause for the specified date-based parameters

We discussed the query classes in WordPress and their usage in brief. As a developer, you should be looking for opportunities to use these classes in custom plugin and theme development to better understand the various parameters.

Limitations and considerations

We have less flexibility with the WordPress built-in database than when we design a database from scratch. Limitations and features unique to WordPress need to be understood clearly to make full use of the framework and avoid potential bottlenecks. Let's find out some of the WordPress-specific features and their usage in web applications.

Transaction support

In advanced applications, we can have multiple database queries, which need to be executed inside a single process. We have to make sure that either all queries get executed successfully or none of them get executed, to maintain the consistency of the data. This process is known as **transaction management** in application development. In simple website development, we rarely get such requirements for handling transactions. As mentioned earlier, MySQL version 5.5 upwards uses **InnoDB** as the table engine, and therefore we are able to implement transaction support. However, WordPress doesn't offer any libraries or functions to handle transactions, and therefore all transaction handling should be implemented manually.

Post revisions

WordPress provides an important feature for keeping the revisions of your posts in the `wp_posts` table. On every update, a new revision of the post will be created in the database. If you have experience of working with software versioning and revision control systems, you probably know the importance of revisions. However, it could create unnecessary performance overheads when executing queries in large databases. In web applications, you should disable this feature or limit the revisions to a certain number, unless it provides potential benefits within your system.

How do you know whether to enable or disable revisions?

Ideally, you should disable this feature in all forms of web application development. Later, you can consider enabling this feature based on your application's requirements.

 It's important to keep in mind that we don't get revisions of the post meta fields. Therefore, the importance of post revisions is restricted to fields such as post title, content, author, and excerpt.

Let's consider a practical scenario for identifying the importance of post revisions. Assume that we have an event management system with a custom post type called events. Each event will span across multiple days, so you can create an event and use the post content to include the activities of the first day. Then, from the next day onwards, you can completely replace the content with the activity of each day and update the event. Finally, we can get all the post revisions with a link to each day for filtering the activities conducted in each day. Therefore, the decision to keep post revisions purely depends on your requirements.

Consider disabling post revisions by placing the following code inside the `wp-config.php` file:

```
define('WP_POST_REVISIONS', false );
```

Autosaving

Autosaving is another feature that goes in combination with post revisions. Autosaving will create a different type of post revision at predefined time intervals. On most occasions, this feature will expand the size of your database rather than provide something useful. Unfortunately, we cannot switch off autosaving without editing the core files. Therefore, we need to extend the interval of autosaving by defining a large value for the `AUTOSAVE_INTERVAL` constant inside the `wp-config.php` file:

```
define('AUTOSAVE_INTERVAL', 600 );
```

The value of the `AUTOSAVE_INTERVAL` constant needs to be configured in seconds. Here, we have used 600 seconds (10 minutes) as the autosave interval.

Using meta tables

The WordPress table structure gives higher priority to meta tables for keeping additional data as key-value pairs. Although meta tables work well in most scenarios, this can become a considerable factor in situations where you need to implement complex select queries and search functionality. Searching for n number of fields means that you create n number of SQL table joins on the metatable. As the number of joins increases, your queries will get slower and slower. In such situations, it's ideal to go with custom tables instead of relying on existing tables.

We have had a brief introduction to the WordPress database and seen the possible ways of using it in web applications. Covering all possible database design and access techniques was beyond the scope of this chapter, so I recommend that you follow online tutorials related to theWordPress database to gain more experience of working with the database.

Summary

Understanding the WordPress database is the key to building successful web applications. Throughout this chapter, we looked at the role of existing tables and the need for custom database tables through practical scenarios.

Database querying techniques and limitations were introduced with the necessary examples. By now, you should have a clear understanding of choosing the right type of table for your next project. We used a theoretical approach with practical scenarios to learn the basics of database design and implementation inside WordPress.

The real excitement begins in the next chapter, where we start the development of our main modules in web applications using the building blocks of WordPress. Stay tuned!

4
Building Blocks of Web Applications

The majority of WordPress-powered systems are either simple websites or blogs. Adapting WordPress for building complex web applications can be a complex task for beginner developers who are used to working with simple websites every day. Understanding the process of handling web application-specific functions becomes vital in such scenarios.

Managing data is one of the most important tasks in web applications. WordPress offers a concept called custom post types for modeling application data and backend interfaces. I believe this is the foundation of most web applications and, hence, named this chapter *Building Blocks of Web Applications*.

While exploring the advanced use cases of custom post type implementations, we will get used to popular web development techniques such as modularizing, template management, data validations, and rapid application development in a practical process.

In this chapter, we will cover the following topics:

- Introduction to custom content types
- Planning custom post types for an application
- Implementing the custom post type settings
- Validating post creation
- Building a simple template loader
- Introduction to custom post type relationships
- Pods framework for custom content types
- Implementing custom post types with popular plugins
- Tasks for practicing custom post types

Let's get started!

Introduction to custom content types

In WordPress terms, custom content types are referred to as custom post types. The term custom post type misleads some people to think of them as different types of normal posts. In reality, these post types can model almost anything in real web applications. This is similar to collections in other web frameworks such as **Ruby** on **Rails** or **Meteor.js**. These post types are stored in the normal posts table and this could well be the reason behind its conflicting naming convention.

Prior to the introduction of custom post types, we only had the ability to use normal posts with custom fields to cater to advanced requirements. The process of handling multiple post types was a complex task. The inability to manage different post types in their own lists and the inability to add different fields to different posts are some of the limitations with the old process. With the introduction of custom post types, we now have the ability to separate each different type of the post type to act as a model to cater to complex requirements. The demand for using these custom post types to build complex applications is increasing every day. The features provided out-of-the-box to cater to common tasks might be one of the reasons behind its popularity in website development.

The role of custom post types in web applications

Even the simplest of web applications will contain a considerable number of models compared to normal websites. Therefore, organizing model data becomes one of the critical tasks in application development. Unless you want complete control over your data processing, it is preferable to make use of custom post types without developing everything from scratch.

Once a custom post type is registered, you will automatically have the ability to execute create, read, update, and delete operations. Default fields enabled in the post creation and custom category types will be saved automatically upon hitting the **Publish** button. Generally, this is all we need to build simple applications. For web applications, we do need the ability to handle a large amount of data with various types of fields. This is where web applications differ from simple websites with the use of custom fields within meta boxes. The rest of this chapter will mainly focus on handling this custom data in different ways to suit complex applications.

Planning custom post types for an application

Having got a brief introduction to custom post types and their roles in web applications, we will find the necessary custom post types for our forum application. The majority of our application and the data will be based on these custom post types. So, let's look at the detailed requirements of a forum application.

The main purpose of this application is to let users create topics and discuss them with other users or get answers from the administrative staff. Therefore, we have to look at two important components: forums and topics. Now, try to visualize the subsections for each of these components. It is obvious that we can sort these components into two custom post types. The following sections illustrate the detailed subcomponents of each of these models.

Forums

A forum is an online discussion where members can discuss important topics with other members. This is the model that holds the members of the forum and the discussed topics as well as the replies. We will limit the implementation of forums to some common fields in order to cover the different areas of custom post types. The following screenshot illustrates the fields for the forum creation screen:

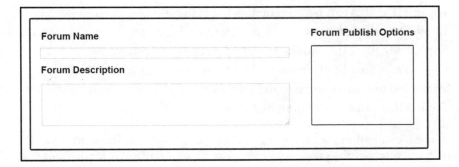

Let's have a look at the components in the screenshot:

- **Forum Name**: this can be matched as the title field of a custom post type
- **Forum Description**: this can be matched as the editor field of a custom post type

Topics

A **topic** is the most important aspect of the application, where the actual conversations happen. A topic is a subcomponent of the forum. For this application, we will model the topics using custom post types. Now, let's look at the following screenshot for the necessary data requirements and their WordPress specific matches:

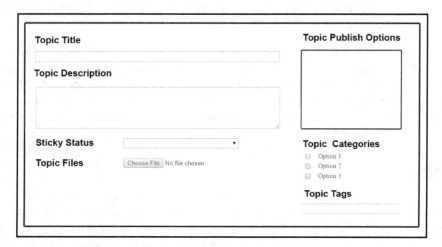

Let's have a look at the components in the screenshot:

- **Topic Title**: this can be matched as the title field of a custom post type
- **Topic Description**: this can be matched as the editor field of a custom post type
- **Topic Category**: this can be matched as custom taxonomies
- **Topic Tags**: this can be matched as custom taxonomies
- **Sticky Status**: this can be matched to a custom drop-down field
- **Topic Files**: this can be matched to a custom file field

I hope you have a clear understanding about the things we will implement in this chapter. We will start by implementing these custom post types inside our forum plugin. While implementing these models, we will also take a look at some advanced techniques for template management, validations, and post relationships.

Implementing custom post types for a forum application

In this section, we will extend the plugin developed in Chapter 3, *Planning and Customizing Core Database*, and implement the custom post type-related functionality. First, we have to create a new file called class-wpwaf-model-manager.php inside the classes directory of the wpwa-forum plugin.

Most web applications will be larger in scale compared to normal websites or blogs. Implementing all custom post functionalities in one file is not the most ideal or practical thing to do. So, our plan here is to keep the initialization and generic configurations in the main file, while separating each of the custom post types into their own class files. Before we go any further, I would like you to have a look at the updated folder structure of the plugin using the following screenshot:

```
▼ wpwa-forum
    ▼ classes
        class-wpwaf-config-manager.php
        class-wpwaf-login.php
        class-wpwaf-model-forum.php
        class-wpwaf-model-manager.php
        class-wpwaf-model-topic.php
        class-wpwaf-registration.php
        class-wpwaf-template-loader.php
    ▶ css
    ▶ img
    ▶ js
    ▼ templates
        info-template.php
        login-template.php
        register-template.php
        topic-meta-template.php
    functions.php
    wpwa-forum.php
```

Now, let's go through each of the new files and folders to identify their roles:

- `class-wpwaf-model-manager.php`: this includes the main initialization and configuration code for the models
- `class-wpwaf-model-forum.php`: this includes the main initialization and configuration code for the forum model
- `class-wpwaf-model-topic.php`: this includes the main initialization and configuration code for the topic model
- `class-wpwaf-template-loader.php`: this includes a `template` file loading and initialization code
- `templates`: this folder contains all the HTML templates required for the plugin

All the custom post type-specific classes are prefixed with the model keyword and located inside the `classes` folder. These files need to be included in the main plugin file prior to their usage. Let's include these files inside the `includes` function of `WPWAF_Forum` class, using the following code:

```
require_once WPWAF_PLUGIN_DIR . 'classes/class-wpwaf-template-
loader.php';
require_once WPWAF_PLUGIN_DIR . 'classes/class-wpwaf-model-
manager.php';
require_once WPWAF_PLUGIN_DIR . 'classes/class-wpwaf-model-forum.php';
require_once WPWAF_PLUGIN_DIR . 'classes/class-wpwaf-model-topic.php';
```

Next, we need to initialize objects from these classes inside the `instance` function of `WPWAF_Forum` class, using the following code:

```
self::$instance->template_loader = new WPWAF_Template_Loader();
self::$instance->model_manager   = new WPWAF_Model_Manager();
self::$instance->forum           = new WPWAF_Model_Forum();
self::$instance->topic           = new WPWAF_Model_Topic();
```

Now, we can move on to the implementation of the custom post type manager.

Implementing the custom post type settings

As planned, we need to implement configurations and general functions in the main class for the custom post types. In the previous section, we looked at the classes needed for our implementation added to the file inclusions and object initializations. Now we have to create the actual class files inside the `classes` folder. Let's start with `WPWAF_Model_Manager` in the `class-wpwaf-model-manager.php` file using the following code:

```
class WPWAF_Model_Manager {
  public function __construct() {
    // Initialization
  }
}
```

This class will be used for common functionalities of all the custom post types of our application. Therefore, all the forum and topic related configurations will be implemented inside the `WPWAF_Model_Manager` class. Now that we have set up everything required for custom post implementation, we can move on to the implementations of those classes.

Creating forum and topic classes

We will start with the `Forum` class, as it is the most simple one of the two custom post types. So, create a file called `class-wpwaf-model-forum.php` inside the `classes` folder and define a blank class called `WPWAF_Model_Forum`, as shown in the following code:

```
<?php
  class WPWAF_Model_Forum {
    public $post_type;
    public function __construct() {
    }
  }
?>
```

Here, we have an instance variable for keeping the custom post type name. This class constructor is responsible for handling all the forum-related function initializations and definitions. The first task is to register a custom post type for a forum. Let's modify the constructor to add the necessary actions for the post type creation:

```
class WPWAF_Model_Forum {
  public $post_type;
  public function __construct() {
    $this->post_type = 'wpwaf_forum';
    add_action('init', array( $this,'create_forums_post_type' ) );
  }
}
```

First, we will assign the name of the post type to the instance variable so that we can use it for registering the post type. With many existing plugins, you will find hardcoded names for the `register_post_type` function.

It's a good practice to use an instance variable or global variable to store the custom post type name and use the variables across all the occurrences of the custom post type name. This will enable you to change the custom post type name anytime with minimum effort without breaking the code.

We use the WordPress `init` action to call the `create_forums_post_type` function for registering new custom post types. Let's look at the implementation of this function:

```
public function create_forums_post_type() {
  global $wpwaf;
  $params = array();
  $params['post_type'] = $this->post_type;
  $params['singular_post_name'] = __('Forum','wpwaf');
  $params['plural_post_name'] = __('Forums','wpwaf');
  $params['description'] = __('Forums','wpwaf');
  $params['supported_fields'] = array('title', 'editor');

  $wpwaf->model_manager->create_post_type($params);
}
```

You might have noticed that familiar custom post type creation code is missing here. We have to define the common settings and all the labels for each and every custom post type. Since we are planning to use multiple custom post types for our project, we have to prevent code duplication. Therefore, we will be implementing the custom post creation in a common function and passing the necessary parameters from the individual models.

In this code, we have defined the necessary labels and supported fields to be passed to the common `create_post_type` function inside the `WPWAF_Model_Manager` class. We can use the global `$wpwaf` object to get an instance of the `WPWAF_Model_Manager` class and execute the `create_post_type` function.

Now we can look at the implementation of the `create_post_type` function for all our models:

```
public function create_post_type($params) {
    extract($params);
    $capabilities = isset($capabilities) ? $capabilities : array();

    $labels = array(
        'name'  => sprintf( __( '%s', 'wpwaf' ), $plural_post_name),
        'singular_name' => sprintf( __( '%s', 'wpwaf' ),
$singular_post_name),
        'add_new' => __( 'Add New', 'wpwaf' ),
        'add_new_item' => sprintf( __( 'Add New %s ', 'wpwaf' ),
$singular_post_name),
        'edit_item' => sprintf( __( 'Edit %s ', 'wpwaf' ),
$singular_post_name),
        'new_item' => sprintf( __( 'New  %s ', 'wpwaf' ),
$singular_post_name),
        'all_items' => sprintf( __( 'All  %s ', 'wpwaf' ),
$plural_post_name),
        'view_item' => sprintf( __( 'View  %s ', 'wpwaf' ),
$singular_post_name),
        'search_items' => sprintf( __( 'Search  %s ', 'wpwaf' ),
$plural_post_name),
        'not_found' => sprintf( __( 'No  %s found', 'wpwaf' ),
$plural_post_name),
        'not_found_in_trash' => sprintf( __( 'No  %s  found in the Trash',
'wpwaf' ), $plural_post_name),
        'parent_item_colon' => '',
        'menu_name' => sprintf( __('%s', 'wpwaf' ), $plural_post_name),
    );

    $args = array(
        'labels'                => $labels,
        'hierarchical'          => true,
        'description'           => $description,
        'supports'              => $supported_fields,
        'public'                => true,
        'show_ui'               => true,
        'show_in_menu'          => true,
        'show_in_nav_menus'     => true,
        'publicly_queryable'    => true,
```

```
            'exclude_from_search'    => false,
            'has_archive'            => true,
            'query_var'              => true,
            'can_export'             => true,
            'rewrite'                => true
        );

        if(count($capabilities) != 0){
            $args['capability_type'] = $post_type;
            $args['capabilities'] = $capabilities;
            $args['map_meta_cap'] = true;
        }else{
            $args['capability_type'] = 'post';
        }
        register_post_type( $post_type, $args );
    }
```

Inside the function, we can use the dynamic data passed as a $params variable. We are using dynamic labels for the custom post type and the supported fields. The most important thing to notice is the use of capability_type and the capabilities settings. This capability_type setting defaults to post and the capabilities setting uses default post capabilities.

In web applications, we need flexibility and custom permission levels, hence using default capabilities might be a limitation. Assume that we want to let our members create topics and restrict them from creating forums. We need to give create_posts capability for members to create topics. However, assigning the create_posts capability also lets them create forums, hence we can't manage the permissions for different post types. As a solution, we use the capabilities setting with an array of custom capabilities.

In our forum application, only admins can create forums, hence we don't need to assign custom capabilities. Administrators have the default post management capabilities, hence they will be able to manage forums.

Now go to the **Permalinks** menu under the **Settings** section in the admin dashboard and save it again to refresh the rewrite rules. You should see the forum creation screen, as shown in the following screenshot:

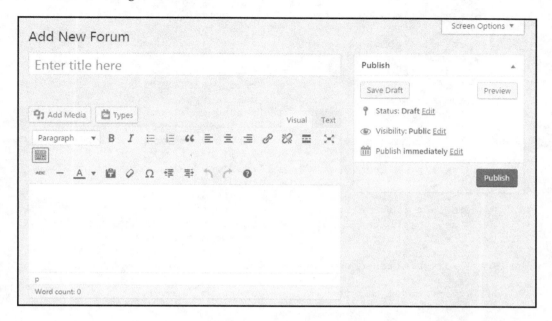

The custom post type for a forum is created to have default post capabilities. So, members of our application need to have these permissions to use the forums section. Since we haven't provided permission to member user roles, you won't be able to view this section as a member.

Now we can create the topic class for our application using the same method. Create a file called `class-wpwaf-model-topic.php` inside the `classes` folder and define a blank class called `WPWAF_Model_Topic`. The topic class should contain the same initialization code for creating the topic post type as shown in the following code:

```
class WPWAF_Model_Topic {
  public $post_type;
  public function __construct() {
    global $wpwaf;

    $this->post_type = 'wpwaf_topic';
    add_action( 'init', array( $this, 'create_topics_post_type' ) );
  }
  public function create_topics_post_type() {
```

```
global $wpwaf;
$params = array();
$params['post_type'] = $this->post_type;
$params['singular_post_name'] = __('Topic','wpwaf');
$params['plural_post_name'] = __('Topics','wpwaf');
$params['description'] = __('Topics','wpwaf');
$params['supported_fields'] = array('title', 'editor');
$params['capabilities'] = array(
    'edit_post'             => 'edit_wpwaf_topic',
    'read_post'             => 'read_wpwaf_topic',
    'delete_post'           => 'delete_wpwaf_topic',
    'create_posts'          => 'create_wpwaf_topics',
    'edit_posts'            => 'edit_wpwaf_topics',
    'edit_others_posts'     => 'edit_others_wpwaf_topics',
    'publish_posts'         => 'publish_wpwaf_topics',
    'read_private_posts'    => 'read',
    'read'                  => 'read',
    'delete_posts'          => 'delete_wpwaf_topics',
    'delete_private_posts'  => 'delete_private_wpwaf_topics',
    'delete_published_posts' => 'delete_published_wpwaf_topics',
    'delete_others_posts'   => 'delete_others_wpwaf_topics',
    'edit_private_posts'    => 'edit_private_wpwaf_topics',
    'edit_published_posts'  => 'edit_published_wpwaf_topics'
        );
    $wpwaf->model_manager->create_post_type($params);
    }
}
```

Here, we have a different post type creation compared to forums. We are using custom capabilities for topics in order to manage the permission levels. So, we have added a custom capability with a `wpwaf` prefix for all the default capabilities. These custom capabilities are not yet associated with any user role in our application, hence even administrators won't be able to see the topics section.

 You can use the members plugin to assign these custom capabilities to administrators until we assign the necessary permission through our plugin.

Now we have to follow the same permalink-saving procedure for topic post types and the screen will look similar to the forum creation screenshot in the initial stages.

Assigning permissions to forums and topics

In general, a moderator user role should be able to handle all the post types created in this application and the member role should have permission for topics. Therefore, we need to provide post-specific capabilities to these user roles. In Chapter 2, *Implementing Membership Roles, Permissions, and Features,* we implemented the user management and permission related features. Now, it's time to update the plugin to add the necessary permissions. Open the class-wpwaf-config-manager.php file in the WPWA Forum plugin. Navigate to the add_application_user_capabilities function and change the existing code as follows:

```php
    public function add_application_user_capabilities() {
        // Section 1
        $custom_member_capabilities = array(
    'edit_wpwaf_topics','publish_wpwaf_topics','delete_wpwaf_topics',
    'edit_published_wpwaf_topics', 'create_wpwaf_topics' );

        $premium_member_role = get_role( 'wpwaf_premium_member' );
        $premium_member_role->add_cap( 'follow_forum_activities' );

        $free_member_role = get_role( 'wpwaf_free_member' );
        $free_member_role->add_cap( 'follow_forum_activities' );

        foreach ($custom_member_capabilities as $capability) {
          $premium_member_role->add_cap($capability);
          $free_member_role->add_cap($capability);
        }

        // Section 2
        $custom_admin_capabilities = array(
    'edit_wpwaf_topics','publish_wpwaf_topics','delete_wpwaf_topics',
    'edit_published_wpwaf_topics', 'create_wpwaf_topics',
    'delete_published_wpwaf_topics','edit_others_wpwaf_topics',
    'delete_others_wpwaf_topics' );

        $moderator_role = get_role( 'wpwaf_moderator' );
        $admin_role = get_role( 'administrator' );

        foreach ($custom_admin_capabilities as $capability) {
          $moderator_role->add_cap($capability);
          $admin_role->add_cap($capability);
        }
    }
```

Let's understand the permission assignment process in two sections.

In Section 1, we have defined an array of topic-related custom capabilities for members. Member user roles need to have the ability to create, edit, delete, and publish their own topics. These user roles should be restricted from managing topics created by other users. So we have assigned the necessary custom capabilities to the array. Then, we get the premium and free user roles and assign all the member-related capabilities using a foreach loop.

In Section 2, we defined an array of topic-related custom capabilities for administrators and moderators. These user roles need to have the ability to create, edit, delete, and publish their own topics, as well as manage the topics of other users. So we have assigned the necessary custom capabilities to the array. Then, we get the admin and moderator user roles and assign all the admin-related capabilities using a foreach loop.

This function is executed within the plugin activation handler, and so you need to deactivate the plugin and activate it again to apply the new capabilities to the users. Once completed, you will be able to manage topics as a member.

Now, we have the necessary permissions and basic fields ready for creating a topic title and description. The most important part of a web application comes with the power of custom fields and custom taxonomies. In the requirements-gathering section, we planned to create custom taxonomies for topic categories and topic tags. So, let's get started on the implementation.

Creating custom taxonomies for topic categories and topic tags

Generally, we use taxonomies to group things that don't get changed often. Here, we are in need of two taxonomies for both topic categories and topic tags. Let's open the class-wpwaf-model-topic.php file and update the WPWAF_Model_Topic class constructor to implement the actions for taxonomy creation:

```php
class WPWAF_Model_Topic {
    public $post_type;
    public $topic_category_taxonomy;
    public $topic_tag_taxonomy;
    public $error_message;
    public function __construct() {
        $this->post_type = "wpwaf_topic";
        $this->topic_category_taxonomy = "wpwaf_topic_category";
        $this-> topic_tag_taxonomy = "wpwaf_topic_tag";
        add_action('init', array($this,'create_topics_post_type'));
```

```
        add_action('init',
    array($this,'create_topics_custom_taxonomies'));
    }
}
```

First, we need two other instance variables to hold the names of custom taxonomies to be reused across all functions. Initialization of these variables is handled through the constructor. Next, we will define custom taxonomies on the `init` action, as we did with custom post types. WordPress offers a function called `register_taxonomy` for creating taxonomies. Similar to custom post types, this function creates code duplication, and so we will be using a common function. First, we will be looking at the model-specific function for defining the necessary data:

```
public function create_topics_custom_taxonomies() {
    global $wpwaf;

    $params = array();

    $params['category_taxonomy'] = $this->topic_category_taxonomy;
    $params['post_type']  = $this->post_type;
    $params['singular_name'] = __('Topic Category','wpwaf');
    $params['plural_name'] = __('Topic Category','wpwaf');
    $params['hierarchical']  = true;
    $wpwaf->model_manager->create_custom_taxonomies($params);

    $params['category_taxonomy'] = $this->topic_tag_taxonomy;
    $params['post_type'] = $this->post_type;
    $params['singular_name']  = __('Topic Tag','wpwaf');
    $params['plural_name']  = __('Topic Tag','wpwaf');
    $params['capabilities'] = array(
        'manage_terms'        => 'manage_wpwaf_topic_tag',
        'edit_terms'          => 'edit_wpwaf_topic_tag',
        'delete_terms'        => 'delete_wpwaf_topic_tag',
        'assign_terms'        => 'assign_wpwaf_topic_tag'
                                );
    $params['hierarchical'] = false;
    $wpwaf->model_manager->create_custom_taxonomies($params);
}
```

We are creating two custom taxonomies for the topics, and so we have called the common create_custom_taxonomies function twice with the necessary parameters. The following code previews the implementation of the common create_custom_taxonomies function inside the WPWAF_Model_Manager class:

```
public function create_custom_taxonomies($params) {
  extract($params);
  $capabilities = isset($capabilities) ? $capabilities : array();

  register_taxonomy(
    $category_taxonomy,
    $post_type,
    array(
      'labels' => array(
        'name'  => sprintf( __( '%s ', 'wpwaf' ) , $singular_name),
        'singular_name' => sprintf( __( '%s
','wpwaf'),$singular_name),
        'search_items' => sprintf(__('Search %s', 'wpwaf' ) ,
$singular_name),
        'all_items'   => sprintf( __( 'All %s ', 'wpwaf' ) ,
$singular_name),
        'parent_item' => sprintf( __( 'Parent %s ', 'wpwaf' ) ,
$singular_name),
        'parent_item_colon' => sprintf( __( 'Parent %s :', 'wpwaf' ) ,
$singular_name),
        'edit_item'  => sprintf( __( 'Edit %s ', 'wpwaf' ) ,
$singular_name),
        'update_item' => sprintf( __( 'Update %s ', 'wpwaf' ) ,
$singular_name),
        'add_new_item' => sprintf( __( 'Add New %s ', 'wpwaf' ) ,
$singular_name),
        'new_item_name' => sprintf( __( 'New %s  Name', 'wpwaf' )
,$singular_name),
        'menu_name' => sprintf(__('%s ', 'wpwaf' ) , $singular_name),
            ),
      'hierarchical' => $hierarchical,
      'capabilities' => $capabilities ,
    )
  );
}
```

The preceding code illustrates the default structure of the custom taxonomy creation function with all the necessary options. There is nothing new in the topic category taxonomy other than the use of instance variables instead of hardcoding. Astute readers might notice the difference in topic tag implementation. We have added a section called `capabilities` to the `Topic` tag. We use topic categories and tags to separate the topics into easily manageable sections. Tags are used to group the topics into any number of sections and keep the categories list to a minimum.

So, we need to provide the ability for members to define any new topic tags in our application. On the other hand, topic categories are fixed and won't get changed regularly. Therefore, we need to block the topic category creation for user roles other than the admin and moderator.

By default, WordPress uses the `manage_categories` permission for all the taxonomies, including default categories and tags. Since we didn't define specific capabilities for topic categories, it will use the default `manage_categories` permission. So, anyone who has the permission to `manage_categories` will have the ability to create new topic categories. Now, let's consider the capabilities of the topic tags:

```
'capabilities' => array(
   'manage_terms'        => 'manage_wpwaf_topic_tag',
   'edit_terms'          => 'edit_wpwaf_topic_tag',
   'delete_terms'        => 'delete_wpwaf_topic_tag',
   'assign_terms'        => 'assign_wpwaf_topic_tag'
)
```

The following four permissions are used to handle default permissions:

* manage_terms
* edit_terms
* delete_terms
* assign_terms

Here, we need to handle the permissions of the topic tags separately from others, hence, we have assigned four custom permission types to respective keys. Now, take a look at the topic creation menu on the admin area. You will notice that the **Topic Category** menu is displayed for admins and the **Topic Tag** menu is not visible. Since we have defined custom capabilities, even the administrator does not have permission until we assign them.

Now you can see the two blocks added to the right of the topic creation screen to define topic categories and topic tags, as shown in the following screenshot:

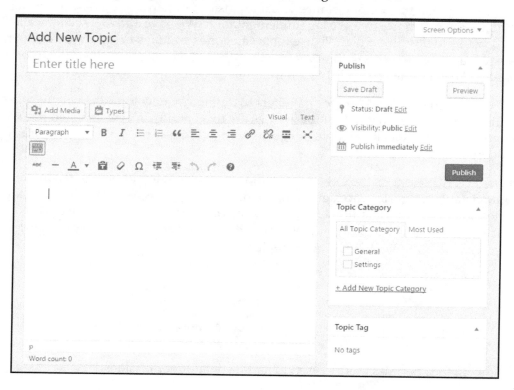

As you can see, an administrator has access to the **Add New Topic Category** link, create tags, since the administrator doesn't have the custom capabilities for topic tags.

Assigning permissions to the topic tags

We added custom capabilities in the topic tags creation process. However, WordPress has no idea about those capabilities until we assign them to a specific user role. In Chapter 2, *Implementing Membership Roles, Permissions, and Features,* we installed the Members plugin to manage user roles. So, you can go to **Users | Roles | Administrator** to see all the available capabilities. You won't see the new capabilities on this screen.

Now, open the `class-wpwaf-config-manager.php` file again in the `WPWA Forum` plugin with the updated code in the preceding section on topic tag permissions. Navigate to the `add_application_user_capabilities` function and change the existing code as follows:

```
public function add_application_user_capabilities() {
    $custom_member_capabilities = array(
'edit_wpwaf_topics','publish_wpwaf_topics','delete_wpwaf_topics',
'edit_published_wpwaf_topics', 'create_wpwaf_topics' ,
'assign_wpwaf_topic_tag');

    // Code for adding capabilities for members

    $custom_admin_capabilities = array(
'edit_wpwaf_topics','publish_wpwaf_topics','delete_wpwaf_topics',
'edit_published_wpwaf_topics', 'create_wpwaf_topics',
'delete_published_wpwaf_topics', 'edit_others_wpwaf_topics',
'delete_others_wpwaf_topics' , 'assign_wpwaf_topic_tag',
'delete_wpwaf_topic_tag', 'edit_wpwaf_topic_tag',  'manage_wpwaf_topic_tag'
);

    // Code for adding capabilities for admins
}
```

 You can get more details about roles and capabilities from the WordPress codex at `http://codex.wordpress.org/Roles_and_Capabilities`.

In this section, we have included additional topic tag-related capabilities to our existing capability arrays. Members only need to assign tags to topics, hence only one capability is included. The administrator and moderator need to manage all the features of the topic tags, hence all four topic tag capabilities are included.

By now, you should know that capabilities cannot be defined without a user role. Finally, we add each of the custom capabilities inside the loop using the `add_cap` function.

Once everything is saved, go to the **Plugins** section and deactivate the WPWA Forum plugin. Then, reactivate the plugin and go to the **Users | Roles | Administrator** section to view the capabilities. Now you should be able to see the custom capabilities assigned to the admin role. Also, you will have access to the **Add New Topic Tag** link in the topic creation screen, as shown in the following screenshot:

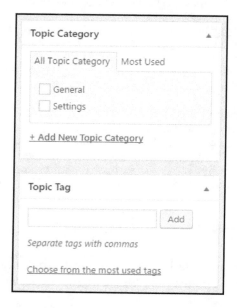

So far, we have created the default fields and taxonomies of the topics creation screen. Now we come to the most important part of creating custom fields for custom post types. Let's get started.

Introduction to custom fields with meta boxes

Being a WordPress user, you should be familiar with custom fields, as it is provided with default posts as well. We can enable custom fields on posts by clicking the **Screen Options** menu at the top of the post creation screen and ticking the checkbox of the **Custom Fields**. Once enabled, you will get a screen similar to the following screenshot:

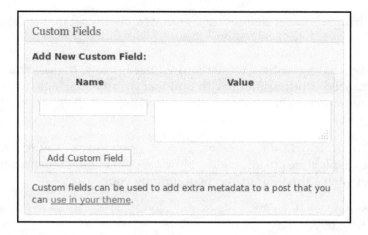

The default **Custom Fields** section allows us to specify any key-value pair with the post. So, the user has complete control over the data created through these fields. In web applications, we need more control over the user input for restricting and validating data, so the default custom fields screen is not ideal for web applications.

Instead, we can use the same custom fields in different approaches using meta boxes. As developers, we have the control to decide the necessary fields on meta boxes rather than allowing users to decide their own key-value pairs. Let's modify the `WPWAF_Model_Topic` class constructor to add the necessary actions for meta box creation for topics post type:

```
add_action('add_meta_boxes', array($this, 'add_topics_meta_boxes'));
```

We can use the `add_meta_boxes` action to define meta box creation functions for WordPress. Now, let's implement the meta boxes inside the `add_topics_meta_boxes` function:

```
public function add_topics_meta_boxes() {
    add_meta_box( 'wpwaf-topics-meta', __('Topic Details','wpwaf'),
array( $this, 'display_topics_meta_boxes' ), $this->post_type );
}
```

It's not possible to directly implement the meta box fields without using the `add_meta_box` function. This function will decide the information and locations for creating meta fields. They are as follows:

- The first parameter defines a unique key to the meta box (the HTML ID attribute of the screen)
- The second and third parameters define the meta box title and function respectively

- The fourth parameter defines the associated post type; in this case, the parameter will be `wpwaf_topic`

 Here, I have mentioned the required parameters. In case you want more advanced configurations with optional parameters, look at the documentation at `http://codex.wordpress.org/Function_Reference/add_meta_box`.

Finally, we need to implement the `display_topics_meta_boxes` function defined in the preceding code to display the custom fields. Now let's look at the most common implementation of such a function using the following code:

```php
public function display_topics_meta_boxes() {
    global $post;

    $html =  "<table class='form-table'>";
    $html .= "<tr>";
    $html .= "<th ><label><?php _e('Sticky Status','wpwaf');
?>*</label></th>";

    $html .= "<td><select class='widefat' name='wpwaf_sticky_status'
id='wpwaf_sticky_status'>";
    $html .= "<option value='0' ><?php _e('Please Select','wpwaf');
?></option>";
    $html .= "<option value='normal' ><?php _e('Normal','wpwaf'); ?>
</option>";
    $html .= "<option value='super_sticky' ><?php _e('Super
Sticky','wpwaf'); ?></option>";
    $html .= "<option value='sticky' ><?php _e('Sticky','wpwaf');
?></option>";
    $html .= "</select></td>";
    $html .= "</tr>";

    $html .= "<tr>";
    $html .= "<th ><label><?php _e('Topic Files','wpwaf');
?></label></th>";
    $html .= "<td><input class='widefat' name='wpwaf_files'
id='wpwaf_files' type='file' value='' /></td>";
    $html .= "</tr>";
    $html .= "</table>";
    echo $html;
}
```

Once you save the code and refresh the topic creation screen, you will get a meta box with a drop-down field and a file field, as defined in the preceding code. It works perfectly and most WordPress developers are comfortable with this technique of including HTML through PHP variables. Most experienced web developers will consider this technique a bad practice. There are certain issues in including HTML in variables, as listed here:

- Difficulty in maintaining proper quotes in the right places; one invalid quote can break everything
- Template and logic codes are scattered in the same function
- Difficulty in debugging the codes

In web applications, we need to separate layers based on their functionality. Therefore, we have to keep logic away from the presentation so that designers know exactly what they are dealing with. So, it's preferable to go with a template engine for complex applications.

What is a template engine?

The template engine is a library or framework that separates logic from template files. These libraries provide their own syntaxes for passing the necessary values to the template from the controllers or models. Once successfully implemented, we shouldn't have complex code inside template files other than simple `if-else` statements and loops.

There are plenty of open source template engines available for PHP. **Smarty**, **Mustache**, and **Twig** are some of the popular ones among them. However, integrating this type of template engine in WordPress is a complex task, compared to using it in other PHP frameworks. The architecture of WordPress is different from any other PHP framework, as it drives on action hooks and filters. Therefore, the integration needs to be capable of handling WordPress-specific things such as actions, filters, widgets, template tags, and so on.

The Twig templates engine created by SensioLabs is one of my favorites, as it offers many unique features compared to other template engines. If you are not familiar with template engines, I suggest that you look at the Twig documentation at `http://twig.sensiolabs.org/documentation`. As I mentioned, integrating Twig with WordPress is beyond the scope of this book. You can use the Timber plugin for WordPress at `https://wordpress.org/plugins/timber-library/` to understand how Twig templates work with WordPress.

Integrating WordPress plugins with the mentioned template engines is not so popular among developers. Even the most popular and well-coded plugins use simple template loading techniques. Throughout this book, we will be using our own template loading technique. Keep in mind that this technique is nowhere close to the features offered by a template engine. Also, this technique partially separates the presentation layer from logic, compared to template engines, which completely separate these two concerns. Let's get started with creating a simple template loading technique used by many developers.

Building a simple custom template loader

As developers, you might be familiar with the WordPress template loading technique using the `get_template_part` function. Basically, this function includes a file behind the scenes. This is similar to executing a `require` or `include` function on a file. However, WordPress recommends using this function instead of manual `require` or `include` function calls. We will use the same technique for building our template loader. This is the most commonly used technique among many popular plugins. Let's start by creating a new file called `class-wpwaf-template-loader.php` inside our plugins/wpwa-forum folder with the following class definition:

```
class WPWAF_Template_Loader{
    // Template loading code
}
```

Now, let's look at the implementation of our `get_template_part` function, similar to the WordPress core function:

```
public function get_template_part($slug,$name= null,$load= true) {
    do_action( 'wpwaf_get_template_part_' . $slug, $slug, $name );
    // Setup possible parts
    $templates = array();
    if ( isset( $name ) ){
        $templates[] = $slug . '-' . $name . '-template.php';
    }
    $templates[] = $slug . '-template.php';
    // Allow template parts to be filtered
    $templates = apply_filters( 'wpwaf_get_template_part',
$templates, $slug, $name );
    // Return the part that is found
    return $this->locate_template( $templates, $load, false );
}
```

The WordPress `get_template_part` function has three parameters with `$slug` being the only required parameter. You can define the template name in two ways, as follows:

- **Templates without parts**: these are standalone templates and so only a slug will be available for these templates. For example, `topics.php` where topics will be the slug without any subtemplate.
- **Templates with parts**: these are partial templates and so both a slug and name will be available in a template name. This is useful when having multiple subtemplates for a specific section: for example, `topic-replies.php` and `topic-members.php`. The topic will be the main slug and replies and members will be the templates.

We will check the availability of the sub or main template with the given filename and assign it to an array called `$templates`.

Note that we have an action called `wpwaf_get_template_part` and a filter called `wpwaf_get_template_part`. These hooks can be used to change the templates array based on different conditions and execute custom code when specific templates are loaded.

Finally, we will call the `locate_template` function for loading the templates inside the `$templates` array. Let's take a look at the implementation of the `locate_template` function:

```
public function locate_template( $template_names, $load = false,
  $require_once = true ) {
  // No file found yet
  $located = false;
  // Traverse through template files
  foreach ( (array) $template_names as $template_name ) {
    // Continue if template is empty
    if ( empty( $template_name ) )
      continue;
    $template_name = ltrim( $template_name, '/' );
    // Check templates for frontend section
    if ( file_exists( trailingslashit(WPWAF_PLUGIN_DIR ) .
'templates/'
  . $template_name ) ) {
      $located = trailingslashit(WPWAF_PLUGIN_DIR ) . 'templates/'  .
  $template_name;
      break;
      // Check templates for admin section
    }
```

```
    }
    if ( ( true == $load ) && ! empty( $located ) )
      load_template( $located, $require_once );
    return $located;
  }
```

We traverse all the templates in the $templates array and look for the existence of a template inside the specified template folders. Here, we are only searching the templates folder. As the project gets larger, we will have to define multiple sublevels inside the templates folder or multiple template folders. In such scenarios, we have to extend this code to include multiple locations for searching templates. Once a template is found, we break the process and return the template file.

Now, we have a basic template loader. In the next section, we will look at how to use this template loader to load the necessary templates.

Creating your first template

Template engines allow us to use pure HTML files or any other file type for templates. However, we are only using a template loader, and therefore we need some PHP code inside the templates. So, let's create the first template file called topic-meta-template.php inside the templates folder for topic metadata. We will be replacing the PHP variable based template code we used earlier with the template loader. Here, we have the complete template code for the topic meta box:

```
<?php
  global $template_data;
  extract($template_data);
?>
<input type="hidden" name="topic_meta_nonce" value="<?php echo
$topic_meta_nonce; ?>" />

<table class="form-table">
  <tr>
    <th style=''><label><?php _e('Sticky Status','wpwaf'); ?>*
</label></th>
    <td><select class='widefat' name="wpwaf_sticky_status"
id="wpwaf_sticky_status">

        <option <?php selected( $topic_sticky_status, '0' ); ?>
value='0' ><?php _e('Please Select','wpwaf'); ?></option>
        <option <?php selected( $topic_sticky_status, 'normal' ); ?>
value='normal' ><?php _e('Normal','wpwaf'); ?></option>
        <option <?php selected( $topic_sticky_status, 'super_sticky'
```

```
); ?> value='super_sticky' ><?php _e('Super Sticky','wpwaf'); ?></option>
            <option <?php selected( $topic_sticky_status, 'sticky' ); ?>
value='sticky' ><?php _e('Sticky','wpwaf'); ?></option>
        </select></td>
    </tr>
    <tr>
        <th style=''><label><?php _e('Topic Files','wpwaf');
?></label></th>
        <td><input class='widefat' name='wpwaf_files' id='wpwaf_files'
type='file' value='' /></td>
    </tr>
</table>
```

Let's get started! Take a look at the following steps:

1. First, we will use a global variable called $template_data to access the data for the templates. We can start the template by defining the nonce value inside a hidden field for securing the form submission. In this technique, we are using PHP variables to assign data to the templates.

2. Then, we have a list of fields for **Sticky Status** and **Topic Files**. Each of these fields uses a PHP variable from the global $template_data variable for displaying data.

- In a modern website design, the HTML table is not such a popular component for creating layouts. We prefer a <div> element-based structure for more flexibility. In the WordPress context, it's ideal to use tables for designs to keep the consistency across all admin screens. Also, you can use a CSS class called widefat on form fields for a better look and feel.

3. The next task will be to assign the created template into a topic screen through meta boxes. So, we have to restructure the display_topics_meta_boxes function to use templates instead of hardcoded HTML elements. Here is the implementation with the use of our new template loader:

```
public function display_topics_meta_boxes() {
    global $wpwaf,$post,$template_data;
    $data = array();
    $topic = $post;
```

```
        $template_data['topic_post_type'] = $this->post_type;
        $template_data['topic_meta_nonce'] = wp_create_nonce('wpwaf-
topic-meta');
        $template_data['topic_sticky_status'] = get_post_meta(
$topic->ID, '_wpwaf_topic_sticky_status', true );

        ob_start();
        $wpwaf->template_loader->get_template_part( 'topic','meta');
        $display = ob_get_clean();
        echo $display;
    }
```

First, we have to get the existing data from the database and assign it to the global `$template_data` variable. The template will only have access to the data specified in this variable. Most of the variables contain data required for the topic screen. However, `topic_meta_nonce` might be new to some of you. WordPress uses nonce value generation for securing and validating form submissions. Therefore, we have assigned the nonce value to the data array with a key called `topic_meta_nonce`.

A nonce is used for security purposes to protect against unexpected or duplicate requests that can cause undesired permanent or irreversible changes to the website, and particularly to its database. Specifically, a nonce is a one-time token generated by a website to identify future requests to that website. When a request is submitted, the website verifies whether a previously generated nonce expected for this particular kind of request was sent along, and decides whether the request can be safely processed or a notice of failure should be returned. This could prevent unwanted repeated, expired, or malicious requests from being processed.

Many developers may not be familiar with this technique, and so let's look at a detailed explanation of the template loading process. As mentioned earlier, the template loader will load the templates using the PHP `require` or `include` statements. Therefore, the output of the template cannot be assigned to a variable, and hence, we need to buffer the output. We will use the `ob_start` function for output buffering. The following is the definition of the `ob_start` function provided by the PHP site:

> *"This function will turn output buffering on. While output buffering is active no output is sent from the script (other than headers), instead the output is stored in an internal buffer."*

4. Then we will use the `$wpwaf` global object to call the `template_loader` object and load the template using our new template loader. Therefore, the content of the template file will be stored in an internal buffer.

5. Finally, we will execute the `ob_get_clean` function to get the current buffer contents and delete the current output buffer. Now, all the contents of the template file will be assigned to the variable and we can easily output it with an `echo` statement.

By now, you will have the complete topic creation screen with default fields, taxonomies, and custom fields, as shown in the following screenshot:

We have managed to create a template loader to separate the logic from the presentation. However, our template loader is far from completely separating the logic from the presentation. In the next section, we will look at the functionality of our template loader and how it differentiates from a perfect template engine.

Comparing the template loader and template engine

We started building a template loader to solve the issue with mixing template code inside PHP variables. We managed to partially solve this problem. Now, the templates are stored as separate files with HTML content and we can reuse these templates from multiple `Model` classes. The `Model` class contains the logic and passes the data to the templates. So, there is no more HTML content inside PHP variables. However, we still have PHP variables inside the template files to output the model data. Let's see how our template loader differentiates from a proper template engine:

- Many template engines compile templates down to plain optimized PHP code and provide cached versions if necessary
- Handles automatic output escaping
- Uses specific syntax for defining data inside templates so that templates can be used without PHP
- Templates can be reused as blocks using inheritance

Considering the preceding points, it is obvious that our template loader only provides basic features for separating the logic from the presentation layer.

Persisting custom field data

You already know that default fields and taxonomies are automatically saved to the database on post publish. In order to complete the topic creation process, we need to save the custom field data to the meta tables. As usual, we have to update the constructor of the `WPWAF_Model_Topic` class to add the necessary actions to match the following code:

```
public function __construct() {
  // Instance variable initializations
  // Other actions
  add_action('save_post', array($this, 'save_topic_meta_data'));
}
```

WordPress doesn't offer an out-of-the-box solution for form validation, as most websites don't have complex forms. This becomes a considerable limitation in web applications. So, let's explore the possible workarounds to reduce these limitations. The action `save_post` inside the constructor will only be called once the post is saved to the database with the default field data. We can do the necessary validations and processing for custom fields inside the function defined for the `save_post` action. Unfortunately, we cannot prevent the post from saving when the form is not validated properly. First, let's figure out the data-saving process for a custom field using the following implementation:

```
public function save_topic_meta_data() {
   global $post,$wpwaf;
   if (isset($_POST['topic_meta_nonce']) &&
!wp_verify_nonce($_POST['topic_meta_nonce'], "wpwaf-topic-
meta")) {
      return $post->ID;
   }
   if (defined('DOING_AUTOSAVE') && DOING_AUTOSAVE) {
     return $post->ID;
   }
   if (isset($_POST['post_type']) && $this->post_type ==
$_POST['post_type'] &&
   current_user_can('edit_wpwaf_topics', $post->ID)) {
      //Implement the validations and data saving
   } else {
   return;
   }
}
```

We begin the custom fields-saving process by verifying the nonce against the value we generated in the form using the `wp_verify_nonce` function. Upon unsuccessful verification, we return the post ID to discontinue the process. Then, we have to execute a similar validation for the autosaving process. Finally, we have to verify the post type and check whether the current user has permission to edit posts of this type.

These validations are common to custom field-saving processes of any post type. Therefore, it's ideal to separate these checks into a common function to be reused across multiple locations.

Once all the validations are successfully completed, we will implement the data-saving process inside the `class-wpwaf-model-topic.php` file, as shown in the following code:

```php
public function save_topic_meta_data() {
    global $post;
    // Common validations
    if (isset($_POST['post_type']) && $this->post_type ==
$_POST['post_type'] &&
    current_user_can(' edit_wpwaf_topics', $post->ID)) {

        // Section 1
        $sticky_status  = isset( $_POST['wpwaf_sticky_status'] ) ?
sanitize_text_field( trim($_POST['wpwaf_sticky_status']) ) : '';

        // Section 2
        if ( $sticky_status == '0' )   {
            $this->error_message .= __('Sticky status cannot be empty.
<br/>', 'wpwaf' );
        }

        // Section 3
        if ( !empty( $this->error_message ) ) {
            remove_action( 'save_post', array( $this, 'save_topic_meta_data'
) );

            $post->post_status = 'draft';
            $post->post_title = isset($_POST['post_title']) ?
sanitize_text_field($_POST['post_title']) : '';
            $post->post_content = isset($_POST['post_content']) ?
($_POST['post_content']) : '';
            wp_update_post( $post );

            add_action( 'save_post', array( $this, 'save_topic_meta_data' )
);

            $this->error_message = __('Topic creation failed.<br/>', 'wpwaf'
```

```
) . $this->error_message;
        set_transient( $this->post_type."_error_message_$post->ID",
$this->error_message, 60 * 10 );

        } else {
        update_post_meta( $post->ID, '_wpwaf_topic_sticky_status',
$sticky_status );
        }

     } else {
       return;
     }
   }
```

The data-saving process looks quite extensive and complex compared to the code we discussed up to now. So, let's break the code into three sections, to simplify the explanation process:

- **Section 1**: the initial code includes the retrieval of form values through the $_POST array to be stored in the variables. Here, we have to validate and filter the POST data to avoid harmful data. Therefore, we have used trim and WordPress escape functions to filter the data. We have only one custom topic field at this stage. You can use the same technique to add more custom fields.

- **Section 2**: in this section, we will implement the form validations for each and every form field. Once validation fails, we can assign the error to the error_message instance variable to be used across the other function of this class. We can implement any type of complex validations in this section.

- If you have a large number of form fields with complex validations, integrating a third-party library for validations might become a better solution than manual time-consuming validations.

- **Section 3**: here, we come to the tricky part of the validation process. Even though we execute validations and generate errors in Section 2, it's not possible to prevent the topic creation. Therefore, we have chosen an alternative way to handle the process:

First, we remove the `save_post` action by using the `remove_action` function. This action should have the same syntax as the `add_action` function used in the constructor for `save_post`. In web applications, it is preferable to work with published data, unless you are implementing a custom application specific status. Hence, we will set the post to draft status upon validation failure.

However, you will lose the topic title and the topic content when errors are generated on the custom posts fields. Therefore, we get the post title and post content from the `POST` data and assign it to the post before updating. So, the post title and post content will be updated in draft even when errors are generated.

Sometimes you may want to save some custom fields even when errors are generated on other fields. In such situations, you can use the same technique to save custom field data into a post meta table.

Then we can update the post to the database and add the `save_post` action back. Even though the post is still saved, we won't see it in the application frontend as we are only focusing on published data. Once the user submits the form without errors, it will revert back to the publish status.

In our application, we are using a post meta field called **Topic Files**. However, we can't directly save this field like other fields, as this field can contain multiple files. So, we need the ability to dynamically add multiple files before a post is updated. Therefore, we will be implementing the **Topic Files** field in upcoming chapters.

Once a topic is successfully updated, WordPress will display the error as `Post draft updated`. Definitely, we need much more user-friendly errors to suit our applications. Therefore, we have to change the existing error messages generated by WordPress. Before this, we have to set the error to the `error_message` variable and save it in the database using the `set_transient` function.

Transient is a WordPress-specific technique for storing cached data in the database for temporary usage. Since WordPress uses a hooks and actions based procedure, it's not possible to get the error message after submission. Therefore, we temporarily save the error message on the database to enable access from the post message handling function, which will be explained in a moment.

When the form is successfully validated without errors, we use the `update_post_meta` function on each field for saving or updating the data to the database. Having understood the code for the custom post saving function, we can revert back to the error message handling process.

Customizing custom post type messages

By default, WordPress uses messages of normal posts for the custom post types. We need to provide our own custom messages to improve the user experience. Customization of messages can be done with the existing filter called `post_updated_messages`. First, we have to update the constructor of the `WPWAF_Model_Topic` class with the following filter hook:

```
add_filter('post_updated_messages',
array($this,'generate_topic_messages'));
```

This filter enables us to add new messages to the existing messages array, as well as alternating the existing messages to suit our requirements. This is another section with duplicate codes, and hence, we will be using a common function to display the messages for all post types. First, we have to look at the model-specific messages function for defining the necessary labels and data, as shown in the following code:

```
public function generate_topic_messages( $messages ) {
    global $wpwaf;
    $params = array();
    $params['post_type'] = $this->post_type;
    $params['singular_name'] = __('Topic','wpwaf');
    $params['plural_name'] = __('Topics','wpwaf');

    $messages = $wpwaf->model_manager-
>generate_messages($messages,$params);
    return $messages;
    }
```

As usual, we will define the necessary data and execute the common function. Implementation of `generate_messages` differs from the commonly used code, since we are handling the form validations manually to improve the process. Let's look at the implementation of the `generate_messages` function inside the `WPWAF_Model_Manager` class:

```
public function generate_messages( $messages, $params ) {
    global $post, $post_ID;
    extract($params);
    $this->error_message = get_transient(
$post_type."_error_message_$post->ID" );

    if ( !empty( $this->error_message ) ) {
      $messages[$post_type] = array();
    } else {

      $messages[$post_type] = array(
      0 => '', // Unused. Messages start at index 1.
      1 => sprintf(__('%1$s updated. <a href="%2$s">View %3$s</a>',
'wpwaf' ),$singular_name,
esc_url(get_permalink($post_ID)),singular_name),

      2 => __('Custom field updated.', 'wpwaf' ),
      3 => __('Custom field deleted.', 'wpwaf' ),
      4 => sprintf( __('%1$s updated.', 'wpwaf' ), $singular_name),

      5 => isset($_GET['revision']) ? sprintf(__('%1$s restored to
revision from %2$s', 'wpwaf' ),$singular_name,
wp_post_revision_title((int) $_GET['revision'], false)) : false,

      6 => sprintf(__('%1$s published. <a href="%2$s">View %3$s</a>',
'wpwaf' ),$singular_name,
esc_url(get_permalink($post_ID)),$singular_name),

      7 => sprintf(__('%1$s saved.', 'wpwaf' ),$singular_name),

      8 => sprintf(__('%1$s submitted. <a target="_blank"
href="%2$s">Preview %3$s</a>', 'wpwaf' ), $singular_name,
esc_url(add_query_arg('preview', 'true', get_permalink($post_ID))),
$singular_name),

      9 => sprintf(__('%1$s scheduled for: <strong>%2$s</strong>. <a
target="_blank" href="%3$s">Preview %4$s</a>', 'wpwaf' ),
      $singular_name,
      date_i18n(__('M j, Y @ G:i'),strtotime($post->post_date)),
      esc_url(get_permalink($post_ID)),
      $singular_name),
```

```
      10 => sprintf(__('%1$s draft updated. <a target="_blank"
href="%2$s">Preview %3$s</a>', 'wpwaf' ), $singular_name,
esc_url(add_query_arg('preview', 'true', get_permalink($post_ID))),
$singular_name),
          );
    }
    return $messages;
  }
```

WordPress uses the messages array with 10 keys to cater for all the messages generated in the custom post screens. Once the **Publish** button is clicked, we can validate the form and save the error messages as transients. However, WordPress will execute the whole process to generate the common error or message without considering our validations. You can find a parameter in the URL with the message as the key and the specific number as the value.

In order to show the validation errors, we need to intercept the WordPress generated message and change it according to our preference.

First, we will get the error message using the get_transient function. If the error message is available, we set the $messages array for this post type to prevent WordPress from generating any kind of message. If the error message is not available, we change the default $messages array to include topic-specific messages instead of post-specific messages. Now we have prevented WordPress from generating messages on errors and changed the messages on successful topic creation. However, we don't have a way to display custom errors on our topic custom fields. Let's look at how we can add custom messages to the topic creation screen.

First, we have to update the constructor of the WPWAF_Model_Topic class with the following code:

```
    add_action( 'admin_notices', array( $this, 'topic_admin_notices' ) );
```

We can use a WordPress built-in action called admin_notices to display custom messages in the post type creation screen. Let's look at the implementation of the topic_admin_notices function using the following code:

```
    public function topic_admin_notices(){
      global $post;
      $this->temp_error_message = get_transient( $this-
>post_type."_error_message_$post->ID" );

      delete_transient( $this->post_type."_error_message_$post->ID" );

      if (!( $this->temp_error_message)){
        return;
      }
```

```
        $message = '<div id="wpwaf-errors" class="error below-h2"><p>';
        $message .= $this->temp_error_message;
        $message .= '</p></div>';

        echo $message;
        remove_action( 'admin_notices', array( $this,'topic_admin_notices')
    );
    }
```

First, we check whether a specific error message exists in the database using the `get_transient` function. Once the errors are assigned to the variable, we delete the error message on the transient to prevent conflicts in the future. In case errors are generated, we add the message to a custom HTML container and echo the output to display it on the topics screen. Finally, we remove the `admin_notices` action added in the constructor to prevent displaying the same errors in other parts of our application.

Now, we have completed the basic foundation for implementing our topics and forums post types. You can use the source code of this chapter to play with the implementations of other post types and I highly recommend that you change the code to understand the various aspects of custom post types.

Introduction to post type templates

A post type template is one of the most valuable features added in recent versions of WordPress. This template allows us to design and style different posts and custom post types with different templates. In Chapter 2, *Implementing Membership Roles, Permissions, and Features*, we discussed page templates and their importance. This is a similar feature for posts instead of pages.

In our forum application, we have a custom post type called topics. In order to display topics on the frontend, we need a template different from the normal post template. So the earlier versions of WordPress allowed us to use the `single-{post_type}.php` file of the theme to design custom post types differently from normal posts. However, this technique only allows us to display all our topics with the same design. Assume that we want to display normal topics with one design and sticky topics with another design. This is not possible with earlier versions of WordPress without modifying the theme files. The introduction of post type templates has made it possible to have unlimited designs for different posts of the same post type.

Creating and using a post type template

This is similar to the page template creation we used earlier. Create a PHP file called `topics-front.php` inside the `TwentySeventeen` theme folder with the following code:

```php
<?php
/*
Template Name: Forum Sticky Topic
Template Post Type: wpwaf_topic
*/
?>
<div>HELLO STICKY TOPICS</div>
```

Here, we have just a basic text to illustrate the use of post templates. Later, we can complete the design needs of our application post types using these templates. Now, go to the topic creation screen and you will find a new section for adding the post template, as shown in the following screenshot:

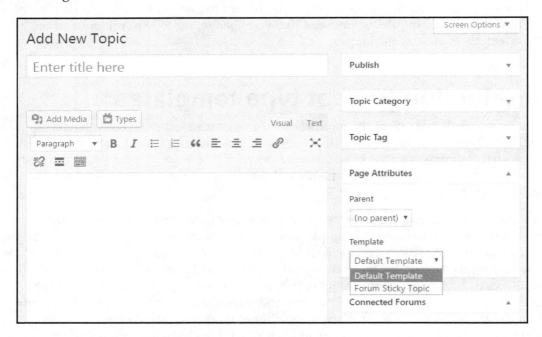

We can assign the new template for all our **Sticky Topics** and use the default template for displaying any other topics.

In this section, we had a brief introduction to post type templates and their importance in working with custom post types in our application. . In `Chapter 8`, *Adjusting Themes for Amazing Frontends*, we will be exploring more about post type templates and how these templates fit into the WordPress template structure.

Introducing custom post type relationships

In general, we use relational databases in developing applications, where our models will be matched to separate database tables. Each model will be related to one or more other modules. However, in WordPress, we have all the custom post types stored in the posts table. Hence, it's not possible to create relationships between different post types with the existing functionality.

WordPress developers around the world have been conducting discussions to get the post relationship capability built into the core. Even though the response from WordPress core development seems positive, we still don't have it on the core version as of 4.7. You can have a look at this interesting discussion at `http://make.wordpress.org/core /2013/07/28/potential-roadmap-for-taxonomy-meta-and-post-relat ionships/`.

Since this is one of the most important aspects of web application development, we have no choice but to look for custom solutions. We have two simple solutions for adding post relationships in our applications:

- Assigning post relationships using custom meta fields
- Using third-party plugins for adding relationships

Let's identify how we can implement these two methods.

We can assign post relationships using the custom post fields we discussed earlier. Currently, we have a field called **Sticky Status** in our topics screen. Similarly, we can add another drop-down field called **Forum** to the topic meta fields section. The only difference here is that we will have to load the existing forums from a database instead of displaying a field with predefined options.

Next, admin needs to select the forum before publishing the topic. Once the `save_post` action is executed, we need to save the custom **Forum** field into a custom table with a forum ID and topic ID, instead of saving the value to the `wp_postmeta` table. This is a very simple method for adding relationships to custom post types.

We choose WordPress for developing web applications in a rapid process. Therefore, we will be using the third-party plugin-based approach for our application to speed up the process, as well as having some additional features in adding relationships.

There are a few competitive plugins among the open source community for providing post relationship functionality. The `Posts 2 Posts` plugin developed by Cristian Burca and Alex Ciobica seems to be the plugin of choice for many developers.

In our forum application, we need to associate topics to forums and vice versa. So, let's see how we can use this cool plugin to implement the necessary features. First, grab a copy of the plugin from `http://wordpress.org/plugins/posts-to-posts/` and get it activated in your WordPress installation. This plugin doesn't offer a GUI for defining post relationships, and so we will need to implement some source code.

Let's get started by updating our `WPWAF_Model_Topic` class constructor with the following code:

```
if ( defined( 'P2P_PLUGIN_VERSION' ) ) {
  add_action( 'p2p_init',array( $this,'join_topics_to_forums' ) );
}
```

Here, we have the `p2p_init` action, which comes built-in with the `Posts 2 Posts` plugin. All the post relationship definitions and configurations go inside the `join_topics_to_forums` function, as illustrated in the following code:

```
public function join_topics_to_forums() {
  global $wpwaf;
  p2p_register_connection_type( array(
      'name'  => 'topics_to_forums',
      'from'  => $this->post_type,
      'to'    => $wpwaf->forum->post_type
          ) );
}
```

The `Posts 2 Posts` plugin provides a function called `p2p_register_connection_type` for defining post type relationships. The first parameter called `name` defines a unique identifier for the relationship. Then, we can define two post types for the connection using the `from` and `to` parameters. This will enable the topics selection section for forums and forums selection section for topics. The following screenshot illustrates the topics screen with the **Connected Forums** box:

First, you have to create forums from the **Forums** item on the left menu. Then, you can add a forum to a topic by clicking on the forum name. Once saved, you will have a screen similar to the following one with the associated forum of a given topic:

This is the most basic implementation of post relationships with this plugin.

If you are curious to learn about advanced usages, you can have a look at the plugin documentation at `https://github.com/scribu/wp-posts-to-posts/wiki`. In the following chapters, we will learn how to retrieve and work with the related posts.

We have set up the foundation of our application backend throughout the chapter. Now, users with the role of a moderator can log into the system and create forums and topics. Throughout the previous sections, we had to work with complicated WordPress functions related to custom post types and taxonomies. In complex applications, we need better quality in the code to avoid duplicate code scattering around hundreds of files.

As a solution, we can develop our own custom post type specific library to simplify the implementations. Ideally, such a library should abstract the custom post type functions into a common interface and let users choose to define their configurations without forcing them to do so. Implementing such a library is a time-consuming and complex task, which is beyond the scope of this book. Therefore, I suggest that you look for existing open source libraries or take the time to plan your own library. An alternative solution will be to take advantage of popular existing frameworks such as `Pods`, which will be introduced shortly.

Pods framework for custom content types

Up until this point, we have explored the advanced usage of WordPress custom post types by considering the perspective of web applications. Although custom post types provide immense power and flexibility for web applications, manual implementation is a time-consuming task with an awful amount of duplicate and complex code. One of the major reasons for using WordPress for web development is its ability to build things rapidly. Therefore, we need to look for quicker and more flexible solutions beyond manual custom post implementations.

Pods is a custom content type management framework, which has been becoming popular among developers in recent years. Most of the tedious functionalities are baked into the framework, while providing us with a simpler interface for managing custom content types. Apart from simplifying the process, Pods provides an extensive list of functionalities that are not available with default WordPress administrative screens.

Let's consider some of the key features of the Pods framework, compared to the manual implementation of custom post types. The Pods framework allows us to:

- Create, extend, and manage custom types and fields, including custom post types, taxonomies, comments, and users
- Use default tables or custom tables for content types
- List built-in form fields and components with necessary validations
- Manage form field-level permissions
- Create settings pages for plugins and themes

Basically, this framework provides out-of-the-box functionalities for common tasks in WordPress application development without much hassle. For example, think of how much effort you need to add a custom field for your comment form. With the Pods framework, you will be able to implement such tasks within a few clicks in under 10 minutes. Pods does have an active community, hence can be recommended for rapid application development with WordPress.

Let's get our hands dirty by implementing something practical with this awesome framework:

1. First, you have to grab a copy of this plugin from `http://pods.io` and get it installed on your WordPress folder.
2. Once activated, you should see the **Pods Admin** menu item inside the left menu.
3. Earlier, we implemented the topics post type by manually implementing custom post type code. Here, we will see how the Pods framework simplifies the same process. Keep in mind that we will create a basic implementation to show the power of Pods, instead of implementing the whole thing we have already completed.
4. Click on the **Create a New Content Type** section to add a new content type and you will get a screen similar to the following screenshot:

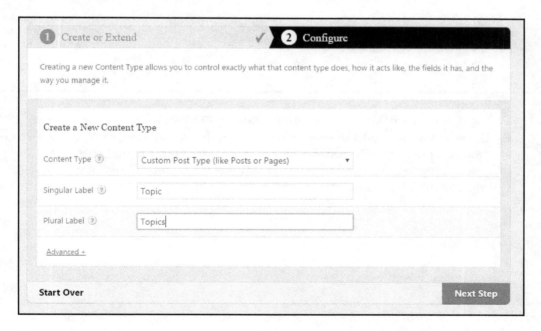

5. In the content type creation screen, you can select a custom post type and add the label as `Topic`, since it's not wise to redefine topics created in our application.

6. Then, move on to the next step to get the screen shown in the following screenshot:

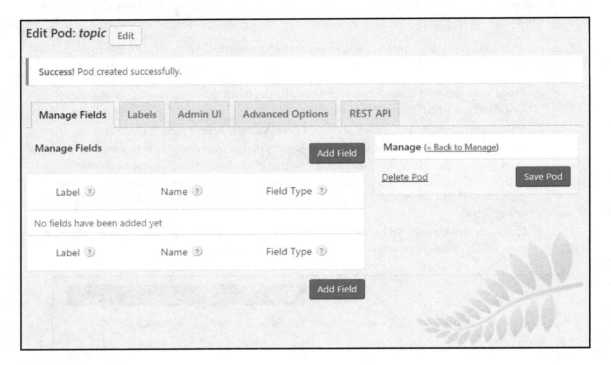

7. Surprisingly, we have the custom post ready in three clicks.

8. The next task is to add the necessary custom fields and associate them with the products post type. Remember the tasks we did in our manual custom field creation process. We had to create HTML for the fields, use template engines, implement validations, and so on.

9. The Pods framework abstracts all these tasks behind the framework, allowing us to focus on application logic. So, click the **Add Field** button to create the first custom field:

10. All the necessary configurations are divided into the four tabs at the top of the screen.

11. You can create the field by defining the necessary labels, validations, and access restrictions. Pods provides over 15 built-in field types, including data pickers, color pickers, file fields, and text editors. You can also allow these fields to be read or written through the new REST API.

12. Once all the fields are created, click on the **Save Pod** button.

13. Now, navigate to the product creation screen and you will find all the custom fields created with Pods, as shown on the following screen:

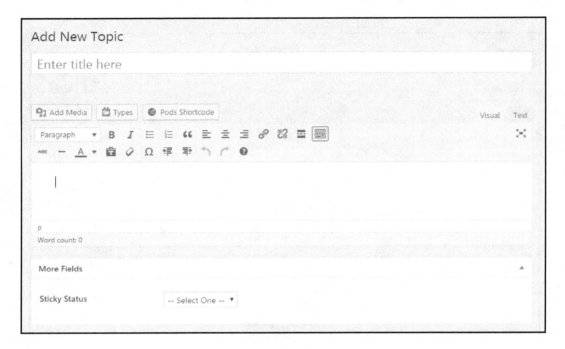

We were able to create a complete custom post type with the necessary fields within 10 minutes. This is one of the most basic usages of the Pods framework. You can find more advanced usages on the official site at `http://podsframework.org/`.

Should you choose Pods for web development?

One can definitely go with the Pods framework for applications that require a rapid development process or low budgets. It's maturing into an excellent framework with the support of the open source community. The Pods framework offers more advantages and fewer limitations compared to similar competitive plugins and frameworks.

The ability to choose between existing tables and custom tables can become quite handy in complex web applications. We have to enable the **Advanced Content Types** component in order to make use of custom tables. It's recommended that you use existing tables in every possible scenario. However, there can be scenarios where custom tables can become a better option to default tables:

- **Extensive data load**: in applications where you have a large number of records with a number of custom post types, it's wise to separate post types into custom tables for better performance.
- **More control**: using existing tables will force us to stick with the features provided in WordPress by default. In situations where you need complete control over your data, it's better to choose custom tables instead of existing ones.

In short, you should be using this framework or similar ones for reducing repetitive work and to focus on application-specific tasks. If you choose not to go with such a framework, you should definitely have your own common library for interacting with custom content type related functions, in order to maintain the quality of code and to build maintainable systems.

There is a popular phrase, which states that:

"With great power comes great responsibility."

We have used some very powerful plugins throughout this chapter and will be continuing to do so in the remaining chapters. As developers, we have a huge responsibility in working with these plugins. It can be dangerous to rely on third-party plugins to build the core of your application. The following are some of the risks of using third-party plugins:

- Plugins can break due to WordPress version upgrades
- Developers might discontinue the development of a plugin
- Plugins might not be updated regularly

That said, all plugins used throughout this book are highly popular and stable. So, it's important to know how these plugins work in order to customize them at later stages if needed. Also, it's better not to rely heavily on third-party plugins and keep alternatives whenever possible.

Implementing custom post type features with popular plugins

Throughout this chapter, we developed common custom post features needed for web applications. Even the implementation of common features from scratch needed considerable effort. As applications grow, we need more custom post types, hence we need features such as managing settings through interfaces, advanced post field types, and managing field saving/validations without coding. In such situations, it's a wise decision to use plugins with these advanced features rather than building everything from scratch.

So, we discussed Pods in the previous section as it's one of the best custom post type management plugins available. Here, are we going to look at two popular alternatives, so that you can compare and use the right solution for your application.

Custom Post Type UI

This is a highly popular plugin by **WebDevStudios** with over 400,000 active installs in the WordPress plugin directory. This plugin can be used to create and manage custom post types and custom taxonomies with all the available settings. So, we can change the way custom post types work without needing to change any code files. Custom Post Type UI focuses more on administrative aspects of custom post types and requires a premium plugin called `Custom Post Type UI Extended` to handle the frontend interfaces for the custom post types.

This is useful when you have simple application requirements for creating and managing custom post types. The `Custom Post Type UI` plugin offers limited functionality compared to the wide range of features available in the Pods framework. You can download Custom Post Type UI from `https://wordpress.org/plugins/custom-post-type-ui/`.

Toolset Types

This is also a highly popular plugin by the team of developers at **OnTheGoSystems**, actively used by over 200,000 sites. Apart from managing custom post types, custom taxonomies, and their settings, this plugin offers a wide range of features including:

- Custom field groups for custom post types
- Custom field groups for custom taxonomies

- Custom fields for users
- 20 custom field types including repeating fields

Similar to Custom Post Type UI, a free version of this plugin doesn't provide the ability to handle frontend views for your post types. It provides a product called **Toolset Package** where you get advanced features for custom post types including:

- Frontend views for custom post types
- Frontend forms to add data to custom post types

So, **Toolset Types** is a great solution compared to Custom Post Type UI and offers similar features to the Pods framework. You can download Toolset Types from `https://wordpress.org/plugins/types/`.

These are the top solutions for managing custom post types, among dozens of other similar plugins. I recommend you use and compare the features of these plugins in order to get a better experience for your future applications.

Time to practice

In this chapter, we discussed the advanced usages of custom post types to suit web application functionalities. Now, I would recommend that you try out the following tasks in order to evaluate the things you learned in this chapter:

- In the `post relationships` section, we enabled relationships using the `join_topics_to_forums` function. With the use of this function, we can generate a new problem considering the possibility of extending. Find the issue and try to solve it by yourself.
- We enabled relationships between custom post types. Research the possibilities of including metadata for relationships.

Summary

In this chapter, we tackled custom post types to learn the advanced usages within web applications. Generally, custom posts act as the core building blocks of any type of complex web application. We went through the basic code of custom post-related functionality, while developing the initial forums and topics post types of the forum management application.

We were able to explore advanced techniques, such as modularizing custom post types, and template engines to cater to common web application requirements. Also, we had to go through a tough process for validating form data due to the limited support offered by WordPress.

We learned the importance of relating custom post types using the `Posts 2 Posts` plugin. Finally, we explored the possibilities of improving the custom post type management process with the use of an amazing framework called Pods.

In the next chapter, we will see how to use the WordPress plugin beyond the conventional use by implementing pluggable and extendable plugins. Until then, get your hands dirty by playing with custom post type plugins.

5
Implementing Application Content Restrictions

In the previous chapter, we looked at the creation of web application content using custom post types and managing various custom post type related features. We can now move into conditionally restricting the content created in previous chapters. Content is the most important aspect of any application. Providing the same features to all users limits your application from gaining exposure as well as causing management nightmares. Therefore, we need at least two user types to manage the application features and use the application features.

WordPress doesn't provide built-in features for restricting content and hence we have to develop everything from scratch or use an existing content restriction plugin. In this chapter, we will be implementing some of the common restriction types while discussing the process for implementing advanced restrictions.

On the one hand, content restrictions provide great benefits to your application and on the other hand, they might cause loop holes in the application, creating major security threats. So, we have a great responsibility in executing the necessary WordPress-specific validations while implementing the content restrictions.

In this chapter, we will cover the following topics:

- Introduction to content restrictions
- Practical usage of content restrictions
- Understanding restriction levels
- Implementing content restrictions in posts/pages
- Enabling restrictions on WordPress core features

- Supplementary content restriction types and techniques
- Useful plugins for content restrictions

Let's get started!

Introduction to content restrictions

Generally, we refer to information in textual, visual, or aural forms as content in websites. In web applications, we can consider content as anything that is used by the administrators of the application or an application's users. The following are some of the commonly used content types in WordPress applications:

- Posts and pages
- Custom post types
- Widgets
- Menus

In applications or websites, we can't provide every feature to everyone. So, we need to identify the various types of users in our application and ascertain what each of these user types can do within our application. Creating limitations of what each user can see within our application is referred to as content restrictions or content permissions.

In WordPress, we need to log in to the backend to create a post or change any settings. This is the most basic form of content restriction, where we limit the backend features to administrative staff with proper authentication. In web applications, we have to manage content restrictions on both the frontend as well as the backend.

In the upcoming sections, we will be looking at various types of content in WordPress web applications and how to implement restrictions.

Practical usage of content restrictions

In normal websites, we provide content access to anyone who visits the website. Modern web applications are built on top of basic content restriction types as well as some innovative restriction types to attract more users to the application. Usage of these restrictions varies based on the type of application and the type of content.

We have to identify the type of restriction to be implemented in an application and the benefits expected from applying the restriction. So, let's look at some of the common uses of content restrictions and their benefits:

- **Restricting individual posts or the entire site**: We use this restriction to keep the privacy of your content from unintended users or to gain monetary benefits for some part of the content.
- **Restricting content behind a social Locker**: We use this type of restriction to increase the exposure of the site in social media to attract more customers and promote your application.
- **Restricting content behind e-mail subscriptions**: This technique is ideal for capturing the e-mails of your application users so that you can send notification about your application features and future promotions.
- **Restricting content such as registration and login**: This technique is not used to gain benefits. Instead, we use it to prevent security threats and spam data into our application.

These are some of the commonly used techniques and their benefits. When exploring web applications, you will find more innovative techniques for content restrictions and useful benefits by adding such restrictions.

The role of membership in content restrictions

Membership plays a vital role in content restrictions. We use memberships to group users into separate levels. In modern applications, content restrictions are commonly used to separate free members from premium members or to offer different feature levels among premium members. So, a membership plan is the commonly used concept along with payments to divide users into separate content restriction levels.

In the next section, we will be looking at the comparison of the restriction levels and how membership works in web applications.

Understanding restriction levels

We have two important aspects in content restrictions. First, we need to identify different content types that need to be restricted and then identify which user types are restricted from accessing this content. So, we group the users and define specific restriction levels for these user groups. Let's identify the most commonly used restriction levels in WordPress web applications:

- User roles-based restrictions
- User groups-based restrictions
- Membership plans-based restrictions
- Unique password-based restrictions

Let's take a look at how these restriction levels are implemented.

User roles-based restrictions

User roles is a default WordPress feature and it's the only technique that we can use as a restriction level without needing custom coding or third-party plugins. As we discussed in Chapter 2, *Implementing Membership Roles, Permissions, and Features*, WordPress gives you six built-in user roles. These user roles also have built-in restrictions to the backend of the application, making it easier to manage restrictions on the backend content.

The implementation of frontend restrictions requires minimum effort as all users have user roles assigned by default. However, a user roles-based restriction is the least flexible way of adding restrictions to your application. User roles are used by many WordPress plugins to provide various features. More often than not, you will be using such third-party plugins for web applications.

In this technique, you will have to change the roles of the users in order to change the restriction levels. So, this process breaks the functionality of other plugins that rely on the user's current role. User role-based restrictions can be used successfully when we have custom user roles and no other plugins depending on these custom user roles.

User groups-based restrictions

This is another commonly used technique to define restriction levels. WordPress doesn't provide user grouping features by default. So, we have to rely on third-party plugins or use our own custom implementation to manage user group-based restrictions.

In this method, an administrator manually assigns users to a group or we provide features for users to join into different groups. This process can be implemented within the user registration or in a separate group management section. Then we assign the permitted groups while creating different types of content in our application. Finally, we have to get the permitted groups and verify whether the current user is part of the permitted groups while displaying the content in the frontend. This is the ideal way of implementing restrictions compared to user role-based restrictions. In this technique, users are separated into actual independent groups instead of relying on user roles used by many plugins.

Membership plans-based restrictions

This technique can be considered as a sub-restriction level of user group-based-restrictions. We group the users with membership plans or membership levels. Often members are required to make a payment to gain access to these special user groups called membership plans. Similar to the user group-based technique, we define the permitted membership levels while creating the content. Finally, we check the membership plan of the logged in user before giving access to the requested content. This technique is ideal when you need users to pay for accessing the content.

Unique password-based restrictions

This is a completely different type of restriction level compared to the other three levels discussed so far. In this technique, a single user or set of users is given a password by the administrative staff. Implementation of this technique is inconvenient as administrators need to regularly provide passwords to users and the users need to enter the password on each request for content. This technique can be used when your application works with a large number of members in a single company.

These are the most common restriction levels for users. You can also find other rarely used restriction levels such as capability-based restrictions and profile field value-based restrictions.

Implementing content restrictions in posts/pages

Posts and pages are the core content types used in any WordPress website. As we discussed in Chapter 4, *Building Blocks of Web Applications*, custom post types play a major role compared to posts and pages in websites. So, understanding how to implement restrictions on these three content types is key to developing a quality application with proper authorization. These content types can be restricted in many common and innovative ways. We will be looking at the most common restrictions on these content types to suit any web application:

- **Shortcode-based restrictions**: This technique is used to restrict a part of the post/page/custom post type from different user levels. We use a shortcode, capable of handling different restrictions, and place it on a post editor. Any content placed between the opening and closing shortcode tags will be restricted based on the restriction level.

- **Individual post/page restrictions**: This technique is used to restrict individual posts/pages/custom post types instead of restricting part of the post. We define the restrictions in a meta box inside the post and use WordPress actions and filters to restrict individual posts to different users.

- **Site lockdown**: This technique is used to restrict an entire site to guest users and only allow access to the members. We use WordPress core actions and filters to restrict the entire site and redirect the user to a different page.

We can develop these restrictions with advanced settings to enhance the flexibility for a wide range of scenarios. Most advanced content restriction plugins provide such flexibility. However, implementing such advanced capabilities is not possible within the scope of this book and hence we will be looking at the theory and most basic implementation. Let's start the implementation of these content restriction techniques.

Shortcode-based restrictions

First, we have to define a shortcode that handles content restrictions. In the forum application, we have several user roles. The shortcode created in this section should be able to provide restrictions for each of these user roles. We can start by creating a new class for content restrictions called `WPWAF_Content_Restrictions` inside the classes folder of our `forum` plugin. Then, we need to include the file inside the `includes` function of the `WPWAF_Forum` class and initialize the object inside the `instance` function of the same class.

Let's start by defining the shortcode inside the constructor, as shown in the following code:

```
class WPWAF_Content_Restrictions{
   public function __construct(){
      add_shortcode( 'wpwaf_private_content', array( $this ,
'private_content_block' ));
   }
}
```

Now, we can move into the implementation of the `private_content_block` function for adding restrictions:

```
public function private_content_block($atts,$content){
   global $wpwaf,$wpdb;

   if(current_user_can('manage_options') ){
      return do_shortcode($content);
   }

   if (!is_user_logged_in())
      return __('Login to access this content','wpwaf');

   foreach ($atts as $sh_attr => $sh_value) {
      switch ($sh_attr) {
       case 'allowed_roles':
         $this->status = $this->allowed_roles_filter( $atts,$sh_value);
         break;
      }

      if(!$this->status){
         break;
      }
   }

   if(!$this->status){
       return __('You don\'t have permission to access this content',
'wpwaf');
   }else{
      return do_shortcode($content);
   }
}
```

First, we check whether the administrator is accessing the content by verifying the `manage_options` capability. We return the content for administrators without applying any restrictions. Next, we check whether the user is not logged in and return a message instead of the actual content. Once these two conditions are successfully verified, we move into the actual restrictions. By default, WordPress passes all the shortcode attributes as the first parameter to the shortcode handler function. So we traverse through all the available attributes using a `foreach` loop.

In this implementation, we are only allowing shortcode content to selected user roles. So, we check for the availability of the `allowed_roles` attribute in the shortcode. We can specify a single role or multiple roles for the `allowed_roles` attribute. Next, we pass the attribute data to a function called `allowed_roles_filter` for verification. This function returns `true` when the logged in user has one of the allowed roles or returns `false` if the user doesn't have any of the allowed roles. If the verification returns `false`, we break the functionality without checking the other attributes since the user doesn't have permission to access the content. Finally, we check the status outside the loop and return a permission restriction message or the actual content depending on the status value.

Now, we can look at the `allowed_roles_filter` function to understand how user role checking works in WordPress:

```php
public function allowed_roles_filter($atts,$sh_value){
  global $wpwaf;
  extract($atts);

  $user_roles = $this->get_user_roles_by_id(get_current_user_id());
  $roles = explode(',',$sh_value);

  if(is_array($roles) && count($roles) > 1){

    foreach ($roles as $role) {
      if(in_array($role, $user_roles)){
        return true;
      }
    }
  }

  return false;
}
```

We passed each attribute and value to this function as parameters. First, we have to get the user roles of the currently logged in user with a custom function, `get_user_roles_by_id`. You can find the implementation of this function in the source code for this chapter. We can access the allowed user roles list with the `$sh_value` parameter. The allowed user role list is converted to an array using the PHP `explode` function. Then we traverse through each of the allowed role(s) using a `foreach` loop and check for matches with the user's roles list. If one of the user's roles matches the roles available in the `allowed_roles` value, we return `true` to provide permission.

Now, we have shortcode-based restrictions set up to work with user roles. We have two member roles in our forum application. Assume that the moderator or admin wants to add separate content inside the topic for free and premium members. In such a scenario, admin can use the following shortcodes inside the forum topic editor to restrict different content to different user roles:

```
[wpwaf_private_content allowed_roles=
"wpwaf_free_member,wpwaf_moderator" ]  Free Member Content
[/wpwaf_private_content]

[wpwaf_private_content allowed_roles=
"wpwaf_premium_member,wpwaf_moderator" ]  Premium Member Content
[/wpwaf_private_content]
```

The first shortcode allows the content within the opening and closing tags to free members and moderators, while restricting it to other user roles. Similarly, the shortcode allows the content within the opening and closing tags to premium members and moderators, while restricting it to other user roles.

This is a simple and flexible way to add different types of content restrictions within the same post/page or custom post type. You can adjust the `switch` statement in the `private_content_block` function to add more restriction attributes such as `blocked_roles`, `allowed_capabilities`, `allowed_users`, and so on.

Individual post/page restrictions

This is a higher level of restriction compared to shortcodes as the entire post/page will be restricted instead of just part of the post/page. Implementing post/page restrictions requires more effort compared to the shortcode-based restrictions as we need an interface to define the restrictions. Using a meta box inside the post creation/edit screen can be considered the simplest way of defining restrictions for each post. In this scenario, we will be implementing forum topic restrictions for guests and members, in order to explain the procedure.

Creating a meta box for topic restrictions

First, we have to update the class constructor with the actions required for displaying meta boxes and saving meta box values, as shown in the following code:

```
class WPWAF_Content_Restrictions{
    public function __construct(){
        // Other actions
        add_action( 'add_meta_boxes', array($this,
'add_topic_restriction_box' ));
            add_action( 'save_post', array($this, 'save_topic_restrictions'
));
    }
}
```

Earlier, we created a meta box to save the custom fields of the topics screen. Similarly, we display another meta box for content restrictions using the add_meta_boxes action. Consider the initialization of the meta box inside the add_topic_restriction_box function:

```
public function add_topic_restriction_box(){
    global $wpwaf;
    if( current_user_can('manage_options')  ){
    add_meta_box(
        'wpwaf-forum-restrictions',
        __( 'Restriction Settings', 'wpwaf' ),
        array($this,'add_topic_restrictions'),
        $wpwaf->topic->post_type,
        'normal',
        'low'
        );
    }
}
```

Here, we have the common meta box initialization with the most basic settings. This meta box is only displayed for the administrator inside the topic create/edit screen. We have an empty meta box that needs to be populated with the restriction settings. So, we can look at the implementation of the add_topic_restrictions function for loading the template:

```
public function add_topic_restrictions($post){
    global $wpwaf,$topic_restriction_params;
    $topic_restriction_params['post'] = $post;
    ob_start();
    $wpwaf->template_loader->get_template_part( 'topic-restriction-
meta');

    $display = ob_get_clean();
```

```
    echo $display;
}
```

This is the implementation of the meta box initialization and hence we have the current post object as a parameter to this function. We use our template loader to retrieve a new template called `topic-restriction-meta`.

Now, we have to create a new template file inside the template folder with the filename of `topic-restriction-meta-template.php`. This template file contains the settings for the restriction type and redirection URL:

```php
<?php
    global $wp_roles,$wpwaf,$topic_restriction_params;
    extract($topic_restriction_params);

    $visibility = get_post_meta( $post->ID,  '_wpwaf_topic_visibility',
true );
    $redirection_url = get_post_meta( $post->ID,
'_wpwaf_topic_redirection_url', true );

?>
<div class="wpwaf_topic_meta_row">
    <div class="wpwaf_topic_meta_row_label"><strong><?php
_e('Visibility','wpwaf'); ?></strong></div>
    <div class="wpwaf_topic_meta_row_field">

        <select id="wpwaf_topic_visibility" name="wpwaf_topic_visibility" >
            <option value='none' <?php selected('none',$visibility); ?>
><?php _e('Please Select','wpwaf'); ?></option>
            <option value='all' <?php selected('all',$visibility); ?> ><?php
_e('Everyone','wpwaf'); ?></option>
            <option value='guest' <?php selected('guest',$visibility); ?>
><?php _e('Guests','wpwaf'); ?></option>
            <option value='member' <?php selected('member',$visibility); ?>
><?php _e('Members','wpwaf'); ?></option>
        </select>
    </div>
</div>

<div class="wpwaf_topic_meta_row">
    <div class="wpwaf_topic_meta_row_label"><strong><?php
_e('Redirection URL','wpwaf'); ?></strong></div>
    <div class="wpwaf_topic_meta_row_field">
        <input type='text' id="wpwaf_topic_redirection_url"
name="wpwaf_topic_redirection_url" value="<?php echo $redirection_url;
?>" />
```

```
        </div>
    </div>
    <?php wp_nonce_field( 'wpwaf_restriction_settings',
'wpwaf_restriction_settings_nonce' ); ?>
```

The initial part of the template contains the necessary global variables and the accessing template data using the `$topic_restriction_params` array. We will be saving the post restriction settings to the `wp_postmeta` table. Therefore, we retrieve the existing values for the content visibility setting and redirection URL in the top section of the template.

Next, we add the **Visibility** setting field using a normal drop-down field and **Redirection URL** setting with the text field. Finally, we include a nonce field for security verification. Now, your topic creation screen will have the content restrictions meta box as shown in the following screenshot:

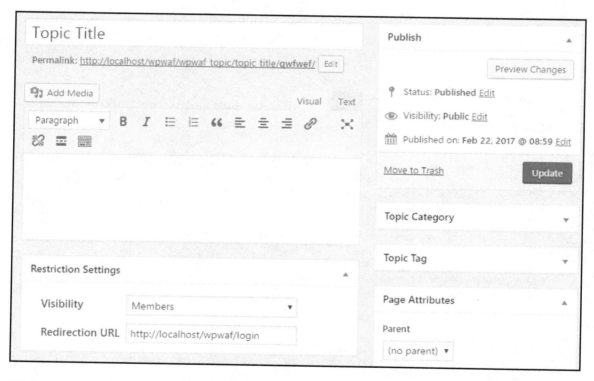

We have four options in the **Visibility** setting for restricting the topic to **Everyone**, **No one**, **Guests**, and **Members**. The **Redirection URL** setting will be used to redirect the users with the restrictions to the topic content.

Saving topic restriction settings

Now we need to save the restrictions on the topic update by using the following implementation of the `save_topic_restrictions` function:

```
public function save_topic_restrictions($post_id){
    if ( ! wp_verify_nonce(   $_POST['wpwaf_restriction_settings_nonce']
, 'wpwaf_restriction_settings' ) ) {
        return;
    }

    if ( defined( 'DOING_AUTOSAVE' ) && DOING_AUTOSAVE ) {
      return;
    }
    if ( ! current_user_can( 'edit_posts', $post_id ) ) {
      return;
    }

    $visibility = isset( $_POST['wpwaf_topic_visibility'] ) ?
$_POST['wpwaf_topic_visibility'] : 'none';
    $redirection_url = isset( $_POST['wpwaf_topic_redirection_url'] )  ?
$_POST['wpwaf_topic_redirection_url'] : '';

    update_post_meta( $post_id, '_wpwaf_topic_visibility', $visibility );
    update_post_meta( $post_id, '_wpwaf_topic_redirection_url',
$redirection_url );

    }
```

The initial sections of the code contain nonce verification, auto-save verification, and verifications for checking the capabilities for editing posts. If one of these verification tests fails, we return the function without saving the content restriction settings. Once verifications are successfully completed, we get the **Visibility** and **Redirection URL** from the $_POST array. Finally, we save these settings to the `wp_postmeta` table using the `update_post_meta` function. The last step of this implementation is to use these settings and apply the restrictions.

Verifying individual post/page restrictions

WordPress executes an action called `template_redirect`, before determining which template to load, based on a user's request. So, we are going to use this action to intercept the default template loading process and redirect the user to a different template when the user doesn't have proper authorization. We can begin the process by updating the class constructer with the `template_redirect` action as follows:

```
class WPWAF_Content_Restrictions{
    public function __construct(){
      // Other actions
      add_action('template_redirect', array($this,
'validate_restrictions' ), 1);
    }
}
```

Next, we need to implement the `validate_restrictions` function to verify the user permission to apply the redirections, as shown in the following code:

```
public function validate_restrictions(){
  global $wpwaf,$wp_query;

  if(current_user_can('manage_options')){
    return;
  }

  if (! isset($wp_query->post->ID) ) {
    return;
  }

  if(is_page() || is_single()){
    $post_id = $wp_query->post->ID;
    $protection_status = $this->protection_status($post_id);

    if(!$protection_status){
      $post_redirection_url = get_post_meta( $post_id,
'_wpwaf_topic_redirection_url', true );
      if(trim($post_redirection_url) == ''){
        $post_redirection_url = get_home_url();
      }
      wp_redirect($post_redirection_url);exit;
    }
  }
  return;
}
```

We start the function by checking whether the administrator is accessing the content and return the original template. Also the existence of a post ID is checked in order to validate the current request. Once these basic validations are completed, we check whether the requested content is a post or page using `is_single` and `is_page` WordPress functions. The WordPress `is_single` function returns `true` for single posts as well as single custom post types. Therefore, we can use it to validate topics custom post types in our application. Next, we get the current post/page ID from the post object and execute the `protection_status` function to verify the permissions. If verification fails for the current user, we grab the redirection URL added earlier in the restriction meta box and redirect the user to the specified URL.

The last part of this implementation is the `protection_status` function where the actual content restrictions are applied, as shown in the following code:

```
public function protection_status($post_id){
    global $wpwaf;

    $visibility = get_post_meta( $post_id, '_wpwaf_topic_visibility',
true );
    switch ($visibility) {
      case 'all':
          return TRUE;
          break;

      case 'guest':
          if(is_user_logged_in()){
              return FALSE;
          }else{
              return TRUE;
          }
          break;

      case 'member':
          if(is_user_logged_in()){
              return TRUE;
          }else{
              return FALSE;
          }
          break;
    }
    return TRUE;
}
```

Implementation of this function is simple compared to the other functions we have used up to now. We take the visibility level defined for the post (in this case `Topic`) using the `_wpwaf_topic_visibility` key in the post meta table. Next, we use a `switch` statement to apply different restrictions based on the visibility. Let's identify the process of each visibility level:

- **Everyone (all)**: This visibility level allows everyone to view content and hence we return the function to display the default template.
- **Guests (guest)**: This visibility level only allows guests to access the restricted content. So, we provide permission by returning `TRUE` when the user is not logged in and restrict any other user from viewing.
- **Members (member)**: This visibility level only allows members to access the restricted content. So, we provide permission by returning `TRUE` when the user is logged in and restrict any other user from viewing.

Now we have completed implementing individual post/page restrictions and you can try this feature by creating a forum topic with a visibility level and accessing the forum topic in the frontend.

We discussed the basic visibility levels in this section to simplify the implementation. It's a must to have advanced restrictions such as user roles and user groups. You can refer to the source code folder for this chapter for the implementation of user roles-based restrictions to individual posts/pages.

Site lockdown

This is the highest level of restriction compared to other restriction types as it blocks the entire site for unauthorized users. Implementing this technique requires many settings and hence we are going to keep it simple by hardcoding the setting values.

Similar to individual post/page restrictions, we can use the `template_redirect` action to implement the site lockdown features. Let's start by adding the action definition to the constructor as following:

```
class WPWAF_Content_Restrictions{
  public function __construct(){
    // Other actions
    add_action( 'template_redirect' , array( $this,
'validate_site_lockdown_restrictions'));
  }
}
```

Basically, we need to restrict the entire site to guest users and allow it to any logged in user. Once the entire site is blocked, users won't be able to even access log in and registration. Therefore, we need to skip certain URLs, posts, and pages from this lockdown and implement the restrictions on any other content. Let's have a look at the implementation of `validate_site_lockdown_restrictions` for the site lockdown:

```php
    public function validate_site_lockdown_restrictions(){
        global $wpwaf,$pagenow;
        $this->user_id = get_current_user_id();

        if(current_user_can('manage_options')){
          return;
        }

        $redirect_url = 'http://www.example.com/login';

        $skipped_urls = array( $redirect_url , wp_login_url(),
wp_registration_url(), wp_lostpassword_url());
        $skipped_custom_urls = array();
        foreach ($skipped_custom_urls as $url) {
          if($url != ''){
              array_push($skipped_urls, $url);
          }
        }

        $url  = @( $_SERVER["HTTPS"] != 'on' ) ?
'http://'.$_SERVER["SERVER_NAME"] :
'https://'.$_SERVER["SERVER_NAME"];
        $url .= $_SERVER["REQUEST_URI"];
        $current_page_url = $url;

        $parsed = parse_url($current_page_url);
        $scheme = isset($parsed['scheme']) ? $parsed['scheme'] . '://' : '';
        $host    = isset($parsed['host']) ? $parsed['host'] : '';
        $port    = isset($parsed['port']) ? ':' . $parsed['port'] : '';
        $user    = isset($parsed['user']) ? $parsedl['user'] : '';
        $pass    = isset($parsedl['pass']) ? ':' . $parsedl['pass']  : '';
        $pass    = ($user || $pass) ? "$pass@" : '';
        $path    = isset($parsed['path']) ? $parsed['path'] : '';

        $current_page_url = $scheme.$user.$pass.$host.$port.$path;

        // Implementation of restrictions
        }
    }
```

First, we get the current user's ID and check for administrator permissions. When the administrator is accessing the content, our function returns without executing any content permission checks. Next, we define a URL for custom redirection when a user doesn't have permission to view content. The next section is the most important one where we define the content to be skipped from site lockdown.

It's obvious that we need to skip the redirection URL along with WordPress backend registration, login, and reset password URLs. We also have an empty array called `$skipped_custom_urls` to add any kind of custom posts/pages/custom post types or links to be skipped from site lockdown. Then we have to construct the current URL of the request by manipulating the content of the PHP `$_SERVER` array. Now we have everything ready to lockdown the site using the remaining code, as shown in the following snippet:

```
public function validate_site_lockdown_restrictions(){
  // Other codes
  if(in_array($current_page_url, $skipped_urls)){
    return;
  }else{
    if($this->user_id == 0){
      wp_redirect($redirect_url);
      exit;
    }
  }
}
```

First, we check whether the current request URL is listed under the set of skipped URLs we defined earlier. Once the skipped URL is matched, we can return the content without applying restrictions. If the skipped URLs are not matched and the user is logged in, we can still return the original content. Finally, when the user is not logged in and the skipped URLs are not matched, we redirect the user to the URL defined earlier to restrict access.

This is the most basic implementation of site lockdown where we restricted the entire site to guests. We can modify the process to lockdown the site to different user roles instead of limiting it to guests. In an ideal implementation, you will need to have settings to define allowed URLs, allowed posts, allowed pages, and allowed custom post types.

Enabling restrictions on WordPress core features

Generally, posts and pages are the common content used for applying restrictions in applications. However, it's important to understand restrictions on other core WordPress features as we need to integrate all the features in order to build a quality application. So, we are going to look at some of the core WordPress features and techniques for applying restrictions.

Restrictions on posts

We have already discussed several content restriction techniques on posts. Apart from these restrictions, we can also implement global post restrictions and post category restrictions:

- **Global post restrictions**: We can restrict all posts or all posts of a single custom post type at once without applying restrictions on individual posts
- **Category restrictions**: We can restrict all posts from a given category at once

Both types of restrictions can be managed with the `template_redirect` action we used in previous sections.

Restrictions on searches

The built-in search features of WordPress allow us to search posts, pages, and custom post types. In some situations, we may want to restrict the content types that can be used in searches for different user types. We can use the `pre_get_posts` filter to apply restrictions on searches. Let's look at the basic usage of this filter:

```
add_action('pre_get_posts', 'search_restrictions');
function search_restrictions($query) {
  if ($query->is_search && $query->is_main_query() && !is_admin())  {
    $search_blocked_ids = array('24','100');
    $search_allowed_types = array('wpwaf_topic','wpwaf_forum');;

    $query->set('post__not_in', $search_blocked_ids );
    $query->set('post_type', $search_allowed_types );
  }
  return $query;
  }
```

There are a few important things to notice. The `pre_get_posts` action is executed even for the normal posts lists generation. So, we have to be able to intercept this action only on searches by using the `$query->is_search` status. Next, we can block certain posts/pages from appearing in search results by using `post__not_in` with the array of the post's ID. Finally, we can restrict the search only to certain post types using the `post_type` attribute.

In this example, we have restricted searches from using two posts and only allowed topics and forums in the results. You can try out many such restrictions on search results with different attributes and values.

Restrictions on menus

It is a common feature to display different menu items based on the functionality available for each user type. We can use the built-in `wp_get_nav_menu_items` filter to apply restrictions and only return menu items based on the permission level. Restrictions on each menu item can be specified using custom menu fields, as shown in the following screenshot:

In this screen, we have the ability to define different visibility levels and select the permitted users inside these visibility levels. Implementing menu restrictions is beyond the scope of this chapter and hence you can use the `WP Private Content Plus` plugin to learn the implementation.

Restrictions on widgets

In normal websites, we populate the sidebars with widgets. However, in web applications, we use widgets in a different way and we still need the ability to display widgets based on different permission levels. Similar to menu restrictions, we can use the built-in `widget_display_callback` filter to check the permissions and apply restrictions. This filter is used in the settings of a particular widget. However, we can use it to check the permission and return the widget instance or return empty on permission failures.

We can use a similar technique as menus to define the restrictions inside each widget as shown in the following screenshot:

Restrictions on archives

We restricted individual posts/pages in previous sections. However, these posts are going to still show up on post archives pages such as post lists, category posts, tag posts, and so on. So, we need to make sure restricted posts are also removed from the archive pages.

Again, the `template_redirect` action comes in handy in this implementation. We can modify the code for individual post/page restrictions to include archive restrictions as displayed in following code:

```
public function validate_restrictions(){
    global $wpwaf,$wp_query;
    // Other code for single post/page restrictions

    if(is_archive() || is_feed() || is_search() || is_home() ){
        if(isset($wp_query->posts) && is_array($wp_query->posts)){
            foreach ($wp_query->posts as $key => $post_obj) {
                $protection_status = $this->protection_status($post_obj->ID);
                if(!$protection_status){
                    $wp_query->posts[$key]->post_content = __('You don\'t have
permission to view the content','wpwaf');
                }
            }
        }
    }
    return;
}
```

First, we check whether a request is made on the archive, feed, search, or home pages. We need to apply these restrictions on all four types. Then we traverse through all the available posts in the list and check for restrictions on each post using the post meta value for the **Visibility** setting. Finally, we replace the post content with a custom message when the user doesn't have permission to view the content.

Supplementary content restriction types and techniques

Up to this point, we discussed the most commonly used content restriction types and their usage. There are many other supplementary restriction types used in modern web applications. We are going to look at some of the important ones among the dozens of restrictions available.

Restrictions on custom generated content

This is one of the most important restriction types and there are limited plugins that support restrictions on custom content. Custom generated content is generally provided by plugins and hence applying restrictions might be difficult in a normal procedure. In Chapter 2, *Implementing Membership Roles, Permissions, and Features,* we created a custom path called /user/login and /user/registration. So, the content generated from these custom URLs can't be restricted with normal content restriction types. The following are some of the popular plugins with custom generated content:

- Woocommerce
- BuddyPress

These popular plugins provide built-in actions and filters for the custom content and hence we can use them to apply restrictions on some of the custom content. In situations where such actions and filters are not available, we can use a URL-based technique for applying restrictions to this custom generated content.

Attachment protection

This is not a commonly used technique in applications. However, it might be important in certain scenarios such as our forum application. Generally, we display text/video/audio content in posts or custom post types. We don't have a way to add separate attachments to posts/custom posts. In the forum application, we need to upload files for certain topics and we may need to restrict them to certain user levels. We can use a meta box on the topics screen to upload the attachments and use post content filters to display attachments with restrictions. You can use the WP Private Content Plus plugin discussed in later sections of this book to apply attachment protection.

Social Locker

This is one of the innovative content restriction techniques used in modern applications. The purpose of this restriction is to let users share application content in their social profiles and increase the exposure to the application content. We add the content to be restricted in a shortcode or in a custom field in a meta box. Then we define the social network interactions required to gain access to the content. Once the user accesses the content for the first time, the Social Locker will be displayed similar to the following screenshot:

Then the user needs to execute one of the requested actions by logging into their social account. Once the action is completed, the user will be redirected back to the application and the restricted content will be displayed instead of the Social Locker screen. You can use the OnePress `Social Locker` plugin at `https://wordpress.org/plugins/social-locker` to understand the implementation of this technique.

E-mail subscription

E-mail subscription is also one of the popular techniques used in application to add user e-mails to a list. However, in recent times this has also been used as a content restriction mechanism similar to `Social Locker`. Similar to `Social Locker`, we can add the content to be restricted in a shortcode or in a setting depending on the implementation you want. Then the user will get the subscription form instead of the actual content when visiting the application. The following screenshot previews a common e-mail subscription form applied for content restrictions:

Once the user provides an e-mail and hits the **SUBSCRIBE** button, the e-mail of the user will be added to a subscription list, most probably on a third-party server. Then the user will have access to the content once a successful response is received from the e-mail subscription list. You can use the `WP Private Content Plus` plugin at `https://wordpress.org/plugins/wp-private-content-plus` to understand the implementation of this technique.

Private page

Private page is another popular technique where we restrict the content to individual users instead of a group of users. This is implemented in an application via the private user profile or normal WordPress page with private restrictions. We will be looking at the private page section. Here, we can create a page and add it to a user using the meta box technique we used in the individual post/page restrictions. Then admin can add user-specific content to this page using the post editor. Only the user assigned to the page will be able to view the restricted content.

The limitation of this technique is the need to create a separate WordPress page for each user, making it difficult to manage pages. As an alternative solution, we can use a shortcode on a single page and let admin add different content to different users using a backend settings section. So, we will only need one private page and each user will have their own private content in this single page. You can use the `WP Private Content Plus` plugin at `https://wordpress.org/plugins/wp-private-content-plus` to understand the implementation of this technique.

We discussed some of the uncommon content restriction techniques in this section. There are more such techniques used in modern applications. Understanding such techniques is useful to gain maximum exposure to your application and hence I recommend you try various content restriction plugins, including the ones discussed in the next section.

Useful plugins for content restrictions

We implemented some of the common restriction types in web applications and discussed the usage of various other restriction types. We kept the implementation to a basic level in order to let you easily understand the core concept. In real web applications, we will need more flexibility and control over the restrictions. So, we are going to look at some of the plugins with advanced content restrictions and settings to cater to advanced application requirements.

Restrict Content

This is a popular free plugin by Pippin Williamson with over 10,000 active installs. Primary functionality of this plugin is the ability to add restrictions to registered users. We can use this plugin to add shortcode-based restrictions and individual post/page/custom post type restrictions. Apart from these two main features, this plugin also provides the ability to restrict content on your WordPress RSS feeds. This is a simple solution when you want to apply basic content restrictions on your site without manual coding.

You can download and check the features of the free version of this plugin at `https://wordpress.org/plugins/restrict-content/`.

WP Private Content Plus

This is another trending plugin in the WordPress plugin directory with over 3,000 active installs. I have added this plugin to this list as I am the developer of this plugin and you can use it to learn basic restrictions on a wide range of content types. `WP Private Content Plus` offers content restrictions on posts, pages, custom post types, menus, widgets, search, and post attachments. Also you will get a wide range of user restriction levels such as guests, members, user roles, user capabilities, and user groups. This plugin is ideal for understanding the implementation of content restrictions, as the source code is similar to the code used in this chapter.

You can download and check the features of the free version of this plugin at `https://wordpress.org/plugins/wp-private-content-plus`.

Membership 2

`Membership 2` is another popular free plugin from the famous WPMU Dev team with over 10,000 active installs. This plugin takes content restriction to the next level by providing membership and payment features. This plugin provides advanced features compared to the other two plugins and offers content restrictions on posts, pages, categories, menus, and URLs. Apart from these basic restrictions, `Membership 2` offers the following advanced content restriction features:

- Dripped content
- Hiding content behind a pay wall
- Restricting media files
- Restricting downloads

You can download this plugin from `https://wordpress.org/plugins/membership/`.

Time to practice

In this chapter, we discussed the basic and advanced techniques for implementing content restrictions. Now, I would recommend that you try out the following tasks in order to evaluate the things you learned in this chapter:

- We enabled user role-based restrictions using the shortcodes technique. Implement the same shortcode-based technique for user capabilities.
- We added individual post/page restrictions for individual posts. Try to implement the same technique for user roles, before checking the source codes for this chapter.

Summary

Content restriction is one of the significant features in applications where you have different type of users. We began this chapter by learning the importance and practical usage of content restrictions. Also, we looked at various user levels used in restrictions.

We implemented the most common restriction types on our forum application while understanding how posts can be restricted in various lower and higher levels. The real power of content restrictions comes with the integration of all the features in an application and hence restrictions on built-in WordPress features were discussed.

Finally, we went through the supplementary content restriction features used in modern applications to increase the exposure while identifying plugins that can be used to automate these restrictions without manual development.

In the next chapter, we will see how to use the WordPress plugin beyond conventional use by implementing pluggable and extendable plugins. Until then, get your hands dirty by playing with custom post types plugins.

6
Developing Pluggable Modules

Plugins are the heart of WordPress, which makes web applications possible. WordPress plugins are used to extend its core features as independent modules. As a developer, it's important to understand the architecture of WordPress plugins and design patterns in order to be successful in developing large-scale applications.

Anyone who has basic programming knowledge can create plugins to meet application-specific requirements. However, it takes considerable effort to develop plugins that are reusable across a wide range of projects. In this chapter, we will build a few plugins to demonstrate the importance of reusability and extensibility. WordPress developers who don't have good experience in web application development shouldn't skip this chapter as plugins are the most important part of web application development.

I will assume that you have sound knowledge of basic plugin development using existing WordPress features in order to be comfortable understanding the concepts discussed in this chapter.

In this chapter, we will cover the following topics:

- A brief introduction to WordPress plugins
- WordPress plugins for web development
- Understanding different types of plugins for web development
- Creating a reusable template loader with plugins
- Creating an extensible file uploading plugin
- Integrating a media uploader to custom fields
- Extending content restrictions with actions and filters
- Exploring the use of pluggable functions
- Time to practice

Let's get started.

A brief introduction to WordPress plugins

WordPress offers one of the most flexible plugin architectures, alongside other similar frameworks such as **Joomla** and **Drupal**. The existence of over 40,000 plugins in the WordPress plugin directory proves the vital role of plugins. In typical websites, we create simple plugins to tweak the theme's functionalities or application-specific tasks. The complexity of web applications forces us to modularize the functionalities to enhance their maintainability. Most application developers will be familiar with the concept of the open-closed principle.

 The open-closed principle states that the design and writing of code should be done in a way that new functionality should be added with minimum changes in the existing code. The design of the code should be done in a way to allow the addition of new functionalities as new classes, keeping as much of the existing code unchanged as possible. You can find more information at http://www.oodesign.com/open-close-principle. html.

We can easily achieve the open-closed principle with WordPress plugins. Plugins can be developed to be open for new features through actions, filters, and pluggable functions, while being closed for modifications. Additional features will be implemented using separate plugins, which can be activated or deactivated anytime without breaking the existing code.

Understanding the WordPress plugin architecture

WordPress is not the most well-documented framework from the perspective of architectural diagrams and processes. Hence, you won't find detailed explanations about how plugins actually work behind the scenes. Plugins need to have a main file that includes the block comment in the predefined format in order for WordPress to identify it as a plugin. The activation and deactivation of plugins can be done anytime by using the **Plugins** section of the admin area. WordPress uses a metafield called active_plugins in the wp_options table to keep the list of existing active plugins.

The following screenshot previews the contents of the `active_plugins` field using the `phpMyAdmin` database browser:

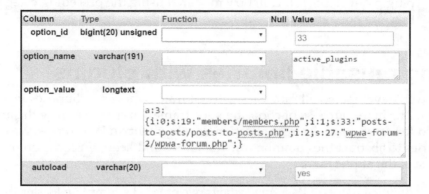

As you can see, we have the list of active plugins in JSON format. In the initial execution process, WordPress loads each and every active plugin through its main file. From there onwards, action hooks and filters will be used to initialize the plugin's functions. We can use built-in hooks as well as custom hooks inside plugins. As a WordPress plugin developer, it's important to understand how the action hooks run during a typical request to avoid conflicts and improve the performance and quality of the plugins. You can visit `ht tp://codex.wordpress.org/Plugin_API/Action_Reference`to understand the action execution procedure and see how plugins fit into the execution process.

WordPress plugins for web development

By default, WordPress offers blogging and CMS functionalities to cater to simple applications. In real web applications, we need to develop most things using the existing features provided by WordPress. In short, all those web application-related features will be implemented using plugins. In this book, we have created a main plugin for the forum management application. This plugin was intended to provide forums and topics specific tasks in our application and is hence not reusable in different projects. We need more and more reusable plugins and libraries as developers who are willing to take long journeys in web application development with WordPress. In this section, we will discuss the various types of such plugins:

- Reusable libraries
- Extensible plugins
- Pluggable plugins

Keep in mind that plugins are categorized into the previously mentioned types conceptually, for the sake of understanding the various features of plugin development. Don't try to search using the preceding categories as they are not defined anywhere.

Creating reusable libraries with plugins

These days, web developers will rarely go without frameworks and libraries in application development. The main purpose of choosing such frameworks is to reduce the amount of time required for common tasks in application development. In WordPress, we do need similar libraries to abstract the common functionalities and keep our focus on the core business logic of the application.

In Chapter 4, *Building Blocks of Web Applications*, we created a template loader to separate the main templates from its core logic. Loading templates is a common functionality for most WordPress plugins, hence template loading is a *must-use* technique. Our template loader was created inside the WPWAF Forum plugin to manage templates for a user account and custom post type-related functionalities. However, it's not reusable across many plugins, as it's located inside our main application plugin.

Usually, advanced WordPress applications are built using a combination of new and existing plugins to make different features independent from one another. Template loaders also fall into the category of independent and reusable modules, hence, we need to convert our template loader to a reusable library using a plugin. In the following sections, we will discuss how to make it reusable and also some tricks to handle plugin dependencies.

Planning the template loader plugin

The main purpose of building this independent plugin is to separate template loader functionalities and reuse it across many WordPress applications or plugins. However, there are other things that need to be considered when planning the plugin. Let's list the main steps of building a template loader plugin:

1. Build a template loader as an independent standalone plugin.
2. Allow the reuse of the template loader from multiple plugins without modifying code.
3. Load the dependent plugins without errors.

With these requirements in mind, let's build the template loader plugin. As usual, create a new folder called `wpwa-template-loader` inside the `wp-content/plugins` folder. Create the main plugin file called `wpwa-template-loader.php` with the following plugin definition:

```php
<?php
/*
  Plugin Name: WPWA Template Loader
  Plugin URI:
  Description: Reusable template loader for WordPress plugins.
  Author: Rakhitha Nimesh
  Version: 1.0
  Author URI: http://www.wpexpertdeveloper.com/
*/
define('wpwa_tmpl_url', plugin_dir_url(__FILE__));
define('wpwa_tmpl_path', plugin_dir_path(__FILE__));
?>
```

We already have a template loader inside the `WPWAF Forum` plugin. So, we will move the files into our new plugin with slight modifications. Consider the following code for the implementation of a template loader class:

```php
class WPWA_Template_Loader{
  public $plugin_path;
  public function set_plugin_path($path){
    $this->plugin_path = $path;
  }
  public function get_template_part( $slug, $name = null, $load =
true ) {
    do_action( 'wpwa_get_template_part_' . $slug, $slug, $name );
    $templates = array();
    if ( isset( $name ) )
    $templates[] = $slug . '-' . $name . '-template.php';
    $templates[] = $slug . '-template.php';
    $templates = apply_filters( 'wpwa_get_template_part',
$templates, $slug, $name );
    return $this->locate_template( $templates, $load, false );
  }
  public function locate_template( $template_names, $load = false,
$require_once = true ) {
    $located = false;
    foreach ( (array) $template_names as $template_name ) {
      if ( empty( $template_name ) )
        continue;
      $template_name = ltrim( $template_name, '/' );
      if ( file_exists( trailingslashit( $this->plugin_path ) .
'templates/' . $template_name ) ) {
```

```
        $located = trailingslashit( $this->plugin_path ) .
'templates/' . $template_name;
            break;
        }
         elseif ( file_exists( trailingslashit( $this->plugin_path )
    . 'admin/templates/' . $template_name ) ) {
            $located = trailingslashit( $this->plugin_path ) .
    'admin/templates/' . $template_name;
            break;
        }
    }
    if ( ( true == $load ) && ! empty( $located ) )
    load_template( $located, $require_once );
    return $located;
    }
}
$wpwa_template_loader = new WPWA_Template_Loader();
```

You might have noticed that we introduced a new class variable called $plugin_path and a new function called set_plugin_path. In the previous chapter, we used the template loader within the plugin, hence, we were able to hardcode the path to the plugins folder to locate the templates. Since we are planning to reuse it across multiple plugins, the path to the templates should be specified dynamically. We can pass the plugin path dynamically using the set_plugin_path function and search the templates inside individual plugins. Now, it's time to use a reusable template loader inside our main plugin.

Template loader is a simple plugin with minor functionality, hence we are using the normal plugin initialization technique instead of the plugin structure used in previous chapters.

Using the template loader plugin

First, we have to remove all the template loader-specific functionalities from our main WPWAF Forum plugin. Let's start by executing the following tasks:

1. Remove the class-wpwaf-template-loader.php file from the main plugin.
2. Remove the require_once statement from the class-wpwa-forum.php file.

Once these two tasks are completed, we are ready to use the template loader. You might have noticed that the only difference between the previous and current implementation of the template loader is the addition of a dynamic plugin path. So, we have to first set the template path of the plugin that relies on the Template Loader plugin.

We can set the template path for the WPWF Forum plugin inside the setup_constants function with the following code:

```
public function setup_constants() {
  global $wpwa_template_loader;
  // Other constants
  $wpwa_template_loader->set_plugin_path(WPWAF_PLUGIN_DIR);
}
```

We can use the global $wpwa_template_loader object of the template loader plugin and execute the set_plugin_path function to set the template location for our forums plugin. Up to this point, we loaded the templates using the global $wpwaf object, as shown in the following code:

```
$wpwaf->template_loader->get_template_part( 'topic','meta');
```

Now, we don't have the template loader class inside the forum plugin, hence we can't use the same technique. So, we have to change each occurrence of the $wpwaf->template_loader->get_template_part function call to use the template loader function of the WPWA Template Loader plugin with the following code:

```
global $wpwa_template_loader;
$wpwa_template_loader->get_template_part( 'topic','meta');
```

After these modifications, our main plugin should function as usual with the new reusable template loader. You can use the same technique to access a template loader from any other plugin.

Handling plugin dependencies

In the previous section, I mentioned that the main plugin should work as usual. However, it won't work as expected and you will get an error with a blank screen, as shown in the following screenshot:

Fatal error: Call to a member function set_plugin_path() on a non-object in C:\wamp\www\www.example.com\wp-content\plugins\wpwa-forum\wpwa-forum.php on line *79*

Call Stack

#	Time	Memory	Function	Location
1	0.0016	258640	{main}( )	..\plugins.php:0
2	0.0026	302224	require_once('C:\wamp\www\www.example.com\wp-admin\admin.php')	..\plugins.php:10
3	0.0032	314976	require_once('C:\wamp\www\www.example.com\wp-load.php')	..\admin.php:31
4	0.0037	321984	require_once('C:\wamp\www\www.example.com\wp-config.php')	..\wp-load.php:37
5	0.0048	419456	require_once('C:\wamp\www\www.example.com\wp-settings.php')	..\wp-config.php:89
6	0.1908	15267488	include_once('C:\wamp\www\www.example.com\wp-content\plugins\wpwa-forum-2\wpwa-forum.php')	..\wp-settings.php:304
7	0.1908	15267504	WPWAF_Forum( )	..\wpwa-forum.php:123
8	0.1908	15267856	WPWAF_Forum::instance( )	..\wpwa-forum.php:120
9	0.1908	15267936	WPWAF_Forum->setup_constants( )	..\wpwa-forum.php:42

You have to enable WP_DEBUG to see the errors. This can be done by setting WP_DEBUG to true in the wp-config.php file.

If you have a sound knowledge of WordPress development, you should have an idea about the cause of this error. I will explain the issue in detail and the solution for those who are not aware of the reason for this error.

Basically, WordPress loads the plugin in a specific order. Dependent plugins should be loaded before the main plugin to prevent any dependency issues. In this scenario, we didn't handle the dependency between the WPWAF Forum plugin and the WPWA Template Loader plugin.

If you check the value `active_plugins` option, `wpwa-forum/wpwa-forum.php` is stored before the `wpwa-template-loader/wpwa-template-loader.php` file. Therefore, the template loader object is not available when the features of WPWAF Forum are executed. We need a solution to delay the loading of the main plugin, until the dependent plugins are fully loaded. Let's update `wpwa-forum.php` to define the necessary dependencies:

```
/* Validating existence of required plugins */
add_action( 'plugins_loaded', 'wpwaf_plugin_init' );
function wpwaf_plugin_init(){
  if(!class_exists('WPWA_Template_Loader')){
    add_action( 'admin_notices', 'wpwaf_plugin_admin_notice' );
  }else{
    WPWAF_Forum();
  }
}
function wpwaf_plugin_admin_notice() {
  echo '<div class="error"><p><strong>WPWAF Forum</strong> requires
<strong>WPWA Template Loader</strong>
  plugin to function properly.</p></div>';
}
```

First, we will use the `plugins_loaded` action to call a custom function called `wpwaf_plugin_init`. This function is executed after all the plugins are loaded, hence, all the plugin files are available for execution. The forum manager plugin is dependent on a Template Loader plugin, hence, we check the existence of the `WPWA_Template_Loader` class. If the Template Loader plugin is activated and fully loaded, we initialize the forum plugin by moving the initialization code from the bottom of the main file to the else statement.

If the Template Loader plugin is not activated, we have to prevent the execution of dependent functionalities and inform the admin about the reason. Therefore, we add a notice to the admin section mentioning that you need to activate the Template Loader plugin before using our main plugin.

The following screenshot shows the message displayed to the admin when the Template Loader plugin is not activated:

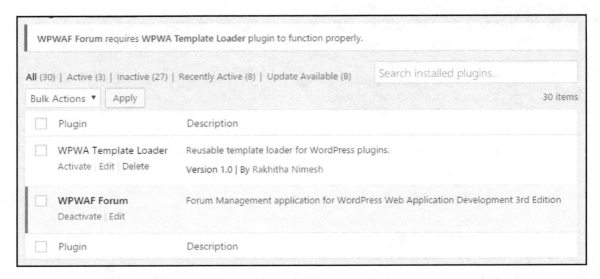

We completed our task on creating a reusable plugin using a Template Loader and identified how to solve the dependencies between plugins. We checked the existence of a class to validate whether the dependent plugin is active. There are a few other techniques for checking the active/inactive status of dependent plugins, listed as follows:

- **Functions**: the existence of a function can be checked similar to the class existence check, as shown in the following code. However, we can only check procedural functions with this technique, hence, this technique can't be used for functions inside classes (methods). Therefore, it's not possible to apply this technique to the Template Loader plugin:

```
if(! function_exists( 'function name' ) ) {
  // Plugin is inactive
}
```

- **Constants**: we can also check the existence of a constant within the dependent plugin. Since we do have constants, this technique can be used for our template loader. We have to use globally available constants such as the plugin version, plugin path, and so on for this validation, as shown in following code:

```
if (! defined(' wpwa_tmpl_path ') ) {
  // Plugin is inactive
}
```

- **Directly checking the plugin status**: WordPress provides a function for providing the active/inactive status of a plugin. However, we have to pass the plugin folder and filename, hence, it's not a reliable solution, unless you are confident that plugins or filenames won't change. The following code shows how to directly check the status of a plugin:

```
if ( is_plugin_active(' wpwa-template-loader/ wpwa-
  template-loader.php') ) {
  // Plugin is active
}
```

Now we have completed the development of a reusable plugin. The next few sections explain the process of creating extendable plugins.

Extensible plugins

In the previous section, we created a reusable plugin for template loading. However, the plugin doesn't allow us to extend the core features, other than providing dynamic parameter passing. Here, we will be exploring the possibility of creating plugins that other developers can extend using their own plugins to change the existing behavior or add a new behavior. WordPress uses its actions and filters techniques for extending the plugins. We can make plugins extendable in two ways:

- Extending plugins with WordPress core actions and filters
- Extending plugins with custom actions and filters

In the following section, we will look at both these techniques using different plugin implementations.

Extending plugins with WordPress core actions and filters

In this section, we will look at actions and filters provided by the WordPress core framework. So, we will create a reusable and extensible plugin for automating the file upload process for custom metafields in our forum application. Let's get started.

Planning a file uploader for the forum application

WordPress offers a built-in media uploader for handling all the file uploading tasks in WordPress core features. The simplicity and adaptability of a media uploader is one of the keys to its success in CMS development. Web applications require the heavy usage of custom metafields and there can be a number of file fields within a single screen. Integrating a media uploader to each and every field can become a tedious and unnecessary task. So, we need a method to automatically integrate file fields with the media uploader. In Chapter 4, *Building Blocks of Web Applications*, we created all the custom post types and fields for the forum management application. However, we skipped the file uploading process for forum topics. Here, we will complete the implementation while building an extensible plugin. So, let's begin with the planning:

- All the meta file fields should be automatically converted to buttons, which opens the media uploader on a click event
- A dynamic container needs to be created to hold multiple files within a single field
- Plugin developers should be able to extend the plugin by customizing the media uploader interface to limit or add the allowed file types

Before we begin the implementation, it's necessary to modify the WPWAF Forum plugin created in the previous chapter, to include the updated file field for uploading topic files. Open the main plugin and navigate to the templates folder. Replace the existing Topic Files field at the end of the topic-meta-template.php file with the following code:

```
<tr>
<th style=''><label><?php _e('Topic Files','wpwaf'); ?></label></th>
<td><input class='widefat wpwaf_files' type="file" name='wpwaf_files'
id='wpwaf_files'  /></td>
</tr>
```

Here, we have modified the previous code to include a CSS class called wpwaf_files and it's used as the identifier for the file field conversion. Once the file uploading plugin is implemented, this file field will be converted into a button and a container for keeping the uploaded files.

Creating the extensible file uploader plugin

As usual, we begin the implementation by creating a new plugin. This time we will name it WPWA File Uploader. Create a folder called wpwa-file-uploader inside the plugins folder and implement the main plugin file as wpwa-file-uploader.php. We will be using the code structure of the forum plugin in this scenario. Since we have already created two plugins, I am going to omit the plugin definition code.

According to the plan, the initial task is to convert the file fields into a button and a container that works with the media uploader. Conversions need to be done from the client side through jQuery or plain JavaScript. Therefore, we have to include the necessary scripts in the File Uploader plugin. Let's look at the initial structure of the File Uploader plugin with the inclusion of the necessary scripts:

```
if( !class_exists( 'WPWA_File_Uploader' ) ) {
   class WPWA_File_Uploader{
      private static $instance;

      public static function instance() {
         if ( ! isset( self::$instance ) && ! ( self::$instance instanceof
WPWA_File_Uploader ) ) {
            self::$instance = new WPWA_File_Uploader();
            self::$instance->setup_constants();

            add_action( 'admin_enqueue_scripts', array( self::$instance ,
'load_admin_scripts' ) );
         }
         return self::$instance;
      }

      public function setup_constants() {
         // Plugin version, path , URL constants
      }

      public function load_admin_scripts (){
         wp_enqueue_script('jquery');

         if (function_exists('wp_enqueue_media')) {
           wp_enqueue_media();
         } else {
           wp_enqueue_style('thickbox');
           wp_enqueue_script('media-upload');
           wp_enqueue_script('thickbox');
         }

         wp_register_script('wpwa_file_upload',
WPWA_FILE_UPLOAD_PLUGIN_URL . 'js/wpwa-file-uploader.js' ,
array('jquery'));
         wp_enqueue_script('wpwa_file_upload');

         $file_upload_options = array(
            'imagePath' => WPWA_FILE_UPLOAD_PLUGIN_URL."img/",
            'addFileText' => __('Add Files','wpwaf') );
         wp_localize_script('wpwa_file_upload', 'WPWAUpload',
```

```
$file_upload_options);
        }
    }
}
```

We have the basic plugin initialization code as usual with single object creation and script inclusion. The `admin_enqueue_scripts` action is used for the script inclusion since we only need the plugin to work on the admin side. Based on your requirements, the `wp_enque_scripts` action can also be used to enable the conversion in the frontend.

Create a new folder called `js` inside the `wpwa-file-uploader` folder and put in an empty JavaScript file called `wpwa-file-uploader.js`. First, we include jQuery in the plugin since the media uploader and the `wpwa-file-uploader.js` file depend on jQuery. The latest version of WordPress uses a modified media uploader, which is simple and interactive compared to the IFRAME-based uploader provided in earlier releases. So, we have to check for the availability of the `wp_enqueue_media` function. Then, we can load the necessary scripts and styles based on the available WordPress version. Finally, we register the `file_uploader.js` file as `wpwa_file_upload` for defining the custom code required for the plugin. We have added the necessary data for the script using the `wp_localize_script` function.

Converting file fields with jQuery

Now, we can begin the conversion of file fields into the media uploader-integrated button and file container. While creating the file field for topics, we assigned a special CSS class called `wpwaf_files`. This class is used to identify the file fields that need to be converted. Let's get started with the implementation inside the `wpwa-file-uploader.js` file:

```
jQuery(document).ready(function($){
    $(".wpwaf_files").each(function(){
        var fieldId = $(this).attr("id");

        $(this).after("<div id='wpwaf_upload_panel_"+ fieldId +"' >
</div>");
        $("#wpwaf_upload_panel_"+ fieldId).html("<input type='button'
value='"+WPWAFUpload.addFileText+"' class='wpwaf_upload_btn' id='"+
fieldId +"' />");
        $("#wpwaf_upload_panel_"+ fieldId).append("<div
style='margin:20px 0' class='wpwaf_preview_box' id='"+ fieldId
+"_panel' ></div>");
        $(this).remove();
    });
});
```

We begin the implementation by traversing through all the elements with the `wpwaf_files` class. Then, we assign the ID of the file field into the `fieldId` variable. Then, we insert a `<div>` container after the file field to keep the button and image container. Next, we assign the button to the main container with a class called `wpwaf_upload_btn`. Then, we can append the file container with a class called `wpwaf_preview_box`. All the containers are given a dynamic ID with a static prefix to be used for media uploader handling. Finally, we remove the file field using the jQuery remove method.

> Make sure you define the `wpwaf_files` class only on file fields to avoid potential conflicts. Otherwise, you need to check the field type for each element with the `wpwaf_files` class.

Now, all the file fields with the CSS class `wpwaf_files` will be converted into a dynamic button and file container. The file container will not be visible until the files are uploaded. Hence, your **Topic Files** field will look something similar to the following screenshot:

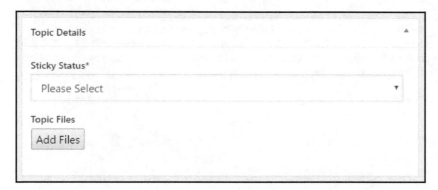

The previous file upload field is removed and we have a button that initializes the WordPress media uploader. Having completed the field conversion, we can now move on to the media uploader integration process.

Integrating the media uploader to buttons

WordPress provides a quick and flexible way of integrating the media uploader to any type of field. The implementation can vary based on the WordPress version. We are using version 4.7.2 throughout the book, hence, we can use the following code snippet for integration:

```
$(".wpwaf_upload_btn").click(function(){
    var uploadObject = $(this);
    var sendAttachmentMeta = wp.media.editor.send.attachment;

    wp.media.editor.send.attachment = function(props, attachment) {
        $(uploadObject).parent().find(".wpwaf_preview_box").append("<img
class='wpwaf_img_prev' style='float:left;with:75px;height:75px' src='"+
WPWAUpload.imagePath +"document.png' />");

        $(uploadObject).parent().find(".wpwaf_preview_box").append("<div
class='wpwaf_prev_file_name' style='margin:25px 0;float:left'>"+
attachment.filename +"</div>");
        $(uploadObject).parent().find(".wpwaf_preview_box").append( "
<input class='wpwaf_img_prev_hidden' type='hidden' name='h_"+
$(uploadObject).attr("id") +"[]' value='"+ attachment.url +"' />");
        $(uploadObject).parent().find(".wpwaf_preview_box").append("<div
style='clear:both' > </div>");

        wp.media.editor.send.attachment = sendAttachmentMeta;
    }

    wp.media.editor.open();
    return false;
});
```

Earlier in the process, we used a class called `wpwaf_upload_btn` for every button. Here, we are using the click event of those buttons to load the media uploader. We start the process by assigning the `wp.media.editor.send.attachment` function into a variable. This function takes two parameters called `props` and `attachment` by default. The path of the uploaded file can be retrieved using the `attachment.url` property. Then, we add the uploaded files to a list with a common file icon and the filename. We also assign the URL to a hidden field to be used in the saving process. Finally, we call the `wp.media.editor.open` function to load the media uploader on the click of a button. Once completed, click on the **Add Files** button in the topic creation screen and you will get the modern media uploader, as illustrated in the following screenshot:

Upload an image to the **Topic Files** field and click the **Insert into page** button on the bottom of the page to add the image to the uploaded files list under the **Add Files** button. You will have something similar to the following screenshot:

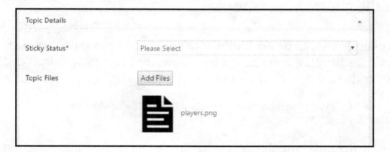

The custom file uploader section created in the preceding sections is fully functional at this stage. We can add any number of images one by one using the **Upload** button. Flexibility adds more value to any type of plugin. Even though we can insert multiple images at the moment, we don't have a method to remove them. Let's create some simple jQuery code to remove the assigned images on a double-click:

```
$("body").on("dblclick", ".wpwaf_img_prev" , function() {
    $(this).next(".wpwaf_img_prev_hidden").remove();
    $(this).next(".wpwaf_prev_file_name").remove();
    $(this).remove();
});
```

In jQuery, dynamically created elements can't be assigned directly to events. We need to use the on function to attach events to dynamically created elements. Here, we have specified the on function on the body tag. You can choose any related element according to your preference. We have assigned the dblclick event to the wpwaf_img_prev class specified inside the dynamically created files. Then, we remove the img tag for the **file** icon and the related hidden field from the preview box. Try uploading a few images and double-click the **file** icon in the preview area to see the effect in action.

Extending the file uploader plugin

Remember that we created this plugin to illustrate the extending capabilities of WordPress plugins for web development. So far, we have completed the core functionality of this plugin to upload images through custom metafields. Now, we have to think about the extensible features and hook points within the plugin. Currently, we have a file upload metafield for topics and we can upload images using the field. Images are useful for discussing forum topics. But the real power comes when we have the ability to upload documents to forum topics. In this section, we will look at the process of extending the file uploader plugin to support other file types.

Customizing the allowed file types

Usually, we do allow the .jpg, .jpeg, .png, and .gif types in the WordPress media uploader. However, there can be occasions where we need more control over the allowed file types. So, let's see how we can change the allowed file types within WordPress. Add the following line of code to the instance function of the WPWA_File_Uploader class:

```
add_filter( 'upload_mimes', array( self::$instance ,
'filter_mime_types' ) );
```

Now, let's consider the implementation of the filter_mime_types function for the file type restricting process:

```
public function filter_mime_types( $mimes ) {
  $mimes = array(
      'jpg|jpeg|jpe' => 'image/jpeg',
 'pdf' => 'application/pdf'
  );
  return $mimes;
}
```

WordPress passes existing mime types as the parameter to this function. Here, we have modified the `mimes` array to restrict the allowed file types to `.jpg` and `.pdf` for each and every post type within WordPress. Ideally, this filtering should be extensible to allow different file types based on application requirements. Usually, WordPress developers tend to redefine the `upload_mimes` filter with another function to cater to such requirements. It's not the best practice to redefine the same filter or action in multiple locations, making it almost impossible to identify the order of execution, unless a specific priority is given.

> Those who are not familiar with priority parameters for actions and filters can take a look at the official documentation at `http://codex.wordpress.org/Function_Reference/add_filter`.

A better solution is to define the filter in a specific place and allow developers to extend through custom actions. Let's consider the modified implementation of the preceding code with the usage of actions:

```
function filter_mime_types($mimes) {
  $mimes = array(
    'jpg|jpeg|jpe' => 'image/jpeg',
    'pdf' => 'application/pdf'
  );
  do_action_ref_array('wpwa_custom_mimes', array(&$mimes));
  return $mimes;
}
```

In the modified version, we have a WordPress action called `wpwa_custom_mimes`. With the use of actions, any developer can extend the function to include their own requirements. In this code, the `mimes` array is passed as a reference variable to the action. Therefore, the original `mimes` array can be modified through the extended versions. WordPress uses global variables for most functionalities. Experienced web developers prefer not to use global variables. Hence, I have used reference passing instead of using global variables.

> The functionality of the WordPress `do_action` and `do_action_ref_array` functions is similar. Usually, most developers will use the `do_action` function. Here, we have used `do_action_ref_array` since reference variable passing is not supported by `do_action`.

Now, let's extend the functionality to support Microsoft Word and rich text file types using custom functions on the specified action hook, as shown in the following code:

```
function wpwa_custom_mimes(&$mimes) {
    $mimes['doc'] = 'application/msword';
    $mimes['rtf'] = 'application/rtf';
}
add_action("wpwa_custom_mimes", "wpwa_custom_mimes");
```

This implementation can be defined inside the theme or any other plugin file. First, we take the `mimes` array as a reference variable. Then, we can add the required mime types back to the `mimes` array. Since we are using reference passing, we don't need to return the `mimes` array. Now, upload files to the topic section and you will notice that `.doc` and `.rtf` formats will also be allowed. For other formats, you will get an error, as shown in the following screenshot:

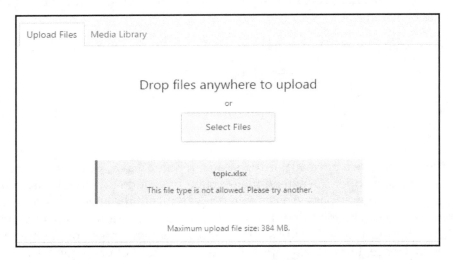

So, we have successfully extended the plugin without touching the code of the core function. In complex application development, make sure you include actions and filters in the proper places to allow extending at later stages. Now, we have built an extensible file uploader plugin for the forum application. Finally, we need to take the necessary steps to save the uploaded files to topics.

Saving and loading topic files

Once again, we have to modify the `WPWAF Forum` plugin to handle the saving and loading process of topic files. In this chapter, we updated the `topic-meta-template.php` template to include the topic files upload field. Now, we have to save the uploaded files to the database. Consider the following code included after the bunch of update meta statements in the `save_topic_meta_data` function in the `class-wpwaf-model-topic.php` file:

```
    $topic_docs = isset($_POST['h_wpwaf_files']) ?
$_POST['h_wpwaf_files'] : "";
    $topic_docs = json_encode($topic_docs);
update_post_meta($post->ID, "_wpwaf_topic_docs", $topic_docs);
```

We can retrieve the list of uploaded files using the hidden field inline with every file. Then, we save all the topic files in a JSON string using a metatable key called `_wpwaf_topic_docs`. Next, we have to retrieve the list of topic files to be displayed on the topic screen load. Here is the updated version of the function for loading existing files:

```
    public function display_topics_meta_boxes() {
        global $wpwaf,$post,$template_data,$wpwa_template_loader;

        $data = array();
        $topic = $post;
        $template_data['topic_post_type']  = $this->post_type;
        $template_data['topic_meta_nonce'] = wp_create_nonce('wpwaf- topic-
meta');
        $template_data['topic_sticky_status']  = get_post_meta( $topic->ID,
'_wpwaf_topic_sticky_status', true );
        $template_data['topic_docs'] = (array) json_decode(get_post_meta(
$topic->ID, '_wpwaf_topic_docs', true ));

        ob_start();
        $wpwa_template_loader->get_template_part( 'topic','meta');
        $display = ob_get_clean();
     echo $display;
    }
```

The display function is updated to include the retrieval of topic files from the database using the `_wpwaf_topic_docs` key. Then, we assign the topic data to the template file, as we did with other metafields.

Finally, we have to modify the template file to display the existing file previews, as shown in the following code of the `topic-meta-template.php` file:

```
<tr>
<th style=''><label><?php _e('Topic Files','wpwaf'); ?></label></th>

    <td><input class='widefat wpwaf_files' type="file"  name='wpwaf_files'
id='wpwaf_files'  />
    <div class='wpwaf_preview_box' id='project_screens_panel' >
    <?php foreach($topic_docs as $doc){
            if(trim($doc) != '') {
        ?>
    <img class='wpwaf_img_prev' style= 'float:left;with:75px;height:75px'
src='<?php echo     WPWA_FILE_UPLOAD_PLUGIN_URL."img/document.png"; ?>' />
    <div class='wpwaf_prev_file_name' style='margin:25px 0;float:left'>
<?php echo basename($doc); ?></div>
    <input class='wpwaf_img_prev_hidden' type='hidden'
name='h_wpwaf_files[]' value='<?php echo $doc; ?>' />
    <div style='clear:both' > </div>
    <?php }} ?>
    </div>
    </td>
    </tr>
```

After the file field, we will include the file preview, filename, file URL hidden field, and the preview box container in the same format we used in the `wpwa-file-uploder.js` file. We include the existing files from the database for the topic. You can delete any existing file and add new files to update the topics screens anytime.

Now, we have completed the topics creation by including the topic files upload section. You can test the plugin by adding and removing files for topics.

Extending plugins with custom actions and filters

In the previous section, we created a separate plugin to explain the extending capabilities with WordPress core actions and filters. In this section, we will be looking at how to use our own custom actions and filters to extend our forum management plugin.

In `Chapter 5`, *Implementing Application Content Restrictions*, we implemented content restrictions on individual topics using several visibility types such as `Members`, `Guests`, and `Everyone`. Here, we are going to look at how to extend those features to enable custom restriction types and visibility levels.

Assume that we want to restrict the topic based on a user meta value of the current user. This is a common requirement in web applications where we provide features based on a user meta value such as activation status, payment statuses, country, or any other custom field value related to your application. Let's identify what we have to change in order to implement this requirement:

- Add new visibilities to the `topic-restriction-meta-template.php` file
- Verify the custom visibilities using the `validate_restrictions` function of the `WPWAF_Content_Restrictions` class

Let's start by adding a custom filter to the `topic-restriction-meta-template.php` file, as shown in the following code:

```php
<select id="wpwaf_topic_visibility" name="wpwaf_topic_visibility"
class="wpwaf-select2-setting">
    <option value='none' <?php selected('none',$visibility); ?>><?php
_e('Please Select','wpwaf'); ?></option>
    <option value='all' <?php selected('all',$visibility); ?>><?php
_e('Everyone','wpwaf'); ?></option>
    <option value='guest' <?php selected('guest',$visibility); ?>><?php
_e('Guests','wpwaf'); ?></option>
    <option value='member' <?php selected('member',$visibility); ?>><? php
_e('Members','wpwaf'); ?></option>
    <option value='role' <?php selected('role',$visibility); ?>><?php
_e('Selected User Roles','wpwaf'); ?></option>

    <?php echo apply_filters('wpwaf_custom_restrictions','',  $visibility);
?>
    </select>
```

As you can see, we have a new custom filter called `wpwaf_custom_restrictions`, along with the built-in visibility levels we discussed earlier. This filter contains two parameters, including an empty display parameter and visibility parameter. We can implement this filter to add custom options to the visibility dropdown.

Next, we are going to look at the modified code of the `protection_status` function for verifying custom visibilities. We need to change the default condition of the `switch` statement as follows, with a new filter:

```php
default:
    return apply_filters('wpwaf_verify_custom_restrictions', TRUE ,
$visibility);
        break;
```

Instead of returning none for the default case, we return the output of our new filter `wpwaf_verify_custom_restrictions`. This filter also takes two parameters including the content visibility status and the visibility level. We have used TRUE as the default value for the first parameter to allow the content to everyone.

Now, we have two custom filters for modifying the individual topic restriction process and apply custom visibilities. Let's implement the `wpwaf_custom_restrictions` filter to include custom visibility for user meta values, as shown in the following code:

```
add_filter('wpwaf_custom_restrictions','wpwaf_custom_restrictions',10,2
);
    function wpwaf_custom_restrictions($display,$visibility){
        $display .= "<option value='user_meta_field' ".
selected('user_meta_field',$visibility) .">". __('User Meta
Field','wpwaf') . "</option>";
        return $display;
    }
```

Now, you will see a new visibility level called **User Meta Field** in the restrictions settings of the topic creation screen.

 We can add these custom filters to the `functions.php` file of your theme or any other custom plugin. In this scenario, we have added this code to our main plugin file, `wpwa-forum.php`.

Finally, we have to implement the restrictions for the **User Meta Field** visibility using the `wpwaf_verify_custom_restrictions` filter, as shown in the following code.

```
    add_filter('wpwaf_verify_custom_restrictions',
'wpwaf_verify_custom_restrictions',10,2);
    function wpwaf_verify_custom_restrictions($status,$visibility){
        $user_id = get_current_user_id();

    if($visibility == 'user_meta_field'){
        $meta_value = get_user_meta($user_id, 'wpwa_activation_status'
, true);

        if($meta_value == 'active'){
          $status = TRUE;
        }else{
          $status = FALSE;
        }
    }
    return $status;
    }
```

First, we retrieve the user ID of the logged in user using the `get_current_user_id` function. Then, we have to check whether the visibility level matches `user_meta_field`. Once it's matched, we retrieve the user metafield value. In this scenario, we are implementing the validation on users who activated their account, hence we use the `wpwa_activation_status` value. If the user has an active value, we return `TRUE` to provide permission to the content, otherwise we return `FALSE` to restrict permission to the content.

So, we have successfully implemented the process for adding custom visibilities to restrictions. You can use the same filters to add more visibility types and verifications. This is how we can make extendable plugins with the use of custom actions and filters.

 In this scenario, we had to add custom HTML and change the restriction status value. Therefore, we used custom filters, as our requirement was modifying the values. Similarly, you can use custom actions when you want to make something happen instead of just modifying the value.

WordPress actions and filters are amazing techniques for creating extensible plugins and allowing customizations for third-party developers. In the next section, we will discuss pluggable plugins with the use of pluggable functions in WordPress.

Pluggable plugins

WordPress provides the ability to use pluggable functions through its pluggable architecture. Pluggable functions are no longer added to the core, due to the limitations in comparison to using actions and filters. WordPress codex defines pluggable functions as functions that let you override certain core functions via plugins. You can find all the pluggable functions in the `pluggable.php` file located inside the `wp-includes` folder of WordPress. The following are some of the popular pluggable functions provided by WordPress:

- `wp_logout`: this is used to log the user out of the system. You can do tasks such as removing custom session variables and recording the user session time to the database by writing a custom `wp_logout` function.
- `wp_mail`: this is used to customize the e-mail settings before sending e-mails through WordPress.
- `wp_new_user_notification`: this is used to customize the subject and contents of the e-mail sent on new user registrations.

However, there are many plugins and themes that take advantage of this technique. These plugins can be considered as different versions of extensible plugins. We used actions and filters to create extensible plugins. Here, we use functions that are pluggable through custom implementations. In web application terms, we can think of it as a very basic version of inheritance. Instead of inheritance, WordPress prefers extending through functions. Let's build a simple test plugin to understand the use of pluggable plugins, using functions.

As usual, we will start with the plugin folder creation and definition. Create a folder called `wpwa-pluggable-plugin` and create a main file called `wpwa-pluggable-plugin.php` with the common plugin definition code:

```
/*
    Plugin Name: WPWA Pluggable Plugin
    Plugin URI:
    Description: Explain the use of pluggable plugins by sending mails on
post saving
    Version: 1.0
    Author: Rakhitha Nimesh
    Author URI: http://www.innovativephp.com/
    License: GPLv2 or later
*/
```

Assume that we need a plugin to send notifications to the author on new topic creation. The following is a basic implementation of such a requirement using the pluggable function:

```
if (!function_exists('wpwa_send_new_topic_notification')) {
   function wpwa_send_new_topic_notification($email,$heading,  $content)
{
      $message = "<p><b>$heading</b><br/></p>";
      $message .= "<p>$content<br/></p>";
      wp_mail($email, "Pluggable Plugins", $message);
   }
}
```

We have created a function called `wpwa_ send_new_topic_notification` to take the e-mail heading and content, and send an e-mail message to the specified address. An important thing to consider is the use of the `function_exists` function. First, it allows us to check whether a function with the same name is already defined. This function will be executed when the other function with same name is not available. So, plugin developers can redefine the function to extend the capabilities of a core function.

In the extensible plugins, we extended a part of the functionality using actions and filters. In pluggable functions, we need to recreate the complete implementation instead of a part.

This function is used to send new topic details to the topic author. Assume we want to extend this feature to do the following:

- Send basic topic details to the topic creator
- Send basic topic details and a topic moderation link to moderators
- Send basic topic details and topic author information to administrators

Now, we can implement these requirements using a plugged version of this function. You can define the modified function inside any other plugin. Here, I have kept both functions inside the same plugin for simplicity. Let's take a look at plugged `wpwa_send_new_topic_notification` with the additional requirements:

```php
    function wpwa_send_new_topic_notification($email, $heading,  $content,
$topic_id = '') {
    // Send notification to user
    $message = "";
    $message = "<p><b>$heading</b><br/></p>";
    $message .= "<p>$content<br/></p>";
    wp_mail($email, "Pluggable Plugins", $message);

    if($topic_id != ''){
      // Send notifications to admins
      $author = get_user_by( 'email', $email );
      $message_admin = $message;
      $message_admin .= "<p>".$author->first_name. "". $author-
>last_name . "<br/></p>";
      $users_query = new WP_User_Query( array(
                'role' => 'administrator',
                'orderby' => 'display_name'
                ) );
      $results_admin = $users_query->get_results();
      foreach($results_admin as $user){
        wp_mail($user->user_email,"Pluggable Plugins", $message_admin);
      }

      // Send notification to moderators
      $message_moderator = $message;
      $message_moderator.= "<p>".$author->first_name. "". $author-
>last_name . "<br/></p>";
      $message_moderator .= get_edit_post_link( $topic_id);
      $users_query = new WP_User_Query( array(
```

```
                    'role' => 'wpwaf_moderator',
                    'orderby' => 'display_name'
                    ) );
        $results_moderator = $users_query->get_results();
        foreach($results_moderator as $user){
          wp_mail($user->user_email,"Pluggable Plugins",
    $message_moderator);
        }
      }
    }
```

In the plugged version, we have an additional parameter to pass the topic ID. We have the same code for sending notification to the topic author, as in the pluggable function. Then, we have two additional sections to send the same notification to administrators and moderators with different content.

Since we have used an additional parameter, existing calls to this function will not be executed properly. Therefore, we make the topic ID as an optional parameter and check the existence before sending additional notifications. Now, all the calls to `wpwa_send_new_topic_notification` will execute the plugged function instead of the pluggable function.

Now, let's look at the execution of the notification sending function on topic save and update:

```
    add_action('save_post', 'wpwa_new_topic_notification');
    function wpwa_new_topic_notification($post_id) {
      $post = get_post($post_id );

      if ( isset($_POST['topic_meta_nonce']) &&
    !wp_verify_nonce($_POST['topic_meta_nonce'], 'wpwaf-topic-meta' ) ) {
            return;
      }

      if (defined('DOING_AUTOSAVE') && DOING_AUTOSAVE){
            return;
      }

      if ( !wp_is_post_revision( $post_id ) && $post->post_type ==
    'wpwaf_topic' ) {
          $post_title = get_the_title($post_id);
          $post_url = get_permalink($post_id);
          $post_author = get_userdata( $post->post_author );
          wpwa_send_new_topic_notification($post_author->user_email ,
    $post_title, $post_url, $post_id);
      }
    }
```

The WordPress `save_post` action allows us to call custom functions on post save or update. Here, we are calling the `wpwa_send_new_topic_notification` function with the post's title as the heading and the post's URL as the content.

 A function can only be reassigned this way once, so you can't install two plugins that plug the same function for different reasons. For safety, it is best to always wrap your functions with `if ( !function_exists() );` otherwise, you will produce fatal errors on plugin activation.

With pluggable functions, we can turn on or off new functionality at any time without affecting the existing code. Since WordPress uses procedural function calling, pluggable plugins through functions makes sense. If you prefer OOP-based plugins, you can choose inheritance over pluggable functions to build pluggable plugins. Once the preceding code is completed and the plugin is activated, you can create some topics to see the usage of pluggable functions.

Tips for using pluggable functions

Pluggable functions seem to be an easy way of extending the functionality of plugins. However, you should be aware of the WordPress file loading process in order to make use of pluggable functions without causing unexpected issues. The following are some of the tips to be considered before creating pluggable functions:

- All the custom pluggable functions should be placed inside plugins, since plugins are loaded first.
- If plugins do not contain pluggable functions, the default core function will be used.
- You shouldn't override core pluggable functions in your theme files, since themes are loaded after pluggable functions. Hence, the default function will be used.

Up to now, we have discussed the various types of reusable plugins suitable for web applications. Using pluggable plugins with procedural functions is not the most popular method amongst developers. Instead, it's recommended that you extend plugins with WordPress actions and filters or use inheritance with object-oriented plugins.

Tips for developing extendable plugins

Plugins are used as the primary components in building web applications. In normal circumstances, we have to use existing plugins as well as develop our own plugins. So it's important to improve the extendibility of plugins to adapt to the custom requirements of different applications. So, let's look at some of the important tips for developing extendable plugins:

- Add custom actions with `do_action` before and after executing major actions in your plugin, such as registration, login, data saving, and so on.
- Add custom filters with `apply_filters` when you have an output for displaying or variables and objects that are worth modifying.
- Use two parameters for filters and keep the second parameter as an array or object, allowing you to add custom attributes without breaking the functionality of existing implementations. It's not wise to add many parameters.
- Use one or two parameters for actions and keep one parameter as an array or object, allowing you to add custom attributes without breaking the functionality of existing implementations. It's not wise to add many parameters.
- Place common functions inside a `functions.php` file and wrap them with the `function_exists` check to allow overriding.
- Add all the HTML display code to the templates and load them through filters, allowing the customization of designs.
- Add the settings section for all the important configurations of your plugin and let the user customize them.

Time to practice

Developing high quality plugins is the key to success in web development using WordPress. In this chapter, we introduced various techniques for creating extensible plugins. Now, it's time for you to take one step further by exploring the various other ways of using plugins. Take some time to try out the following tasks to get the best out of this chapter:

- In this chapter, we integrated a media uploader to custom fields and restricted the file types using actions. However, restrictions will be global across all types of posts. Try to make the restrictions based on custom post types and custom fields. We should be able to customize the media uploader for each field.

- Use the `wp_handle_upload` function to implement a manual file uploading to cater to complex scenarios which cannot be developed using the existing media uploader.
- Create pluggable plugins using inheritance without considering pluggable functions.

Summary

We began this chapter by exploring the importance and architecture of WordPress plugins. Here, we identified the importance of creating reusable plugins by categorizing such plugins into three types called reusable libraries, extensible plugins, and pluggable plugins.

While building these plugins, we learned the use of actions, filters, and pluggable functions within WordPress. The integration of a media uploader was very important for web applications, which works with file-related functionalities. Also, we looked at how we can extend our content restrictions module with custom actions and filters. Finally, we discussed some important tips for building extendable plugins.

In the next chapter, Chapter 7, *Customizing the Dashboard for Powerful Backends*, we will master the use of the WordPress admin section to build highly customizable backends using existing features. Stay tuned, as this will be important for developers who are planning to use WordPress as a backend system without using its theme.

Customizing the Dashboard for Powerful Backends

Usually, full-stack PHP frameworks don't provide built-in admin sections. So, developers have to build an application's backend from scratch. WordPress is mainly built on an existing database, which makes it possible to provide a prebuilt admin section. Most of the admin functionality is developed to cater to the existing content management functionality. As developers, you won't be able to develop complex applications without having the knowledge of extending and customizing the capabilities of existing features.

The structure and content of this chapter is built in a way that enables the tackling of the extendable and customizable components of admin screens and features. We will be looking at the various aspects of an admin interface while building the forum management application.

In this chapter, we will cover the following topics:

- Understanding the admin dashboard
- Customizing the admin toolbar
- Customizing the main navigation menu
- Adding features with custom pages
- Building options pages
- Using feature-packed admin list tables
- Adding content restrictions to admin list tables
- Awesome visual presentation with admin themes
- The responsive nature of the admin dashboard

Understanding the admin dashboard

WordPress offers one of the most convenient admin sections among similar frameworks, such as **Drupal** and **Joomla**, for building any kind of application. In the previous chapters, we looked at the administration screens related to various areas such as user management, custom post types, and posts. Here, we will look at some of the remaining components from the perspective of web application development. Let's identify the list of sections we will consider:

- The admin toolbar
- The main navigation menu
- Option and menu pages
- Admin list tables
- Responsive design capabilities

Customizing the admin toolbar

The admin toolbar is located at the top of the admin screen to allow direct access to the most used parts of your website. Once you log in, the admin toolbar will be displayed on the admin dashboard as well as at the frontend. Typical web applications contain separate access menus for the frontend and backend. Hence, web developers might find it difficult to understand the availability of the admin toolbar at the frontend from the perspective of the functionality as well as the look and feel. In web applications, it's your choice whether to remove the admin toolbar from the frontend or customize it to provide a useful functionality. In this section, we will look at both methods to simplify your decision about the admin toolbar. First, let's preview the admin toolbar at the frontend with its default settings, as shown in the following screenshot:

Let's add a new class called `class-wpwaf-dashboard.php` to our main forum manager plugin for functionalities in the admin section:

```
class WPWAF_Dashboard {
  public function __construct() { }
}
?>
```

As usual, we need to include the `class-wpwaf-dashboard.php` file and initialize an object of this class inside the `WPWAF_Forum` class. Now, we are ready to get started with the implementation of admin features.

Removing the admin toolbar

WordPress allows us to configure the visibility settings of the admin toolbar at the frontend. Unfortunately, it does not provide a way to remove the toolbar from the backend. Let's consider the following implementation for removing the admin toolbar from the frontend:

```
class WPWAF_Dashboard {
  public function __construct() {
    $this-> set_frontend_toolbar(FALSE);
  }
  public function set_frontend_toolbar($status) {
    show_admin_bar($status);
  }
}
```

Here, we use a function called `set_frontend_toolbar` to dynamically set the visibility of the admin toolbar at the frontend. WordPress uses the `show_admin_bar` function with a Boolean condition to implement this functionality. You might have noticed the difference in implementation compared to the plugins developed in the previous chapters. Earlier, we used to initialize all the functions using actions and filters. Setting the admin toolbar can be implemented as a standalone function without actions or filters. Hence, we call the `set_frontend_toolbar` function on the `admin_dashboard` object. Here, we used the `FALSE` value to hide the admin toolbar at the frontend.

Managing the admin toolbar items

Default items in the admin toolbar are designed to suit generic blogs or websites, and hence it's a must to customize the toolbar items to suit web applications. The profile section in the top-right corner is suitable for any kind of application as it contains common functionalities such as the editing profile, log out, and setting a profile picture. Hence, our focus should be on the menu items on the left side of the toolbar. First, we have to identify how menu items are generated in order to make the customizations. So, let's look at the following code for retrieving the available toolbar menu items list:

```
add_action( 'wp_before_admin_bar_render', array( $this,
  'customize_admin_toolbar' ) );
```

Let's have a look at the following steps:

1. As usual, we start by adding the necessary actions to the constructor of the dashboard plugin, as shown in the following code:

    ```
    public function customize_admin_toolbar() {
      global $wp_admin_bar;
      $nodes = $wp_admin_bar->get_nodes();
      echo "<pre>";
      var_dump($nodes);
      exit;
    }
    ```

    We have access to the wp_admin_bar global object inside the customize_admin_toolbar function. All the toolbar items of the current page will be returned by the get_nodes function.

2. Then, we can use print_r() on the returned result to identify the nodes. The following code is a part of the returned nodes list, and you can see the main item IDs called user-actions and user-info:

    ```
    Array
    (
    [user-actions] => stdClass Object
    (
    [id] => user-actions
    [title] =>
    [parent] => my-account
    [href] =>
    [group] => 1
    [meta] => Array()
    ```

```
        )
        [user-info] => stdClass Object
        (
        [id] => user-info
        [title] =><img alt=''
src='http://1.gravatar.com/avatar/d3e0fb2e11ff3767d1359c559afbe304?
s=64&d=mm&r=g' /><span class='display-name'>Free Member</span>
        [parent] => user-actions
        [href] => http://localhost/packt/wordpress-web-
        develop-test/wp-admin/profile.php
         )
        )
```

3. We need to use those unique IDs to add or remove menu items. Now we will remove all the items other than the first item and create menu items specific to the forum application. So, let's remove the preceding code and modify the `customize_admin_toolbar` function as follows:

```php
public function customize_admin_toolbar() {
  global $wp_admin_bar;
  $wp_admin_bar->remove_menu('updates');
  $wp_admin_bar->remove_menu('comments');
  $wp_admin_bar->remove_menu('new-content');
  $wp_admin_bar->remove_menu('customize');
}
```

4. By default, the admin toolbar contains four items for site updates, comments and new posts, pages, customize, and so on. Explore the result from `print_r` and you will find the respective keys for the preceding items such as `updates`, `comments`, `customize`, and `new-content`.

5. Then, use the `remove_menu` function on the `wp_admin_bar` object to remove the menu items from the toolbar. Now, the toolbar should look like the following screenshot:

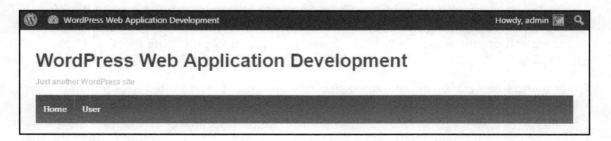

6. Next, we need to add application-specific items to the toolbar. Since we are mainly focusing on forums, we can have a menu called Forums to contain links to forums and topics, as shown in the following updated code of the `customize_admin_toolbar` function:

```
public function customize_admin_toolbar() {
    global $wp_admin_bar;
    // Remove menus
    if ( current_user_can('edit_wpwaf_topics') ) {
        $wp_admin_bar->add_menu( array(
            'id' => 'wpwaf-forums',
            'title' => __('Forum Components','wpwaf'),
            'href' => admin_url()
                ));

        $wp_admin_bar->add_menu( array(
            'id' => 'wpwaf-new-topics',
            'title' => __('Topics','wpwaf'),
            'href' => admin_url() . "post-
new.php?post_type=wpwaf_topic",
            'parent' => 'wpwaf-forums'
                ));
    }

    if ( current_user_can('edit_posts') ) {
        $wp_admin_bar->add_menu( array(
            'id' => 'wpwaf-new-forums',
            'title' => __('Forums','wpwaf'),
            'href' => admin_url() . "post-new.php?post_type=wpwaf_forum",
            'parent' => 'wpwaf-forums'
                ));
    }
}
```

The WordPress `wp_admin_bar` global object provides a method called `add_menu` to add new top menus as well as submenus. The preceding code contains the top menu item for administrators, containing two submenu items for forums and topics. We restrict free members and premium members to one menu item called **Topics** using the respective capabilities.

Other menu items can be implemented similarly and have been omitted here for simplicity. When defining submenus, we have to use the ID of the top menu for the parent attribute. It's important to make the menu item IDs unique to avoid conflicts. Finally, we define the URL to be invoked on the menu item click using the `href` attribute. We can use any internal or external URL for the `href` attribute.

Make sure you check the necessary permission levels while building custom admin toolbars. The following screenshot previews the admin toolbar with custom menu items:

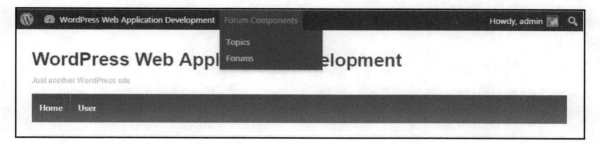

Now we have the ability to extend the admin toolbar to suit various applications. Make sure to add or remove menu items for the forum application to understand the process of the admin toolbar.

Customizing the main navigation menu

In WordPress, the main navigation menu is located on the left-hand side of the screen where we have access to all the sections of the application. In a similar way to the admin toolbar, we have the ability to extend the main navigation menu with customized versions.

Let's start by adding the admin menu invoking an action to the constructor:

```
add_action('admin_menu',array( $this,'customize_main_navigation') );
```

Now, consider the initial implementation of the customize_main_navigation function:

```
public function customize_main_navigation(){
    global $menu,$submenu;
    echo "<pre>";print_r($menu);echo "</pre>";exit;
}
```

The preceding code uses the global variable menu for accessing the available main navigation menu items. Before we begin the customizations, it's important to get used to the structure of the menu array using a print_r statement. A part of the output generated from the print_r statement is shown in the following section:

```
Array
 (
 [2] => Array
 (
 [0] => Dashboard
```

```
[1] => read
[2] => index.php
[3] =>
[4] => menu-top menu-top-first menu-icon-dashboard
[5] => menu-dashboard
[6] => none
)
[4] => Array
(
[0] =>
[1] => read
[2] => separator1
[3] =>
[4] => wp-menu-separator
)
)
```

The structure of the menu array seems to be different compared to the admin toolbar items array. Here, we have array indexes instead of unique keys, and hence the altering of the menu will be done using index values.

Up until this point, we have used existing WordPress features for the functionality of the forum management application, and hence the main navigation menu is constructed based on user roles and permissions. Therefore, we don't need to alter the menu at this point. However, we will see how menu items can be added and removed to cater to advanced requirements in the future. Let's get started by removing the **Dashboard** menu item using the following code:

```
public function customize_main_navigation() {
  global $menu, $submenu;
  unset($menu[2]);
}
```

We can use the unset function to remove items from the `$menu` array. Now your `Dashboardmenu` item will be removed from the menu. Similarly, we can use the global submenu variable to remove submenus when needed.

As of WordPress 3.1, we can use the `remove_menu_page` and `remove _submenu_page` functions to remove the existing menu items. I suggest that you try the preceding method to get an understanding of the menu slugs and links before moving onto these functions.

The following code contains the functionality for removing the **Dashboard** menu item with the latest technique:

```
remove_menu_page('index.php');
```

Creating new menu items

The latest versions of WordPress use `add_menu_page` or `add_sub_menu_page` to create custom menu pages. In the preceding section, we removed items from the existing menu. Adding new menu items is not as simple as removing a menu item. We have to provide functionality and a display code for the menu page while adding them to the menu. The implementation of `add_menu_page` will be discussed in the next section on the **Settings** page.

Adding features with custom pages

WordPress was originally created as a blogging platform and evolved into a content management system. Hence, most of the core functionality is implemented on the concept of posts and pages. In web applications, we need to go way beyond these basic posts and pages to build quality applications. Custom menu pages play a vital role in implementing custom functionalities within the WordPress admin dashboard. Let's consider the two main types of custom pages in the default context:

- **Custom menu pages**: Generally, these pages are blank by default. We need to implement the interface as well as implementation for catering for custom requirements that can't take advantage of the core features of WordPress.
- **Options pages**: These are used to manage the options of the application. Even though options pages are generally used for theme options, we can manage any type of applications-specific settings with these pages.

Building options pages

The theme options page is implemented in each and every WordPress theme by default. However, the design and the available options may vary based on the quality and features of the theme. We selected a theme called **Responsive** (`https://wordpress.org/themes/responsive/`) for the purpose of this book. So, let's take a look at the default theme options panel of the Responsive theme using the following screenshot:

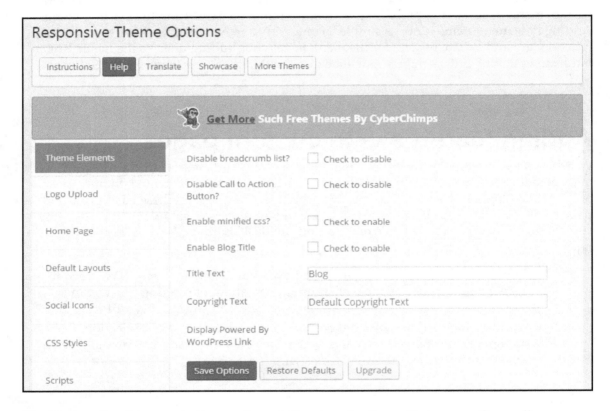

The Responsive theme uses its own layout structure for the options page. Generally, we have two ways of creating options pages for plugins:

- Using custom menu pages with our own template and processing
- Using WordPress options pages with the options and settings API

Both techniques can be effectively used for web applications. However, most developers will pick custom menu pages for large scale applications. Let's identify the differences between the two techniques:

- Custom menu pages create a separate menu item on the left menu, while the options page adds a submenu to the **Settings** menu.
- Options created with the options and settings API will be stored as individual options in the `wp_options` table. When using custom menu pages, we can save all the options inside one field and also options can be stored in any database table according to our preferences.
- Options pages with the settings API will automatically save all the options, while custom menu pages require the manual implementation of the options saving process.
- Custom menu pages provide more flexibility in design as well as the options saving process for large applications.

Basically, options pages with the options and settings API are useful for simple applications, while custom menu pages with our own implementations will be more suited for complex large-scale web applications. Having identified the differences, we can now move on to the implementation of our application settings panel with custom menu pages.

Creating a custom layout for options pages

We decided to create our own layout instead of using the default WordPress options pages. Therefore, the design of the settings panel can be created based on our preference without any restrictions on HTML elements as well as CSS classes. Let's create a new template file inside the template folder of our main plugin as `settings-template.php`.

Once completed, we can start defining the options required for our application. Here, we will create two main sections called **Topic Subscription Settings** and **Content Restriction Settings**. So, add the following code to the `settings-template.php` file for basic options for the forum management application:

```
<div id="wpwaf-settings-panel">
<h2><?php echo __('Forum Management Application Settings','wpwaf');
?></h2>
<form name="wpwaf-settings-frm" id="wpwaf-settings-frm" method="POST">
<div id="wpwaf-subscription-setting" class="wpwaf-settings-tab"><?php
echo __('Topic Subscription Settings','wpwaf'); ?></div>
<div class="wpwaf-settings-content">
<div id="wpwaf-subscription-setting-content" class="wpwaf-settings-tab-
content">
```

```
    <div class="label"><?php echo __('Topic Subscription Limit','wpwaf');
?></div>
    <div class="field"><input type='text' id="wpwaf_topic_susbcribe_limit"
name="wpwaf[topic_susbcribe_limit]" value="<?php echo
$wpwaf_topic_susbcribe_limit; ?>" /></div>
    </div>
    </div>


    <div id="wpwaf-widget-setting" class="wpwaf-settings-tab"><?php echo
__('Content Restriction Settings','wpwaf'); ?>
    </div>
    <div class="wpwaf-settings-content">
    <div id="wpwaf-widget-setting-content" class="wpwaf-settings-tab-
content">
    <div class="label"><?php echo __('Site Lockdown Status','wpwaf');
?></div>
    <div class="field"><select id="wpwaf_lockdown_status"
name="wpwaf[lockdown_status]" class="">
    <option <?php selected('enabled',$wpwaf_lockdown_status); ?>
value="enabled"><?php _e('Enabled','wpwaf'); ?></option>
    <option <?php selected('disabled',$wpwaf_lockdown_status); ?>
value="disabled"><?php _e('Disabled','wpwaf'); ?></option>
    </select>
    </div>
    </div>
    <div id="wpwaf-widget-setting-content" class="wpwaf-settings-tab-
content">
    <div class="label"><?php echo __('Individual Topic Restriction
Status','wpwaf'); ?></div>
    <div class="field"><select id="wpwaf_single_topic_restrict_status"
name="wpwaf[single_topic_restrict_status]" class="">
    <option <?php selected('enabled',$wpwaf_single_topic_restrict_status);
?> value="enabled"><?php _e('Enabled','wpwaf'); ?></option>
    <option <?php selected('disabled',$wpwaf_single_topic_restrict_status);
?> value="disabled"><?php _e('Disabled','wpwaf'); ?></option>
    </select>
    </div>
    </div>
    </div>


    <div >
    <div class="wpwaf-settings-tab-content">
    <div class="label"> </div>
    <div class="field"><input type="submit" id="wpwaf_settings_submit"
name="wpwaf_settings_submit" class="" value="<?php echo __('Save
Settings','wpwaf'); ?>" /></div>
    </div>
    </div>
```

```
</form>
</div>
```

We have two main tabs called **Topic Subscription Settings**, with an option called **Topic Subscription Limit** and another tab called **Content Restriction Settings** with two options called **Site Lockdown Status** and **Individual Topic Restrictions**. Next, we can move on to the implementation of the options panel and the options saving process using the `settings` template.

Building an application options panel

Create a new class called the `class-wpwaf-settings.php` file inside the `classes` folder of the forum application plugin. Be sure to include and initialize an object of this class as usual. First, we need to register the menu page for the forum management application settings. WordPress offers functions called `add_menu_page` and `add_sub_menu_page` for manually creating blank menu pages. Let's take a look at the initial implementation of the `WPWAF_Settings` class with menu page creation, as shown in the following code:

```
class WPWAF_Settings{
   public function __construct(){
      add_action('admin_menu', array($this, 'add_menu'), 9);
   }
   public function add_menu(){
      add_menu_page(__('WPWAF Settings', 'wpwaf'), __('WPWAF
Settings', 'wpwaf'),'manage_options','wpwaf-
settings',array($this,'settings'));
   }
   public function settings(){}
}
```

We have to use the `admin_menu` action to create a unique menu page for the settings panel. Inside the `add_menu` function, we define the **WPWAF Settings** page and the function called `settings` to handle the settings panel. The `settings` function should be used to load the template we created earlier in creating the custom layout section. The following code previews the `settings` function with the updated code:

```
public function settings(){
   global $wpwa_template_loader,$template_data_settings;
   $wpwaf_options = (array) get_option('wpwaf_options');

   $template_data_settings['wpwaf_topic_susbcribe_limit'] =
isset($wpwaf_options['topic_susbcribe_limit']) ?
$wpwaf_options['topic_susbcribe_limit'] : '';
```

```
    $template_data_settings['wpwaf_lockdown_status'] =
isset($wpwaf_options['lockdown_status']) ?
$wpwaf_options['lockdown_status'] : '';

    $template_data_settings['wpwaf_single_topic_restrict_status'] =
isset($wpwaf_options['single_topic_restrict_status']) ?
$wpwaf_options['single_topic_restrict_status'] : '';

    ob_start();
  $wpwa_template_loader->get_template_part( 'settings');
    $display = ob_get_clean();
    echo $display;
  }
```

As usual, we will use the `$wpwa_template_loader` object created from our reusable plugin to load the settings template into the menu page. You will also notice the use of the `$wpwaf_options` and `$template_data_settings` variables in this code. We use an option called `wpwaf_options` to save all the options inside a single meta key in the `wp_options` table. This option will be empty until we save the options for the first time. Then, we use the `$template_data_settings` variable to pass the data to the templates using a global variable.

Now, we need to apply the styles to our template design. You can find the CSS styles for the settings template inside the `settings.css` file inside the `css` folder. Let's update the constructor with the following code to include the CSS file:

```
    add_action('admin_enqueue_scripts', array($this, 'add_scripts'),
  9);
```

Then, we can register and include the CSS file using the implementation of the `add_scripts` function, as shown in the following code:

```
    public function add_scripts(){
      wp_register_style('wpwaf_settings_styles', WPWAF_PLUGIN_URL.
  'css/settings.css');
      wp_enqueue_style('wpwaf_settings_styles');
    }
```

We should be able to see the new menu page for **WPWAF Settings** on the left menu. Once you click on the menu item, you should see the settings page similar to the following screenshot:

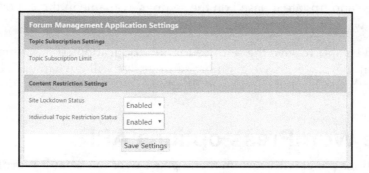

The final part of this task is the implementation of the options saving process. Since we are using custom menu pages, we have to develop the code from scratch to save the options. Let's begin by updating the class constructor with the following action:

```
add_action('init', array($this, 'save_settings'));
```

Usually, we use the init action to intercept the GET or POST requests in WordPress. Our settings panel works on normal form submission, and hence we have to extract data from the $_POST array and store the options in the database. Let's consider the implementation of the save_settings function with the options saving code:

```php
public function save_settings(){
   if(isset($_POST['wpwaf_settings_submit'])){
     $wpwaf_options = (array) get_option('wpwaf_options');
     foreach($_POST['wpwaf'] as $setting=>$val){
       $wpwaf_options[$setting] = $val;
     }

     update_option('wpwaf_options',$wpwaf_options);
     add_action( 'admin_notices', array($this,'settings_notice' ));
   }
}
public function settings_notice() {
   ?>
<div class="updated">
<p><?php _e( 'Settings Updated!', 'wpwa' ); ?></p>
</div>
<?php
   }
```

First, we check the availability of the submit button using the `wpwaf_settings_submit` key in the `POST` array. You might have noticed that we defined all the form field names inside an array called `wpwaf` for simplified access. We can get the existing setting from the `wp_options` table and update it based on the settings available in the `$_POST['wpwaf']` variable. Finally, we add an admin notice to display the success message.

Now, you should be able to save the settings for our application. This settings panel is at the most basic level at this stage. As we get more settings, we will have to update the options saving process with conditional checks and filtering.

Using the WordPress options API

We chose the options panel with custom menu pages over the default WordPress options managing technique. However, it's important to know how to use the WordPress options and settings API in situations where you need a simple options panel. We have to use the `wp_options` table for storing custom options for our plugins and themes. WordPress provides a set of built-in functions for working with the `wp_options` tables. Let's look at the most commonly used functions of the WordPress options API:

- `add_option`: This is used to save new option/value pairs into the database. It doesn't do anything if the option already exists in the database.
- `delete_option`: This is used to remove existing option/value pairs from the database. It returns `true` when the option is deleted successfully and `false` on failure or when the option does not exist.
- `get_option`: This is used to retrieve option/value pairs from the database. It returns `false` if the options don't exist in the database.
- `update_option`: This is used to update option/value pairs in the database. First, it checks for the existence of the option and updates it accordingly. If the option does not exist, it will be added using the `add_option` function.

Be sure to use these functions whenever you need to work with the `wp_options` table, instead of writing your own queries. These functions come with built-in filters and validations, and hence are considered the safest way of working with the `wp_options` table. You can look at the complete WordPress options API at http://codex.wordpress.org/Options_API.

Let's start building a simple options page with the default technique. First, we have to define the admin settings page or menu page, as shown in the following code:

```
add_action('admin_menu', 'wpwaf_options_menu');
function wpwaf_options_menu() {
    add_options_page('WPWAF Options', 'WPWAF Options',
'administrator', __FILE__, 'wpwaf_options_page');
    add_action( 'admin_init', 'wpwaf_register_settings' );
}
```

Then, we have to define the options of our page using the `register_setting` function by WordPress. Let's consider the implementation of the `wpwaf_register_settings` function:

```
function wpwaf_register_settings() {
    register_setting( 'wpwaf-settings-group', 'option1' );
    register_setting( 'wpwaf-settings-group', 'option2' );
}
```

Here, we have two fields in the options panel called **Option1** and **Option2**. We can define them inside a single group with the `register_setting` function. Next, we can move into the HTML implementation of the form using the following code:

```
function wpwaf_options_page() {
?>
<div class="wrap">
<form method="post" action="options.php">
<?php settings_fields( 'wpwa-settings-group' ); ?>
<table class="form-table">
<tr valign="top">
<th scope="row">Option1</th>
<td><input type="text" name="option1" value="<?php echo
get_option('option1'); ?>" /></td>
</tr>
<tr valign="top">
<th scope="row">Option2</th>
<td><input type="text" name="option2" value="<?php echo
get_option('option2'); ?>" /></td>
</tr>
</table>
<?php submit_button(); ?>
</form>
</div>
<?php } ?>
```

It's important to define the form action as `options.php` to get the default functionality provided by WordPress. Then, we pass the previously defined options group name to the `settings_fields` function. This function will generate a set of hidden variables needed for saving the options. Next, we define the existing values of the two options by using the `get_option` function. We have to make sure that we use the same names for the field name as well as the `register_setting` function. Finally, we call the `submit_button` function to generate the submit button.

Once the form is submitted, WordPress will look for the field names that match the settings registered through the `register_setting` function. Then, it will automatically save the data into the `wp_options` table. This process is quite useful in scenarios where you don't want to rely on third-party plugins for creating options panels. Make sure to test both the techniques to identify the pros and cons of each.

Using feature-packed admin list tables

In web applications, you will find a heavy usage of CRUD operations. Therefore, we need tables to display the list of records. These days, developers have the choice of implementing common lists using client-side JavaScript as well as PHP. These lists contain functionalities such as pagination, selections, sorting, and so on. Building these types of lists from scratch is not recommended unless you are planning to build a common library. WordPress offers a feature-packed list for its core features using the `WP_List_Table` class located in the `wp-admin/includes/wp-list-table.php` file. We have the ability to extend this class to create application-specific custom lists. First, we'll look at the default list used for core features, as shown in the following screenshot:

As you can see, most of the common tasks, such as filtering, sorting, custom actions, searching, and pagination, are built into this list, which is easily customized by creating child classes. In the next section, we will discuss the default admin lists and how we can customize them in our applications.

Working with default admin list tables

We have two ways of working with admin list tables. First, we can customize the existing admin lists for posts, users, comments, and so on using the available actions and filters. The second method is to use the WordPress code for admin list tables and create our own tables with all the built-in features. The first option is the easiest and most recommended of the two options. In this section, we will be looking at how to customize the default list tables available in the WordPress admin section.

The post list

The post list can be accessed using the **Posts** | **All Posts** menu item; it contains all the available posts in the WordPress database. By default, it will display the data for the following fields:

- Title
- Author
- Categories
- Tags
- Number of comments
- Date

On a normal WordPress site, blog posts will be listed in this list, and hence we rarely need to make any customizations. However, WordPress custom post types are frequently used in web application development. You won't find the custom posts inside the default WordPress post list. Instead, WordPress provides a separate list of each custom post type. Assume that we have a custom post type called **Topic**. Then we can access the topic post list from the **Topics** | **All Topics** menu item. We can customize the admin list features for custom post types. Let's look at the customizable features for custom post types and practical use cases:

- Custom actions for custom post types
- Custom filters for custom post types

- Post status links
- Post list columns

Creating custom actions for custom posts

We can find the actions list for custom post types in the top-left corner of the list in the **Bulk Actions** drop-down. The default actions for custom posts are **Edit** and **Move To Trash**. In web applications, we need custom actions to manage custom posts. So, let's see how we can create and execute custom actions for the topics list:

```
add_filter( 'bulk_actions-edit-wpwaf_topic', 'topic_action_buttons' );
function topic_action_buttons($bulk_actions) {
    $bulk_actions['wpwaf_topic_normal_switch'] = __( 'Mark Topic as
Normal', 'wpwaf');
    $bulk_actions['wpwaf_topic_sticky_switch'] = __( 'Mark Topic as
Sticky', 'wpwaf');
    $bulk_actions['wpwaf_topic_super_sticky_switch'] = __( 'Mark Topic as
Super Sticky', 'wpwaf');
    return $bulk_actions;
}
```

WordPress didn't offer filters or actions for changing the default **Bulk Actions** list until the recent 4.7 version, so we had to make use of other actions with some workarounds. Now we have a filter called `bulk_actions-{screen_id}` and we can use it on the `edit-wpwaf_topic` screen to add custom actions. So, we add the new options to the existing bulk actions field with unique values. Now, you should see three new options inside the **Bulk Actions** drop-down for the topic post type.

The next part is to use the custom options to execute some custom tasks. Let's take a look at the code:

```
add_filter( 'handle_bulk_actions-edit-wpwaf_topic',
'topic_action_handler', 10, 3 );
function topic_action_handler( $redirect_to, $do_action, $post_ids ) {
    if ( !in_array($do_action,
  array('wpwaf_topic_normal_switch','wpwaf_topic_sticky_switch',
    'wpwaf_topic_super_sticky_switch' ) ) ) {
        return $redirect_to;
    }

    foreach ( $post_ids as $post_id ) {
      switch ($do_action) {
        case 'wpwaf_topic_normal_switch':
          update_post_meta($post_id, '_wpwaf_topic_sticky_status',
'normal');
```

```
            break;

        case 'wpwaf_topic_sticky_switch':
            update_post_meta($post_id, '_wpwaf_topic_sticky_status',
'sticky');
            break;

        case 'wpwaf_topic_super_sticky_switch':
            update_post_meta($post_id, '_wpwaf_topic_sticky_status',
'super_sticky');
            break;
        }
    }
    $redirect_to = add_query_arg( 'bulk_emailed_posts', count( $post_ids
), $redirect_to );
    return $redirect_to;
    }
```

Recent WordPress versions also offers another useful filter called `handle_bulk_actions-{screen_id}` for executing actions on **Bulk Action** custom options. First, you have to select some topics from the list and then select **Mark Topic** as **Sticky** from the **Bulk Actions** drop-down. Once you click the **Apply** button, we check the proper action using the `$do_action` variable passed to this function. Topic IDs are passed as the third parameter to this function. We can traverse through topic IDs and identify the correct action using a `switch` statement. Then we update the `post_meta` table based on the action and return the default redirect parameter.

This is a great feature for quickly working on a large number of custom post type ietms at once.

Creating custom filters for custom post types

The admin list provides another useful feature for filtering custom post types. By default, we can filter the custom post types by date. In web applications, we can use this feature to create our own filters by using a technique similar to the custom action creation. Let's see how we can add a filter for topic statuses:

```
    function wpwaf_topic_list_filters() {
        global $typenow, $wpwaf;
        $topic_sticky_status = isset($_GET['wpwaf_topic_sticky_status']) ?
$_GET['wpwaf_topic_sticky_status'] : '';
        if( $typenow == $wpwaf->topic->post_type ){

            $display  = "<select name='wpwaf_topic_sticky_status'
id='wpwaf_topic_sticky_status' class='postform'>";
```

```
        $display .= "<option value=''>"__('Show All Topics',
'wpwaf')."</option>";
        $display .= "<option ". selected( $topic_sticky_status ,
'normal',false) ." value=''>".__('Normal Topics', 'wpwaf') ."</option>";
        $display .= "<option ". selected($topic_sticky_status,
'sticky',false) ." value=''>".__('Sticky Topics', 'wpwaf')."</option>";
        $display .= "<option ". selected($topic_sticky_status,
'super_sticky',false) ." value=''>".__('Super Sticky Topics',
'wpwaf')."</option>";

        $display .= "</select>";
        echo $display;
    }
}
add_action( 'restrict_manage_posts','wpwaf_topic_list_filters' );
```

We can find an action called `restrict_manage_posts` inside the WordPress core files to filter the records of normal posts as well as custom post types. In this scenario, we create a custom filter by defining a drop-down field with the necessary filters. We can get the selected filter value from the `$_GET` array and display it as the selected value for the filter. It's important to check the post types using the `$typenow` global variable to prevent new filters for all post types. Now, we have the input fields to filter topics from our list. The next task is to apply the filters into a topics list query. Consider the following code for filtering topics based on the status value:

```
add_filter( 'parse_query', 'wpwaf_topic_list_filter_query' );
function wpwaf_topic_list_filter_query( $query ){
  global $pagenow,$wpwaf;
  $type = $wpwaf->topic->post_type;
  if (isset($_GET['post_type'])) {
    $type = $_GET['post_type'];
  }

  if ($wpwaf->topic->post_type == $type && is_admin() &&
$pagenow=='edit.php' && isset($_GET['wpwaf_topic_sticky_status']) &&
$_GET['wpwaf_topic_sticky_status'] != '') {
    $query->query_vars['meta_key'] = '_wpwaf_topic_sticky_status';
    $query->query_vars['meta_value'] =
$_GET['wpwaf_topic_sticky_status'];
  }
}
```

We have to use the WordPress `parse_query` filter to apply our custom filters into the post list query.

The `parse_query` filter is an action triggered after `WP_Query->parse_query()` has set up query variables (such as the various `is_` variables used for conditional tags). We can use this action to modify the queries in the current page or post.

As usual, we have to check the proper post type and current page. The topics list is loaded from the `edit.php` file, and hence we have to use it for the conditional check. In this scenario, we are filtering the topic status, and hence we should also check the availability of the `wpwaf_topic_sticky_status` key inside the `$_GET` array. If all conditions are satisfied, we change the default query variables to include the meta key and meta value for the topic status. Now the modified query will only return the topics matching the specified status.

 We created the sticky status as a custom field, and hence it's stored in the `wp_postmeta` table. Therefore, we can directly change the query by using the meta key and value. If you store these values on a different database table or you are filtering a value from a different table, custom filtering will be complex and will require manual queries.

Now, you can select a specific status from the new drop-down field and click on the **Filter** button to filter the topics by status. You can repeat the same technique to create more filters as required.

Creating custom post status links

WordPress posts can have one of the many statuses at any given time, and this is used to determine how the post is handled. We have eight post statuses by default for normal posts as well as custom post types. The following are the default post statuses with their meaning within a post life cycle:

- **Published**: The post is published and viewable for everyone
- **Future**: The post is scheduled to be published on a future date
- **Draft**: The incomplete post is viewable by anyone with the proper user level
- **Pending**: The post is awaiting the approval of a user with the `publish_posts` capability to publish
- **Private**: The post is viewable only to WordPress users at an administrator level
- **Trash**: The posts in **Trash** are assigned the trash status
- **Auto-Draft**: These are the revisions that WordPress saves automatically while you are editing
- **Inherit**: This is used with a child post (such as attachments and revisions) to determine the actual status from the parent post (`inherit`)

These post statuses will be displayed on top of the topics list. However, it only displays statuses with at least one post. This is another way of filtering posts by post statuses. In this application, we used default post statuses and created a meta key to manage the topic sticky status. We can also have used post statuses for topics by removing the default statuses and creating custom statuses. Let's see how we can create a status link for the custom post status using the following code:

```
add_action('admin_footer-post-new.php',
  'wpwaf_create_post_status_list');
add_action('admin_footer-post.php','wpwaf_create_post_status_list'
);
function wpwaf_create_post_status_list(){
   global $post,$wpwaf;
   $complete = '';
   $label = '';
   if($post->post_type == $wpwaf->topic->post_type){
      $complete = ' selected=selected ';
      $label = "<span id='post-status-display'>".__('Resolved',
'wpwaf')."</span>";
   ?>
   <script>
      jQuery(document).ready(function($){
         $("select#post_status").append("<option
value='wpwaf_topic_resolved' <?php echo $complete; ?>>".__('Released
Status', 'wpwaf'). "</option>");
         $(".misc-pub-section label").append("<?php echo $label;
 ?>");
      });
   </script>
   <?php
   }
}
```

We have to use `admin_footer-post-new.php` and `admin_footer-post.php` to include custom statuses on the topic creation screen as well as the topics list. As usual, we embed the new status into the post status drop-down using JavaScript. Now, the new status will be available automatically as a link in the topics list.

We can create a new post status by using the `register_post_status` function on the `init` action. You should never create new post statuses before the `init` action. You can find complete guidelines at `http://codex.wordpress.org/Function_Reference/register_post_stat us`.

Once you click on the link, topics with the `wpwaf_topic_resolved` status will be displayed. This is a useful feature for applications with many custom post statuses.

Displaying custom list columns

We have discussed all the major features of the admin post list, such as custom actions, filtering, and post statuses. Finally, we will complete this section by using custom columns in post lists. The custom post list usually displays title and date columns in the post list. Consider our forum application with managing topics. Generally, we would need the topic sticky status and date in the list to make it easier to manage multiple topics at the same time. Let's take a look at the following code for adding custom columns to the list:

```
add_filter( 'manage_edit-wpwaf_topic_columns',
'wpwaf_topic_list_columns' ) ;
  function wpwaf_topic_list_columns( $columns ) {
    $columns = array(
      'cb' => '<input type="checkbox" />',
      'title' => __( 'Topic' ,'wpwaf' ),
      'status' => __( 'Sticky Status' ,'wpwaf' ),
      'date' => __( 'Date' ,'wpwaf' ),
    );
    return $columns;
  }
```

We can decide the columns in the post list using the `manage_edit-{custom post type}_columns` filter. In this scenario, we are trying to add a new custom column called `Sticky Status`. If needed, we can remove the existing columns by removing them from the array. Now, you should see the new columns in the topics list with empty values. Next, we have to retrieve and display the values for those new columns. Consider the following code for displaying values:

```
add_action( 'manage_wpwaf_topic_posts_custom_column',
'wpwaf_manage_topic_columns', 10, 2 );
  function wpwa_manage_topic_columns( $column, $post_id ) {
    global $post;
    switch( $column ) {
      case 'status' :
        $status = get_post_meta( $post_id,
'_wpwa_topic_sticky_status', true );
        if ( empty( $status ) )
          echo __( '-' );
        else
          echo $status;
        break;
      default :
        break;
    }
  }
```

We have a built-in action called `manage_{custom post type}_posts_custom_column` for managing and filtering the values in the post list. All the available columns are passed as a parameter to this function. We can switch the columns and get the values from the `wp_postmeta` table using the respective meta keys. If needed, we can also filter and format the values before sending them to the list. Now you should see the new columns and values inside the topics list. The following screenshot previews the topics list after all the customizations are completed:

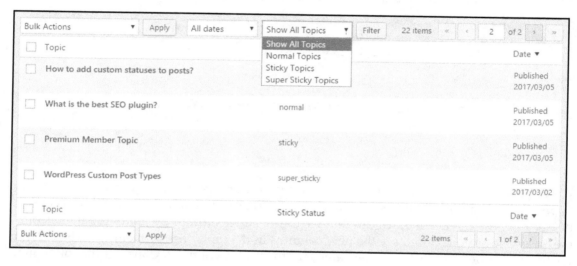

We have covered all the major features in the post list throughout the previous sections, and now you should be able to customize any custom post list according to your preference. You can find the code for this section inside the `wpwa_actions_filters.php` file.

The user list

We can access the backend user list by navigating to **Users** | **All Users** in the admin panel. The WordPress user list is also built on top of the `WP_List_Table` class, and hence we can have most of the features we discussed in the previous section on the post lists. I won't discuss all those features for the user list as the code is similar to the variation of actions and filters.

We will discuss the practical usages of these features in the user list instead of discussing the code. The user list only contains `Delete` as a custom action for deleting multiple users at once. In large applications, we will need features such as:

- Confirming the e-mail address after registration

- Receiving user approval before login
- Enabling and disabling users

In such scenarios, we can use these as custom actions in the **Bulk Actions** drop-down to work with multiple users instantly.

> You can use the `admin_footer` action for adding custom actions to the drop-down field and the `load-users.php` action for updating the users after selecting a specific action.

Adding dynamic columns to the user list is similar to the technique used in the post list, and hence we won't discuss it in detail. Next, we have user roles as links on the top instead of post statuses. We have custom user roles in our forum application and those will be added as links for filtering users. Finally, we can create custom filters in the user list to filter approved/unapproved, confirmed/unconfirmed, and enabled/disabled users based on the scenario we discussed.

> You can use the `restrict_manage_users` action for creating the new filter drop-downs for users and the `pre_user_query` action for customizing the query based on the filter values.

We have discussed the practical customization of the user list and mentioned the filters for implementing them. Make sure that you try these implementations on your own.

The comments list

Comments is the other major list used for web applications and can be accessed using the **Comments** menu in the admin panel. Similar to what we did with the user list, we will only be discussing the practical usage instead of code.

First, we can consider the custom actions for comments. By default, we have **Unapprove, Approve**, **Mark as Spam**, and **Move to Trash** as the custom actions. Let's recall our example from Chapter 1, *WordPress as a Web Application Framework*. We used comments to provide answers to questions created through custom post types. So, we can have custom actions, such as **Mark answer as correct**, **Mark answer as incorrect**, and so on.

> You can use the `admin_footer` action for adding custom actions to the drop-down field and the `init` action for updating the comments after selecting a specific action.

Next, we can add new filters to the comments list. We can add a filter for correct/incorrect answers. Also, we can add another filter for answers from a specific user. Finally, we might need a filter for answers to a specific question. These are some of the use cases in our simple example, and you will find many such filters in advanced applications.

 You can use the `restrict_manage_comments` action for creating the new filter drop-downs for comments and the `pre_get_comments` action for customizing the query based on the filter values.

Finally, we have comment status links on top instead of post status links. However, WordPress doesn't provide a function for adding new custom comment statuses, and hence we can't change the filtering links available on the top of the list.

Throughout the previous three sections, we discussed how to customize the default user, post, and comments list. However, we haven't covered the most important part of creating our own lists with the admin list table. In large web applications, we will be using custom database tables more than the default tables, and hence custom list building is a vital feature. We will be covering the `WP_List_Table` class and its usage in the next section.

Building extended lists

The extended version of `WP_List_Table` can be created by manually overriding each and every function in the base class. However, we will take a simpler approach by using an existing template to extend the lists. The WordPress plugin directory contains a useful plugin called `Custom List Table Example` for the reusable template of the `WP_List_Table` class. This plugin is not updated for the recent WordPress version. However, the code is still useful for building a custom list table. You can grab a copy of the plugin at `http://wordpress.org/plugins/custom-list-table-example/` and get used to the code before we get started.

Create a new class called `class-wpwaf-list-table.php` and copy the `list-table-example.php` file from the downloaded plugin. Then, you can change the plugin descriptions and information if necessary. Now we are ready to customize the template.

Using the admin list table for forum topics

In requirements planning, we identified the need for a notification service where we send notifications to users on subscribed topic updates. Here, we are going to develop the first part of this requirement where users subscribe to forum topics. There are several ways of implementing such requirements within WordPress. Here, we will be using a custom list table to manage the subscription process. The following is the list of identified tasks for this implementation:

- Topics should be listed for subscriptions
- Any user with a `follow_forum_activities` capability should be able to select multiple topics for subscriptions
- Selected topics should be saved in a custom database table with subscribed user details, on executing a custom action

Let's get started.

 We need to use the `wp_topic_subscriptions` table for implementing this feature.

Step 1 – defining the custom class

Change the name of the `TT_Example_List_Table` class to a new unique name. Here, we have used `WPWAF_List_Table` as the class name.

Step 2 – defining the instance variables

The template offered by the `Custom List Table Example` plugin uses hardcoded data in a variable called `$example_data`. In real web applications, we need to dynamically get this data from the database, file, or any external source. Therefore, set the `$example_data` variable to an empty array as follows:

```
var $example_data = array();
```

Step 3 – creating the initial configurations

We need to configure the necessary settings inside the `WPWAF_List_Table` class constructor, as given in the following code:

```
function __construct() {
  global $status, $page;
  parent::__construct(array(
  'singular' => 'topic',
  'plural' => 'topics',
  'ajax' => false
  ));
}
```

Inside the array of configurations, we have to define a singular and plural name for the records. This should be a unique name and have no relation to database tables or columns. We can also define the support for AJAX, although it will be not discussed here.

Step 4 – implementing the custom column handlers

In this step, we need to define the methods for handling each of the columns to be displayed in the list. The topics list will contain a single column called `Topic Title`, and hence we need only the following function implementation:

```
function column_topic_title($item) {
  return sprintf('%1$s ', $item['topic_title'] );
}
```

Before explaining the code, I would like you to have a look at the structure of our final data set using the following code:

```
Array(
  [0] => Array
  (
    [ID] => 24
    [topic_title] => How to use WordPress Custom Posts?
  )
  [1] => Array
  (
    [ID] => 22
    [topic_title] => What is the best SEO plugin?
  )
)
```

The preceding dataset is generated manually to contain custom keys. When we are using the direct database result for the dataset, these keys will be replaced by database columns.

Here, we are using a column name called `topic_title`, which doesn't actually exist in the database, so the `column_topic_title` function returns the contents of the `topic_title` key in the dataset.

 Don't forget to create the `column_{column name}` functions for each and every column in your list in case you decide to include multiple columns.

Step 5 – implementing the column default handlers

In the previous step, we created column functions for available columns in the list. If you skip the definition of specific function for a column, we should create a default callback function called `column_default`, as shown in the following code:

```
function column_default($item, $column_name) {
  switch ($column_name) {
    case 'topic_title':
      return $item[$column_name];
    default:
      return print_r($item, true);
  }
}
```

Here, we need to define each and every column that will not be defined separately. Even though we have defined `topic_title`, it won't be used as we have a specific function called `column_topic_title`.

Step 6 – displaying the checkbox for records

Apart from the custom columns, we need to have a column with a checkbox for every record in the list. This checkbox will be used to select the records and execute specific actions on the **Bulk Actions** drop-down menu. Let's consider the implementation using the `column_cb` function inside the template:

```
function column_cb($item) {
  return sprintf(
<input type="checkbox" name="%1$s[]" value="%2$s" />',
    $this->_args['singular'], $item['ID']  );
}
```

The first parameter in the preceding statement uses a singular label that we created inside the constructor to set the name of the checkbox as an array. The second parameter contains the ID for the row as defined in our dataset. This value should be the ID of the record in the database table.

 We can define any key for the ID in the dataset. However, consistency is important in developing reusable stuff, and hence I prefer using an ID for all the record IDs in each of the lists I create. You may decide to reuse your own key across all the custom lists.

Step 7 – listing the available custom columns

Now, we need to define all the columns available to create the custom list by modifying the existing `get_columns` function, as illustrated in the following code:

```
function get_columns() {
  $columns = array(
    'cb' => '<input type="checkbox" />',
    'topic_title' => __('Topic Title','wpwaf')
    );
  return $columns;
}
```

This is an in-built function that returns an array of columns. We don't need to change the details of the checkbox column as it's common to all the lists. Later, we have to define all the custom columns using the column name as the key and the display name as the value.

Step 8 – defining the sortable columns of list

The `get_sortable_columns` function is pretty straightforward like the previous one, where we define the columns to be sortable. Consider the following modified implementation of this function for our requirements:

```
function get_sortable_columns() {
  $sortable_columns = array(
    'topic_title' => array('topic_title', false)
    );
  return $sortable_columns;
}
```

Here, we have only a single entry based on our requirements. You can add all the available columns for custom lists. The key of the array item contains the column name, and the value contains the database column. Since we will be using a manually created data set from the database, the key and value will be same.

Step 9 – creating a list of bulk actions

In the default post list, we can see different options called **Edit**, **Move to Trash**, and so on inside the **Bulk Actions** drop-down. Similarly, we can include custom actions in custom lists. This is one of the most powerful features of this list, in implementing complex requirements in web applications. Consider the modified implementation of the get_bulk_actions function:

```
function get_bulk_actions() {
    $actions = array(
        'subscribe' => __('Subscribe','wpwaf'),
        'unsubscribe' => __('Unsubscribe','wpwaf')
    );
    return $actions;
}
```

The preceding function is prebuilt and returns a list of actions to be included in the drop-down. In this scenario, we need users to subscribe and unsubscribe to topics. Hence, we use custom actions called subscribe and unsubscribe.

Step 10 – retrieving the list data

Up until now, we have carried out the configuration part of the list, and now, we are moving onto the exciting part by adding real data and executing actions. The default template contains a function called prepare_items to set the data required for the custom table. We can include the necessary SQL queries inside this function to generate data. However, I prefer keeping the function in its default state and providing the data through the example_data instance variable.

 You can use the extensive code comments of this function to understand the functionality of each section and make the customizations when necessary.

Step 11 – adding a custom list as a menu page

Having created the list, we need a specific location to access this list as it's not available in any of the navigation menus. So, we will include the list on the left-hand side of the navigation menu as an admin menu page. The following code should be placed in `class-wpwaf-list-table.php` after the `WPWAF_List_Table` class:

```
function wpwaf_subscribers_menu() {
    add_menu_page( __('Subscribe to Topics','wpwaf'), __('Subscribe to
Topics','wpwaf'), 'follow_forum_activities', 'wpwaf_subscriptions',
'topics_list_page');
    }
    add_action('admin_menu', 'wpwaf_subscribers_menu');
```

The new menu page is created on the `admin_menu` action using the `add_menu_page` function. Only users with the user capability of `follow_forum_activities` will have the access to this function since we have specified the capability on `add_menu_page`.

Finally, we have defined the callback function as `topics_list_page` to generate the HTML contents for the list.

Step 12 – displaying the generated list

First, we have to set the database results to the list table. So, consider the initial part of the `topics_list_page` function for querying the database, as shown in the following code:

```
function topics_list_page() {
    $testListTable = new WPWA_List_Table();
    $topics_query = new WP_Query(array('post_type' =>
'wpwaf_topic','post_status' =>'publish' ));

    if($topics_query->have_posts()) :
        while($topics_query->have_posts()) : $topics_query->the_post();
        array_push($testListTable->example_data, array("ID" =>
get_the_ID(), "topic_title" => get_the_title()));
        endwhile;
    endif;

    $testListTable->prepare_items();
}
```

We can begin the implementation by initializing an object of the `WPWAF_List_Table` class. Then, we execute a WordPress query using a built-in `WP_Query` class to retrieve the list of topics in all forums. We have chosen to manually create the dataset by traversing through the database results and assigning it to the dataset structure defined earlier. Keep in mind that we are passing the dataset to the `WPWAF_List_Table` class by using an instance variable called `$example_data`. Finally, we call the `prepare_items` function to get the data ready with features such as sorting, paginations, and so on.

Having completed the explanations on the initial part, we can move into the HTML generation part of the `topics_list_page` function, as illustrated in the following code:

```html
<div class="wrap">
<div id="icon-users" class="icon32"><br/></div>
<h2><?php echo __('Subscribe to Topics','wpwaf'); ?></h2>

<form id="topics-filter" method="POST">
<input type="hidden" name="page" value="<?php echo $_REQUEST['page']
?>" />
<?php $testListTable->display() ?>
</form>
</div>
```

Here, we have a basic HTML form and the necessary heading and labels. The actual list generation is done through the `display` function of `WPWAF_List_Table`. This function is available on the `WP_List_Table` class and hasn't been overridden on the template class. Hence, a call to display will use the function in the parent class. You can also override the display function on the child class to provide a different behavior to the default design.

Now, your custom list should look something similar to the following screenshot:

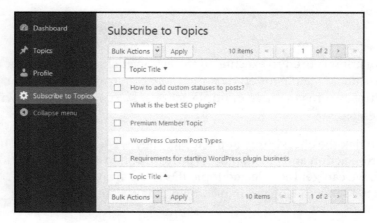

Even though we have completed the custom list implementation, the list doesn't have any functionality until we implement the custom action to allow the users to subscribe and unsubscribe to the developers. Let's move back to the `process_bulk_action` function of the `WPWAF_List_Table` class, as shown in the following code:

```
function process_bulk_action() {
    global $wpdb;
    if ('subscribe' === $this->current_action()) {
        $subscribed_topics = $_POST['topic'];

        $user_id = get_current_user_id();
        $topic_subscriptions_table = $wpdb->prefix.'topic_subscriptions';

        foreach ($subscribed_topics as $subscribed_topic) {
            $wpdb->insert(
                $topic_subscriptions_table,
                array(
                    'topic_id' => $subscribed_topic,
                    'user_id' => $user_id
                ),
                array(
                    '%d',
                    '%d'
                )
            );
        }

        $msg = __('Succefully completed.','wpwaf') ."<a href='" .
admin_url() . "?page=wpwaf_subscriptions'>". __('Subscribe to More
Topics','wpwaf') . "</a>";

        wp_die($msg);
    }
}
```

The preceding function is used to execute all the actions defined in the **Bulk Actions** drop-down. We can use an `if` statement on `current_action` to add the code for different actions. In scenarios where you have multiple actions, `switch` statements will be ideal over `if-else` statements.

The users have to tick the checkboxes of the topics they wish to subscribe. Then, they can select the **Subscribe** action and click on the **Apply** button to execute the action. Once the button is clicked, we can get the selected topic IDs as an array using `$_POST['topic']`. Also, we can get the ID of the logged in user using the `get_current_user_id` function.

In Chapter 3, *Planning and Customizing the Core Database,* we created a custom table called topic_subscriptions to be used for topic-subscription management. Now, we need to insert records to this table using a custom query, as shown in the preceding code. Finally, we display the message on the same page with a link back to the topics list.

Managing the subscribe and unsubscribe status

We have implemented the subscribe process for topics. However, we also need the unsubscribe functionality and we need to highlight whether a given topic is subscribed or not. So, let's update the process_bulk_action function for adding another action for unsubscribe, as shown in the following code:

```
function process_bulk_action() {
  global $wpdb;
  // Subscription code

  if ('unsubscribe' === $this->current_action()) {
    $subscribed_topics = $_POST['topic'];
    $user_id = get_current_user_id();
    $topic_subscriptions_table = $wpdb->prefix.'topic_subscriptions';
    foreach ($subscribed_topics as $subscribed_topic) {
      $wpdb->delete(
        $topic_subscriptions_table,
        array( 'topic_id' => $subscribed_topic, 'user_id' => $user_id),
array( '%d','%d' )
      );
    }

    $msg = __('Succefully completed.','wpwaf') ."<a href='" .
admin_url() . "?page=wpwaf_subscriptions'>
". __('Subscribe to More Topics','wpwaf') . "</a>";

    wp_die($msg);
  }
}
```

The only difference in the unsubscribe part is that we delete the record instead of inserting it to the table. The remaining code is exactly the same as subscribe and hence explanations are not included here. Now, we can update our column_cb function as follows to display subscribed topics as being checked:

```
function column_cb($item) {
  global $wpdb,$wpwaf;
  $user_id = get_current_user_id();
```

```
    $topic_id = $item['ID'];
    $checked = '';
    $topic_subscriptions_table = $wpdb->prefix.'topic_subscriptions';
    $sql = $wpdb->prepare( "SELECT * FROM $topic_subscriptions_table
  WHERE topic_id = %d AND user_id = %d ", $topic_id , $user_id );
    $result = $wpdb->get_results($sql);
    if($result){
      $checked = ' checked ';
    }

    $checkbox_field = '<input type="checkbox" '.$checked.' name="%1$s[]"
value="%2$s" />';

    return sprintf(
      $checkbox_field, $this->_args['singular'], $item['ID']
          );
  }
```

First, we check whether the current user has active subscription to a topic by searching for a matching record in the `topic_subscriptions` table. If a record is available, we set the `$checked` variable to checked and add it to the checkbox field. Now the subscribed topics will be displayed with a checked ID column.

Adding content restrictions to admin list tables

We now have a fully functional admin list table for the topic subscription process. But one of the most important things is missing in our implementation. We displayed the list of all the topics and the content restrictions added in Chapter 5, *Implementing Application Content Restrictions* are missing. So, users have access to all the topics regardless of restrictions.

Now we need to make sure the users can only subscribe to the topics with permission. Therefore, we have to display the subscribe checkbox for the topics with permission and remove the checkbox for restricted topics. Let's take a look at the modified implementation of the `column_cb` function with the topic restrictions:

```
    function column_cb($item) {
      global $wpdb,$wpwaf;
      // Other code

      $topic_visiblity = $wpwaf->restrictions-
  >protection_status($topic_id);
      if($topic_visiblity){
        $checkbox_field = '<input type="checkbox" '.$checked.'
name="%1$s[]" value="%2$s" />';
      }else{
```

```
        $checkbox_field = '';
    }

    $checkbox_field = '<input type="checkbox" '.$checked.' name="%1$s[]"
value="%2$s" />';
    return sprintf(
      $checkbox_field,$this->_args['singular'], $item['ID'] );
  }
```

We have a slight modification to the previous version. First, we pass the topic ID to the `protection_status` function of the `WPWAF_Content_Restrictions` class through the global `$wpwaf` object. This function returns whether the current user has permission to view the topic. If the user has the necessary permission, we display the checkbox field similar to earlier code. If the topic is restricted, we remove the checkbox and add a blank value, preventing users from subscribing to the topic.

Now, we have a fully featured custom list with all the basic grid functionalities. We can create as many lists as possible by creating new templates or creating a reusable class for this library. It's for the future, but for now, you can test the list by subscribing to forum topics.

An awesome visual presentation for admin screens

In general, users who visit websites or applications don't understand the technical aspects. Such users evaluate systems based on the user friendliness, simplicity, and richness of the interface. Hence, we need to think about the design of the admin pages. Most WordPress clients don't prefer the default interface as it is seen commonly by users. This is where admin themes become handy in providing application-specific designs. Even with admin themes, we cannot change the structure as it affects the core functionality. However, we can provide eye-catching interfaces by changing the default styles of the admin theme.

Using existing themes

WordPress Version 3.8 and higher provides the ability to change the color theme of the admin section using eight different color schemes. This is a great feature for changing the look and feel of admin screens in WordPress. Users are allowed to pick their own color scheme for the site, making it flexible for different users with different color preferences. You can change the color theme from the **Your Profile** section of the **Users** menu in the WordPress admin screen.

The following screenshot previews the available color themes in the user profiles section:

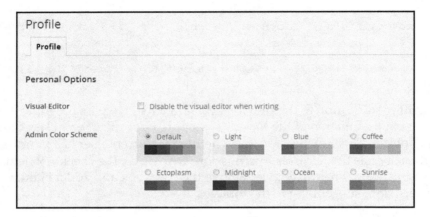

This is the most basic version of admin design customization as it only changes the color scheme of the admin section. Other features such as elements, dimensions, icons, and so on won't be changed. These features let users choose their color scheme. However, most of you will need a simplified admin design or feature-rich modern dashboards. This is where the admin theme plugin comes into action. We will be covering admin theme plugins in the next section.

Using plugin-based third-party admin themes

Experienced WordPress developers will know that the theme is designed to provide the frontend functionality of a WordPress site. You can change the theme as you wish and create custom themes based on your preference. However, the WordPress admin features and design templates are stored inside the WordPress core files. WordPress doesn't provide a feature for changing the admin theme or designing your own admin theme. So, we can't provide the admin designs as part of a normal WordPress theme. As a solution, we use plugins to customize admin designs. You can find many free and premium third-party plugins for admin themes.

The following are some of the most popular admin theme plugins available in the WordPress plugin directory:

- **Blue Admin**: This is a simple admin design that makes your WordPress administration section more clear and relaxed (`https://wordpress.org/plugins/blue-admin/`)
- **Slate Admin theme**: A clean, simplified WordPress admin theme (`https://wordpress.org/plugins/slate-admin-theme/`)

We will look at one of the listed admin theme plugins to understand how it changes the look and feel of admin screens. We will be using the Slate Admin theme as it's free and compatible up to WordPress 4.7.2. The following screen previews the post creation screen using the Slate Admin theme:

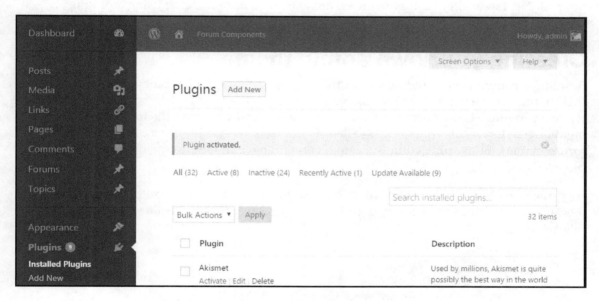

Once this plugin is activated, you may notice that the design of the post creation screen looks different from the default design and provides a much cleaner interface. However, all the fields, text, and structure of the page still look the same.

As a developer, it's important for you to understand how an admin theme plugin works and how you can create an admin theme plugin. We have already seen that admin templates are generated from the core. So, the elements and structure are fixed to certain elements, CSS classes, and IDs.

In WordPress themes, we can completely change the design of the frontend posts and pages by using our own templates and elements. Unfortunately, we can't use the same procedure for admin themes as we don't have access to backend templates, and we may lose some features by changing the elements on the WordPress admin dashboard. In simple terms, it's not possible to change the elements of admin templates using plugins. We can only change the design using CSS and JavaScript. Admin theme plugins offer great features for changing the design of admin screens. However, they are not flexible enough to create admin dashboards with advanced components and designs. If we need a unique admin screen with our own features, we need to remove the default admin menus and screens using filters and implement all the features by using our own templates inside custom menu pages.

So far, we have looked at default color schemes and changing designs using admin theme plugins. Next, we will discuss how to create your own admin theme using a plugin.

Creating your own admin theme

Building a complete admin theme is a time-consuming task, which is beyond the scope of this chapter, as we need to define custom styles for all the existing CSS selectors. Therefore, we will provide a head start to the admin theme design by altering the main navigation menu. Let's start by creating a class called `class-wpwaf-admin-theme.php` inside the forum management application. As usual, you will have to require the file inside the main plugin file.

As usual, we need to include this function and initialize an object from this class inside the `WPWAF_Forum` class. Let's start by defining the style sheet for the admin theme using the following code:

```php
<?php
class WPWAF_Admin_Theme {
  public function __construct() {
    add_action('admin_enqueue_scripts', array($this,
'wpwa_admin_theme_style'));
    add_action('login_enqueue_scripts', array($this,
'wpwa_admin_theme_style'));
  }
  public function wpwa_admin_theme_style() {
    wp_enqueue_style( 'my-admin-theme', WPWAF_PLUGIN_URL .'css/wp-
admin.css');
  }
}
```

We begin the implementation by defining the necessary actions for including the CSS file. Usually, we use `admin_enqueue_scripts` to include scripts and styles in the admin area. The `login_enqueue_scripts` action is used to enable styles on the login screen. You can omit the `login_enqueue_scripts` action if you are not intending to customize the login screen.

Then, we add the CSS file specific to the plugin, using the `wp_enqueue_style` function. That's all we need to implement in order to create admin themes. The rest of the designing stuff will be handled through the CSS file. So, make sure to create a new CSS file called `wp-admin.css` inside a folder called `css`.

 The CSS file used for an admin theme is loaded after the default WordPress admin stylesheets. Therefore, it will override the existing styles provided by the default stylesheet.

In this section, we will style the main navigation menu of WordPress. You can update the CSS file with menu-specific styles, as illustrated in the following code:

```
#adminmenuback,#adminmenuwrap { background: #000; }
#adminmenu a{ color : #FFF; }
#adminmenu a.menu-top, #adminmenu .wp-submenu .wp-submenu-head {
  border-bottom-color: #191A1B;
  border-top-color: #191A1B;
}
#adminmenu .wp-submenu, .folded #adminmenu a.wp-has-current-
  submenu:focus + .wp-submenu, .folded #adminmenu .wp-has-current-
  submenu .wp-submenu {
  background-color: #363636;
}
#adminmenu li.wp-menu-separator {
  background: none repeat scroll 0 0 #DFDFDF;
  border-color: #454545;
}
#adminmenu div.separator { background:#000; }
#adminmenu li.wp-menu-separator {
  background: none repeat scroll 0 0 #000;
  border-color: #000;
}
#adminmenu .wp-submenu li.current, #adminmenu .wp-submenu
  li.current a, #adminmenu .wp-submenu li.current a:hover {
  color: #FFFFFF;
}
#adminmenu .wp-submenu a:hover,
#adminmenu .wp-submenu a:focus {
  background-color: #d54e21;
```

```
    color: #fff;
}
#adminmenu li.menu-top:hover,#adminmenu li.opensub > a.menu-top,
#adminmenu li > a.menu-top:focus {
    background-color: #d54e21;
    color:#fff;
    font-weight:bold;
}
```

Now, you can preview the navigation menu of the admin section using the following screenshot:

Customizing the menu was a very simple task, and now, we have a slightly different interface with a different color scheme. Similarly, we have to define the styles for all the available themes to make a complete admin theme.

The main style file of WordPress is the `wp-admin.css` file, located in the `wp-admin/css` directory. I suggest that you have a look at this file to understand the styles of the various components in WordPress. The following is the content of this file:

```
@import url(common.css);
@import url(forms.css);
@import url(admin-menu.css);
@import url(dashboard.css);
@import url(list-tables.css);
@import url(edit.css);
@import url(revisions.css);
```

```
@import url(media.css);
@import url(themes.css);
@import url(about.css);
@import url(nav-menus.css);
@import url(widgets.css);
@import url(site-icon.css);
@import url(l10n.css);
```

All the main components are separated into their own CSS files. Inside the CSS file for each component, you will find the necessary styles and comments to understand where the styles are used. Here, we added all the CSS styles into one CSS file called `wp-admin.css`. Ideally, you can create separate CSS files for each component and load them within our `Forum` plugin. Use the content and comments of these CSS files to style the remaining components to build a complete admin theme.

The responsive nature of the admin dashboard

The responsive design has become one of the major trends in web application development with an increase in the usage of mobile-based devices. Responsive applications are built using style sheets that adapt to various screen resolutions with the help of media queries. Fortunately, the WordPress admin dashboard is responsive by default, and hence we can make responsive backends without major implementations.

Let's consider the following screenshot of an admin dashboard in its default resolution to understand its responsive nature:

Now, let's preview the mobile version of the same screen using the following screenshot:

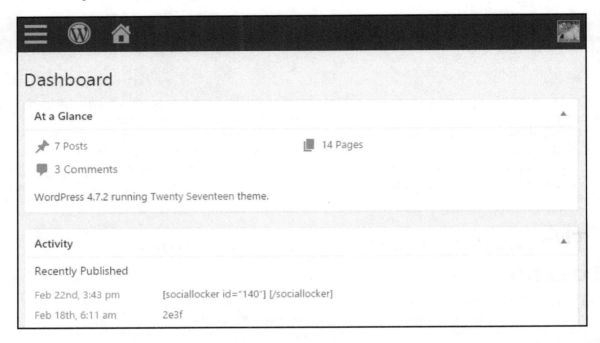

With the low screen resolution, the theme has made adjustments to keep the responsiveness by minimizing the main navigation menu and increasing the size of the dashboard widgets. This is an example of the responsive nature of the WordPress admin section. Try other screens to get an idea of how elements are adjusted to keep the responsive nature.

Since the admin section is responsive by default, we don't have to do anything else to make it responsive. However, keep in mind that the plugins we create and use will not be responsive by default. Hence, it's important to design your plugin screens using percentage dimensions to keep the responsive nature.

Supplementary admin dashboard features

We have discussed some of the most important admin features in this chapter. There are many other supplementary features that add benefits to applications. In this section, we are going to briefly introduce some of the useful admin features available in WordPress.

Dashboard widgets

By default, the WordPress dashboard will be displayed on initial login and it contains default widgets such as At a glance, Quick Draft, WordPress News, Welcome, and so on. The WordPress admin dashboard is a great place to display important information in a summarized way. We have the ability to remove existing widgets as well as add new widgets from plugins and themes. So, it's the ideal place to keep the most commonly used functionality as well as the most commonly needed data displays.

Screen options menu

The **Screen Options** menu is displayed near the top right-hand section of your screen along with the **Help** menu. This menu is displayed only on screens where additional options are available. This menu shows the features available in the current screen and the data available for displaying. You can use the checkboxes to enable/disable these features, as shown in the following screenshot.

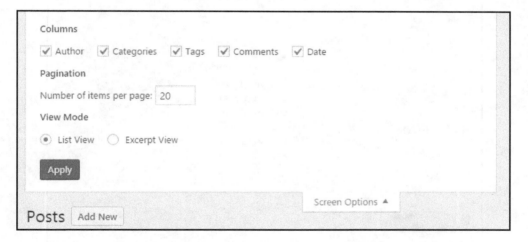

Help menu

You can see a **Help** menu near the top right-hand corner for most of the WordPress backend screens. This section explains the features available in the current screen. Novice developers can use this menu to understand the components and functionality of each admin screen and directly go to the documentation at `https://codex.wordpress.org`, when they want to learn the features in detail.

User language control

This is one of the more recently introduced features in the WordPress admin section. Until the recent version, only an administrator had the capability to change the application language and users had to use it regardless of whether they were comfortable with it or not. Now an administrator has the ability to define multiple languages and users can choose the preferred language from their WordPress account. Assume that we have the application in English. In this case, an administrator can go to WordPress **Settings** | **General** | **Site Language**, select another language from the **Available** list, and save. Then you have multiple languages in the **Installed** section as shown in the following screenshot:

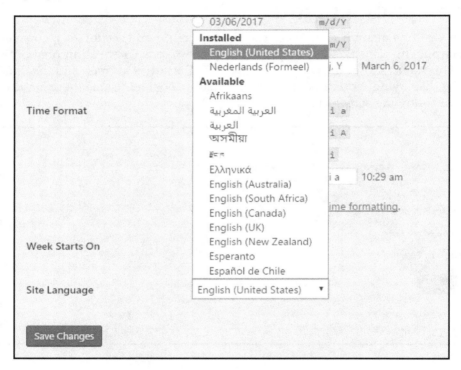

In this scenario, we have added **English** and **Nederlands** to the **Installed** languages list. You can add any number of languages as you need. Now when the user is logged into the WordPress backend profile, there will be option for selecting one of these two languages, as shown in the following screenshot:

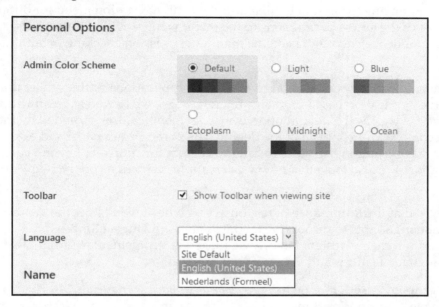

User language features allow users to use the application in their preferred language, increasing the flexibility of your application for users from different countries.

Time for action

In this chapter, we covered the basics of an admin panel-related functionality to be compatible with web applications. Now, it's time for you to take these things beyond the basics by implementing the following actions:

- We created a default type of the admin list table to allow subscriptions. Now, try to include an AJAX-based star rating system to allow users to rate topics by implementing a custom column in the existing list.
- We started the implementation of the custom admin theme by setting up styles for the left navigation menu. Try to complete the theme by styling the remaining components.
- Add custom actions, filters, and custom columns for the user list similar to the features we used for post lists.

Summary

Throughout this chapter, we looked at some of the exciting features of the WordPress admin dashboard, and how we can customize them to suit complex applications. We started by customizing the admin toolbar and the main navigation menu for different types of users. Most of the access permissions to the menu were provided through user capabilities, and hence we didn't need the manual permission checking in building the menu.

Typical web applications contain a large amount of applications settings to let users customize the application based on their preferences. So, we looked at creating our own options pages as well as the default options management features provided by the WordPress core. Also, we looked at the default lists in the admin panel and extended the existing WordPress admin list tables to cater to custom functionality beyond core implementation. We also looked at how we can apply restrictions on the items in admin list tables.

Next, we looked at the importance of responsive web design and how the WordPress admin dashboard adapts to responsive layouts while showing a glimpse into the WordPress admin theme design. Finally, we looked at supplementary admin features and how user language features add value to your application.

In the next chapter, Chapter 8, *Adjusting Theme for Amazing Frontends*, we will explore how we can manage existing WordPress themes to build complex web application layouts using modern techniques.

8
Adjusting Theme for Amazing Frontends

Generally, users who visit web applications don't have any clue about the functionality, accuracy, or quality of the code of the application. Instead, they decide the value of the application based on its user interfaces and the simplicity of using its features. Most expert-level web developers tend to give more focus on development tasks in complex applications. However, the application's design plays a vital role in building the initial user base. WordPress uses themes that allow you to create the frontend of web applications with highly extendable features that go beyond conventional layout designs. Developers and designers should have the capability to turn default WordPress themes into amazing frontends for web applications.

In this chapter, we will focus on the extendable capabilities of themes while exploring the roles of the main theme files for web applications. Widgetized layouts are essential for building flexible applications, and hence we will also look at the possibilities of integrating widgetized layouts with WordPress action hooks. It's important to have a very good knowledge of working with WordPress template files to understand the techniques discussed in this chapter. By the end of this chapter, you will be able to design highly customizable layouts to adapt future enhancements.

In this chapter, we will cover the following topics:

- A basic file structure of the WordPress theme
- Understanding the template execution hierarchy
- Web application layout creation techniques
- Building a forum application home page
- Widgetizing application layouts
- Generating the application frontend menu

- Managing options and widgets with a customizer
- Creating pluggable templates
- Planning action hooks for layouts

An introduction to the WordPress application frontend

WordPress powers its frontend with a concept called themes, consisting of a set of predefined template files to match the structure of default website layouts. In contrast to web applications, a WordPress theme works in a unique way. In `Chapter 1`, *WordPress as a Web Application Framework*, we had a brief introduction to the role of a WordPress theme and its most common layout. Preparing a theme for web applications can be one of the more complicated tasks, not discussed widely in the WordPress development community. Usually, web applications are associated with unique templates, which are entirely different from the default page-based nature of websites.

A basic file structure of the WordPress theme

As a WordPress developer, you should have a fairly good idea about the default file structure of WordPress themes. Let's briefly introduce the default files before identifying their use in web applications. Think about a typical web application layout where we have a common header, footer, and content area. In WordPress, the content area is mainly populated by pages or posts. The design and the content for pages are provided through the `page.php` template, while the content for posts is provided through one of the following templates:

- `index.php`
- `archive.php`
- `category.php`
- `single.php`

Basically, most of these post-related file types are developed to cater to the typical functionality of blogging systems, and hence can be omitted in the context of web applications. Since custom posts are widely used in application development, we need to focus more on templates such as `single-{post_type}` and `archive-{post_type}` rather than `category.php`, `archive.php`, and `tag.php`.

 Even though default themes contain a number of files for providing default features, the `style.css` and `index.php` files are enough for implementing a WordPress theme. Complex web applications themes are possible with the standalone `index.php` file.

In normal circumstances, WordPress sites have a blog built on posts, and all the remaining content of the site is provided through pages. When referring to pages, the first thing that comes to mind is static content. However, WordPress is a fully functional CMS, and hence, the page content can be highly dynamic. Therefore, we can provide complex application screens by using various techniques on pages. Let's continue our exploration by understanding the theme file execution hierarchy.

Understanding the template execution hierarchy

WordPress has quite an extensive template execution hierarchy compared to general web application frameworks. However, most of these templates will be of minor importance in the context of web applications. Here, we will illustrate the important template files in the context of web applications. The complete template execution hierarchy can be found at `http://codex.wordpress.org/images/1/18/Template_Hierarchy.png`.

The following diagram shows the template execution hierarchy in brief:

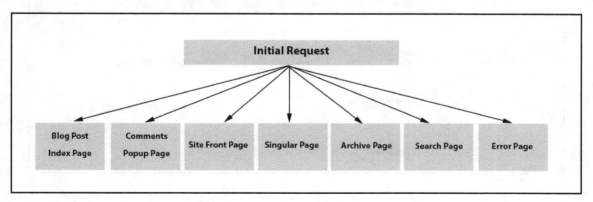

Once the initial request is made, WordPress looks for one of the main starting templates, as illustrated in the preceding diagram. It's obvious that most of the starting templates, such as the front page, comments popup, and index pages, are specifically designed for content management systems. In the context of web applications, we need to put more focus into both singular and archive pages, as most of the functionality depends on those templates. Let's identify the functionality of the main template files in the context of web applications:

- **Archive pages**: These are used to provide summarized lists of data as a grid.
- **Single posts**: These are used to provide detailed information about the existing data in the system.
- **Single pages**: These are used for any type of dynamic content associated with applications. Generally, we can use pages for form submissions, dynamic data display, and custom layouts.

Let's dig deeper into the template execution hierarchy on the singular page path, as illustrated in the following diagram:

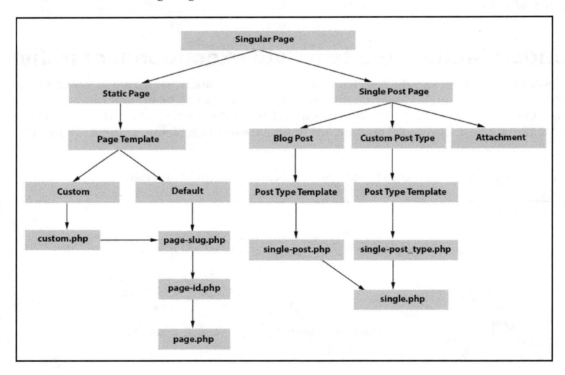

A singular page is divided into two paths that contain posts or pages. The static page is defined as custom or default page templates. In general, we will use default page templates for loading website pages. WordPress looks for a page with the slug or ID before executing the default `page.php` file. In most scenarios, web application layouts will take the other route of custom page templates, where we create a unique template file inside the theme for each of the layouts and define it as a page template using code comments. We can create a new custom page template by creating a new PHP file inside the `theme` folder and using the `Template Name` definition in code comments, illustrated as follows:

```
<?php/*  Template Name: My Custom Template*/?>
```

To the right of the preceding diagram, we have a single post page, which is divided into three paths called the blog post, custom post, and attachment post. Both attachment posts and blog posts are designed for blogs and hence they will not be used frequently in web applications. However, the custom post template will have a major impact on application layouts. As with a static page, the custom post looks for custom post type templates or single post type templates before looking for a default `single.php` file. The template hierarchy was changed in Custom WordPress version 4.7 to support custom post type templates.

The execution hierarchy of an archive page is similar in nature to posts, as it looks for post-specific archive pages before reverting to the default `archive.php` file.

Now, we have had a brief introduction to the template loading process used by WordPress. In the next section, we will look at the template loading process of a typical web development framework to identify the differences.

The template execution process of web application frameworks

Most stable web application frameworks use a flat and straightforward template execution process compared to the extensive process used by WordPress. These frameworks don't come with built-in templates, and hence every template will be generated from scratch:

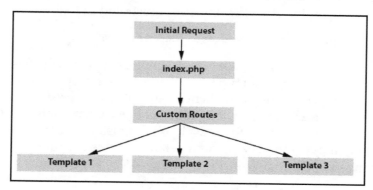

In this process, the initial request always comes to the index.php file, which is similar to the process used by WordPress or any other framework. This process is known as the **Front Controller** pattern in most PHP frameworks. It then looks for custom routes defined within the framework. It's possible to use custom routes within a WordPress context, even though it's not used generally for websites. Finally, the initial request looks for the direct template file located in the templates section of the framework. As you can see, the process of a normal framework has very limited depth and specialized templates.

 Keep in mind that index.php, referred to in the preceding section, is the file used as the main starting point of the application, not the template file. In WordPress, we have a specific template file named index.php located inside the theme folder as well.

Managing templates in a typical application framework is a relatively easy task when compared to the extensive template hierarchy used by WordPress. In web applications, it's ideal to keep the template hierarchy as flat as possible with specific templates targeted towards each and every screen.

In general, WordPress developers tend to add custom functionalities and features by using specific templates within the hierarchy. Having multiple templates for a single screen and identifying the order of execution can be a difficult task in large-scale applications, and hence should be avoided in every possible instance.

Web application layout creation techniques

As we move into developing web applications, the logic and screens will become complex, resulting in the need for custom templates beyond the conventional ones. There are a wide range of techniques for putting such functionality into the WordPress code. Each of these techniques have their own pros and cons. Choosing the appropriate technique is vital in avoiding potential bottlenecks in large-scale applications. Here is a list of techniques for creating dynamic content within WordPress applications:

- Static pages with shortcodes
- Page templates
- Custom templates with custom routing

Shortcodes and page templates

We discussed static pages with shortcodes and page templates in Chapter 2, *Implementing Membership Roles, Permissions, and Features*. The shortcode technique should be used carefully in web applications due to the lack of control it displays within the source code.

In the preceding two techniques, the site admin has the capability of changing the structure and core functionality of an application through the dashboard by changing the database content. Usually, the site admin is someone who is capable of managing the site, not someone who has a knowledge of web application development. As developers, we should always keep the controlling logic and core functionality of an application within our control by implementing it inside the source code files. The site admin should only be allowed to change the application data and behavior within the system rather than the application's control logic. Let's consider the following scenario to help you understand the issues that occur in the preceding techniques.

Assume that we want to create a sign-up page for our application. So we create a page named sign-up from the admin dashboard and assign a shortcode or page template to it to display the sign-up form. Later, users can use the sign-up page from the frontend to get registered. Then, we get a new requirement to add some information to the sign-up page. While updating the page, we get the part of shortcode that was deleted by mistake and save it without even knowing. Now the application's sign-up page is broken, and the users will not be able to use the system. This is the risk of using the preceding techniques where we can easily break the core controlling functionality of an application.

Instead, we should be allowing both data and behavior changes using the admin dashboard; for example, we can allow the admin to choose the necessary fields for the sign-up form using settings. We can alter the behavior of the sign-up form, but we can never break the sign-up page. Therefore, the preceding two techniques are not ideal in large-scale web application layouts.

Custom templates with custom routing

The custom routing technique allows us, as developers, to have complete control over the template generation process. In Chapter 2, *Implementing Membership Roles, Permissions, and Features*, we looked at the basics of custom templates with routing while creating the frontend login and registration pages. Now, let's move on by inspecting advanced aspects of custom template techniques.

Using pure PHP templates

Pure PHP templates are a widely used technique within popular frameworks, including WordPress. In this technique, template files are created as separate PHP files to contain the visual output of the data. The separation of models, views, and controllers allows us to manage each concern of the application development independently from each other, thus increasing maintainability and extensibility. In ideal situations, views should have a very limited business logic, or, if possible, no logic at all. Most probably, designers who don't have much of an idea about PHP coding will be working with views. Therefore, it's important to keep the views as simple as possible with display logic and data. The data required for the views should be generated from models by executing the business logic.

Even though this technique is widely used, it doesn't fulfill the expectation of using views completely. These PHP templates will always have some PHP code included. The main problem with this technique is when someone who doesn't have PHP knowledge makes a mistake in the PHP code placed inside templates; the application will break. PHP was originally meant to be a template engine, and hence, we won't have many problems in using PHP templates other than the preceding issue.

The WordPress way of using templates

WordPress uses a function called `get_template_part` for reusing templates as pure PHP files. This function locates the given template parts inside your theme files and makes a file inclusion under the hood. Consider the following code for understanding the use of the `get_template_part` function:

```
get_template_part( $slug, $name );
```

The first parameter, `$slug`, is mandatory, and it is used to load the main template. The second parameter, `$name`, is optional, and it is used to load a specialized version of the template. Let's look at some different usages of this function:

```
get_template_part("topic");
get_template_part("topic", "wordpress");
```

The first line of code will include the `topic.php` file inside the `themes` folder. The second line of code will include the `topic-wordpress.php` file, which will be a specialized version of the `topic.php` file in typical scenarios. Typically, we pass the necessary data to templates when using template systems. However, the `get_template_part` function does not provide the option of passing data as it's a pure file inclusion. However, we have access to the data within this context, as this is a pure file inclusion. Also, we have the option of accessing the necessary data through global variables.

> If you decide to use the WordPress technique of using template files, make sure you create each and every template file inside your `theme` folder.

Direct template inclusion

Developers who don't prefer the WordPress method of including templates can create their own style of template inclusion. In `Chapter 2`, *Implementing Membership Roles, Permissions, and Features*, we used the direct template method with custom routing. Let's recall the implementation to understand the process:

```
add_action('template_redirect', array($this, 'front_controller'));
public function front_controller() {
global $wp_query,$wpwaf;
  $control_action = isset( $wp_query->query_vars['control_action'] ) ?
$wp_query->query_vars['control_action'] : '';

  switch ( $control_action ) {
    // Other case statements
```

```
case 'activate':
    do_action( 'wpwaf_before_activate_user' );
    $wpwaf->registration->activate_user();
    do_action( 'wpwaf_after_activate_user' );
    break;
    }
}
```

We intercepted the default template-locating procedure using the `template_redirect` action and used a `query` variable to switch routes. Then, we used the `activate_user` function for template inclusion, as shown in the following code:

```
public function activate_user() {
    // Implementingnecessary functions and data generation
    includeWPWAF_PLUGIN_DIR. 'templates/info-template.php';
    exit;
}
```

In this scenario, the `info-template.php` template has access to all the data generated inside the `activate_user` function. Developers should execute all the business logic in the top section of the `activate_user` function. Even though `info-template.php` has access to all the data, it's good practice to put the data necessary for the template inside a specific array so that anyone can identify the data used in the template just by looking at the `activate_user` function.

With this technique, we can create the template files inside the `themes` or `plugins` folder and load it where necessary, making it more flexible compared to the `get_template_part` technique of WordPress.

Theme versus plugin-based templates

In typical web applications, templates will be created inside a separate folder from the other main components such as models and controllers. WordPress is mainly used for general websites and content management systems. So the visual representation is much more important than a web application. Hence, theme templates become the top priority in WordPress development.

Now, the most important question is whether to place web application templates within the `themes` or `plugins` folder. The decision between the theme and plugin templates purely depends on your personal preference and the type of application. First, we have to keep in mind that most existing theme templates are used for generating CMS-related functionality, and hence, they will have a lesser impact in advanced web applications. Most web application templates need to be created from scratch. So answering the following question will simplify your decision making process.

Are you planning to create an application-specific theme?

What I mean by an application-specific theme is that you are willing to change the structure and code of the existing templates to suit your application. These kinds of themes will not be reused across multiple applications, and switching themes will almost be impossible. The following list illustrates some of the tasks to be executed on existing files to make application-specific themes:

1. The heavy usage of custom fields.
2. Removing existing components such as sidebars, comments, and so on.
3. Using custom action and filter hooks with templates.
4. Using custom widgetized areas.

If your answer is yes, all the templates should be placed inside the `themes` folder as they will not be used for any other application. On the other hand, if you are planning to design new templates for the application while keeping the existing templates without major customizations, it's a good practice to create the application-specific templates inside the `plugins` folder. This technique separates application-specific templates from the core templates, allowing you to switch the theme anytime without breaking the application. Also, maintenance becomes easier as core templates and application-specific templates are easily tracked separately.

Building the forum application home page

So far, we have learned the theoretical aspects of creating templates inside WordPress themes. Now, it's time to put them into practice by creating the home page for the forum application. In this section, we will talk about the importance of widget-based layouts for web applications while building the home page. Our home page consists of two major parts:

- Forums list of the application
- Various widgets for forum application data

Let's implement these two parts starting with the forums list.

Building the forum list using shortcode

The **Forums list** on the home page is the main entry point to our application where we list all the available forums with the link to the individual forum page. We can implement the forum list using a custom template, shortcode, or a widget. In this scenario, we are going to use a shortcode to develop the forums list since it can be reused in many other parts of the application. Let's start by updating the constructor of the WPWAF_Model_Forum class to include the new shortcode:

```
add_shortcode('wpwaf_forums_list', array( $this, 'display_forums_list'
) );
```

Next, we are going to implement the forums list using the display_forums_listfunction as illustrated in the following code:

```
public function display_forums_list($attr){
    global $wpdb,$wpwa_template_loader, $wpwaf_forum_list_params;
    $topics_to_forums = $wpdb->prefix.'p2p';
    $sql   = $wpdb->prepare( "SELECT wppost.*, count(wpp2p.p2p_to) as
topics_count from $wpdb->posts as wppost inner join $topics_to_forums as
wpp2pon wppost.ID = wpp2p.p2p_to where wppost.post_type = '%s' and
wppost.post_status = 'publish'group by wpp2p.p2p_to", 'wpwaf_forum');

    $wpwaf_forum_list_params['forums'] =array();
    $result = $wpdb->get_results($sql);
    if($result){
      $wpwaf_forum_list_params['forums'] =$result;
    }
    ob_start();
    $wpwa_template_loader->get_template_part('forums','list');
    $display = ob_get_clean();
    return $display;
}
```

We have to retrieve the forums list as well as the topic count for each forum. So we need a custom query, which is complex compared to the queries we have used until now. Earlier, we created topic-to-forum relationships by using the Posts 2 Posts plugin. Therefore, the topics for each forum are stored in the wp_p2p_to database table.

First, we join the default WordPress `posts` table and the `p2p_to` table using a left join while checking the topics post type and post status. We also use the group by statement to capture the number of topics in each forum. Next, we add the results to a global parameter variable and pass it to a new template called `forums-list`.

Our next task is creating the `forums-list-template.php` file inside the `templates` folder of the plugin and adding the necessary display HTML for the forums list. The following code previews the implementation of the forums list template:

```php
<?php global $wpwaf_forum_list_params; ?>
<div class='wpwaf_forum_list'>
    <div class='wpwaf_forum_list_header'><?php _e('Forums','wpwaf');
?></div>
        <div class='wpwaf_forum_list_panel'>
        <div class='wpwaf_forum_list_item_head'>
    <div class='wpwaf_forum_list_name'><?php _e('Forum Title','wpwaf');
?></div>
        <div class='wpwaf_forum_list_count'><?php _e('Topics
Count','wpwaf'); ?></div>
        </div>

        <?phpforeach ($wpwaf_forum_list_params['forums'] as $forum) { ?>
        <div class='wpwaf_forum_list_item'>
    <div class='wpwaf_forum_list_name'>
        <a href='<?php echo get_permalink($forum->ID); ?>'><?php echo
$forum->post_title; ?></a></div>
        <div class='wpwaf_forum_list_count'><?php echo $forum->topics_count;
?></div>
        </div>
    <?php } ?>
    </div>
    </div>
```

Here, we use the forum results passed from the model to initialize the `foreach` loop and generate the items for the forums list. We have a basic HTML design and the necessary CSS is included in the `style.css` file of the forum plugin. So we have the forum names with the link to the default forum single page, and the topic count for each forum.

We have a reusable shortcode for generating the forums list of the application. The next task is to integrate this shortcode into the application home page. However, you might be wondering why we used a shortcode since we discussed the risks of using shortcodes for application logic in Chapter 2, *Implementing Membership Roles, Permissions, and Features.*

In this scenario, we are going to integrate the shortcode directly into a template, instead of adding it through the post/page editor. So there is no risk for conflicts when content is modified by the administrator, unless they modify the code of the template. Since the administrator is not responsible for editing template code, we can add this functionality through a shortcode to make it reusable. In the next few sections, we will be integrating the shortcode with the template.

Widgetizing home page

The home page is the main entry point to any application and hence we have to make sure to display all the valuable information in the home page. We can build a static home page with fixed content or we can include widgetized areas to make it dynamic and flexible. So we need both widgets and widgetized areas to for such an implementation.

Let's identify the importance of widgetizing:

- Widget placements can be changed without touching the source code
- Ability to reuse components in different widgetized areas of applications
- Apply settings or add dynamic content to all widgets at once

What is a widget?

A widget is a dynamic module that provides additional features to your website. WordPress uses widgets to add content to website sidebars. In most web applications, we won't get sidebars while creating layouts. However, we can take widgets beyond their conventional sidebar usage by creating fully widgetized layouts for increased flexibility.

Let's plan the structure of the home page layout by using widgets, as shown in the following diagram:

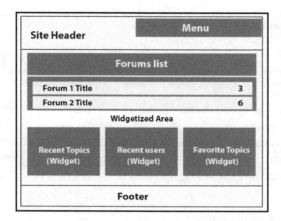

According to the preceding diagram, the home page will be partly widgetized by using a single widget area. At this stage of the project, we will include three widgets within the widgetized area to display **Recent Topics**, **Recent Users**, and **Favorite Topics**. There is no limitation on the number of widget areas allowed per screen, and hence, you can define multiple widget areas wherever necessary. Also, we have kept the top part of the layout static while widgetizing the other parts.

In web applications, widgets play an important role compared to websites. By widgetizing layouts, we allow the content to be dynamic and flexible for future enhancements.

Widgetizing application layouts

As mentioned earlier, we have the option of creating template files inside a theme or a plugin. Here, we will create the templates inside the plugins folder to improve flexibility. So let's begin the process by creating a file called class-wpwaf-theme.php within the root directory of our main plugin. Then, we have to do the usual file inclusion and object initialization inside the WPWAF_Forum class. Next, we can update the constructor code as follows to register the widgetized area for the home page:

```php
class WPWAF_Theme {
  public function __construct() {
    $this->register_widget_areas();
  }
  public function register_widget_areas() {
    register_sidebar(array(
```

```
                  'name' => __('Home Widgets','wpwaf'),
                  'id' => 'home-widgets',
                  'description' => __('Home Widget Area', 'wpwaf'),
                  'before_widget' => '<div id="one" class="home_list">',
                  'after_widget' => '</div>',
                  'before_title' => '<h2>',
                  'after_title' => '</h2>'     ));
              }
          }
```

Surprisingly, we don't have to use an action hook to create the widget areas. WordPress widgets are designed to work on sidebars, and hence the function name, `register_sidebar`, is used for defining widgetized areas. However, we don't need an actual sidebar to define widget areas for various purposes. Most of the configurations used for this function are important for working with the widget areas. The configuration options are explained as follows:

- `name`: This is used to define the name of the widgetized area. It will be used to load the widgetized area on frontend templates
- `id`: This is used to uniquely identify the widget area
- `before_widget` and `after_widget`: These are used to provide additional HTML content before and after the widget contents
- `before_title` and `after_title`: These are used to provide additional HTML content before and after the widget title

Once the previous code is implemented, you will get a dynamic widgetized area in the admin dashboard widgets section, as shown in the following screenshot:

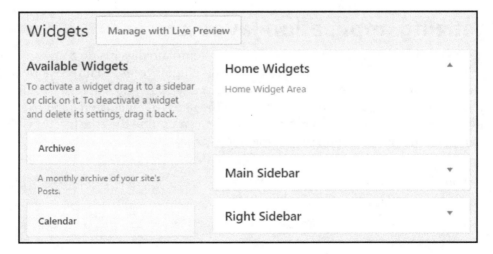

Creating widgets

Having defined the widget area, we can create some dynamic widgets to populate the home page content. Registering widgets is similar to the process used for registering widgetized areas. Let's create a function for including and registering widgets into the application:

```
public function register_widgets() {
    $base_path = WPWAF_PLUGIN_DIR;
    include $base_path . 'widgets/class-wpwaf-home-list-widget.php';
    register_widget('WPWAF_Home_List_Widget');
}
```

We will create all three widgets required for the home page using the class-wpwaf-home-list-widget.php file inside the widgets folder of our plugins folder. First, we have to include the widgets file inside the register_widgets function. Second, we have to register each and every widget using the register_widget function. We can create three separate widgets for the home page. However, we will create a single widget to illustrate the power of reusability for complex web applications.

So we have limited the widget's registration to a single widget named WPWAF_Home_List_Widget. This will be the class of the widget that extends the WP_Widget class. Finally, we have to update the constructor with the widgets_init action, as shown in the following code:

```
add_action('widgets_init', array($this, 'register_widgets'));
```

In general, widgets contain a prebuilt structure that provides their functionality. Let's understand the process and functionality of a widget using its base structure, as illustrated in the following code:

```
classWPWAF_Home_List_Widget extends WP_Widget {
    function __construct() { }
    public function widget($args, $instance) { }
    public function form($instance) { }
    public function update($new_instance, $old_instance) {  }
}
```

First, each widget class should extend the WP_Widget class as the parent class. Then, we need four components, including the constructor, to make a widget. Let's see the role of each of these functions within widgets:

- __construct: This function is used to register the widget by calling the parent class constructor with the necessary parameters
- widget: This function is used to construct the frontend view of the widget using the processed data

- `form`: This function is used to create the backend form for the widget to define the necessary configurations and options
- `update`: This function is used to save and update the fields inside the form function to the database tables

Now we have a basic idea about the prebuilt functions within widgets. Let's start the implementation of `WPWAF_Home_List_Widget` to create the home page content. Basically, this widget will be responsible for providing the home page content such as the recent topics, recent users, and favorite topics. Considering the current requirements, we need two form fields for defining the widget title and choosing the type of widget. Let's get things started by implementing the constructor as follows:

```php
public function __construct {
    parent::__construct(
        'home_list_widget', // Base ID
        'Home_List_Widget', // Name
    array('description' => __('Home List Widget', 'wpwaf'),)
    );
}
```

Here, we call the parent class constructor by passing ID, nayme, and `description`. This will initialize the main settings of the widget. We can then have a look at the implementation of the `form` function using the following code:

```php
public function form($instance) {
if (isset($instance['title'])) {
    $title = $instance['title'];
  } else {
    $title = __('New title', 'wpwaf');
  }
if (isset($instance['list_type'])) {
    $list_type = $instance['list_type'];
  } else {
    $list_type = 0;
  }
?>
<p>
<label for="<?php echo $this->get_field_name('title');
 ?>"><?php _e('Title:'); ?></label>
<input class="widefat" id="<?php echo $this-
  >get_field_id('title'); ?>" name="<?php echo $this-
  >get_field_name('title'); ?>" type="text" value="<?php echo
  esc_attr($title); ?>" />
</p>
<p>
<label for="<?php echo $this->get_field_name('list_type');
```

```
     ?>"><?php _e('List Type:'); ?></label>
    <select class="widefat" id="<?php echo $this-
    >get_field_id('list_type'); ?>" name="<?php echo $this-
    >get_field_name('list_type'); ?>" >

    <option <?php selected( $list_type, 0 ); ?>
     value='0'>Select</option>
    <option <?php selected( $list_type, "rec_topic" ); ?>
  value='rec_topic'><?php echo __('Recent Topics','wpwaf'); ?></option>
    <option <?php selected( $list_type, "rec_users" ); ?>
  value='rec_users'><?php echo __('Recent Users','wpwaf'); ?></option>
    <option <?php selected( $list_type, "fav_topics" ); ?>
  value='fav_topics'><?php echo __('Favorite Topics','wpwaf'); ?>
  </option>
    </select>
    </p>
    <?php
    }
```

Let's get started!:

1. First, we will check the existing values of the form fields using the `$instance` array. This array will be populated with the existing values of the form fields from the database. Initially, these fields will contain empty values.

   Next, we have defined the form fields required for the widget. The **Title** of the widget is implemented as a text field, while the **List Type** is implemented as a drop-down field with recent topics, recent users, and favorite topics as the options.

   You might have noticed the use of the `get_field_name` and `get_field_id` functions inside the `name` and `ID` attributes of the form fields. These two functions are located in the parent class and are used to generate dynamic names in a common format. Using the view source of the browser window, you will find the field names are similar to the following code:

   ```
   widget-home_list_widget[1][title]
   widget-home_list_widget[1][list_type]
   ```

   These types of field names and IDs are assigned to make the automation easier. The widgets' data-saving method is completely automated, and hence we have to only define the necessary form fields. Saving the data to the database will be done automatically by WordPress.

2. Next, we need to implement the form-updating function, as shown in the following code:

```
public function update($new_instance, $old_instance) {
  $instance = array();
  $instance['title'] = (!empty($new_instance['title']) )
 ? strip_tags($new_instance['title']) : '';
  $instance['list_type'] =
 (!empty($new_instance['list_type']) ) ?
 strip_tags($new_instance['list_type']) : '';
 return $instance;
 }
```

The `update` function is relatively simpler than other functions, as we just have to define the form field keys inside the `$instance` array.

3. The rest of the database updating will be done automatically behind the scenes. Once those fields are defined, you will get a new widget item named `Home_List_Widget` in the **Available Widgets** area. You can drag the widget into **Home Widget** to include the widget on the home page. Now, your screen should look like the following screenshot:

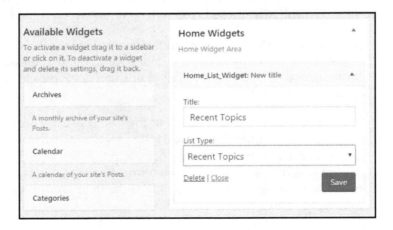

We need to implement the `form` function to complete the development of the home page widgets. Here, we want to display a list of recent topics, users, or favorite topics. We will construct the recent topics list for the purpose of this explanation, and you can find the remaining widget implementations within the source code. This function generates the frontend display contents.

Throughout this book, we have given higher priority to separating templates from business logic. Therefore, we need to use separate templates for generating the HTML required for a widget's frontend display. Here, we will use the `template loader` plugin that we developed earlier.

Now we can move back to the implementation of the `widget` function of the home page widget, as given in the following code:

```
public function widget($args, $instance) {
  global $wpwa_template_loader,$home_list_data;
  extract($args);
  $title = apply_filters('widget_title', $instance['title']);

  $list_type = apply_filters('widget_list_type',
$instance['list_type']);
  echo $before_widget;
  if (!empty($title))
    echo $before_title . $title . $after_title;
  switch ($list_type) {
    case 'rec_topic':
      // Get list of recent topics from the database
      $topics_query = new WP_Query(array('post_type' =>
'wpwaf_topic','post_status' =>'publish', 'order' => 'desc', 'orderby' =>
'date' ));

      $home_list_data = array();
      $home_list_data["records"] = array();

      if($topics_query->have_posts()){
        while($topics_query->have_posts()) : $topics_query-
>the_post();
          array_push($home_list_data["records"], array("ID"
=>get_the_ID(), "title" =>get_the_title(), "type"=>"favorite"));
  endwhile;
      }
      $home_list_data["title"] = $title;

      ob_start();
    $wpwa_template_loader->get_template_part("home","list");
      echo ob_get_clean();
      break;
  }
  echo $after_widget;
}
```

Let's look at the code in detail:

1. The first three lines of this function extract the arguments passed to the widget function and retrieve the widget option values by applying the necessary filters.
2. The next three lines are used to wrap the widget with dynamic content.
3. Then, we come to the most important part of the function where we generate the front layout and the data. The `template loader` class, `WPWA_Template_Loader`, is accessed using the global variable named `$wpwa_template_loader` for dynamic template loading.
4. Then, we check the value of the drop-down field using the `switch` statement. In the widget form, we included `rec_topic` as the key for recent topics.
5. The other two option values can be found in the source code. Inside the `rec_topic` case, we query the database to retrieve the recently created topics using `WP_Query`. The `wpwaf_topic` post type is used to filter the values.
6. Then, we add the generated results into the `$home_list_data` array to pass them into the template.
7. Finally, we call the `get_template_part` function of the template loader object by passing the template name as `home-list`. You can create a PHP file named `home-list-template.php` inside the `templates` folder. The implementation of the home page widgets template is given in the following code:

```php
<?php global $home_list_data; ?>
<div class='home_list_item'>
<div class='list_panel'>
<?php foreach($home_list_data["records"] as $record){ ?>
<div class='list_row'>
<a href=''><?php echo $record['title']; ?></a>
<?php do_action('wpwaf_home_widgets_controls',$record['type'],$record['ID']); ?>
</div>
<?php } ?>
</div>
</div>
```

The preceding template generates the recent topics list using the data passed into the template. So far, we have created the necessary widgets and the widget areas for the home page. The final task in this process is to create the home page template itself.

Designing a home page template

We have to create a file named `home-template.php` inside the `templates` folder. At the beginning of the widget creation process, we planned the structure of the home page using a wireframe. Now we need to adhere to the structure while designing the home page, as shown in the following code:

```php
<?php get_header(); ?>
<?php echo do_shortcode('[wpwaf_forums_list]'); ?>
<?php if ( !function_exists('dynamic_sidebar') ||
 !dynamic_sidebar('Home Widgets') ) :
endif;?>
<?php get_footer(); ?>
```

These four lines of code make the complete design and the data for the home page. Usually, every page template contains a WordPress header and footer using the `get_header` and `get_footer` functions. The second line of code contains the execution of our forums list shortcode, created earlier in this chapter. We integrate it to the template and use the `WordPressdo_shortcode` function to execute it. Since shortcode is directly embedded to the template, we can prevent the conflicts created by modifying post/page content.

The next lines of code check for the existence of the `dynamic_sidebar` function for loading dynamic widget areas. Then, we load the widgetized area created in the *Widgetizing application layouts* section using the sidebar name. This area is populated with the widgets assigned in the admin section.

The design and functionality of the home page are now completed and ready to be displayed in the application. However, we haven't given instructions to WordPress to load it as the home page. So let's go to the `WPWAF_Theme` class to define the home page. First, we have to add the following code to the plugin constructor to customize template redirection:

```php
add_action('template_redirect', array($this,
'application_controller'));
```

The implementation of the `application_controller` function will look like the following code:

```php
public function application_controller() {
  global $wp_query,$wpwa_template_loader;
  $control_action = isset( $wp_query-
>query_vars['control_action'] ) ? $wp_query-
>query_vars['control_action'] : '';
  if (is_home () && empty($control_action) ) {
    ob_start();
    $wpwa_template_loader->get_template_part("home");
```

```
        echo ob_get_clean();
        exit;
    }
}
```

WordPress allows us to check the home page of the application using the `is_home` function. Our plan is to redirect the default home page to the custom home template created in the preceding sections. Hence, we intercept the default routing process and use the template loader class to dynamically use the home template using the `get_template_part` function. Also, we have to make sure that the `control_action` query variable is empty before rendering the home page.

Now you can log in as the admin, add the recent topics, recent users, and favorite topic widgets to the widgetized area in the admin section, and save the changes. The final output of the home page will look like the following screenshot:

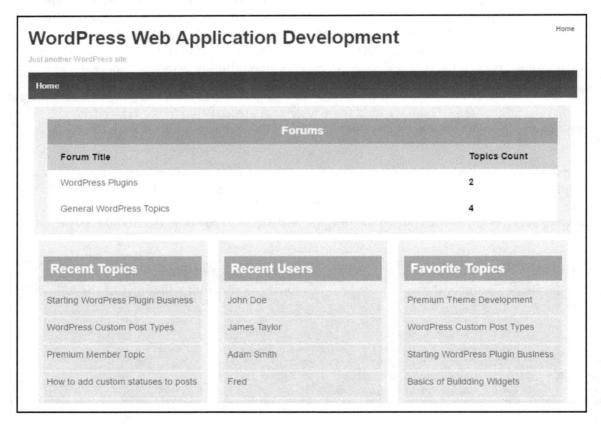

Generating the application frontend menu

Typically, a web application's frontend navigation menu varies from the backend menu. WordPress has a unique backend with the admin dashboard. Logged-in users will see the backend menu on the top of the frontend screens as well. In the previous chapter, we looked at various ways of customizing the backend navigation menu. Here, we will look at how the frontend menu works within WordPress.

Navigate to the `themes` folder and open the `header.php` file of the Responsive theme. You will find the implementation for the frontend menu using the `wp_nav_menu` function. This function is used to display the navigation menus generated from the **Appearance** section of the WordPress admin dashboard. As far as the forum application is concerned, we may need four different frontend menus for free members, premium members, moderators, and normal guest users. By default, WordPress uses the assigned menu or the default page list to display the menu. Here, we need to create four different navigation menus based on the user role.

Creating a navigation menu

We have to log in to the forum application as the administrator and navigate to **Appearance | Menus** to create new frontend menus. Now enter a menu name and click on the **Save Menu** button to create the menu. Now, your screen will look something similar to the following screenshot:

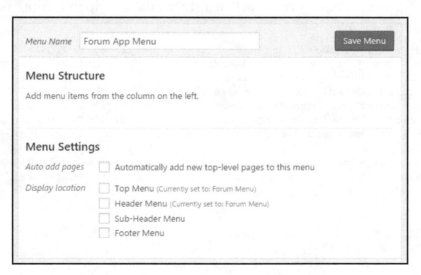

Once created, we have to add the menu items one by one using the items on the left side such as **Posts**, **Pages**, **Categories**, **Custom Links**, and so on. In this scenario, we need user role-specific menus. So, we have two ways of implementing the user role-based menus:

- Create four separate menus and load them based on the user role
- Use a single menu and add each menu item based on the user role

The first technique uses four separate menus and hence common menu items for all user roles will be duplicated. Therefore, we are going to discuss the second technique of creating a single menu and assign menu items to user roles. The first thing we need is the ability to define the allowed user roles for menu items. We can use custom menu fields to add these settings.

WordPress uses the `Walker_Nav_Menu_Edit` class for generating the settings for each menu item. However, it doesn't support custom menu fields by default. So we have to extend this class using our own class and add the necessary actions to support custom menu fields. Create a new class called `WPWAF_Walker_Nav_Menu_Edit` inside the `classes` folder by copying the contents of the WordPress `Walker_Nav_Menu_Edit` class. This class should extend the base class, as shown in the following code:

```php
<?php
class WPWAF_Walker_Nav_Menu_Edit extends Walker_Nav_Menu_Edit { }
?>
```

Then, we need to modify the sub class by including the `wp_nav_menu_item_custom_fields` action just after the description setting, as shown in the following code:

```
<p class="field-description description description-wide">
<label for="edit-menu-item-description-<?php echo $item_id; ?>">
<?php _e( 'Description' ); ?><br />
<textarea id="edit-menu-item-description-<?php echo $item_id; ?>"
class="widefat edit-menu-item-description" rows="3" cols="20"
name="menu-item-description[<?php echo $item_id; ?>]"><?php echo
esc_html( $item->description ); // textarea_escaped ?></textarea>

<span class="description"><?php _e('The description will be
displayed in the menu if the current theme supports it.'); ?></span>
</label>
</p>

<?php do_action( 'wp_nav_menu_item_custom_fields', $item_id, $item,
$depth, $args ); ?>
```

Now, we have to make WordPress of about the existence of this class. Let's add the `wp_edit_nav_menu_walker` filter and implement it inside the `WPWAF_Theme` class to include our custom `menu walker` class:

```
class WPWAF_Theme {
  public function __construct() {
     // Other actions and filters
     add_filter( 'wp_edit_nav_menu_walker', array( $this,
'edit_nav_menu_walker' ) );
  }
  public function edit_nav_menu_walker( $walker ) {
     require_once(WPWAF_PLUGIN_DIR . '/classes/class-wpwaf-walker-
nav-menu-edit.php' );
     return 'WPWAF_Walker_Nav_Menu_Edit';
  }
}
```

Now, we have to implement the `wp_nav_menu_item_custom_fields` action added inside the `WPWAF_Walker_Nav_Menu_Edit` class to include the settings for user role-based menu item restrictions. Let's update the constructor of the `WPWAF_Theme` class to include the following action:

```
add_action( 'wp_nav_menu_item_custom_fields', array( $this,
'menu_item_custom_fields' ), 10, 4 );
```

Next, we need to add the settings for restrictions after the description setting. Let's add the necessary HTML by implementing the `menu_item_custom_fields` function. The following code previews the implementation of this function:

```
   public function menu_item_custom_fields($item_id, $item,
$depth, $args ) {
      global $wp_roles;

      $user_roles = apply_filters( 'nav_menu_roles', $wp_roles-
>role_names, $item );

      $roles = (array) get_post_meta( $item->ID,
'wpwaf_nav_menu_roles', true );
      $visibility_level = get_post_meta( $item->ID,
'wpwaf_nav_menu_visibility_level', true );

      if($visibility_level == ''){
        $visibility_level = '0';
      }
   ?>

   <input type="hidden" name="nav-menu-role-nonce" value="<?php
```

```
       echo wp_create_nonce( 'nav-menu-nonce-name' ); ?>" />

          <div class="description-wide">
          <span class="description"><?php _e( "Visibility", 'wpwaf' );
?></span><br />
          <input type="hidden" class="nav-menu-id" value="<?php echo
   $item->ID ;?>" />

          <div class="logged-input-holder" style="float: left; width: 35%;">
          <select class="wpwaf_menu_visibility"
name='wpwaf_menu_visibility_<?php echo $item->ID ;?>'
id='wpwaf_menu_visibility_<?php echo $item->ID ;?>' >

          <option value='0' <?php selected('0',$visibility_level); ?>><?
php _e('Everyone','wpwaf'); ?></option>

               // Other options omitted here
          <option value='3' <?php selected('3',$visibility_level); ?>><?
php _e('By User Role','wpwaf'); ?></option>
          </select>
          </div>
          </div>
       // User role selection checkboxes
          <?php
    }
```

First, we get the available WordPress user roles using the global $wp_roles object and filtering with nav_menu_roles. Next, we get the saved user roles and visibility setting from the database for each menu item. Initially, we won't have any data and hence we set the **Visibility** to **0** to make it visible to everyone. Next, we add the nonce variable and HTML for the **Visibility** setting with existing database values. Finally, we have to include the checkboxes for user role selection.

User role selection code is omitted here as it's similar to the code we discussed in individual post restrictions. You can find the full source code inside the code folder for this chapter. Now you will see the settings to restrict menu items, as shown in the following screenshot:

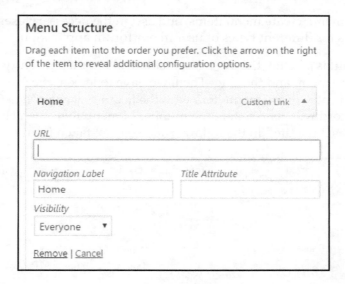

We can use this **Visibility** setting to define different restrictions for each menu item.

Saving menu item restrictions

The next task of this process is saving the restrictions for menu items. We can use the `WordPresswp_update_nav_menu_item` action to save the restriction details to the `wp_postmeta` table, as shown in the following implementation:

```
    public function update_nav_menu_item( $menu_id, $menu_item_db_id, $args
) {
        $new_visibility_level = isset(
$_POST['wpwaf_menu_visibility_'.$menu_item_db_id] ) ?
$_POST['wpwaf_menu_visibility_'.$menu_item_db_id] : '0';

        $visibility_roles = isset( $_POST['wpwaf_menu_roles']
[$menu_item_db_id] ) ? $_POST['wpwaf_menu_roles'][$menu_item_db_id] :
array();
update_post_meta( $menu_item_db_id, 'wpwaf_nav_menu_visibility_level',
$new_visibility_level );
    update_post_meta( $menu_item_db_id, 'wpwaf_nav_menu_roles',
$visibility_roles );
    }
```

This is a very basic function where we capture **Visibility** and **User Roles** from the form submission and save the values in the `wp_postmeta` table with plugin-specific keys. Now, we have the ability to add restrictions to menu items.

So, you can go the menu, create menu items, and assign the necessary user roles or other visibility conditions for different types of user in our forum application.

Once a custom menu is created, the `wp_terms` table will have a new entry for the menu with the name of the menu and the slug. Then, we have to look at the `wp_term_taxonomy` table for the related entry of the menu item with the taxonomy column defined as `nav_menu`. This record will also contain the number of menu items, which is displayed in the count column, as illustrated in the following screenshot taken from `phpMyAdmin`:

	term_taxonomy_id	term_id	taxonomy	description	parent	count
Edit Copy Delete	1	1	category		0	7
Edit Copy Delete	2	2	link_category		0	0
Edit Copy Delete	3	3	wpwaf_topic_category		0	0
Edit Copy Delete	5	5	wpwaf_topic_category		0	0
Edit Copy Delete	6	6	wpwaf_topic_tag		0	0
Edit Copy Delete	7	7	wpwaf_topic_tag		0	0
Edit Copy Delete	8	8	nav_menu		0	3

Finally, we have to look for the information about each and every menu item stored in the `wp_posts` table. All the menu items are stored as table rows in the `wp_posts` table with a `post_type` column named `nav_menu_item`. The `post_status` column stored as publish means that the menu item is active, while draft means that the menu item is inactive or deleted. Developers can use a combination of these three database tables with user roles and permissions to automate the menu creation process.

Displaying user-specific menus on the frontend

After having created user-specific menu items in the WordPress admin section, we can now move on to displaying them on the frontend. Open the `header.php` file of the Responsive theme and you will find the main menu defined as `header-menu` using the `theme_location` parameter. The main menu generation code is defined as follows:

```php
<?php  wp_nav_menu( array(
    'container'       => 'div',
    'container_class' => 'main-nav',
```

```
'fallback_cb'     => 'responsive_fallback_menu',
'theme_location'  => 'header-menu'    ) ); ?>
```

By default, this code will load the menu used for the **Header Menu** drop-down box in
Appearance | **Menus** | **Manage Locations**. We implemented the menu restriction-saving
process in earlier sections. However, we didn't restrict menu items based on those
conditions. So now we have to apply the restrictions to menu items on the header menu.
Let's start by adding the following code to the constructor of the WPWAF_Theme class:

```
if ( ! is_admin() ) {
add_filter( 'wp_get_nav_menu_items', array( &$this,
'restrict_nav_menu_items' ), 10, 3 );
}
```

We can use the wp_get_nav_menu_items filter to filter each menu item of the menu. This
filter returns all valid menu items. So all we have to do is verify the restrictions and remove
the menu items with restricted access. Let's look at the implementation of the
restrict_nav_menu_items function:

```
public function restrict_nav_menu_items( $items, $menu, $args ) {
  $hide_children_of = array();
  foreach ( $items as $key => $item ) {
    $visible = true;
    $visibility_level = get_post_meta( $item->ID,
'wpwaf_nav_menu_visibility_level', true );
    if(in_array( $item->menu_item_parent, $hide_children_of ) ){
      $visible = false;
      $hide_children_of[] = $item->ID;
    }

    if( $visible &&isset( $visibility_level ) ) {
    switch( $visibility_level ) {
      case '3' :
        $visibility_roles = (array) get_post_meta( $item->ID,
'wpwaf_nav_menu_roles', true );
        $visible = false;
        foreach ( $visibility_roles as $role ) {
          if ( current_user_can( $role ) )
            $visible = true;
        }
        break;
      }
    }

    $visible = apply_filters( 'nav_menu_roles_item_visibility',
$visible, $item );
    if ( ! $visible ) {
```

```
        $hide_children_of[] = $item->ID; // store ID of item
        unset( $items[$key] ) ;
      }
    }
    return $items;
}
```

First, we traverse through each menu item and get the visibility level that we saved in previous sections. Then, we check whether any menu item is predefined to be restricted and set the visible status to FALSE. Next, we use a `switch` statement to check the different visibility levels we created. Here, I have only included the code for user roles since it's our main requirement. Then, we check the added user roles with the user roles of the current user. If the user roles are matched, we set the visibility to TRUE and return the menu items. If the user roles are not matched, we set visibility to FALSE and remove the menu item from the array using unset. Finally, we will only have the permitted menu items on the array.

In web applications, we need user role-specific menus, and hence, we used restrictions on each menu item. Once logged in, each user will see the header menu with menu items specific to their user role. Now, we have a basic user role-based menu for the application.

Managing options and widgets with customizer

The WordPress theme customizer is a great feature for customizing a theme's settings and components from the frontend. This feature lets you preview those changes in real time and hence is useful for administrators. Generally, customizer is capable of editing the following sections in real time:

- **Site title** and **Tagline**
- **Colors**
- **Header Image**
- **Background Image**
- **Navigation**
- **Widgets**

The sections of the customizer are theme-dependent, and hence, you will see more or fewer sections in various themes. You can access the theme customizer by navigating to the **Appearance | Customize menu**. The following screenshot previews the default customizer screen of the **Responsive** theme for our forum application:

All these sections play a part in designing a website with WordPress. However, theme options and widgets are the most important components from the web development perspective, and hence, we will discuss the usage of options and widgets.

Adding custom options to the theme customizer

Apart from widgets, all other sections mentioned in the previous section are related to theme options. These are built-in options of any given theme. In web applications, we need the custom options panel to configure their features and design. In this section, we will learn how to add custom options to the theme customizer. After this chapter is completed, you can use these techniques to integrate the complete options page into the theme customizer.

Assume that we want to let an admin customize the text color of one of the application-specific components. First, we need to add a custom options section to the theme customizer. Then, we can add the necessary options as settings into the main section. Let's modify the constructor of `WPWAF_Theme` to add the following actions:

```
add_action('customize_register',array($this,'customize_panel'));
add_action( 'wp_head', array($this,'apply_custom_settings'));
```

WordPress uses the `customize_register` action to add custom sections to the theme customizer. Next, we use the `wp_head` action to apply the options to our application. We can start by implementing the `customize_panel` function, as shown in the following code:

```
public function customize_panel( $wp_manager ){
  $wp_manager->add_section( 'wpwaf_settings_section', array(
    'title' => __('WPWAF Settings','wpwa'),
    'priority' => 35 ) );
  $wp_manager->add_setting( 'color_setting', array(
    'default' => '#000000' ) );
  $wp_manager->add_control( new WP_Customize_Color_Control(
    $wp_manager, 'color_setting', array(
    'label' => __('Text Color','wpwaf'),
    'section' => 'wpwaf_settings_section',
    'settings' => 'color_setting',
    'priority' => 6  ) ) );
}
```

First, we add a custom section called **WPWAF Settings** for our custom options. This code will add an additional tab to the customizer tabs on the left. Then, we add a setting called `color_setting` to specify the text color of a specific element within the application. Finally, we add an input control for the setting using the `add_control` function. In this scenario, we are using the `WP_Customize_Color_Control` class as we need a color picker. You can find other available input control types at `http://codex.wordpress.org/Class_Reference/WP_Customize_Manager/add_control`.

Now, refresh the theme customizer and you will see our new **WPWAF Settings** section, as shown in the following screenshot:

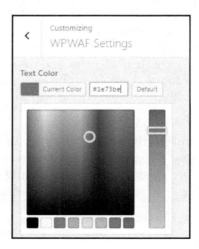

Once the setting is defined, we have to apply it to the website. Here, we are changing the text color, and hence, our CSS should be updated while changing the color of this setting. Consider the following implementation of the `apply_custom_settings` function to apply the setting to the website:

```
function apply_custom_settings(){  ?>
  <style>  body {
  color: <?php echo get_theme_mod('color_setting' ); ?>;
  }  </style>
<?php
}
```

We can get the value of settings by passing the settings field key to the `get_theme_mod` function. In this example, we are applying the color to the page `<body>` tag. Ideally, you should target application-specific design elements using these settings. Now, you can change the text color from our new setting control and the font color of the page will be changed in real time. This technique can be used to add advanced settings panels into the theme customizer to simplify the customizing process and saving time on backend operations.

Handling widgets in the theme customizer

Widgets are heavily used in web application development, and hence, we need to know how to use them within the theme customizer. We can access widgets by clicking on the **Widgets** tab in the customizer panel. The following screenshot previews the default widget areas of our application:

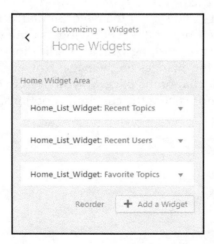

We created a custom widget area called **Home Widgets**, and it contains the three widgets assigned in the previous sections. Changing widget configurations is quite a simple task. Take a look at the following steps:

1. Click on the arrow on the right side to open the **Recent Topics** widget. You will get a screen similar to the following one with available widget options:

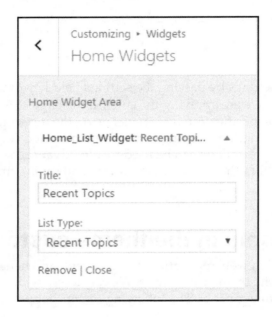

2. Now, change the **Title** or **List Type** values and it's immediately applied to the widget on the right-hand side of the page. Similarly, we can check any type of advanced widget settings and test our widgets until we get the expected output. In this scenario, we are working with an application-specific widget area, and hence, you can see the changes on the page. However, normal widgets are displayed on the sidebar of the page. So you need to open a normal post/page with the sidebar before using the customizer options.

3. The last task in this section is to identify how we can add new widgets into widget areas without using the backend functionality. You can click the **Add a Widget** button and it will open up a screen similar to the following one:

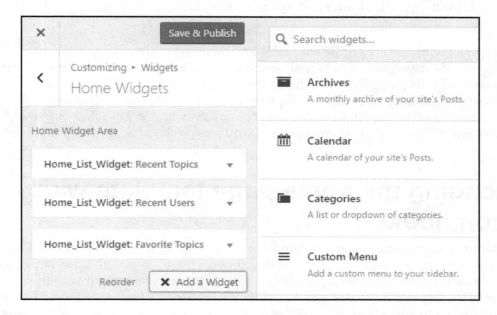

We can search widgets from the available list and click on one to add it to the selected widgets area.

 All changes made through the theme customizer are temporary for previewing purposes and will not be saved until you click the **Save and Publish** button.

We discussed the importance of the theme customizer and how we can adapt and customize it for web applications. Now, it's time for you to integrate the application options panel into the theme customizer.

Creating pluggable templates

Templates can be categorized into several types based on their functionality. Each of these types of template plays a different role within complex applications. The proper combination of these template types can result in highly maintainable and reusable applications. Let's explore the functionality of the various template types.

The simplest type of template contains the complete design for each and every screen in the application. These types of template are not reusable. We can also have template parts that get included into some other main templates. These types of template are highly reusable across multiple templates. Header and footer are the most common examples of such templates.

These types of template are highly adaptable and flexible for future enhancements or the modification of existing features. WordPress provides the capability to create similar types of templates with its pluggable architecture by using action hooks. There is a drastic difference between the way reusable templates work in WordPress and normal web applications. However, the final output is quite similar in nature. Let's find out how pluggable templates are created and used in WordPress web applications.

Extending the home page template with action hooks

Let's identify the practical usage of action hooks in pluggable templates for extending web application layouts. In earlier sections, we developed a home page with three widgets with a reusable template inside a dynamic widget area. Now, we have to figure out the extendable locations of those widgets. Consider the following scenario--Assume that we have been asked to add a button in front of each topic in the home page **Recent Topics** widget. Users who are logged in to the application can click on the button to instantly mark topics as favorites. The implementation of this requirement needs to be done without affecting or changing the other two widgets. Also, we have to plan for similar future requirements for other widgets.

The most simple and preferred way of many beginner-level developers is to create three separate templates for the widgets and directly assign the button to the widget by modifying the existing code. As a developer, you should be familiar with the open-closed principle. Let's see the Wikipedia definition of the open-closed principle:

"software entities (classes, modules, functions, etc.) should be open for extension, but closed for modification."

This means we should never change the working components of the application. Hence, changing the widget to add the new requirement is not the ideal method. Instead, we should be looking at extending the existing components. So, we need to make use of WordPress action hooks to define extendable areas in the widget.

Customizing widgets to enable extendable locations

The following are the steps to customize widgets to enable extendable locations:

1. First, let's modify the widget template with extendable hooks. Ideally, this should have been done in the initial stage of widget creation. Open the `home-list-template.php` file inside the `templates` folder and replace the existing code with the following code:

```
<div class='home_list_item'>
<div class='list_panel'>
<?php foreach($home_list_data ["records"] as $record){
 ?>
<div class='list_row'>
<a href=''><?php echo $record['title']; ?></a>
<?php
do_action('wpwaf_home_widgets_controls',$record['type'],$record['ID']);
?></div>
<?php } ?>
</div>
</div>
```

   Here, we included an action hook named `wpwaf_home_widgets_controls`, which takes two parameters for the action type and ID of the record. This widget layout is applied for multiple widgets, and hence, we don't want the action to be executed for all available widgets. Therefore, we use the type parameter to check for widgets that require the `do_action` call. The second parameter is that an ID will be used to execute functions for these records. Here, it will be used to identify the topic to be marked as favorite.

2. Next, we have to change the widget code to pass the type parameter. We must pass a value for widgets that require `wpwaf_home_widgets_controls`. Otherwise, keep it blank to skip the action execution. In this scenario, we will be passing a value named favorite as the type parameter.

3. Then, we need to implement the `wpwaf_home_widgets_controls` action by including an `add_action` definition. Place the following action inside the constructor of the `WPWAF_Theme` class in the main plugin:

```
add_action('wpwaf_home_widgets_controls', array($this,
'home_widgets_controls'), 10, 2);
```

The preceding code defines the `wpwaf_home_widgets_controls` action with the default priority of the `10` and `2` parameters. Finally, we have to implement the `home_widgets_controls` function to output the `Mark Favorite` button to the widget list, as shown in the following code:

```
public function home_widgets_controls($type, $id) {
    if ($type == 'favorite') {
        echo "<input type='button' class='$type' id='" . $type .    "_"
. $id . "' data-id='$id' value='" . __('Mark Favorite','wpwaf') .    "' />";
    }
}
```

This function uses the two parameters passed by the `do_action` call. After validating the type, we can output the `Mark Favorite` button with the necessary attributes and CSS classes. Now, you will have a screen similar to the following screenshot with the new **Mark Favorite** button:

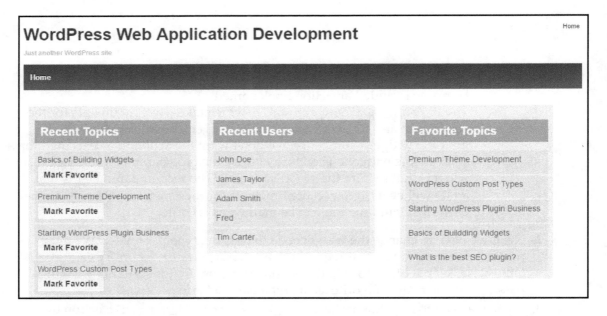

Once the button is clicked, we can use the `data-id` attribute to get the topic ID and make an AJAX request to execute the **Mark Favorite** operation.

With the latest modifications, the home page widgets have become highly flexible for future modifications. Now, developers have the ability to add more functionality through the control buttons without changing the existing source code. Let's summarize the list of tasks for adding new features to the widgets:

- Pass a type value to the template with widget data
- Implement the action using the `add_action` function with the necessary parameters
- Use the priority value to change the order of the control buttons
- Check the type value and generate the necessary HTML code

WordPress action hooks are a powerful technique for extending themes and plugins with dynamic features. Developers should always look to create extendable areas in their themes and plugins. Basically, you need to figure out the areas where you might get future enhancements and place action hooks upfront for easier maintenance.

Planning action hooks for layouts

Usually, WordPress theme developers build template files using unique designs and place the action hooks later. These hooks are mainly placed before and after the main content of the templates. This technique works well for designing themes for websites. However, a web application requires flexible templates, and hence, we should be focusing on optimizing the flexibility as much as possible. So the planning of hook points needs to be done prior to designing. Consider the following sample template code of a typical structure of a hook-based template:

```php
<?php do_action('before_menu'); ?>
<div class='menu'>
<div class='menu_header'>Header</div>
<ul><li>Item 1</li>
<li>Item 2</li></ul>
</div>
<?php do_action('after_menu'); ?>
```

The preceding code is well structured for extending using action hooks. However, we can only add new content before and after the menu container. There is no way to change the content inside the menu container. Let's see how we can increase the flexibility using the following code:

```php
<?php do_action('before_menu'); ?>
<?php do_action('menu'); ?>
<?php do_action('after_menu'); ?>
```

Now, the template contains three action hooks instead of hardcoded HTML. So the original plugin or theme developer must implement the action hook using the following code:

```
add_action('menu','create_dynamic_menu');
function create_dynamic_menu(){
  echo "<div class='menu'>
  <div class='menu_header'>Header</div>
  <ul><li>Item 1</li>
  <li>Item 2</li></ul>
  </div>";
}
```

So the base theme also uses hooks to embed the template code. Now it's possible to change the inner components of the menu using another set of action hooks.

> Even though the echo statement is used to simplify explanations, this HTML code needs to be generated using a separate template file in ideal scenarios.

Let's see how we can override the original menu template with our own template at runtime using the following code:

```
remove_action('menu','create_dynamic_menu');
add_action('menu','create_alternative_dynamic_menu');
function create_alternative_dynamic_menu (){
  echo "<div class='menu'>
  <div class='menu_header'>Header</div>
  <ol><li>Item 1</li>
  <li>Item 2</li></ol>
  </div>";
}
```

First, we have to remove the original implementation of the menu using the remove_action function. The syntax of remove_action should match exactly with the add_action definition to make things work. Once removed, we implement the same action with a different function to provide a different template to the original template. This is a very useful way of extending and overriding an existing functionality. In order to use this technique, you have to plan the action hooks from the initial stage of the project. Now, you should have a clear idea about advanced template creation techniques in WordPress.

Managing custom CSS with live preview

Generally, we use customized versions of themes and plugins to build applications without developing all features from scratch. Even in this book, we had to use a theme and some plugins while developing the major requirements from scratch. So, when using combinations of themes and other plugins, we tend to get styling issues as these plugins and themes are not fully compatible with one another. Therefore, it's almost a must that we customize features and designs of these plugins to create a uniform design.

Custom CSS plays a major role in customizing the styles of these themes and plugins. Until recently, we had to use a style sheet of child theme or external plugins to add custom CSS. WordPress 4.7 introduced a feature for custom CSS, where we can add CSS through theme customizer and preview the changes instantly. Let's look at how we can add and preview CSS using the following screenshot:

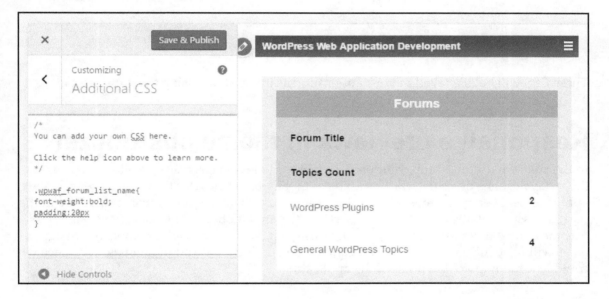

You can find the **Additional CSS** section in the bottom of the left menu in the theme customizer. We can add dynamic CSS in the left area and it will be instantly updated on the right side as shown in the screenshot. Once testing is completed, you can **Save & Publish** the changes and it will be saved permanently. This is not a theme-specific feature and this CSS section is generated from the WordPress core using the following code in the wp-includes/class-wp-customize-manager.php file:

```
$custom_css_setting = new WP_Customize_Custom_CSS_Setting( $this,
sprintf( 'custom_css[%s]', get_stylesheet() ), array(
    'capability' => 'edit_css',
    'default' =>sprintf( "/*\n%s\n*/", __( "You can add your own CSS
here.\n\nClick the help icon above to learn more." ) ),) );

$this->add_setting( $custom_css_setting );
$this->add_control( 'custom_css', array(
    'type'     => 'textarea',
    'section'  => 'custom_css',
    'settings' => array( 'default' => $custom_css_setting->id ),
    'input_attrs' =>array(
            'class' => 'code',      ),) );
```

These CSS will be displayed in your application as inline styles using the <style> tag.

Responsive previews in theme customizer

In the past, we used desktop computers or laptops to access large web applications. But these days users tend to use various kinds of mobile-based devices to access large web applications. Even e-commerce based applications are available on mobile and, unlike in the past, users are not afraid of doing transactions through mobiles. So responsive design has become a must in website and application design. If we don't consider responsive design, users will have major limitations in accessing the application through mobiles and hence we could lose many potential users of the application.

Until recently, we had to use other plugins or third-party services to check the responsiveness of your application screens. WordPress 4.5 introduced responsive previews in the theme customizer where we can check different screen sizes instantly without needing any other service. We can go to **Theme Customizer** and you will see the various screen icons at the bottom of the left menu, as shown in the following screenshot:

As you can see, we have selected the smallest icon for mobiles and the screen on the right is adjusted to show our application in a mobile screen. Now, we can instantly change CSS, fix any issues, and check again in all the screen sizes.

This is an awesome and time-saving feature to fix issues in your designs. You can also add/remove different screen sizes using the filters available in WordPress.

Time for action

In this chapter, we discussed some of the advanced techniques in WordPress themes. Developers who don't have any exposure to advanced application development with WordPress might find it a bit difficult to understand these techniques. Therefore, I suggest you to try the following tasks to get familiar with the advanced theme creation techniques:

- Automate the process of frontend menu item creation. The admin should be able to add menu items to multiple navigation menus in a single event or the complete menu should be generated based on permission levels.
- Complete the process of marking topics as favorites using AJAX and the necessary WordPress actions.
- We implemented user role-based restrictions for menu items. Try to use the same technique to add user role-based restrictions to widgets.

Summary

The frontend of an application presents the backend data to the user in an interactive way. The possibility of requesting frontend changes in an application is relatively high as compared to the backend. Therefore, it's important to make the application's design as stylish and as flexible as possible. Advanced web applications will require complex layouts that can be extended by new features. Planning for the future is important, and hence, we prioritized the content of this chapter to talk about extending the capabilities of WordPress theme files using a widgetized architecture and custom action hooks.

We also had a look at the integration of custom hooks with widgetized areas while building the basic home page for the forum application. A navigation menu is vital for providing access to templates based on user roles and permissions. Here, we looked at how we can manage frontend menu items based on user roles and how to display them on the frontend. Finally, we looked to how to use the WordPress theme customizer with instant previews.

In the next chapter, we will look at the use of an open source plugin within WordPress. In web application development, developers usually don't get enough time to build things from scratch. So it's important to make use of existing open source libraries for rapid development. Get ready to experience the usage of popular, open source libraries within WordPress.

9
Enhancing the Power of Open Source Libraries and Plugins

WordPress is one of the most popular open source frameworks, serving millions of people around the world. The WordPress core itself uses dozens of open source libraries to power existing features. Web application development is a time-consuming affair compared to generic websites. Hence, developers get very limited opportunities for building everything from the ground up, creating the need for using stable open source libraries.

With the latest versions, WordPress has given higher priority for using stable and trending open source libraries within its core. Backbone.js, Underscore.js, and jQuery masonry are recent popular additions among such open source library. Inclusion of these types of libraries gives a hint about the improvement of WordPress as a web development framework.

We will discuss the various use of these existing open source libraries within the core and how to adapt them into our applications. This chapter also includes some popular techniques such as social logins, to illustrate the integration of external libraries that don't come with the core WordPress framework.

In this chapter, we will cover the following topics:

- Open source libraries inside WordPress core
- Open source JavaScript libraries in WordPress core
- Creating a forum user profile page with Backbone.js
- Integrating Backbone.js and Underscore.js
- Understanding the importance of code structuring
- Using PHPMailer for custom e-mail sending
- Implementing user authentication with OpenAuth

- Building a LinkedIn app
- Authenticating users to our application

So, let's get started!

Why choose open source libraries?

Open source frameworks and libraries are taking control of web development. On the one hand, they are completely free and allow developers to customize and create their own versions, while on the other, large communities are building around open source frameworks. Hence, these frameworks are improving in leaps and bounds at an increasing speed, providing developers with more stable and bug-free versions. WordPress uses dozens of open source libraries and there are thousands of open source plugins in its plugins directory. Therefore, it's important to know how to use these open source libraries in order to make our lives easier as developers. Let's consider some of the advantages of using stable open source products:

- A large community support
- The ability to customize existing features by changing source code
- No fees are involved based on per-site or per-person licensing
- Usually reliable and stable

These reasons prove why WordPress uses these libraries to provide features, and why developers should be making use of them to build complex web applications.

Open source libraries inside the WordPress core

As mentioned earlier, there are several libraries available within the core that have yet to be noticed by many WordPress developers. Most beginner-level developers tend to include such libraries in their plugins when it's already available inside the core framework. This happens purely due to the nature of WordPress development, where most development is done for generic websites with very limited dynamic content.

As we move into web application development, we should understand the need for using existing libraries whenever possible due to the following reasons:

- WordPress contains libraries that are more stable and compatible
- Using a WordPress built-in library prevents conflicts in using different version of the same library
- This also prevents the duplication of libraries and reduces the size of project files

I am sure you are familiar with libraries and plugins such as `jQuery` and `TinyMCE` within WordPress. Let's discover lesser-known and recently added libraries in order to make full use of them with web applications.

Open source JavaScript libraries in the WordPress core

Most open source JavaScript libraries are located inside the `wp-includes/js` folder of your WordPress installation. Let's take a look at the following screenshot for JavaScript libraries available with WordPress 4.7:

crop	customize-preview.js	media-grid.js	wp-auth-check.js	wp-pointer.min.js
imgareaselect	customize-preview.min.js	media-grid.min.js	wp-auth-check.min.js	wp-util.js
jcrop	customize-preview-nav-menus.js	media-models.js	wp-backbone.js	wp-util.min.js
jquery	customize-preview-nav-menus.min.js	media-models.min.js	wp-backbone.min.js	zxcvbn.min.js
mediaelement	customize-preview-widgets.js	media-views.js	wp-custom-header.js	zxcvbn-async.js
plupload	customize-preview-widgets.min.js	media-views.min.js	wp-custom-header.min.js	zxcvbn-async.min.js
swfupload	customize-selective-refresh.js	quicktags.js	wpdialog.js	
thickbox	customize-selective-refresh.min.js	quicktags.min.js	wpdialog.min.js	
tinymce	customize-views.js	shortcode.js	wp-embed.js	
admin-bar.js	customize-views.min.js	shortcode.min.js	wp-embed.min.js	
admin-bar.min.js	heartbeat.js	swfobject.js	wp-embed-template.js	
autosave.js	heartbeat.min.js	twemoji.js	wp-embed-template.min.js	
autosave.min.js	hoverIntent.js	twemoji.min.js	wp-emoji.js	
backbone.min.js	hoverIntent.min.js	tw-sack.js	wp-emoji.min.js	
colorpicker.js	imagesloaded.min.js	tw-sack.min.js	wp-emoji-loader.js	
colorpicker.min.js	json2.js	underscore.min.js	wp-emoji-loader.min.js	
comment-reply.js	json2.min.js	utils.js	wp-emoji-release.min.js	
comment-reply.min.js	masonry.min.js	utils.min.js	wplink.js	
customize-base.js	mce-view.js	wp-a11y.js	wplink.min.js	
customize-base.min.js	mce-view.min.js	wp-a11y.min.js	wp-list-revisions.js	
customize-loader.js	media-audiovideo.js	wp-ajax-response.js	wp-list-revisions.min.js	
customize-loader.min.js	media-audiovideo.min.js	wp-ajax-response.min.js	wp-lists.js	
customize-models.js	media-editor.js	wp-api.js	wp-lists.min.js	
customize-models.min.js	media-editor.min.js	wp-api.min.js	wp-pointer.js	

As you can see, there are a large number of built-in libraries inside the `wp-includes/js` folder. WordPress uses jQuery for most of its core features, and hence, there is a separate folder for jQuery-related libraries, for example, `jQuery UI`, `Masonry`, `jQuery Form` plugin, and many more. Developers can use all of these libraries inside their own plugins and themes without duplicating the files. `Backbone.js` and `Underscore.js` are the latest additions to the WordPress core. These two libraries are becoming highly popular among web developers for building modularized client-side code for large-scale applications. WordPress integration with `Backbone.js` and `Underscore.js` has been rarely explained in online resources. So we will look at the integration of these two libraries into the forum application and to identify the use of JavaScript libraries included in the WordPress core.

What is Backbone.js?

`Backbone.js` has been one of the most trending open source libraries in the last few years for building large-scale JavaScript-based applications. It's a light-weight library that depends on `Underscore.js` and `jQuery`. Let's look at the official definition from `http://backbonejs.org/` to identify its importance:

> *"Backbone.js gives structure to web applications by providing* **models** *with key-value binding and custom events,* **collections** *with a rich API of enumerable functions,* **views** *with declarative event handling, and connects it all to your existing API over a RESTful JSON interface."*

The preceding definition contains a number of important aspects required for web application development. We already discussed the importance of separating concerns in web application development throughout the first few chapters of this book. The MVC architecture is heavily used in server-side implementation for separating these concerns. However, most developers, including experienced ones, don't use such techniques in client-side scripting, which results in code that is very hard to manage. `Backbone.js` provides a very flexible solution by structuring client-side code to work in the MVC type process. Backbone is neither a truly MVC/MVP nor MVVM framework, and it's restricted to models and views, as the role of controllers is ambiguous. Generally, `Backbone.js` views play the role of controllers as well. Although it's not pure MVC, it's good enough to handle complex code structuring on the client side.

The last part of the `Backbone.js` definition mentions the RESTful JSON interface. **Representational State Transfer** (**REST**) is emerging as a popular architectural style and will become the trend in future with the use of JavaScript-based applications. You can learn more about RESTful architecture at
`http://www.restapitutorial.com/lessons/whatisrest.html`.

The future of web application development will heavily depend on JavaScript and HTML5, and hence it's a must to get a head start as developers to learn these popular frameworks.

Understanding the importance of code structuring

Typically, WordPress developers tend to focus more on design aspects of the application compared to development aspects. Hence, we can find a large number of WordPress plugins with messy client-side code filled up with jQuery events. Let's see the importance of structuring code by looking at a practical scenario. Consider the following screenshot for displaying the forum member profile of the forum management application:

Personal Information

Full Name
John Doe

Topics

Add New

Topic Title	Topic Description	Sticky Status
Starting WordPress Plugin Business		normal
WordPress Custom Post Types		normal
Premium Member Topic		normal
What is the best SEO plugin?		normal

Consider the **Topics** section of the screenshot where we have a data grid generated on a page load using AJAX. There is an **Add New** button that creates new records on the database using another AJAX request. Even though it's not shown, we need edit and delete actions in the future to complete the functionality of the grid. So, let's see how developers implement these tasks with jQuery:

```
$(document).ready(function(){
    // Create the AJAX request to load the initial data
    // Generate the HTML code to update the grid
    $("#add_btn").click(function(){
        // Create the AJAX request to save the data
```

```
      // Generate the HTML code to update the grid
    });
    $("#edit_btn").click(function(){
      // Create the AJAX request to update the data
      // Generate the HTML code to update the grid
    });
    $("#del_btn").click(function(){
      // Create the AJAX request to save the data
      // Generate the HTML code to update the grid
    });
});
```

There are four events to implement the given tasks. As the application scales, we will have hundreds of such events within the JavaScript files. The HTML code is placed all over, inline with these event handling functions. It's almost impossible for another developer to identify the code required for any given screen.

Now, let's see how `Backbone.js` solves this issue in combination with `Underscore.js`. Let's take a look at the advantages of using `Backbone.js`, compared to the events-based structure of jQuery:

- Separates concerns using models, views, and collections
- Template generation is done separately with Underscore.js
- Matching client-side data with server-side database models
- Organizing data into collections and synchronizing with the server
- The ability to listen to changes in models instead of UI elements

Basically, `Backbone.js` offers all the features required for building scalable applications. Also, we can use other libraries with `Backbone.js` to cater to a specific functionality such as DOM handling.

Integrating Backbone.js and Underscore.js

We started the process of integrating `Backbone.js` and `Underscore.js` to identify the use of the JavaScript libraries provided with the WordPress core. Let's begin the integration by loading these libraries into WordPress. The following code illustrates how we can include these existing libraries into plugins:

```
function include_scripts() {
  wp_enqueue_script('backbone');
}
add_action('wp_enqueue_scripts', 'include_scripts');
```

The preceding code loads the `Backbone.js` library on the frontend of the application with the necessary dependencies such as `jQuery` and `Underscore.js`. We can load all the other libraries with a similar technique. Take a look at the available JavaScript libraries by visiting the *Default Scripts Included and Registered by WordPress* section of `http://codex.wordpress.org/Function_Reference/wp_enqueue_script`. You can use the value of the **Handle** column as the parameter for the `wp_enqueue_script` function to load the library into the plugin.

Creating a forum user profile page with Backbone.js

We looked at the basic structure for a forum user profile page at the beginning of the *Understanding the importance of code structuring* section. In this section, we will implement the mentioned tasks with the use of `Backbone.js` and `Underscore.js`. As usual, we will update our main forum management plugin with the necessary code.

Our first task will be to load the personal information of forum users. First, we need some custom rewrite rules to handle the routing for the `Backbone.js`-based user profile screen. Let's start by creating the necessary action hooks to handle the custom routing. We already have a custom route handler function called `manage_user_routes` in the `WPWAF_Config_Manager` class of the forum plugin. Let's update the function to include the new custom rewrite rules, as shown in the following code:

```
public function manage_user_routes() {
    add_rewrite_rule('^user/([^/]+)/([^/]+)/?',
    'index.php?control_action=$matches[1]&record_id=$matches[2]',
'top');
    add_rewrite_rule( '^user/([^/]+)/?',
'index.php?control_action=$matches[1]', 'top' );
    }
```

In this scenario, we need another rewrite rule for working with the ID parameter. Hence, we have introduced another rule to match the `user /([^/]+)/([^/]+)`. The first parameter will take the control action, while a second parameter called `record_id` is used for the ID of the forum user. This rule can be reused across all the editor load functions by ID.

 The forum user frontend profile can be accessed by using `/user/profile/ID` where ID is the unique ID in the `wp_users` table.

We have to also register a new query variable for `record_id`. So we can update our existing `manage_user_routes_query_vars` function, as shown in the following code:

```
public function manage_user_routes_query_vars( $query_vars ) {
    $query_vars[] = 'control_action';
    $query_vars[] = 'record_id';
    return $query_vars;
}
```

Next, we have to load the profile page through a custom controller. We already have a controller in the `WPWAF_Config_Manager` class using the `front_controller` function. Let's update the existing `front_controller` function to include the new control action for this section:

```
public function front_controller() {
    global $wp_query,$wpwaf;
    $control_action = isset ( $wp_query->query_vars['control_action'] ) ?
$wp_query->query_vars['control_action'] : '';

    switch ( $control_action ) {
      // Other actions

      case 'activate':
        do_action( 'wpwaf_before_activate_user' );
        $wpwaf->registration->activate_user();
        do_action( 'wpwaf_after_activate_user' );
        break;

      case 'profile':
        do_action( 'wpwaf_before_create_profile' );
        $record_id = isset($wp_query->query_vars['record_id']) ?
$wp_query->query_vars['record_id'] : '' ;
        $forum_member_id = $record_id;
        $wpwaf->user->create_forum_member_profile($forum_member_id);
        do_action( 'wpwaf_after_create_profile' );
        break;

     default:
        break;
     }
    }
```

This is the same technique that we used in Chapter 2, *Implementing Membership Roles, Permissions, and Features*, for working with custom routing. We will introduce a new control action called profile. Here, we have an additional query parameter for the forum member ID named record_id. We have called the create_forum_member_profile function on an object called user. So we need a new class to handle user-specific functions. Create a new class called WPWAF_User inside the classes folder. We have to use the usual file inclusion and object creation for the WPWAF_User class.

Finally, we can look at the create_forum_member_profile function of the WPWAF_User class for generating forum member profile data:

```
    public function create_forum_member_profile($forum_member_id) {
        global $wpwaf,$wpwaf_topics_data,$wpwa_template_loader;

        $user_query = new WP_User_Query(array('include' => array(
$forum_member_id)));

        $wpwaf_topics_data = array();
        foreach ($user_query->results as $forum_member) {
          $wpwaf_topics_data['display_name'] =
$forum_member->data->display_name;
        }

        $current_user = wp_get_current_user();

        $wpwaf_topics_data['forum_member_status'] = ($current_user->ID ==
$forum_member_id);
        $wpwaf_topics_data['forum_member_id'] = $forum_member_id;
        $wpwaf_topics_data['forum_list'] = $wpwaf->forum->get_forum_list();

        $wpwa_template_loader->get_template_part("forum-member");
        exit;
    }
```

First, we use the WP_User_Query class to get the profile details of the forum member. At this stage, we only have the name of the forum member in the profile. So we will assign the name to the $wpwaf_topics_data array to be passed into the template.

Next, we will check whether the member of this profile is logged into the application to show or hide the **Add New** button on the topics screen. We also need to pass the available forums list to the template since a forum is required for creating a topic. So we need to create a new function called `get_forum_list` in the `WPWAF_Model_Forum` class, as shown in the following code:

```php
public function get_forum_list(){
    $forums = new WP_Query(array('post_type' => 'wpwaf_forum',
                    'post_status' => 'publish'));
    $data = array();

    if ($forums->have_posts()) : while ($forums->have_posts()) :
$forums->the_post();
        array_push($data, array("ID" => get_the_ID(), "forum_title" =>
get_the_title()));

    endwhile;
    endif;
    return $data;
}
```

Finally, we render the member template with the `$wpwa_template_loader` global object. This object is provided by the reusable template loader plugin that we created earlier in this book. In order to complete the initial page loading, we need to create the `forum-member-template.php` template inside the `templates` folder.

Here are the initial contents of the `forum-member-template.php` template:

```php
<?php
    global $wpwaf_topics_data;
    get_header();
?>
<div class='main_panel'>
<div class='forum_member_profile_panel'>
<h2><?php echo __('Personal Information','wpwaf'); ?></h2>
<div class='field_label'><?php echo __('Full Name','wpwaf'); ?></div>
<div class='field_value'><?php echo
esc_html($wpwaf_topics_data['display_name']); ?></div>
</div>
<?php get_footer(); ?>
```

At this stage, our forum member profile seems pretty simple as we only have one field to display. Now, we come to the complex part of the template, where we load the topics to the profile.

Update the `load_scripts` function of the `WPWAF_Forum` class to include the `Backbone.js` library and the script to handle forum member profile features, as shown in the following code snippet:

```
public function load_scripts(){
  global $wp_query;
  // Other scripts and styles

  wp_register_script('wpwaf-forum-member', WPWAF_PLUGIN_URL .'js/wpwaf-
forum-member.js', array('backbone'));
  wp_enqueue_script('wpwaf-forum-member');

  $member_id = isset($wp_query->query_vars['record_id']) ?
$wp_query->query_vars['record_id'] : '0';

  $config_array = array(
    'ajaxUrl' => admin_url('admin-ajax.php'),
    'memberID' => $member_id,
    'nameRequired' => __('Topic Title is required','wpwaf'),
    'descRequired' => __('Topic Content required','wpwaf'),
    'forumRequired' => __('Forum is required','wpwaf') );

  wp_localize_script('wpwaf-forum-member', 'wpwaForumMemberData',
$config_array);

}
```

We create a new JavaScript file called `wpwaf-forum-member.js` inside the `js` folder by providing the dependent library as `Backbone.js`. Now, you will have both `Backbone.js` and `Underscore.js` included. We have also used the `wp_localize_script` function to pass the WordPress AJAX URL and other necessary parameters into the `wpwa-forum-member.js` file.

Structuring with Backbone.js and Underscore.js

Here, we come to the most exciting part of working with `Backbone.js` inside WordPress. Defining the models, views, and collections are a major part of working with `Backbone.js`. Let's plan the structure before we get into the implementation.

The forum member profile should contain a list of topics created by the member. So the model in this scenario is `Topic` and the collection will be topics. The list of topics needs to be loaded as a dynamic table, and hence, we need a view/template for the topics list. First, we need to define these three components to get started with `Backbone.js`. Let's start with the creation of a model, as shown in the following code:

```
jQuery(document).ready(function($){
  var Topic =  Backbone.Model.extend({
    defaults: {
      topic_title: '',
      topic_content: '',
      topic_forum :'0',
    },
  });
});
```

Here, we have a very simple model named `Topic` for working with topics in the forum application. The details of the topics have been limited to title, content, and forum to simplify the explanations. Next, we can look at the collection of topics using the following code:

```
var TopicCollection = Backbone.Collection.extend({
  model: Topic,
  url:
wpwaForumMemberData.ajaxUrl+"?action=wpwaf_process_topics&forum_member_id="
+wpwaForumMemberData.memberID
  });
```

`Backbone.js` uses collections to store lists of models and listens to changes in specific attributes. So we have assigned the `Topic` model to the `TopicCollection` collection. Next, we have to define a URL for working with the model data from the server. Generally, this URL will be used to save, fetch, delete, and update data on the server.

These requests work in a RESTful manner. We will use the WordPress AJAX handler URL to manipulate the various requests from models. Therefore, we have used the AJAX handler URL with an action named `wpwaf_process_topics`, which will be responsible for handling all the requests for the `Topic` model.

This is not the place for learning basics of `Backbone.js`. So, I suggest that you familiarize yourself with the basic concepts of `Backbone.js` using the official documentation at `http://backbonejs.org`.

Now, let's look at the view for displaying a topic list for forum members:

```
var topicsList;
var TopicListView = Backbone.View.extend({
  el: $('#forum_member_topics'),
  initialize: function () {
    topicsList = new TopicCollection();
  }
});
var topicView  = new TopicListView();
```

Finally, we have the `Backbone.js` view for generating template data to the user screen. Here, you can see that the initialization of these components is handled by creating a new object of the `view` class. Therefore, we can assume that the view acts as the controller on most occasions.

The main container of the view is defined by the `el` attribute. Then, we initialized the collection of topics using the `TopicCollection` class. Now let's take a look at the remaining sections of the `forum-member-template.php` file for understanding the view. The following code is included after the profile information section:

```
<div id='forum_member_topics'>
<h2><?php echo __('Topics','wpwaf'); ?></h2>
<div >
<table id='wpwaf_list_topics'>
</table>
</div>
</div>
```

As defined in the view, this will be the main container used for displaying the topics list. Now, we have the definition of all the `Backbone.js` components required for this scenario.

Displaying the topics list on page load

Once the page load is completed, we need to fetch the topics from the server to be displayed on the profile page. So let's update the view with the necessary functions, as shown in the following code:

```
var TopicListView = Backbone.View.extend({
  el: $('#forum_member_topics'),
  initialize: function () {
    topicsList = new TopicCollection();
    topicsList.bind("change", _.bind(this.getData, this));
    this.getData();
  }
```

```
getData: function () {
  var obj = this;
  topicsList.fetch({
    success: function () {
      obj.render();
    }
  });
},
});
```

Inside the `initialize` function, we bind an event named `change` for the `topicsList` collection, to call a function named `getData`. This event will get fired whenever we change the items in the collection. Next, we call the `getData` function inside the `initialize` function.

The `getData` function is responsible for retrieving topics from the server. So we call the `fetch` function on the `topicsList` collection to generate a GET request to the server. Since the request is asynchronous, we have to wait until the `success` function is fired before proceeding with the callback to fetch topics. Once the request is completed, the `topicsList` collection will be populated with the list of topics from the server. Finally, we execute the `render` function to load the templates.

We have to understand the server-side implementation of this request before moving into the `render` function. So let's update the constructor of the `WPWAF_Model_Topic` class by adding the following action to enable AJAX requests on topics:

```
add_action('wp_ajax_nopriv_wpwaf_process_topics', array($this,
'process_topics'));
add_action('wp_ajax_wpwaf_process_topics', array($this,
'process_topics'));
```

Afterwards, we can look at the following code for the implementation of the `process_topics` function:

```
public function process_topics() {
    $request_data = json_decode(file_get_contents("php://input"));
    $forum_member = isset ($_GET['forum_member_id']) ?
$_GET['forum_member_id'] : '0';
    if (is_object($request_data) && isset ($request_data->topic_title ))
{
        // Saving and updating models
    } else {
        $result = $this->list_topics($forum_member);
        echo json_encode($result);
```

```
            exit;
        }
    }
```

All the requests to the server will be made by `Backbone.js` in a RESTful manner. So we have to use PHP input stream accessing techniques to get the data passed by `Backbone.js`. Here, we have used `php://input`, which allows us to read raw data of the request body.

The `php://input` stream is a read-only stream that allows you to read raw data from the request body. In the case of `POST` requests, it is preferable to use `php://input` instead of `$HTTP_RAW_POST_DATA` as it does not depend on the special `php.ini` directives. Moreover, for those cases where `$HTTP_RAW_POST_DATA` is not populated by default; it is a potentially less memory-intensive alternative to activating `always_populate_raw_post_data`. The `php://input` stream is not available with `enctype="multipart/form-data"`. More information on accessing various input/output streams can be found at `http://php.net/manual/en/wrappers.php.php`.

The backbone `fetch` function uses the `GET` request with no parameters, and hence, the `$request_data` variable will be empty. So the else part of the code will be invoked to call the `list_topics` function, to generate the topics list, as shown in the following code:

```php
    public function list_topics($forum_member_id) {
        $topics = new WP_Query(array('author' => $forum_member_id,
'post_type' => 'wpwaf_topic',
            'post_status' => 'publish','posts_per_page' => 15,  'orderby' =>
'date'));
        $data = array();

        if ($topics->have_posts()) : while ($topics->have_posts()) :
$topics->the_post();
        $topic_id = get_the_ID();
        $topic_content = get_the_content();
        $sticky_status = get_post_meta($topic_id,
'_wpwaf_topic_sticky_status', TRUE);

        array_push($data, array("ID" => $topic_id, "topic_title" =>
get_the_title(), "topic_status" => $sticky_status, "topic_content" =>
$topic_content));

        endwhile;
        endif;
        return $data;
    }
```

The latest topics of the specified forum member are retrieved using the `WP_Query` class. Each topic is set up as an array to be used as a model from the client side. Having completed the server-side code, now we can move back to the rendering part in Backbone. The latest versions of `Backbone.js` and `Underscore.js` require us to define the template upfront. So we can modify the initial view code as follows to include the `topic-list-template` template:

```
var TopicListView = Backbone.View.extend({
    el: $('#forum_member_topics'),
    template : _.template($('#topic-list-template').html()),
    initialize: function () {
      topicsList = new TopicCollection();
      topicsList.bind("change", _.bind(this.getData, this));
      this.getData();
    }
    // getData function
});
```

Now, we can look at the `render` function of the view, for populating data into the template, as shown in the following code:

```
render: function () {
    var header_data = $('#topic-list-header').html();
    template_data = this.template({ topics: topicsList.toJSON() });
                              $(this.el).find("#wpwaf_list_topics"
).html( header_data +template_data);
    return this;
  }
```

We start the `render` function by adding the topic list header content into the `header_data` variable using the jQuery `html` function.

Next, we pass the data returned from the fetch request into the `Underscore` template using a variable named `topics`. It's hard to understand the rest of the `render` function without looking at the template. So let's take a look at the two templates stored inside the `forum-member-template.php` file:

```
<script type="text/template" id="topic-list-template">
<% _.each(topics, function(topic) { %>
<tr class="topic_item">
<td><%= topic.topic_title %></td>
<td><%= topic.topic_content %></td>
<td><%= topic.topic_status %></td>
</tr>
<% }); %>
</script>
```

```
<script type="text/template" id="topic-list-header">
<tr >
<th><?php echo __('Topic Title','wpwaf'); ?></th>
<th><?php echo __('Topic Description','wpwaf'); ?></th>
<th><?php echo __('Sticky Status','wpwaf'); ?></th>
</tr>
</script>
```

Using `text/template` as the `script type` parameter is a common way of defining templates inside HTML files. The browser doesn't execute these client-side scripts due to the `text/template` type. Here, we have two templates, where the first one generates the list of topics using `Underscore.js` template variables. We can access the topics variable passed from the `render` function to generate the list. The data from the `Backbone.js` models can be accessed directly inside the template as objects using dot notation. The second template is used for the table header of the topics list.

Now, let's get back to the `render` function. The `render` function loads both of the preceding templates with necessary data. Then, we use the `el` element of the view to find the `#wpwaf_list_topics` table, and populate the output generated from the templates as the content using the `html` function. Now, we will get the data grid populated with the topics list on page load. So far, we have discussed the usage of the `Backbone.js` model, view, and collection. Next, we need the ability for the forum member to create new topics from the frontend.

Creating new topics from the frontend

The forum member profile page should be visible to all types of users, including the ones who are not logged in. So far, we have displayed the topics list on the initial page load. The owner of the profile page should be able to add, edit, or delete topics from the frontend after logging in to the application. This improves the user experience by avoiding the need to switch between the backend and frontend to update and preview data. Here, we will implement topic creation from the frontend. Therefore, the logged in forum member should get an **Add New** button on top of the topics list, as shown in the following screenshot:

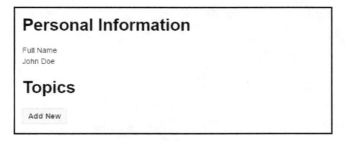

Let's update the `forum-member-template.php` template to include the **Add New** button, as illustrated in the following code:

```
<div id="msg_container"></div>
<?php if ($wpwaf_topics_data['forum_member_status']) { ?>
<input type='button' id="wpwaf_add_topic" value="<?php echo __('Add
New','wpwaf'); ?>" />
<?php } ?>
```

The preceding code is placed after the `Topics` heading in the `#forum_member_topics` container. We want the button to be displayed only for the owner of the profile. So we use the `forum_member_status` value passed from the `create_forum_member_profile` function. Once the button is clicked, the member should get a form for saving new topics.

Initially, the form is hidden and will be displayed on the click event of the button. So, let's add the hidden form to the `forum-member-template.php` template after the preceding code:

```
<div id='wpwaf_topic_add_panel' style='display:none' >
<div class='field_row'>
<div class='field_label'><?php echo __('Topic Title','wpwaf'); ?></div>
<div class='field_value'><input type='text' id='wpwaf_topic_title'
/></div>
</div>

<div class='field_row'>
<div class='field_label'><?php echo __('Topic Content','wpwaf');
?></div>
<div class='field_value'><textarea id='wpwaf_topic_content'
></textarea></div>
</div>
<div class='field_row'>
<div class='field_label'><?php echo __('Forum','wpwaf'); ?></div>
<div class='field_value'>
<select id="wpwaf_topic_forum">
<option value="0"><?php echo __('Select','wpwaf'); ?></option>
<?php foreach ($wpwaf_topics_data['forum_list'] as $forum_id => $forum)
{ ?>
<option value="<?php echo $forum['ID']; ?>"><?php echo
$forum['forum_title']; ?></option>
<?php } ?>
</select>
</div>
</div>

<div class='field_row'>
<div class='field_label'><input type='hidden'
```

```
id='wpwaf_topic_forum_member' value='<?php echo
$wpwaf_topics_data['forum_member_id']; ?>' /></div>
    <div class='field_value'><input type='button' id='wpwaf_topic_create'
value='<?php echo __('Save','wpwaf'); ?>' /></div>
    </div>
    </div>
```

The CSS `display:none` attribute is used to hide the `wpwaf_topic_add_panel` container on the initial page load. Inside the container, we have three fields for topic title, topic content, and forum with a save button called `#wpwaf_topic_create`. Now, we have to display the form by clicking the **Add New** button. Generally, we use a jQuery event handler on the button to cater to such requirements. However, we have already looked at how the code becomes hard to understand with the usage of jQuery events. So, we will use `Backbone.js` events to structure the code properly.

Integrating events to Backbone.js views

`Backbone.js` allows you to define events on each view, making it possible to restrict the scattering of events. This technique allows developers to quickly understand the events used for any given screen without having to search through all the code. Here, we need two events to display the topic creation form and submit the data to the server. Let's add the following code to the `TopicListView` variable created previously:

```
events: {
  'click #wpwaf_add_topic': 'addNewTopic',
  'click #wpwaf_topic_create': 'saveNewTopic'
},
addNewTopic: function(event) {
  $("#wpwaf_topic_add_panel").show();
}
```

As you can see, all the events are separated into a section called `events` inside the view. We have used a click event on `#wpwaf_add_topic` and `#wpwaf_topic_create` to call the `addNewTopic` and `saveNewTopic` functions, respectively. The `addNewTopic` function uses the jQuery `show` function to make the topic creation form visible to the forum member.

Once the button is clicked, your screen should look like the following screenshot:

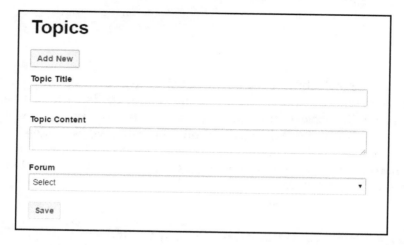

Next, we need to concentrate on the saving and validating process for new topics.

Validating and creating new models for the server

Form validation is very important in web development to avoid harmful invalid data and to keep the consistency in the database. Backbone.js automatically calls a validation function on the execution of the create function on a collection. Let's add the validate function to the Topic model with basic validations on topic title, topic content, and, forum, as shown in the following code:

```
var Topic =  Backbone.Model.extend({
   defaults: {
      topic_title: '',
      topic_content: '',
      topic_forum :'0'   },

   validate: function(attrs) {
      var errors = this.errors = {};

      if (!attrs.topic_title) errors.topic_title =
wpwaForumMemberData.nameRequired;
      if (attrs.topic_content == '') errors.topic_content =
wpwaForumMemberData.descRequired;
      if (attrs.topic_forum == '0') errors.topic_forum =
wpwaForumMemberData.forumRequired;

      if (!_.isEmpty(errors)){
```

```
            return errors;
        }
    }
});
```

The `validate` function is automatically executed before saving data to the server, by passing the attributes of the model as a parameter. We can execute the necessary validation within this function and return the errors as an object.

Creating new models in the server

This is the final section of the process for saving new topics to database. Now, we have to implement the `saveNewTopic` function defined in the events section, as shown in the following code:

```
saveNewTopic: function(event) {
  var options = {
    success: function (response) {
      if("error" == response.changed.status){ }
    },
    error: function (model, error) {
      console.log(error);
    }
  };

  var topic = new Topic();
  var topic_title = $("#wpwaf_topic_title").val();
  var topic_content = $("#wpwaf_topic_content").val();
  var topic_forum = $("#wpwaf_topic_forum").val();
  var forum_member_id = $("#wpwaf_topic_forum_member").val();

  topicsList.add(topic);
  topicsList.create({
    topic_title: topic_title,
    topic_content:topic_content,
    topic_forum : topic_forum,
    forum_member_id : forum_member_id
  },options);
}
```

First, we have a variable called `options` for defining success and failure functions for the topic creation. Here, we are logging the result values to the browser console. In real implementations, the result should be displayed to the user as a message.

Then, we create a new object of the `Topic` model by passing the data retrieved from the form fields. Later, the newly created model is assigned to the original topics collection retrieved in the initial page load. Remember that we defined the following line of code while implementing the `initialize` function of the view:

```
topicList.bind("change", _.bind(this.getData, this));
```

This event gets fired whenever the items in the collection are changed. Here, we have assigned a new model to the collection, and hence, this event will get fired. So the topics list will be updated without refreshing the page to contain the new model. Finally, we execute the `create` function on the collection to save a new topic to the database. This will generate a POST request to the AJAX action handler called `wpwaf_process_topics`. Finally, we complete the process by implementing the rest of the `process_topics` function, as shown in the following code:

```
public function process_topics() {
    global $wpdb;
    // Initialization code
    if (is_object($request_data) && isset($request_data->topic_title)) {
        $topic_title = isset($request_data->topic_title) ?
$request_data->topic_title : '';
        $topic_content = isset($request_data->topic_content) ?
$request_data->topic_content : '' ;
        $topic_forum = isset($request_data->topic_forum) ?
$request_data->topic_forum : '' ;

        $err = FALSE;
        $err_message = '';

        if ($topic_title == '') {
            $err = TRUE;
            $err_message .= __('Topic Title is required.','wpwaf');
        }
        if ($topic_content == '') {
            $err = TRUE;
            $err_message .= __('Topic Description is required.','wpwaf');
        }
        if ($topic_forum == '') {
            $err = TRUE;
            $err_message .= __('Topic Forum is required.','wpwaf');
        }
        if ($err) {
            echo json_encode(array('status' => 'error', 'msg' =>
$err_message));
            exit;
        } else {
```

```
            $current_user = wp_get_current_user();
            $topic_details = array(
                'post_title' => esc_html($topic_title),
                'post_content' => esc_html($topic_content),
                'post_status' => 'publish',
                'post_type' => 'wpwaf_topic',
                'post_author' => $current_user->ID );

            $result = wp_insert_post($topic_details);
            if (is_wp_error($result)) {
              echo json_encode(array('status' => 'error', 'msg' => $result));
            } else {
              update_post_meta($result, "_wpwaf_topic_sticky_status",
    'normal');
              $topic_relations_table = $wpdb->prefix.'p2p';
                $wpdb->insert(
                  $topic_relations_table,
                  array(
                    'p2p_from' => $result,
                    'p2p_to' => $topic_forum,
                    'p2p_type' => 'topics_to_forums',
                  ),
                  array(
                    '%d',
                    '%d',
                    '%s'
                  )
                );
              echo json_encode(array('status' => 'success'));
            }
          }
        }
      exit;
    } else {
    // Generating topics list and sending to template
    }
  }
```

Earlier, we discussed the initial request data gathering technique and the `else` statement while fetching data from server. Now, we will look at the `if` statement for saving new topic data. We can get the topic data from the `$request_data` object. It's important to validate data on both the client side as well as the server side. Earlier, we implemented client-side validation using `Backbone.js`. Here, we have used the server-side validations for all the input parameters. In case validation errors are generated, we pass a JSON array containing the status and the error message.

When the input data is successfully validated, we create a new topic using the `wp_insert_post` function with the basic topic details. Once the topic is successfully saved, we can execute `update_post_meta` functions to save additional metadata. So we save the topic sticky status as normal since users are creating topics from the frontend. Then the admin can verify the topics and modify the sticky status as needed. Here, we also have forum input, which is considered as the relationship between topic and forum. Therefore, we use a custom insert query on the **p2p** table in order to add a topics-forums relationship and make it compatible with the `Posts 2 Posts` plugin.

So we have come to the end of a long process identifying the basic usage of `Backbone.js` and `Underscore.js` in WordPress frontend. In the last part, we learned the uses of the `Backbone.js` create and validate functions plus handling effects.

Keep in mind that edit and delete functionalities will also go through the `if` statement of the `process_topics` function. We need to figure out a way to separate these functions by filtering the request data sent on create, update, and delete events.

Now, you should be able to understand the value of `Backbone.js` for creating well-structured client-side code. In the next section, we will look at the integration of existing PHP libraries inside WordPress.

Using PHPMailer for custom e-mail sending

In the previous section, we looked at the use of `Backbone.js` and `Underscore.js` to identify the usage of open source JavaScript libraries within the WordPress core. Now, it's time to identify the use of open source PHP libraries within the WordPress core, so we will choose `PHPMailer` among a number of other open source libraries. `PHPMailer` is one of the most popular e-mail sending libraries used inside many frameworks as a plugin or library. This library eases the complex tasks of creating advanced e-mails with attachments and third-party account authentications.

`PHPMailer` has been added to GitHub to improve its development process. You can get more information about this library at https://github.com/PHPMailer/PHPMailer.

WordPress has a copy of this library integrated into the core for all e-mail-related tasks. We can find the `PHPMailer` library inside the `wp-includes` folder within the file called `class.phpmailer.php`.

Usage of PHPMailer within the WordPress core

Basically, the functionality of this library is invoked using a common function called `wp_mail` located in the `pluggable.php` file inside the `wp-includes` folder. This function is used to handle all the e-mail sending tasks within WordPress. The `wp_mail` function is very well structured to cater to various functionalities provided by `PHPMailer`. Customizations to the existing behavior of this function can be provided through various types of hook as listed here:

- `wp_mail_from`: Changing the e-mail of the sender, which defaults to `wordpress@{sitename}`
- `wp_mail_from_name`: Changing the name of the sender, which defaults to WordPress
- `wp_mail_content_type`: Changing the e-mail content type, which defaults to text/plain
- `wp_mail_charset`: Changing the e-mail character set, which defaults to the charset assigned in settings

In web applications, we might need advanced customizations that go beyond the capabilities of these existing hooks. In such situations, we have to use a customized e-mail sending functionality. The existing `PHPMailer` library can be easily used to create custom versions of e-mail sending functionalities. There are two ways of creating custom e-mail sending functionality, as listed here:

- Creating a custom version of the pluggable `wp_mail` function
- Loading `PHPMailer` inside plugins and creating custom functions

Creating a custom version of a pluggable wp_mail function

We briefly introduced pluggable functions in `Chapter 6`, *Developing Pluggable Modules*. These functions are located inside the `pluggable.php` file inside the `wp-includes` folder. As developers, we can override the existing behavior of these functions by providing a custom implementation. `wp_mail` is a pluggable function, and hence, we can create custom implementations within plugins. We just duplicate the contents of existing functions within a plugin and change the code as necessary to provide custom features.

Loading PHPMailer inside plugins and creating custom functions

This is a straightforward task, where we have to include the files and initialize the PHPMailer class, as shown in the following code:

```
require_once ABSPATH . WPINC . '/class-phpmailer.php';
require_once ABSPATH . WPINC . '/class-smtp.php';
$mailer = new PHPMailer( true );
```

Then, we can use the $mailer variable object to configure and send e-mails as described in the official documentation.

 By default, WordPress uses the default mail server of your web host to send e-mails. This doesn't involve sender e-mail authentication, and hence, is the reason behind spam e-mails.

We can prevent e-mail spamming by authenticating the e-mail through **Simple Mail Transfer Protocol (SMTP)**. Here, we will implement the custom PHPMailer function while implementing a notification process for new topic creation in our forum management application. Let's list the tasks for this process:

- Creating custom functions to use PHPMailer
- Sending e-mails in SMTP using an authenticated account
- Sending notifications on new topic creation

We can start the process by creating a new class called WPWAF_Email_Manager in a file called class-wpwaf-email-manager.php. Then, include the following action inside the constructor of the WPWAF_Email_Manager class:

```
add_action('new_to_publish', array($this, 'send_topic_notifications'));
add_action('draft_to_publish', array($this,
'send_topic_notifications'));
add_action('pending_to_publish', array($this,
'send_topic_notifications'));
```

Here, we have used three actions related to the post status transfer. Topic creators, moderators, and admins should get notifications about all the topics, once they are published. So we use the preceding post status transfer actions to execute a custom function on publish status change. Let's look at the `send_topic_notifications` function for sending e-mail notifications with `PHPMailer`:

```php
    public function send_topic_notifications($post) {
        global $wpdb;
        $permitted_posts = array('wpwaf_topic');
        if (isset($_POST['post_type']) && in_array($_POST['post_type'],
$permitted_posts)) {

            require_once ABSPATH . WPINC . '/class-phpmailer.php';
            require_once ABSPATH . WPINC . '/class-smtp.php';
            $phpmailer = new PHPMailer(true);
            $phpmailer->From = "admin@gmail.com";
            $phpmailer->FromName = __("Forum Application","wpwaf");

            $phpmailer->SMTPAuth = true;
            $phpmailer->IsSMTP(); // telling the class to use SMTP
            $phpmailer->Host = "ssl://smtp.gmail.com"; // SMTP server
            $phpmailer->Username = "admin@gmail.com";
            $phpmailer->Password = "password";
            $phpmailer->Port = 465;
            $phpmailer->addAddress('admin@gmail.com', 'John');
            $phpmailer->Subject = __("New Topic on Forum Application","wpwaf");

            $subscribers = array();
            $user_query = new WP_User_Query(array('role__in' => array(
'administrator','wpwaf_moderator'), 'number' => 10, 'orderby' =>
'registered', 'order' => 'desc'));
            foreach ($user_query->results as $member) {
                $subscribers[] = $member;
            }

            $author_id=$post->post_author;
            $author = get_userdata($author_id);
            $subscribers[] = $author;

            foreach ($subscribers as $subscriber) {
                $phpmailer->AddBcc($subscriber->user_email,
$subscriber->user_nicename);
            }

            $phpmailer->Body = __("New Topic is available","wpwaf") .
get_permalink($post->ID);
```

```
        $phpmailer->Send();
    }
}
```

We start the `send_topic_notifications` function by filtering the necessary post types to prevent code execution for unnecessary post types. In this case, we are only sending notifications on new forum topics. Next, the `PHPMailer` and `SMTP` class will be included to load the library, as discussed in an earlier section. Once the `$phpmailer` object is created, we can define the necessary parameters for sending e-mails. So we start by defining from the sender e-mail and sender display name.

Next, we have configured the SMTP settings for e-mail authentication and sending through a custom SMTP server. We define the SMTP authentication by using `true` for the `SMTPAuth` parameter. Then, we have to define the `Host`, `Username`, `Password`, and `Port` of the SMTP account that will be used to authenticate e-mails. In this scenario, we will be using Gmail as the SMTP server for sending emails.

Next, we need to send this notification to administrators, moderators, and the topic creator. The custom SQL query is used to retrieve the respective administrators and moderators from the database. Also we need to get the topic creator using the author details of the `$post` object. Then, we add the e-mail of each of those users into the `$phpmailer` object, while looping through the query results. Here, we need to use the `AddBcc` function to keep the confidentiality of the e-mail addresses. Finally, we send the notification with common e-mail content using the permalink of the published topic. So we have a very basic notification system for members about new forum topics.

This technique works fine for basic scenarios where we have a limited number of members. In situations where we have large amounts of members, we can't use this technique as it will delay the publishing of topics. So let's look at other possible solutions for these situations:

- We can track the latest published topics in a separate database table and schedule a cron job for sending notification periodically.
- We can create a member-specific RSS feed with a custom feed URL. Subscribers can then use third-party e-mail services to get notifications on feed updates.

We used the most basic implementation of `PHPMailer` to customize the default mail sending process. This library allows advanced e-mail related feature configurations and might be useful in applications that need extensive use of e-mail related features. In general applications we can also use features such as CC emails, BCC emails, custom reply to e-mail, and various attachments. I suggest you to look into the `PHPMailer` code to understand the other available features.

Implementing user authentication with OpenAuth

Log in with open authentication has become a highly popular method among application users as it provides quicker authentication compared to the conventional registration forms. So many users prefer the use of social logins to authenticate themselves and try the application before deciding to register. Let's take a look at the definition of **OAuth** by Wikipedia:

> *"OAuth is an open standard for authorization. OAuth provides client applications a 'secure delegated access' to server resources on behalf of a resource owner. It specifies a process for resource owners to authorize third-party access to their server resources without sharing their credentials. Designed specifically to work with Hypertext Transfer Protocol (HTTP), OAuth essentially allows access tokens to be issued to third-party clients by an authorization server, with the approval of the resource owner, or end-user. The client then uses the access token to access the protected resources hosted by the resource server."*

OpenAuth is becoming the standard third-party authentication system for providing such functionality. Most existing web applications offer the user authentication using OpenAuth, and hence, it's important to know how we can integrate OpenAuth login into WordPress. Here, we will upgrade our plugin to let users log in and register through popular social networking sites such as Twitter, Facebook, and LinkedIn. We will use third-party OAuth connection libraries to build this functionality as creating an OAuth library from scratch beyond the scope of this book.

Now, we are ready for implementing the OpenAuth login integration for our forum application. The forum will contain the OpenAuth login using Twitter, Facebook, and LinkedIn. So we need three links or buttons just under our login screen.

Basically, we have two ways of assigning these links into the login screen:

1. Directly embed the HTML code under the default login button.
2. Define an action hook and implement the hook within a plugin.

Even though both techniques do the same job, we have more advantage in choosing the action hooks technique as it allows us to add or remove any number of login-related components without affecting existing functionality. So we have to modify the `login-template.php` file inside the `templates` folder of our main plugin. The following code previews the last part of the login template with the new action for social logins:

```
<form method="post" action="<?php echo site_url(); ?>/user/login"
id="wpwaf_login_form" name="wpwaf_login_form">
<!-- Rest of the HTML fields -->
<li>
<label class="wpwaf_frm_label"> </label>
<input  type="submit" name="submit" value="<?php echo
__('Login','wpwaf'); ?>" />
</li>
</ul>
</form>
<?php do_action('wpwaf_social_login'); ?>
```

Here, we execute an action called `wpwaf_social_login` with the `do_action` function. This allows the possibility of adding dynamic content to the login screen using plugins. Next, we have to generate the necessary login links to populate the `wpwaf_social_login` area. Create a new class called `WPWAF_Social` in a file called `class-wpwaf-social.php` for including the functions related to social login links. The first task is to create the login links for different social networks and add them to the login form. Let's look at the initial version of the `WPWAF_Social` class:

```
<?php
class WPWAF_Social{
  public function __construct(){

    add_action('wpwaf_social_login',
array($this,'wpwaf_social_login_buttons'));
    }

  public function wpwaf_social_login_buttons($html){
    $allowed_networks = array('Twitter','Linkedin','Facebook');
    if (get_option('users_can_register') == '1') {
      $html = '<div align="center" style="margin:10px">';

      foreach ($allowed_networks as $key => $network) {
        $link =
'?wpwaf_social_login='.$network.'&wpwaf_social_action=login';

        $html .= '<a class="wpwaf-social-link" href="'.$link .'">
              '. __('Login with ','wpwaf'). $network .'</a>';
      }
```

```
        $html .= '</div>';
      }
      echo $html;
    }
  }
```

We have implemented the `wpwaf_social_login` action with the use of the `wpwaf_social_login_buttons` function inside the `WPWAF_Social` class. The simplicity of the HTML code made me output it using an echo statement. Ideally, we should be using template parts for loading the display code. The `href` attribute contains the action to be executed and the name of the social network. We will need both parameters for the upcoming implementation.

Configuring login strategies

We need to implement the login strategy for each social network. So we need a base class for handling common functionality for all the social networks. Let's create a new class called `WPWAF_Social_Connect` inside a new file called `class-wpwaf-social-connect.php`. This file needs to be created in the root of our `plugins` folder. As usual, we need to include this file inside the `WPWAF_Forum` class. The following code contains the initial version of the `WPWAF_Social_Connect` class:

```php
<?php
class WPWAF_Social_Connect{
  public function callback_url(){
    $url = 'http://' . $_SERVER["HTTP_HOST"] .
$_SERVER["PHP_SELF"];
    if(strpos($url, '?')===false){
      $url .= '?';
    }else{
      $url .= '&';
    }
    return $url;
  }
  public function redirect($redirect){
    wp_redirect($redirect);exit;
  }
  public function register_user($result){}
}
```

These are the most common functions for all social networks at this stage. However, we might need additional functions as we cater to advanced requirements for social login. First, we have a function called `callback_url` for defining the return page after completing the authentication with the social network. We use the current page URL as the callback URL.

Then, we have a generic function for making the redirections using the `wp_redirect` function. Finally, we have the `register_user` function. This function will be used to either register a new user or log in existing users, after successful authentication with social networks. Now, we have the base functionality to implement the social login.

In this chapter, we will implement a social login with LinkedIn. We omit other networks, as the process is similar. So first we need to find an OAuth library and LinkedIn API library. We have used the `OAuth.php` class in a single file and placed the `OAuth.php` class inside the `lib` folder. We need to require it in our main plugin file as usual.

Then, you can grab a PHP library for executing the LinkedIn API functions based on your preference. Here, I am using a library class at `https://code.google.com/p/simple-linkedinphp/` since it's a simpler choice for our basic features. You can download and copy the `linkedin_3.2.0.class.php` file into the `lib\LinkedIn` folder. As usual, we need to require this file from our main plugin class, `WPWAF_Forum`. In scenarios where you have advanced LinkedIn API features, you can find more recent and powerful LinkedIn API libraries for PHP.

Now we are ready for the implementation of social login with LinkedIn. We created a class called `WPWAF_Social` for all the common functionality for social login. So we need to create a class for each social network and extend the `WPWAF_Social` class for the common functionality. Let's create a new class called `WPWAF_LinkedIn_Connect` in a file called `class-wpwaf-linkedin-connect.php`. This file needs to be included after the `Oauth.php` and `linkedin_3.2.0.class.php` files in the `WPWAF_Forum` class. First, we need to identify the functionality of the `WPWAF_LinkedIn_Connect` class as follows:

1. This class should redirect the user to the LinkedIn network to authorize the account with our application.
2. Once the account is authorized and redirected to our site, we need to verify the account details and log in or create a new account for the user.
3. We need to handle any errors generated from the social network.

We will implement these features one by one.

Implementing LinkedIn account authentication

Let's start with redirecting to LinkedIn and authorizing the application. The following code shows the initial implementation of the WPWAF_LinkedIn_Connect class with the login function:

```
class WPWAF_LinkedIn_Connect extends WPWAF_Social_Connect{
    public function login(){

        $callback_url = wpwaf_add_query_string($this->callback_url(),
'wpwaf_social_login=Linkedin&wpwaf_social_action=verify');
        $wpwaf_social_action = isset($_GET['wpwaf_social_action']) ?
$_GET['wpwaf_social_action'] : '';
        $response = new stdClass();

        $app_config  = array(
'appKey' =>   '81ivwylq9ym6u8',
'appSecret' =>   'Xqr8K0vlFoEtTJLO',
'callbackUrl' => $callback_url);

        @session_start();
        $linkedin_api = new LinkedIn($app_config);

        if ($wpwaf_social_action == 'login'){
            $response_linkedin =
$linkedin_api->retrieveTokenRequest(array('scope'=>'r_emailaddress'));
            if($response_linkedin['success'] === TRUE) {
        $_SESSION['oauth']['linkedin']['request'] =
$response_linkedin['linkedin'];
        $this->redirect(LINKEDIN::_URL_AUTH .
$response_linkedin['linkedin']['oauth_token']);

        }else{
           // Handle Errors
        }
    }
    return $response;
  }
}
```

We start the implementation by extending the `WPWAF_Social_Connect` class. Consider the first three lines of the login function. We add the `wpwaf_social_login` and `wpwaf_social_action` parameters to the callback URL generated from the `parent` class. Here, we have used a custom function called `wpwaf_add_query_string`, to add the query variables to the callback URL. Implementation of the `wpwaf_add_query_string` function can be found inside the `functions.php` file of the forum plugin. Then, we assign the action to the `$wpwaf_social_action` variable and create a `stdClass` object to handle the response.

Afterwards, we have to define the LinkedIn APP Key and LinkedIn APP Secret in the `$app_config` array, along with the callback URL. We will cover more details on the app key and secret in the next section on *Building a LinkedIn app*.

Now, we can start the process of authenticating user accounts with our application. First, we start a new session using `session_start` to hold the data retrieved from LinkedIn. Then, we initialize the third-party LinkedIn class by passing the `$app_config` array. We have to check for the proper action using `$wpwaf_social_action` as we have multiple actions in this process. If the action is login, we call the `retrieveTokenRequest` function of the LinkedIn API class with a scope called `r_emailaddress`. You can learn more about scope in the LinkedIn API at

`https://developer.linkedin.com/documents/authentication`.

Then, we save the information to the session and redirect the user to LinkedIn on a successful response from the `retrieveTokenRequest` function execution. If this function generates any errors, we need to handle it using a custom function. We will be omitting the error handling part considering the scope of this chapter. You will find a complete implementation in the source code for this chapter. After redirecting to LinkedIn, the user can authenticate the application with their LinkedIn account. Once the authentication is completed, the request will be redirected to our application using the callback URL. So we need to start the implementation to verify account details and log in the user, as we discussed in the functionality of the `WPWAF_LinkedIn_Connect` class.

Verifying a LinkedIn account and generating a response

We created an if statement in the previous code to check for the availability of the `login` action. Now, we need to extend it with the `else if` statement to check for the response from LinkedIn. The following code contains the implementation of the account verification process:

```
elseif(isset($_GET['oauth_verifier'])){
    $response_linkedin = $linkedin_api->retrieveTokenAccess(
```

```
$_SESSION['oauth']['linkedin']['request']['oauth_token'],
 $_SESSION['oauth']['linkedin']['request']['oauth_token_secret'],
 $_GET['oauth_verifier']);

       if($response_linkedin['success'] === TRUE){
           $linkedin_api->setTokenAccess($response_linkedin['linkedin']);
           $linkedin_api->setResponseFormat(LINKEDIN::_RESPONSE_JSON);
           $user_result = $linkedin_api->profile('~:(email-
address,id,first-name,last-name,picture-url)');

           if($user_result['success'] === TRUE) {
              $data = json_decode($user_result['linkedin']);
              $response->status  = TRUE;
              $response->wpwaf_network_type = 'linkedin';
              $response->first_name  = $data->firstName;
              $response->last_name  = $data->lastName;
              $response->email  = $data->emailAddress;
              $response->error_message = '';
           }else{
              /* Handling LinkedIn specific errors */

           }
       }else{
       /* Handling LinkedIn specific errors */

       }
    }
```

The LinkedIn API redirects the request to our application with a URL parameter called `oauth_verifier`, and hence, we check the existence of the parameter before proceeding. Once it's set, we call the `retrieveTokenAccess` function of the API class with session parameters and the value of `oauth_verifier`. This function verifies the request and requests the user's access token from the Linkedin API. Once successful, the response is returned and we call the `setTokenAccess` and `setResponseFormat` functions of the API class. Having completed the verification process, we can now request the user details using the access tokens generated earlier. So we execute the profile function of the API class with the necessary information such as `email-address`, `id`, `first-name`, `last-name`, `picture-url`, and so on. Once the profile information request is successful, we assign the necessary profile data to our response object.

 We have omitted all the error handling conditions in this function. You can use the source code for this chapter to look at the implementation of handling errors.

We have completed the process requesting profile information from LinkedIn. However, we didn't create a LinkedIn app for our application. Now, let's build an app to generate these keys for LinkedIn. App creation for these social networking sites mentioned here is explained commonly in many online resources. Hence, we will create a LinkedIn app to define a new strategy.

Building a LinkedIn app

First, you have to log in to your existing LinkedIn account. Then, you have to visit the developer section using `https://www.linkedin.com/secure/developer`. You will get a screen similar to the following with the existing apps, if there are any:

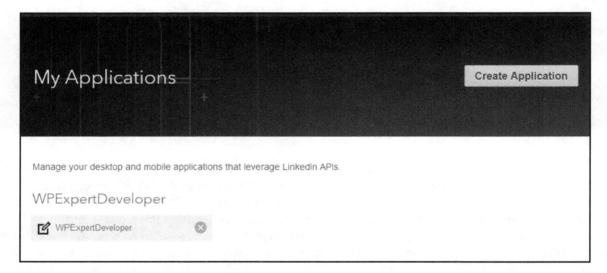

You can click on the **Create Application** link to get the following screen:

Make sure that you fill out all the mandatory values in the given form. Once you hit the **Submit** button, you will get a screen with all the application-specific details, including **API Key** and **Secret key**. Also this screen will have the settings to define **Default Application Permissions** and OAuth redirect URL's for your application. The following screenshot previews the application **Settings** section:

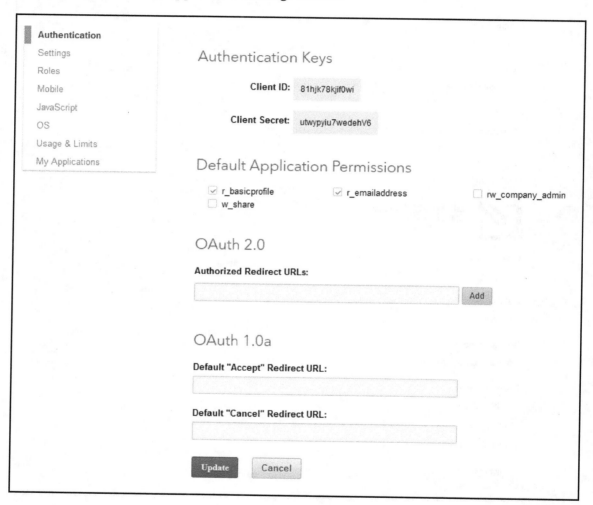

Now, we can move back to the configuration array in the `login` function of the `WPWAF_LinkedIn_Connect` class and include the LinkedIn configuration details, as shown in the following code:

```
$app_config = array(
  'appKey' => '81hjk78kjif0wi',
  'appSecret' => 'utwypyiu7wedehV6',
  'callbackUrl' => $callback_url);
```

We have completed the implementation of the `WPWAF_LinkedIn_Connect` class. Now, we need to initialize this process and log in the users into our application.

The process of requesting the strategies

We have the login links assigned to the login screen buttons with `href` values. Each network is added to the link using `wpwaf_social_login` as Facebook, Twitter, and LinkedIn. The URL of the login screen is `http://www.yoursite.com/user/login/`, and once you click the link for LinkedIn, you will get a URL such as `http://www.yoursite.com/user/login/?wpwaf_social_login=Linkedin&wpwaf_social_action=login`. The verification and authentication process will be processed based on these parameters.

Initializing the library

We have implemented all the functionality for authenticating users from LinkedIn, using the `WPWAF_LinkedIn_Connect` and `WPWAF_Social` classes. However, nothing will work yet as we haven't initialized the social login library class. So we have to implement the initialization code inside the `WPWAF_Social` class. Let's start the process by including a `wp_loaded` action to execute the initialization. The following code displays the modified constructor of the `WPWAF_Social` class:

```
public function __construct(){
    add_action('wp_loaded', array($this,
'wpwa_social_login_initialize' ));
    add_action('wpwa_social_login', array($this,
'wpwa_social_login_buttons'));
  }
```

Next, we need to implement the `wpwaf_social_login_initialize` function, as shown in the following code:

```
public function wpwaf_social_login_initialize(){
   $wpwaf_social_login_obj = false;
   $wpwaf_social_login = isset($_GET['wpwaf_social_login']) ?
$_GET['wpwaf_social_login'] : '';
   $wpwaf_social_action = isset($_GET['wpwaf_social_action']) ?
$_GET['wpwaf_social_action'] : '';

   if('' != $wpwaf_social_login ){
      switch ($wpwaf_social_login) {
         case 'Linkedin':
            $wpwaf_social_login_obj = new WPWAF_LinkedIn_Connect();
            break;

      }

      if($wpwaf_social_login_obj){
         $login_response = $wpwaf_social_login_obj->login();
         $wpwaf_social_login_obj->register_user($login_response);
      }
   }
}
```

First, we retrieve the `wpwaf_social_login` and `wpwaf_social_action` variables from the `$_GET` array. We check the existence of the `wpwaf_social_login` variable before proceeding further. Then, we switch the `wpwaf_social_login` variable to identify the social network. Here, we have only included LinkedIn as we are only implementing the LinkedIn version in this chapter. You can add the remaining networks with similar code.

So, we initialize the `WPWAF_LinkedIn_Connect` class using the `$wpwaf_social_login_obj` object. Finally, we check the availability of valid objects in the `$wpwaf_social_login_obj` variable. Then, we call the login function to start the authentication process for social login.

When the user is redirected to LinkedIn, the following screen will appear asking the user to authenticate the application by logging in:

LinkedIn will redirect the user to our application once a user grants the permissions for the application. The callback URL configured in the $app_config file will be used as the redirection path. The next step in this process is to handle the response and authenticate the user into our application.

Authenticating users to our application

Once a user is successfully authenticated inside LinkedIn, the request will be redirected to our application with the profile details of the user. However, each of these services will provide different types of data, and hence, it's difficult to match them into a common format. As developers, we should be relying on the most basic and common data across all services for OpenAuth login and registrations. Let's understand the process of authentication before moving on to the response handling part:

1. The user clicks on the LinkedIn link.
2. The user is redirected to LinkedIn for granting permissions to our application.

3. The user is redirected back to our application on successful authentication with profile details.
4. The application checks whether a user already exists using the username.
5. Existing users will be automatically logged into the WordPress application.
6. Non-existing users will be saved in the application as a new user, using the details retrieved from LinkedIn, and redirected to profile for completing remaining details.

Now, let's see how we can handle the response object generated from the `WPWAF_LinkedIn_Connect` class, to authenticate users into our application. First, we have to update the `wpwaf_social_login_initialize` function as follows to include the call to the `register_user` function:

```
public function wpwaf_social_login_initialize(){
  // Rest of the code

  if('' != $wpwa_social_login ){
    // Rest of the code
    if($wpwa_social_login_obj){
      $login_response = $wpwa_social_login_obj->login();
      $wpwa_social_login_obj->register_user($login_response);
    }
  }
}
```

Now, we can take a look at the implementation of the `register_user` function inside `WPWAF_Social_Connect`. Let's start with the first part of this function using the following code:

```
public function register_user($result){
  if($result->status){
    if(isset($result->email)){
      $user = get_user_by('email',$result->email);
    }else{
      $user = get_user_by('login',$result->username);
    }

    // Remaining Code
  }else{
  // Handle Errors
  }
}
```

We start the process by checking the status of the `$result` object. This is the response object generated after authenticating the account with LinkedIn. If a successful response is received, we check the network type for login. We assigned the network type inside the login function of the `WPWAF_LinkedIn_Connect` class. We have to do the error handling part for unsuccessful responses. There are some key points that we need to know about the username before moving forward.

 Both the LinkedIn and Facebook APIs provide the e-mail address of the user, and hence, we use it to verify the users. However, the Twitter API doesn't provide the e-mail address by default. We have to specially request the email address using the **Additional Permissions** section. Even if permissions are requested, we may not get the e-mail when the user has made it private through their Twitter account.

So we check the existence of email addresses in the response object. However, if permissions are not configured, we won't get the e-mail from Twitter. In such a case we get the user by `login` (username) for Twitter and user by `email` for other social networks. If the user is already registered with the given `login` or `email`, we will get a valid `$user` object. Otherwise, it will return `false`. Now, we can move onto the next section of the `register_user` function:

```
public function register_user($result){
  if($result->status){
    // Retrieving the user from the database
    if(!$user){
      // Create a new user for the application
    }else{
      // Automatically authenticating existing users
    }
    wp_redirect(admin_url('profile.php'));
  }else{
    // Handle Errors
  }
}
```

A valid object for `$user` means that the existing user is trying to log in through the LinkedIn connect. So we authenticate and automatically log on the user and redirect them to the profile page of the WordPress backend. If a valid user is not found, the user is trying to log in through LinkedIn connect for the first time, and hence, we have to create a new account for the user. Let's start by looking at the user creation process inside the `if` statement:

```
if($result->wpwaf_network_type != 'twitter'){
  $username = strtolower($result->first_name.$result->last_name);
  if(username_exists($username)){
```

```
      $username = $username.rand(10,99);
    }
  }else{
    $username = $result->username;
  }

  $sanitized_user_login = sanitize_user($username);
  $user_pass = wp_generate_password(12, false);

  $user_id = wp_create_user($sanitized_user_login, $user_pass,
$result->email);
  if (!is_wp_error($user_id)) {
    update_user_meta($user_id, 'user_email', $result->email);
    update_user_meta($user_id, 'wpwaf_network_type', $result-
>wpwa_network_type);
    wp_update_user( array ('ID' => $user_id, 'display_name' =>
$result->first_name.' '.$result->last_name) ) ;
    wp_set_auth_cookie($user_id, false, is_ssl());
  }
```

We have already mentioned that the Twitter API provides the username for the user, and hence, we can use the same username for our application. The LinkedIn APIs don't provide a username. So we have to build a dynamic custom username using a combination of first and last names, or use email addresses as the username.

 Building usernames can be done in various ways and different plugins use their own techniques. This is only one way of generating the username and it might not be the best method. You can implement your own technique based on your application requirements.

However, the first and last name combination may not be a unique username. In such cases, we add a dynamic random number to the end of the username to make it unique. Then, we use the sanitize_user function for stripping out unsafe characters and generate the password using the wp_generate_password function.

Finally, we create a new user by passing the username, password, and e-mail to the wp_create_user function. If the user creation is successful, we update the user with first and last names in the wp_users table. We also add the user e-mail and network type to the wp_usermeta table. Next, we will use the wp_set_auth_cookie function to create the authentication cookies for WordPress and log on the user automatically. Once registered, the user will be authenticated by setting the WordPress authenticate cookie and redirected to the profile page to fill out their details. At this stage, the user will have a default password. Therefore, it's mandatory to update the user profile with a new password to complete the registration.

Now, we can have a look at the `else` part of the code for existing users. It's pretty simple as we only have to automatically log on the existing users. So we use the following line to create authenticate cookies and log on the user:

```
wp_set_auth_cookie($user->ID, false, is_ssl());
```

We have completed the user registration and login process using social networks. The intention of this implementation was to learn how to integrate third-party open source libraries into WordPress web applications. Now, let's take a look at the importance points in implementing social login for Facebook and Twitter:

- **Implementing Facebook login**: We can implement a Facebook login by including a PHP library for the Facebook API and creating a similar class called `WPWAF_Facebook_Login` with the Facebook app requests. The following are some of the important points in implementing Facebook login:

  1. We can request Facebook permissions using `$facebook->get('/me?fields=id,first_name,last_name,email,picture.type(large)',$accessToken);`.

  2. Facebook allows us to create accounts with emails as well as mobile numbers. So mobile number-based accounts may not have email addresses and hence we may need to dynamically create the email address when it's not available.

  3. We can construct the email to use `@facebook.com`.

- **Implementing Twitter login**: We can implement a Twitter login by including a PHP library for the Twitter API and creating a similar class called `WPWAF_Twitter_Login` with the Twitter app requests. The following are some of the important points in implementing Twitter login:

  1. The email is not provided by default and you have to specially request it using the APP settings section.

  2. Twitter may or may not provide the email of the user and hence we should be prepared to create a dynamic email when it's not available in the response.

Now, we have completed the library integration and OpenAuth login. Make sure that you test the user registration and log in using different services. Having completed this process, you should be capable of integrating other libraries for networks such as Facebook and Twitter into WordPress applications.

Using third-party libraries and plugins

We discussed the importance of open source libraries in detail. Most WordPress developers prefer the creation of web applications by installing a bunch of third-party plugins. Ideally, developers should be focusing on limiting the number of plugins within an application to improve the structure of code and possible conflicts.

In web applications, we will need to use third-party resources, no matter how much we want to develop our own code. So it's important to identify stable plugins to be used for applications and ensure that these plugins are safe to use.

Using open source plugins for web development

There are hundreds of quality free and premium plugins that can be used extensively in web development. Before using any plugin, you should check the popularity of the plugin, the quality of the code, and the support provided by the plugin developers. In this section, we are going to look at some useful and stable plugins for adding functionality to your web applications:

- **Advanced Custom Fields**: User data input, process, and output are the main functionality of most web applications and hence we need custom fields to capture the details. This plugin is the ideal solution to capturing custom data to your posts, pages, and custom post types. This plugin offers over 15 field types and a visually simple data adding process. You can download this plugin and check the available features at `https://wordpress.org/plugins/advanced-custom-fields/`.

- **Ninja Forms**: ACF plugins allowed us to capture custom data for posts, pages, and custom post types. These types of forms plugin are even more useful in web applications since we can capture data using dynamic forms without needing to use WordPress core post/page features. This plugin offers features such as unlimited forms, data formatting, data validation, import/export user submissions, Ajax-based form submissions, and over 40 add-ons for additional features. You can download this plugin and check the available features at `https://wordpress.org/plugins/ninja-forms/`.

- **Easy Digital Downloads**: Selling products or services is also one of the major requirements of many web applications and hence we need an e-commerce solution. This plugin allows us to easily sell any digital product with minimum effort and manages all the features related to selling. This plugin offers shopping cart, payment gateways, reports, and a wide range of addons for supporting the various aspects of online product/service selling. You can download this plugin and check the available features at `https://wordpress.org/plugins/easy-digital-downloads/`.

In this section, we discussed three plugins that can be directly used to build the main functionality of our web applications. However, there are several other non-functional plugin types such as security, caching, performance, SEO, and translation for supporting the development of web applications. These aspects will be discussed in upcoming chapters.

Using plugins for checking security of other plugins

WordPress is the most used framework for building websites in the world and hence it's the framework with the most security threats. Third-party libraries can contain malicious code that enables security holes in your applications allowing attackers to easily create exploits. Even though there are some tools for checking malicious code, none of them are 100% accurate, and we can't guarantee the results. The following are some plugins for checking malicious code of your plugins and themes:

- `Exploit Scanner`: You can find this plugin at `https://wordpress.org/plugins/exploit-scanner/`
- `Plugin Security Scanner`: You can find this plugin at `https://wordpress.org/plugins/plugin-security-scanner/`
- `Theme Check`: You can find this plugin at `https://wordpress.org/plugins/theme-check/`
- **Theme Authenticity Checker** (**TAC**): You can find this plugin at `https://wordpress.org/plugins/tac/`

As developers, we should be always looking for stable and consistent libraries for our projects. So it's preferable to work with existing WordPress libraries and stable third-party plugins as much as possible when developing web applications.

Time for action

As usual, we discussed plenty of practical usages for open source libraries within WordPress. We completed the implementation of a few scenarios and left out some tasks for future development. As developers, you should take this opportunity to get experience in integrating various third-party libraries:

- Track the latest published topics in a separate database table and schedule a cron job for sending notification periodically
- Create a member-specific RSS feed for topics and let users subscribe to get updates
- Implement edit and delete functionality for a topic list using `Backbone.js`
- Integrate OpenAuth login for Facebook and Twitter

Summary

The open source nature of WordPress has improved developer engagement to customize and improve existing features by developing plugins, and contributing to the core framework. Inside the core framework, we can find dozens of popular open source libraries and plugins. We planned this chapter to understand the usage of trending open source libraries within the core.

First, we looked at the open source libraries inside the core. `Backbone.js` and `Underscore.js` are trending as popular libraries for web development and hence have been included in the latest WordPress version. Throughout this chapter, we looked at the use of `Backbone.js` inside WordPress while building the forum member profile page of the forum application. We looked into `Backbone.js` concepts such as models, collections, validation, views, and events.

Later on, we looked at the usage of existing PHP libraries within WordPress by using `PHPMailer` to build a custom e-mail sending interface. In web applications, developers don't always get the opportunity to build everything from scratch. So it's important to make use of existing libraries as much as possible.

As developers, you should have the know-how to integrate the third-party libraries as well as the existing ones. Hence, we chose the LinkedIn API library and OAuth for integrating social network logins into our application. We integrated the LinkedIn login feature into the forum application. Finally, we looked at some of the useful open source plugins for application development and code-related plugins to check the security threats in other plugins.

In the next chapter, we will look at both WordPress XML-RPC and new REST API functions to build simple yet flexible API's for the forum application. Until then, make sure that you try out the actions given in this chapter.

10
Listening to Third-Party Applications

The complexity and size of web applications prompts developers to think about rapid development processes through third-party applications. Basically, we use third-party frameworks and libraries to automate the common tasks of web applications. Alternatively, we can use third-party services to provide functionalities that are not directly related to the core logic of the application. Using APIs is a popular way of working with third-party services. The creation of an API opens the gates for third-party applications to access the data of our applications.

WordPress provides the ability to create an API through its built-in APIs powered by **XML-RPC** and **REST**. Also, WordPress is moving completely toward the JSON REST API, and it's available in core with WordPress 4.7. The existing XML-RPC and REST APIs cater to the blogging and CMS functionalities, while allowing developers to extend the APIs with custom functionalities. This chapter covers the basics of an existing API, while building the foundation of a forum management system API. Here, you will learn the necessary techniques for building complex APIs for larger applications.

In this chapter, we will cover the following topics:

- Introduction to APIs
- The WordPress XML-RPC API for web applications
- Building the XML-RPC API client
- Creating the custom XML-RPC API methods
- Integrating user authentication for XML-RPC
- Integrating the API access tokens for XML-RPC
- Providing the API documentation
- REST API for web applications

- Working with built-in REST endpoints
- Using custom post types in REST API
- Creating custom REST routes and endpoints
- Building REST API clients
- User authentication techniques for REST API
- Integrating the API access tokens for REST API
- Time for action

Let's get started!

Introduction to APIs

API is the acronym for **Application Programming Interface**. According to the definition on Wikipedia, an API specifies a set of functions that accomplishes specific tasks or allows working with specific software components. As web applications grow larger, we might need to provide the application services or data to third-party applications. We cannot let third-party applications access our source code or database directly due to security reasons. So, APIs allow the access of data and services of the application through a restricted interface, where users can only access the data provided through the API. Typically, users are requested to authenticate themselves by providing usernames and necessary passwords or API keys. So, let's look at the advantages of having an application-specific API.

The advantages of having an API

Often, we see the involvement of APIs with popular web and mobile applications. As the owner of the application, you have many direct and indirect advantages by providing an API for third-party applications. Let's go through some of the distinct advantages of having an API:

- Access to the API can be provided to third-party applications as a free or premium service
- User traffic increases as more and more applications use the API
- By offering an API, you get free marketing and popularity among people who normally don't know your application
- Generally, APIs automate tasks that require user involvement, allowing much better and quicker experience for the users

With the increasing use of mobile-based devices, API-based applications are growing faster than ever before. Most of the popular web applications and services have opened up their API for third-party applications, and others are looking to build their API to compete in this rapidly changing world of web development. Here are some of the most popular existing APIs used by millions of users around the world:

- **Twitter REST API**: https://dev.twitter.com/rest/public
- **Facebook Graph API**: https://developers.facebook.com/docs/graph-api
- **Google Maps API**: https://developers.google.com/maps/
- **Amazon Product Advertising API**: http://goo.gl/6iLxfw
- **YouTube API**: https://developers.google.com/youtube/

Considering the future of web development, it's imperative to have knowledge of building an API to extend the functionalities of web applications. So, we will look at the WordPress APIs in the next section.

The WordPress XML-RPC API for web applications

With the latest versions, the WordPress API has matured into a secure and flexible solution that easily extends to cater to complex features. This was considered to be an insecure feature that exposed the security vulnerabilities of WordPress; hence, was disabled by default in earlier versions. As of Version 3.5, XML-RPC is enabled by default and the enable/disable option from the admin dashboard has been completely removed.

The existing APIs mainly focus on addressing functionalities for blogging and CMS-related tasks. In web applications, we can make use of these API functions to build an API for third-party applications and users. The following list contains the existing components of the WordPress XML-RPC API:

- Posts
- Taxonomies
- Media
- Comments
- Options
- Users

The complete list of components and respective API functions can be found in the WordPress codex at `http://codex.wordpress.org/XML-RPC_WordPress_API`.

Let's see how we can use the existing API functions of WordPress.

Building the API client

WordPress provides support for its API through the `xmlrpc.php` file located inside the root of the installation directory. Basically, we need two components to build and use an API:

- **The API server**: This is the application where the API function resides
- **The API client**: This is a third-party application or service that requests the functionality of an API

Since we will be using the existing API functions, we don't need to worry about the server, as it's built inside the core. So, we will build a third-party client to access the service. Later, we will improve the API server to implement custom functionalities that go beyond the existing API functions. The API client is responsible for providing the following features:

- Authenticating the user with the API
- Making XML-RPC requests to the server through the curl command
- Defining and populating the API functions with the necessary parameters

With the preceding features in mind, let's look at the implementation of an API client:

```php
class WPWA_XMLRPC_Client {
    private $xml_rpc_url;
    private $username;
    private $password;
    public function __construct($xml_rpc_url, $username, $password)
{
        $this->xml_rpc_url = $xml_rpc_url;
        $this->username = $username;
        $this->password = $password;
    }
    public function api_request($request_method, $params) {
        $request = xmlrpc_encode_request($request_method, $params);
        $ch = curl_init();
        curl_setopt($ch, CURLOPT_POSTFIELDS, $request);
        curl_setopt($ch, CURLOPT_URL, $this->xml_rpc_url);
        curl_setopt($ch, CURLOPT_RETURNTRANSFER, 1);
        curl_setopt($ch, CURLOPT_TIMEOUT, 1);
        $results = curl_exec($ch);
```

```
      $response_code = curl_getinfo($ch, CURLINFO_HTTP_CODE);
      $errorno = curl_errno($ch);
      $error = curl_error($ch);
      curl_close($ch);
      if ($errorno != 0) {
        return array("error" => $error);
      }
      if ($response_code != 200) {
        return array("error" => __("Request Failed : ","wpwa") .
$results);
      }
      return xmlrpc_decode($results);
    }
  }
```

Let's have a look at the following steps to build the API client:

1. First, we will define three instance variables for API URL, username, and password. The constructor is used to initialize the instance variables through the parameters provided by users in object initialization.

2. Next, we have the `api_request` function for making the curl requests to the API. Here, we take two parameters as request method and attributes. The WordPress API provides the request method for each API function. A user can pass the necessary parameter values for the API call through the `$params` array.

> -   `curl` is a command-line tool and library for transferring data with URL syntax, supporting various protocols, including HTTP and FTP. This is the most popular tool used in API requests and responses. On some servers, curl might not be enabled, so make sure that you enable curl on your server.

3. Inside the `api_request` function, we use the `xmlrpc_encode_request` function provided by PHP to generate an XML file from the passed parameters and request data.
4. Then, we can pass the converted XML file to a curl request to invoke the API functions on the server.
5. Based on the server response, we can generate an error or retrieve the decoded result by using the `xmlrpc_decode` function. Generally, the result returned from the server will be in the string, integer, or array format.

• The official PHP documentation states that the `xmlrpc_encode_request` and `xmlrpc_decode` functions are experimental and should be used at our own risk. We have used those functions here, considering the scope of this chapter.

We can create the XML request manually or use a third-party XML-RPC library to provide a much more stable solution. In case you decide to implement manual XML request creation, use the following format to generate the parameters:

```xml
<?xml version="1.0"?>
<methodCall>
  <methodName>subscribeToTopics</methodName>
    <params>
      <param>
        <value><string>username</string></value>
      </param>
    </params>
</methodCall>
```

6. Now, we have the basic API client for requesting or sending server data.

7. Next, we need to define functions inside the client for invoking various API functions. Here, we will implement the API functions for accessing the forums and topics of the forum management system. So, let's update the API client class with the following two functions:

```php
function getLatestTopics() {
    $params = array(0, $this->username, $this->password,
array("post_type" => "wpwaf_topic"));
    return $this->api_request("wp.getPosts", $params);
}
function getLatestForums() {
    $params = array(0, $this->username, $this->password,
array("post_type" => "wpwaf_forum"));
    return $this->api_request("wp.getPosts", $params);
}
```

8. Now, we have implemented two functions with similar code for accessing WordPress custom post types.

WordPress provides the ability to access any post type through the `wp.getPosts` request method. The request is invoked by passing the request method and parameters to the `api_request` function created in the earlier section.

The parameters array contains four values for this request:

- The first parameter of 0 defines the blog ID.
- Next, we have the username and password of the user who wants to access the API.
- Finally, we have an array with optional parameters for filtering results. It's important that you pass the values in the preceding order as WordPress looks for parameter values by its index.

Here, we have used `post_type` as the optional parameter for filtering forums and topics from the database. The following is a list of allowed optional parameters for the `wp.getPosts` request method:

- `post_type`
- `post_status`
- `number`
- `offset`
- `orderby`
- `order`

In the codex, it is mentioned that the response of `wp.getPosts` will only contain posts that the user has permission to edit. Therefore, the user will only receive the permitted post list. If you want to allow public access to all the post details, the custom API function needs be developed to query the database.

Now, let's see how to invoke the API function by initializing the API client, as illustrated in the following code:

```
$wpwaf_api_client = new
WPWAF_XMLRPC_Client("http://www.yoursite.com/xmlrpc.php",
"username", "password");
$topics = $wpwaf_api_client->getLatestTopics();
$forums = $wpwaf_api_client->getLatestForums();
```

We can invoke the API by initializing the `WPWAF_XMLRPC_Client` class with the three parameters we discussed at the beginning of this process. So, the final output of the `$topics` and `$forums` variables will contain an array of posts.

Keep in mind that the API client is a third-party application or service. So, we have to use this code outside the WordPress installation to get the desired results.

The XML-RPC client code is included in the `xml-rpc-client.php` file of the source code folder for this chapter. So far, we have looked at the usage of existing API functions within WordPress. Next, we will look at the possibilities of extending the API to create custom methods.

Creating a custom API

Custom APIs are essential for adding web application-specific behaviors, which go beyond the generic blogging functionality. We need the implementation for both the server and client to create a custom API. Here, we will build an API function that outputs the list of topics of a specified forum in the forum application. Here, we will use a separate plugin for API creation as an API is usually a separate component from the application. Let's get started by creating another plugin folder called `wpwa-xml-rpc-api` with the main file called `class-wpwa-xml-rpc-api.php`. Since this is a plugin with a basic set of functions, we don't use the plugin coding structure used in the forum plugin.

Let's look at the initial code to build the API server:

```
class WPWAF_XML_RPC_API {
    public function __construct() {
        add_filter('xmlrpc_methods', array($this, 'xml_rpc_api'));
    }
    public function xml_rpc_api($methods) {
        $methods['wpwaf.getForumTopics'] = array($this,
'forum_topics_list');
        return $methods;
    }
}
new WPWAF_XML_RPC_API();
```

First, we use the plugin constructor to add the WordPress filter called `xmlrpc_methods`, which allows us to customize the API functions assigned to WordPress. The preceding filter will call the `xml_rpc_api` function by passing the existing API methods as the parameter. The `$methods` array contains both the existing API methods as well as the methods added by plugins.

The `xmlrpc_methods` filter allows for the customization of the methods exposed by the XML-RPC server. This can be used to both add new methods and remove built-in methods.

Inside the function, we need to add new methods to the API. WordPress uses `wp` as the namespace for the existing methods. Here, we have defined the custom namespace for application-specific functions as `wpwaf`. The preceding code adds a method called `getForumTopics` in the `wpwaf` namespace to call a function called `forum_topics_list`.

The following code contains the implementation of the `forum_topics_list` function to generate the entire topics list as the output:

```
public function forum_topics_list( $args ) {
    global $wpdb;
    $forum_id = isset($args['forum_id']) ? $args['forum_id'] : 0;

    $topics_to_forums = $wpdb->prefix.'p2p';
    $sql   = $wpdb->prepare( "SELECT wppost.* from $wpdb->posts as wppost
inner join $topics_to_forums as wpp2p on wppost.ID = wpp2p.p2p_from where
wppost.post_type = '%s' and wppost.post_status = 'publish'  and p2p_type=
'topics_to_forums' and p2p_to = %d ", 'wpwaf_topic', $forum_id);

    $result = $wpdb->get_results($sql);
    return $result;
}
```

The list of topics for a given forum is generated through a custom query by joining a WordPress posts table with a custom `p2p` table. Now, we have the API server ready with the custom function. Consider the following code to understand how custom API methods are invoked by the client:

```
function getForumTopics($forum_id) {
    $params = array("forum_id" => $forum_id);
    return $this->api_request("wpwaf.getForumTopics", $params);
}
$wpwaf_api_client = new
WPWAF_XMLRPC_Client("http://www.yoursite.com/xmlrpc.php",
    "username", "password");
$forum_topics = $wpwaf_api_client->getForumTopics(231);
```

As we did earlier, the definition of the `getForumTopics` function is located inside the client class and the API is initialized from outside the class. Here, you will receive a list of all the topics for the given forum in the system.

Now, we know the basics of creating a custom API with WordPress. In the next section, we will look at the authentication for custom API methods.

Integrating API user authentication

Building a stable API is not one of the simplest tasks in web development. However, once you have an API, hundreds of third-party applications will be requesting to connect to the API, including potential hackers. So, it's important to protect your API from malicious requests and avoid an unnecessary overload of traffic. Therefore, we can request an API authentication before providing access to the user. Also, providing the API through SSL is almost a must to secure your API.

The existing API functions come built-in with user authentication; hence, we had to use user credentials in the section where we retrieved a list of forums and topics. Here, we need to manually implement the authentication process for custom API methods. Let's create another API method for subscribing to the topics of the forum application. This feature is already implemented in the admin dashboard using admin list tables. Now, we will provide the same functionality for the API users.

Let's get started by modifying the xml_rpc_api function as follows:

```
public function xml_rpc_api($methods) {
    $methods['wpwaf.subscribeToTopics'] = array( $this,
'topic_subscriptions' );
    $methods['wpwaf.getForumTopics'] = array( $this, 'forum_topics_list'
);
    return $methods;
}
```

Now, we can build the subscription functionality inside the topic_subscriptions function using the following code:

```
public function topic_subscriptions( $args ) {
    global $wpdb;
    $username = isset( $args['username'] ) ? $args['username'] : '';
    $password = isset( $args['password'] ) ? $args['password'] : '';

    $user = wp_authenticate( $username, $password );
    if (!$user || is_wp_error($user)) {
        return $user;
    }

    $follower_id = $user->ID;
    $topic_id = isset( $args['topic_id'] ) ? $args['topic_id'] : 0 ;
```

```
    $topic_subscriptions_table = $wpdb->prefix.'topic_subscriptions';

    $sql   = $wpdb->prepare( "SELECT * FROM $topic_subscriptions_table
WHERE topic_id = %d AND user_id = %d ", $topic_id , $follower_id );

    $result = $wpdb->get_results($sql);
    if(!$result){
        $wpdb->insert(
            $topic_subscriptions_table,
            array(
                'topic_id' => $topic_id,
                'user_id' => $follower_id
            ),
            array(
                '%d',
                '%d'
            )
        );

        return array("success" => __("Subsciption Completed.","wpwaf"));
    }else{
        return array("error" => __("Already subscribed to
topic.","wpwaf"));
    }
    return $args;
}
```

Let's have a look at the steps:

1. First, we will retrieve the username and password from the arguments array and call the built-in `wp_authenticate` function by passing them as parameters. This function will authenticate the user credentials against the `wp_users` table. If the credentials fail to match a user from the database,
2. we return the error as an object of the `WP_Error` class.

- Notice the use of array keys for retrieving various arguments in this function. By default, WordPress uses array indexes as 0, 1, 2 for retrieving the arguments, and, hence, the ordering of arguments is important. Here, we have introduced key-based parameters so that users have the freedom of sending parameters without worrying about the order.

3. Once the user is successfully authenticated, we can access the ID of the user to be used as the follower. We also need the ID of a preferred topic through the method parameters.

4. Next, we check whether a subscription already exists using a custom query on `wp_topic_subscriptions` table by passing the user and topic ID.

5. Finally, we insert the record into the `wp_topic_subscriptions` table to create a new user subscription for a forum topic.

The other parts of the code contain the necessary error handlings based on various conditions. Make sure that you keep a consistent format for providing error messages.

Now, we can implement the API client code by adding the following code into the API client class:

```
function subscribeToTopics($topic_id, $api_token) {
    $params = array( "username" => $this->username, "password" =>
$this->password, "topic_id" => $topic_id, "token" => $api_token);
    return $this->api_request("wpwaf.subscribeToTopics", $params);
}
```

Here, we call the custom API method called `wpwaf.subscribeToTopics` with the necessary parameters. As usual, we invoke the API by initializing an object of the `WPWAF_XMLRPC_Client` class, as shown in the following code:

```
$wpwaf_api_client = new
WPWAF_XMLRPC_Client("http://yoursite.com/xmlrpc.php", "follower",
"follower123");
$subscribe_status = $wpwaf_api_client->subscribeToTopics(1);
```

Once implemented, this API function allows users to subscribe to the forum topics.

Integrating API access tokens

In the preceding section, we introduced API authentication to prevent unnecessary access to the API. Even the authenticated users can overload the API by accessing it unnecessarily. Therefore, we need to implement user tokens for limiting the use of the API. There can be many reasons for limiting requests to an API. We can think of two main reasons for limiting the API access as listed here:

- To avoid the unnecessary overloading of server resources
- To bill the users based on API usage

If you are developing a premium API, it's important to track its usage for billing purposes. Various APIs use unique parameters to measure the API usage. Here are some of the unique ways of measuring API usage:

- The Twitter API uses the number of requests per hour to measure API usage
- Google Translate uses the number of words translated to measure API usage
- Google Cloud SQL uses input and output storage to measure API usage

Here, we won't measure the usage or limit the access to the forum API. Instead, we will be creating user tokens for measuring the usage in future. First, we have to create an admin menu page for generating user tokens. Let's update the `WPWAF XML-RPC API` plugin constructor by adding the following action:

```
public function __construct() {
  add_filter('xmlrpc_methods', array($this, 'xml_rpc_api'));
  add_action('admin_menu', array($this, 'api_settings'));
}
```

The following code contains the implementation of the `api_settings` function to create an admin menu page for token generation:

```
public function api_settings() {
    add_menu_page(__('API Settings','wpwaf'), __('API Settings','wpwaf'),
  'follow_forum_activities', 'wpwaf-api', array( $this, 'user_api_settings')
);
    }
```

We will not discuss the preceding code in detail as we have already done it in the previous chapters. Only users with `follow_forum_activities` capability are allowed to access the API through tokens. Now, we can look at the `user_api_settings` function for the implementation of the token generation screen as follows:

```
public function user_api_settings() {
    global $wpwa_template_loader,$api_data;
    $user_id = get_current_user_id();
    if ( isset( $_POST['api_settings'] ) ) {
      $api_token = $this->generate_random_hash();
      update_user_meta( $user_id, "api_token", $api_token );
    } else {
    $api_token = (string) get_user_meta($user_id, "api_token",
TRUE);
      if ( empty($api_token) ) {
        $api_token = $this->generate_random_hash();
        update_user_meta( $user_id, "api_token", $api_token );
      }
    }
```

```
        $api_data['api_token'] = $api_token;
        ob_start();
        $wpwa_template_loader->get_template_part('api-settings');
        $html = ob_get_clean();
        echo $html;
    }
```

In the preceding code, the same `user_api_settings()` function is used to generate the screen as well as to handle the form submission. We have a HTML form for the API settings in a template called `api-settings-template.php`. We can use our reusable template loader plugin to load the template through the global `$wpwa_template_loader` object. Let's look at the template file using the following code:

```
    <?php global $api_data;
      extract($api_data);
    ?>
    <div class="wrap"><form action="" method="post" name="options">
      <h2><?php _e('API Credentials','wpwa'); ?></h2>
      <table class="form-table" width="100%" cellpadding="10">
        <tbody>
          <tr>
            <td scope="row" align="left">
            <label><?php _e('API Token :','wpwaf'); ?><?php echo
$api_token; ?></label>
            </td>
          </tr>
        </tbody>
      </table>
      <input type="submit" name="api_settings" value="<?php _e('Update',
'wpwaf');?>"
    /></form>
    </div>
```

Here, we have a HTML form with a submit button and a label for displaying the API key. We don't have any input fields as the key is generated automatically. Once the form is submitted, a new token needs to be generated as a hashed string.

Now, both the template and loading part are ready. However, this template resides outside our main plugin, and hence, the template loader object will not be able to identify the `templates` folder of this plugin. So, we need to use the extendable features to add the necessary template locations. First, we have to update the constructor to include the following code:

```
    add_filter('wpwaf_template_loader_locations',array( $this,
'api_template_locations' ));
```

Next, we can have a look at the implementation for the `api_template_locations` function to include custom template locations, as shown in the following code:

```
public function api_template_locations($locations){
    $location = trailingslashit( plugin_dir_path(__FILE__) ) .
'templates/';
    array_push($locations,$location);
    return $locations;
}
```

So, we add the path of the `templates` folder of our new plugin to the existing template locations array. Now, the template loader should be able to identify the `templates` folder.

Now, we can move back to the API key generation process:

1. First, we check for the submission of the form.
2. Then, we generate a new token using a custom function called `generate_random_hash`. The following code shows the implementation of the `generate_random_hash` function inside the `WPWAF_XML_RPC_API` class:

```
public function generate_random_hash($length = 10) {
    $characters =
    '0123456789abcdefghijklmnopqrstuvwxyzABCDEFGHIJKLMNOPQRSTUV
WXYZ';
    $random_string = '';
    for ($i = 0; $i < $length; $i++) {
        $random_string .= $characters[rand(0,
strlen($characters) - 1)];
    }
    $random_hash = wp_hash($random_string);
    return $random_hash;
}
```

3. We can generate a dynamic hashed string by passing a random string to the existing `wp_hash` function provided by WordPress.
4. Then, we update the generated token using the `update_user_meta` function. If a user is loading the screen without submission, we will display the existing token to the user.

5. Now, you will have a menu item called `API Settings` in the admin menu bar to generate the API Token screen, as shown in the following screenshot:

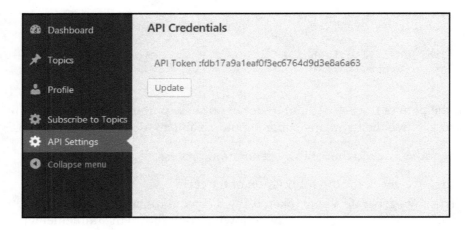

6. Having created the token, we now have to check for the token values before providing access to the API. So, consider the updated version of the `topic_subscriptions` function, as shown in the following code:

```
public function topic_subscriptions( $args ) {
    global $wpdb;
    $username = isset( $args['username'] ) ? $args['username'] : '';
    $password = isset( $args['password'] ) ? $args['password'] : '';
    $user = wp_authenticate( $username, $password );

    if (!$user || is_wp_error($user)) {
        return $user;
    }

    $follower_id = $user->ID;
    $api_token = (string) get_user_meta($follower_id, "api_token",
TRUE);

    $token = isset( $args['token'] ) ? $args['token'] : '';
    if ( $args['token'] == $api_token) {
        $topic_id = isset( $args['topic_id'] ) ? $args['topic_id'] : 0
;
        $topic_subscriptions_table =
$wpdb->prefix.'topic_subscriptions';

        $sql  = $wpdb->prepare( "SELECT * FROM
$topic_subscriptions_table WHERE
            topic_id = %d AND user_id = %d ", $topic_id , $follower_id
```

```
);

            $result = $wpdb->get_results($sql);
            if(!$result){
                $wpdb->insert(
                        $topic_subscriptions_table,
                        array(
                            'topic_id' => $topic_id,
                            'user_id' => $follower_id
                        ),
                        array(
                            '%d',
                            '%d'
                        )
                );

                return array("success" => __("Subsciption
Completed.","wpwaf"));
            }else{
                return array("error" => __("Already subscribed to
topic.","wpwaf"));
            }

        } else {
            return array("error" => __("Invalid Token.","wpwaf"));
        }

        return $args;
    }
```

7. Now, the user will have to log in to the WordPress admin page, and generate a token before using the API. In a premium API, you can either bill the user for purchasing the API token or bill the user based on their usage.

8. So now, the API client code also needs to be changed to include the token parameter. The following code contains the updated call to the API with the inclusion of tokens:

```
$wpwaf_api_client = new
WPWAF_XMLRPC_Client("http://www.yoursite.com/xmlrpc.php",
"username", "password");
$subscribe_status = $wpwaf_api_client-
>subscribeToTopics("topic id", "api token");
```

Providing the API documentation

Typically, most popular APIs provide complete documentation for accessing the API methods. Alternatively, we can use a new API method to provide details about all the other API methods and parameters. This allows third-party users to request an API method and get the details about all the other functions.

 WordPress uses the API method called `system.listMethods` for listing all the existing methods inside the API. Here, we will take one step further by providing the parameters of API methods with the complete list.

We can start the process by adding another API method to the `xml_rpc_api` function, as shown in the following code:

```
public function xml_rpc_api($methods) {
    $methods['wpwaf.subscribeToTopics']  = array( $this,
'topic_subscriptions' );
    $methods['wpwaf.getForumTopics']= array( $this, 'forum_topics_list'
);
    $methods['wpwaf.apiDoc'] = array( $this, 'api_doc' );
    return $methods;
}
```

Once updated, we can use the following code to provide details about the API methods:

```
public function api_doc() {
    $api_doc = array();

    $api_doc["wpwaf.subscribeToTopics"] = array("authentication" =>
"required", "api_token" => "required","parameters" => array("Topic ID",
"API Token"),"result" => __("Subscribing to Topics","wpwaf")
        );

    $api_doc["wpwaf.getForumTopics"] = array("authentication" =>
"optional", "api_token" => "optional", "parameters" => array("Topic
ID"),"result" => __("Retrive List of Topics of given Forum","wpwaf")
        );
    return $api_doc;
}
```

Here, we have added all the custom API functions with all the necessary details for making use of them. The `authentication` parameter defines whether a user needs to provide login credentials for accessing the API. The `api_token` parameter defines whether the user needs a token to proceed. A list of allowed parameters to the API method is defined by `parameters`, and finally, the result parameter defines what a user will get after accessing the API method.

Now that we have completed the process of working with the XML-RPC API in WordPress, You should be able to build complex APIs for web applications by using the discussed techniques. In the next section, we are going to look at the latest addition to the WordPress APIs.

WordPress REST API for web applications

REST APIs have become a popular way of providing application features as a service in all types of web application. It's already become the standard for providing third-party access and could well be the future of web application development. Most popular online applications such as Facebook, Twitter, Google, LinkedIn, and Amazon provide features to application developers through a well defined REST API. Let's take a look at the Wikipedia definition to identify what REST is and how it works:

> *"Representational state transfer (REST) or RESTful Web services are one way of providing interoperability between computer systems on the Internet. REST-compliant Web services allow requesting systems to access and manipulate textual representations of Web resources using a uniform and predefined set of stateless operations."*

Basically, REST API is a set of functions that can be accessed through HTTP protocol using HTTP methods such as `GET`, `POST` , `PUT`, `DELETE`. It has been a long time since the discussions started about the need for REST API in WordPress. So, the REST API was introduced in a external plugin for testing. Finally, it's included in WordPress core in WordPress 4.7 and now it fully supports REST API endpoints for all the major data models in WordPress.

Let's identify some of the common terms used in REST API operations:

- **Route**: This is a well defined URL which can be mapped to a HTTP method in API
- **Endpoint**: The process of matching a specific route to a HTTP method
- **Request**: The call to an API endpoint with the necessary data
- **Response**: The data provided by an API to a specific request
- **Schema**: Used to structure API data and provide info on the available properties and input parameters for API requests

Introduction to WordPress REST API endpoints

We already identified the meaning of endpoints. WordPress version 4.7 provides well defined endpoints for accessing all the main data types. Let's identify the main data needed for web applications with the endpoints provided by WordPress:

- **Posts**: `/wp/v2/posts`
- **Categories**: `/wp/v2/categories`
- **Tags**: `/wp/v2/tags`
- **Pages**: `/wp/v2/pages`
- **Comments**: `/wp/v2/comments`
- **Taxonomies**: `/wp/v2/taxonomies`
- **Users**: `/wp/v2/users`

These are the most important endpoints for web applications. You can check all the available endpoints and additional information in WordPress REST API documentation at `https://developer.wordpress.org/rest-api/reference/`.

WordPress REST API is enabled by default. You can check whether API is enabled on your site by accessing `http://www.example.com/wp-json` in the browser. If the API is enabled, you will get a large JSON string with available settings and endpoints.

Next, it's important to identify how different endpoints work in the REST API. The simplest way to test API requests is by using an API testing tool. There are many such tools and we are going to use the Postman extension for Google Chrome browser. You can install the extension in your chrome browser from `https://www.getpostman.com/`. Once installed, you will get a standalone app as shown in the following screenshot:

You will get the initial screen in white or black depending on the theme you use for the tool. Now, we are ready to test API requests with WordPress REST API.

Testing GET requests

This is the simplest request type and information in GET requests are provided for any application or user without permission. You can just type the URL `http://www.example.com/wp-json/wp/v2/posts` in the **Enter request URL** section and click the **Send** button to view the results as shown in the following screenshot:

The tab on the bottom section of the screen will contain the normal post details available in your site.

Testing POST requests

Testing POST requests require more work compared to using GET requests. These requests always require some authentication and return an error when valid authentication is not available. So, first you have to add the URL in **Enter request URL** and select the method as POST. Next, go to **Authorization** tab and select **Basic Auth** as the type. Then add the **Username** and **Password** of a user in your site with post creation and edit capabilities. Generally, POST requests need additional parameters and values. Here, we are trying to create a post and hence you can add the post details as key-value pairs in the **form-data** section of **Body** tab. Finally, click on the **Send** button to send the API request. However, you will get the following error message instead of creating the post:

```
{  "code": "rest_cannot_create",
   "message": "Sorry, you are not allowed to create posts as this
user.", "data": { "status": 401  } }
```

You might be confused why it's returning a permission error even when we have provided basic authentication details. WordPress considers basic auth as an unsafe way of handling REST API requests and, hence, **Basic Auth** is disabled by default. So, we have to use a plugin called `JSON Basic Authentication` by WordPress API Team. This plugin is included in the source code folder for this chapter. Once this plugin is activated, you can send the request again and will see the response and form parameters as shown in the following screenshot:

The response will contain the details about the newly created post from our request. You can use `UPDATE` and `DELETE` operations similarly by changing the request type and providing necessary parameter values.

Basic Auth is not a recommended way of authenticating the REST API since we have to transfer username and password details in each request in plain text format. So, the WordPress team suggests that we should only use Basic Auth for testing purposes or in highly secured private networks only.

Disabling REST API

Unlike XML-RPC API, WorPress REST API GET requests are enabled by default and accessible without authentication. This could create potential security risks since anyone can access the information with default routes. So, we can easily get the user information on any WordPress site including the usernames. Therefore, it's important to disable the REST API when we don't need it, and when we feel it's a security threat for our site.

Unfortunately, WordPress doesn't offer the features for disabling REST API, which is a major drawback at this stage. So, we have to either use an external plugin or add our own custom code to disable the REST API.

First, we will create new plugin called WPWAF REST API to handle the API operations for these sections. Create a new file called wpwa-rest-api.php. Since we have a basic implementation, we will be using a single file instead of the code structure used in the forum plugin. Let's add the code to wpwa-rest-api.php file for disabling REST API:

```
add_filter('rest_authentication_errors','wpwaf_disable_rest_api' );
function wpwaf_disable_rest_api( $access ) {
  if(! is_user_logged_in() || !current_user_can('manage_options')) {
      return new WP_Error( 'rest_cannot_access', __( 'Only authenticated
users can access the REST API.', 'wpwaf' ), array( 'status' =>
rest_authorization_required_code() ) );
      }
    return $access;
  }
```

WordPress uses the rest_authentication_errors filter for adding errors to REST API operations. This filter is not intended to disable the the REST API. However, we can use it as a workaround for disabling the API. We execute a custom function on this filter and check whether user is a guest or user is not an admin. In such cases, we return WP_Error object with restricted access error. So, now the logged in administrators will be allowed to access the API and it will be disabled for any other users or external requests.

Custom content types with REST API

In the previous chapters, we discussed the importance of custom post types in web applications compared to normal posts. Similarly, custom post types play a vital role in REST API as well. However, custom post types are not enabled by default in WordPress REST API. So, we have to apply the necessary settings and enable them as needed for our applications.

We can try whether given custom post type is enabled using the
`http://www.example.com/wp-json/wp/v2/{custom post type}` format in our
Postman app. Since REST is not enabled by default, you should get the following response:

```
{"code":"rest_no_route","message":"No route was found matching the URL
and request method","data":{"status":404}}
```

So, we have to enable support for each custom post type in the configuration. Let's see how
we can enable forums and topics of our application through REST API. We have to modify
the registration of custom post type as following in `WPWAF_Model_Manager` class:

```
public function create_post_type($params) {
    extract($params);
    $capabilities = isset($capabilities) ? $capabilities : array();
    // Define labels

    $args = array(
      // other configuration settings
      'can_export'              => true,
      'rewrite'                 => true,
      'show_in_rest'            => true,
    );
    // Assigning arguments
    register_post_type( $post_type, $args );
}
```

Basically, we can just set show_in_rest attribute as true to enable REST API support for any
given custom post type. Now, if you send the previous request, you will get a JSON string
with the available custom post type items. There are two other important parameters that
we can use in registering a custom post type:

- `rest_base`: This setting lets you define a custom base for accessing the custom
  post type. Usually, we access forum topic using `/wp-json/wp/v2/wpwaf_topic`. We can change this route using a custom route such
  as `/wp-json/wp/v2/forum_topic`. This is useful when you want to provide a
  user friendly route or keep the routes private by using non-default rest base.
- `rest_controller_class`: This setting allows us to define a custom controller
  class to generate the results for REST API requests for this custom post type. We
  can create our own class by extending `WP_REST_Controller` class and we can
  change the way we provide results or add our own custom rotes and endpoints
  to existing custom post types.

Implementation of this setting is beyond the scope of this book and hence not discussed here. You can learn more about custom rest controller classes at
https://developer.wordpress.org/rest-api/extending-the-rest-api/
controller-classes/.

Once custom post types are enabled in REST API, users can publicly access all the custom post details similar to normal posts. This could be a limitation in web applications where custom post types are restricted based on user types. This is applicable to our forum application since we are only allowing forum topics based on the user permissions we set in edit topics screen. In such scenarios, we need to disable default routes and only provide the data through custom routes or apply authentication mechanism as discussed in the last section of this chapter.

Managing custom routes and endpoints

The real power of REST API in web applications comes with the usage of custom routes and endpoints. There are certain limitations in adjusting existing routes and endpoints to our applications. In some scenarios, we may have to create our own classes and extend the WordPress core classes to achieve custom functionality. So, custom routes and endpoints allow us to implement custom REST API features with minimum work, without interfering with WordPress core REST API features.

In this section, we are going to implement the following features for our forum application while learning the basics of custom REST API routes and endpoints:

1. Disable default forum and topic endpoints and use custom endpoints to provide application topics with necessary permissions.
2. Provide REST API access to custom table data by sending topics of a given forum.

Let's start the implementation of these two features.

Creating custom routes and endpoints for forum topics

In the previous section, we enabled forum and topics post types in REST API using the `show_in_rest` attribute. However, we have limitations when using the default REST API features for custom post types. First, we only get the standard data and we need to make lot of modifications to provide custom data such as **Sticky Status** for our forum topics. Also all the topics will be available to the public and we have to make considerable changes to implement forum topic restrictions. So, we are going to create our own routes and endpoints for topic related features.

 We have to disable forums and topics in REST API by removing the `show_in_rest` attribute added earlier.

Let's add a custom route to provide forum topics through the REST API. Add the following code to the main file of `WPWAF REST API` plugin:

```
add_action( 'rest_api_init', 'wpwaf_topics_route' );
function wpwaf_topics_route() {
    register_rest_route( 'wpwaf/v1', '/read_topics', array(
        'methods'  => WP_REST_Server::READABLE,
        'callback' => 'wpwaf_prepare_read_topics',
        'permission_callback' => function () {
          return TRUE;
        }
    ) );
}
```

We start by implementing a function call on `rest_api_init` action. This action is called when the server is preparing to serve a REST API request. Inside the function, we use the `register_rest_route` function to create new routes for our application. Let's identify the basic parameters used in `register_rest_route` function:

- `namespace`: This will be the first URL segment after the main REST API URL. Here, we have used `wpwaf/v1` and, hence, it will replace the `wp/v2` we used for accessing core WordPress routes.
- `route`: This is the base URL for the route. Here, we have used `read_topics` as the route and it will replace the default route of `wpwa_topic`.
- `methods`: Here we have used the method as `WP_REST_Server::READABLE`. It makes sure that our custom route works when `WP_REST_Server` changes our readable endpoints.

- `callback`: This is the function that gets executed when a route is matched to a given endpoint. We have defined a callback function called `wpwaf_prepare_read_topics`. All the topic data that should be sent in REST API response is prepared within this function.

- `permission_callback`: This is the function used to check the permission of the request before executing the callback function. We have returned TRUE to provide permission. In real scenarios, we need to check user permission and return TRUE or FALSE.

Now, we can look into the implementation of our callback function for generating the topics list for the application. Consider the following implementation of the `wpwaf_prepare_read_topics` function:

```
function wpwaf_prepare_read_topics() {
    $topics_query = new WP_Query(array('post_type' =>
'wpwaf_topic','post_status' =>'publish',  'order' => 'desc', 'orderby' =>
'date', 'meta_key'     => '_wpwaf_topic_sticky_status', 'meta_value'    =>
'normal', 'meta_compare' => '=' ));

    $data = array();
    if($topics_query->have_posts()){
        while($topics_query->have_posts()) : $topics_query->the_post();
            $sticky_status = get_post_meta(get_the_ID(),
'_wpwaf_topic_sticky_status', true);
            array_push($data, array("ID" => get_the_ID(), "title" =>
get_the_title(), "sticky_status"=> $sticky_status ));
        endwhile;
    }
    return rest_ensure_response(($data));
}
```

In the initial part, we use `WP_Query` to generate a list of topics published in our application. We are only retrieving the **Normal** topics and omitting **Sticky** and **Super Sticky** topics for the public API. As you can see, we have full control over the data available through the REST API, compared to the previous method of enabling custom post types in the API.

Next, we traverse through the list of topics and add it to an array. In this scenario, we have also added a custom topic field value of sticky statuses to the response data. Finally, we pass the resulted data array to the `rest_ensure_response` function. This function converts our data to JSON and returns the response compatible with `WP_REST_Response`.

Creating custom routes and endpoints for custom table data

You learned how to create custom routes and endpoints for existing WordPress data. As discussed in previous chapters, custom tables play a major role in web applications. The default WordPress REST APIs don't have any routes or endpoints for working with custom table data. So, we have to always use our own custom routes and endpoints for manipulating custom table data.

In our forum application, we stored the connection between topics and forums using the Posts 2 Posts plugin in wp_p2p custom table. Now, we are going to create a custom API endpoint that allows us to retrieve the topics for a given forum. Let's start by adding another custom route to our REST API plugin as shown in the following code:

```
register_rest_route( 'wpwaf/v1', '/read_forum_topics/(?P<id>\d+)',
    array(
        'methods' => 'POST',
        'callback' => 'wpwaf_prepare_read_forum_topics',
        'args' => array(
          'id' => array(
            'validate_callback' => function($param, $request, $key) {
                return ($param != 5 );
            }
          ),
        ),
    ) );
```

We use the same namespace as on the last occasion and use read_forum_topics as the new route. Also we have an additional parameter in brackets where we can pass the ID of the forum. We have also set the method to POST instead of using GET. Since we are retrieving records and passing the ID in URL, we could have used GET as the method. However, we have enabled POST method so that we can pass additional parameters and filter the results. We have used a new callback function, wpwaf_prepare_read_forum_topics, to handle the new custom route.

In this scenario, there is an additional parameter called args compared to the previous custom route. This args array is used to validate the parameters passed to the endpoint. Assume we want to restrict a certain forum(s) from being available through the REST API. So, we execute the validate_callback function on the id parameter. If you pass forum ID as 5, you will get the following invalid parameter error:

```
{"code":"rest_invalid_param","message":"Invalid parameter(s):
id","data":{"status":400,"params":{"id":"Invalid parameter."}}}
```

We can use this technique to validate multiple parameters with different conditions and make sure Requests only contain the data in requested formats. Now, we can move into the implementation of the `wpwaf_prepare_read_forum_topics` function for handling the request to the new route:

```
function wpwaf_prepare_read_forum_topics($data){
   global $wpdb;
   $data = $data->get_params();
   $forum_id = isset($data['id']) ? $data['id'] : 0;

   $topics_to_forums = $wpdb->prefix.'p2p';
   $sql  = $wpdb->prepare( "SELECT wppost.* from $wpdb->posts as wppost
inner join $topics_to_forums as wpp2p on wppost.ID = wpp2p.p2p_from where
wppost.post_type = '%s' and wppost.post_status = 'publish' and p2p_type=
'topics_to_forums' and p2p_to = %d ", 'wpwaf_topic', $forum_id);

   $result = $wpdb->get_results($sql);
   $topics = array();
   if($result){
      foreach ($result as $key => $value) {
         $topics[] = array('ID'=> $value->ID, 'post_title' =>
$value->post_title, 'post_content' => $value->post_content);
      }
   }

   return rest_ensure_response(($topics));
}
```

The REST API request object is passed to this function as a parameter. So, we use the `get_params` function of the `$data` object to retrieve the available parameters in the request. Next, we capture the forum ID using the `id` attribute of the `$data` object. Next, we execute a custom query on the **p2p** table while joining it with the posts table. The result will contain the published topics for the given forum. Then, we traverse through the results and assign the topic details in to an array. Finally, we use the `rest_ensure_response` function to pass the topic data in JSON format to the response.

There are also some disadvantages in using custom routes and endpoints, in situations where we have the ability to use existing routes and endpoints. We need to implement our own pagination and sorting for custom endpoints while WordPress provides them by default for existing endpoints.

We can use user permission checks by default in WordPress core endpoints while we need to pass additional nonce parameters to check user permissions.

Now, we can call this new route and retrieve the topics list for a given forum.

Building the REST API client

API client is the user or service that uses the data provided by the REST API. We can have two types of REST API clients:

- **REST API client in the same site**: We use REST API features within the same site using other plugins or themes. So, the plugin handles the necessary features by calling the REST API routes instead of manually querying the database.
- **REST API client from external site**: We use the client and access the REST API of another site. The client site could be WordPress or non-WordPress site. The client can also be implemented in different programming language without using PHP.

There are several benefits of using both of these methods in different scenarios. Let's identify the usage of API clients.

REST API client in the same site

The simplest way is to use the REST API in the same site. This technique is valuable in scenarios where we use multiple plugins for application development. Assume, we have two plugins called A and B. We want to work with some of the features of plugin A within plugin B. In such scenarios, we will have to look for available filters/actions or directly change the code to implement it. Instead, if plugin A provides REST API routes for its features, we can easily access them through plugin B to achieve the requirements.

Also, another important thing is that we may miss some of the necessary validations, unless we completely understand the code of plugin A. With the REST API of plugin A, we don't need to worry about any such validations. All we need to do is execute the API route with necessary parameters and plugin A will handle the internal stuff. So, using the API client within the same site is quite useful and allows us to use WordPress default features such as user permission checking and Backbone models.

There are plans for providing the entire functionality of the WordPress admin section through REST API requests. We will see this in future versions of WordPress and it will be the best scenario for understanding the need for the API client within the same site.

Now, we can start building a simple API client within the site using the WordPress core features and core REST API routes. We can develop the client using PHP or JavaScript libraries provided by WordPress. In the modern world, building single page applications with JavaScript frameworks such as Backbone and Node.js has become a popular choice. That's also one of the major reasons why we need REST API features. So, we are going to look at basic implementation of a `Backbone.js`-based client instead of developing a PHP based client.

We will be using the `WPWAF REST API` plugin to add the `Backbone.js` based API client functionality. First, we need to use the following code to load the `wp-api` script in WordPress:

```
add_action('wp_enqueue_scripts','add_rest_api_scripts');
function add_rest_api_scripts(){

    wp_register_script('WPWAF_REST', WPWAF_REST_PLUGIN_URL."rest.js" ,
array( 'wp-api' ) );
    wp_enqueue_script('WPWAF_REST');
}
```

In this code, we load a custom script to handle REST API functionality while loading `wp-api` script as a dependency.

In `Chapter 9`, *Enhancing the Power of Open Source Libraries and Plugins*, we discussed the importance of `Backbone.js` in web applications. Here, we can understand the importance further by looking at the `Backbone.js` support for WordPress REST API operations.

WordPress provides `Backbone.js` models for all the major endpoints in REST API. We can access these models using `wp.api.models` object and directly execute the CRUD operations in these models. So, let's look at the implementation of a `rest.js` file inside our plugin, where we do REST API operations with `Backbone.js`:

```
wp.api.loadPromise.done( function() {
  var post = new wp.api.models.Post( { id: 280 } );
  post.fetch();

  var post = new wp.api.models.Post( { title: 'This is a REST API
post', content: 'REST API post content' } );
  post.save();
} );
```

Before executing any API operations, we have to make sure `wp.api.models` are loaded properly. Therefore, we use the `loadPromise.done` function of the API. Inside this function, we can execute any type of operation since all the models are loaded properly.

We can access WordPress posts related API endpoints using the `wp.api.models.Post` object. In the first two lines, we initialize the Post with the ID `280` and call `Backbone.jsfetch` function on the post object to retrieve the details about the given post. We can refresh the site and see the JSON response for fetching the post using the browser console.

In the next two lines of code, again we initialize a post object. However, this time we are planning to create a new post through REST API and hence we pass the necessary attributes and values to the post model. Then, we call the `Backbone.jssave` function on the model to create a new post on the site. If you are already logged in as a user with post creation permission, you will see a new post on your site once the code is executed. If you are not logged in as a permitted user, this will generate the following error:

```
{"code":"rest_cannot_create","message":"Sorry, you are not allowed to
create posts as this user.","data":{"status":401}}
```

So, it's important to note that user authentication is necessary to access REST API features through built-in `Backbone.js` models. Therefore, we can understand that `Backbone.js` based API clients are most suitable when working with existing WordPress REST API endpoints and executing API operations within the site.

Now, we can complete this section by looking at update and delete operations with `Backbone.js` as shown in the following code:

```
wp.api.loadPromise.done( function() {
  var post = new wp.api.models.Post( { id: 282, title: 'Updated REST
API post', content: 'Updated REST API post content' } );
  post.save();

  var post = new wp.api.models.Post( { id: 280 } );
  post.destroy();
} );
```

In the first two lines, we add the post details and load it as a model similar to previous example. However, we use post id on this occasion. So, the post with existing an ID will be loaded instead of creating a new post model. Then, we use the `save` function to save the data. Since this is done on an existing post, the `save` function will update the post instead of creating new posts. The next two lines are used to delete a post from the site. We load the post to a model using the ID and execute the `Backbone.js` destroy function to delete the post from the site.

In this section, we learned how to use `Backbone.js` based REST API operations while using an API client within the same site. We can also build a PHP based API client to execute such operations within the site.

REST API client from external site

This is where REST API is used to its maximum potential, even though we use it to build functionality of the same site. The main intention of creating a REST API is to provide access to third-party WordPress and non-WordPress based applications. So, the API client can be implemented in any programming language. In this section, we will be building a PHP based API client for accessing REST APIs of other applications with the support of CURL.

Let's add the API client implementation with CURL. You should place this code in a PHP file and access it from a source external to your application:

```php
function rest_api_client($url,$post_data = ''){
    $api_route = $url;
    $ch = curl_init($api_route);
    $headers = array(
        'Authorization:Basic YWRtaW46dTh1OHU4dTg='// <---
    );
    curl_setopt($ch, CURLOPT_HTTPHEADER, $headers);
    curl_setopt($ch, CURLOPT_SSL_VERIFYHOST, false);
    curl_setopt($ch, CURLOPT_RETURNTRANSFER, 1);
    curl_setopt($ch, CURLOPT_POST, true);
    curl_setopt($ch, CURLOPT_SSL_VERIFYPEER, false);

    if($post_data != ''){
        curl_setopt($ch, CURLOPT_POSTFIELDS, $post);
    }
    curl_setopt($ch, CURLOPT_VERBOSE, 1);
    $return = curl_exec($ch);
    echo "<pre>";
    print_r($return);
    exit;

}

$post_data = array();
$post_data = json_encode($post_data);
$api_route =
"http://www.example.com/wp-json/wpwaf/v1/read_forum_topics/100";
rest_api_client($api_route,$post_data);
```

We create a function called `rest_api_client` to accept two parameters for the API endpoint URL and the post data. Then we initialize a curl request using the REST API operations require `curl_init` function on the specified route. Then we add the `Authorization` header with a base 64 encoded string containing the combination of `username:password`. We need some sort of a authenticate method to execute `POST`, `DELETE` requests. We should only use an `Authorization` header for testing purposes. We will be discussing various authentication techniques in the next section.

Then, we specify the necessary curl parameters and add the post data to the request in case it's provided. Finally, we execute and print the API response returned from the server. Now, we have a basic API client function and we can call the function with necessary parameters to execute REST API requests as shown in the preceding code.

In this case, we are retrieving the topics of the forum with the ID `100` and it will return the JSON string with the topic results. If we request the ID `5`, we will get an invalid parameter error since its validated and restricted in our route.

So, we have identified the process of using both JavaScript and PHP for executing REST API functions within the site and from external sources.

REST API authentication and access tokens

As we discussed earlier, all `POST` and `DELETE` REST API operations require authentication. In some scenarios, we may have to use authentication even for the `GET` requests in providing private data. So, authentication becomes the most important and must use aspect in REST API operations in web applications. We identified that Basic Auth is not a secure or recommended way of authenticating your API operations. In this section, we are going to look at the possible ways of integrating REST API authentication:

- **Basic authentication**: We used this technique while testing the API requests with Postman app. In this technique, we pass the username and password in a base 64-encoded string within the request header. Since, these details are passed in plain text, it's not considered secure for real use.
- **Cookie-based authentication**: In this technique, we use the browser cookies created in user login and nonce value to authenticate the user. We can pass the nonce value through `_wpnonce` parameter or `X-WP-Nonce` header. This technique requires a valid nonce value and the user to be logged in to WordPress. It means we can only use this technique within the site with valid users and, hence, it's not the ideal method in providing access to third-party clients.

- **OAuth authentication**: This is the recommended way of authenticating third party requests to the API. In this technique we use OAuth token credentials to verify the requests. We have to create OAuth app and authenticate the application to use the REST API similar to the social login apps we created earlier. Since, these tokens have a short lifetime, it's considered as the most secure way. However, the implementation of this technique is very complex compared to other techniques and, hence, beyond the scope of this book.

- **Token authentication**: In this technique, we use a custom token similar to the one used in XML-RPC. This is similar to the the OAuth technique. However, this is simpler and less secure compared to OAuth technique. These tokens are also sent in plain text. However, we don't expose user account details and we can frequently regenerate the token to make the process secure.

Let's see how we can implement token-based authentication for our read forum topics functionality of REST API. We can use the same token generated in the XML-RPC section for authenticating requests. The following code contains the updated version of the `wpwaf_prepare_read_forum_topics` function using `api` token authentication:

```
function wpwaf_prepare_read_forum_topics($data){
    global $wpdb;
    $post_data = json_decode($data->get_body());
    $data = $data->get_params();
    $api_token = isset($post_data->api_token) ? $post_data->api_token :
'';
    $sql_token  = $wpdb->prepare( "SELECT * from $wpdb->usermeta where
meta_key = 'api_token' and   meta_value = '%s'", $api_token);
    $result_token = $wpdb->get_results($sql_token);
    if(!$result_token){
        return new WP_Error( 'rest_cannot_access', __( 'Only authenticated
users can access the REST API.', 'wpwaf' ), array( 'status' =>
rest_authorization_required_code() ) );
    }

    $forum_id = isset($data['id']) ? $data['id'] : 0;
    $topics_to_forums = $wpdb->prefix.'p2p';
    $sql  = $wpdb->prepare( "SELECT wppost.* from $wpdb->posts as wppost
inner join $topics_to_forums as wpp2p on wppost.ID = wpp2p.p2p_from where
wppost.post_type = '%s' and wppost.post_status = 'publish' and p2p_type=
'topics_to_forums' and p2p_to = %d ", 'wpwaf_topic', $forum_id);

    $result = $wpdb->get_results($sql);
    $topics = array();
    if($result){
      foreach ($result as $key => $value) {
        $topics[] = array('ID'=> $value->ID, 'post_title' =>
```

```
$value->post_title, 'post_content' => $value->post_content);
        }
    }
    return rest_ensure_response(($topics));
}
```

We have changed the initial part of the code to get the post data using the `get_body` function of the request object. Then we use the `json_decode` function and extract the provided API token into a variable. Next, we execute a custom query on the `wp_usermeta` table to check whether a given token is assigned to any user. If the token is matched, we continue the function and, if it's not matched, we return a permission error.

Now, we can look at the modifications in the client function call to include the `api` token as shown in the following code:

```
    $post_data = array('api_token' => 'fdb17a9a1eaf0f3ec6d3e8a6a63' );
    $post_data = json_encode($post_data);
    $api_route =
"http://www.example.com/wp-json/wpwaf/v1/read_forum_topics/231";
    rest_api_client($api_route,$post_data);
```

We call the REST API route using the same process as earlier. However, we include the API token generated from the **API Settings** section, in a post data array. Now, we have proper authentication to the route. We can implement the same authentication checks to other routes as well.

 In this scenario, we assigned tokens to the users and checked the tokens from external sources. So, a valid user account was necessary even though user login credentials are not used. If we need to provide complete third party access without users, we can store the token details on a custom table instead of a user table and send the tokens to the necessary people.

REST API is becoming the trend in modern web applications and hence WordPress seems to provide more and more features to build fully functional REST APIs for applications. So, in the future, we will see the emergence of REST as a must use WordPress feature and deprecation of XML-RPC API based functionalities.

Time for action

Throughout this chapter, we looked at the various aspects of the WordPress XML-RPC API and REST API while developing practical scenarios. In order to build stable and complex custom APIs, you should have practical experience of the preceding techniques. I recommend that you try the following tasks to extend the knowledge gathered in this chapter:

- You can measure the API usage through the number of requests.
- We created an API function to list all the forums and topics of the application. Try to introduce the filtering of results with additional parameters.
- The XML-RPC API created in this chapter returns an array as the result. Introduce different result formats such as JSON, XML, and array, so that developers can choose their preferred format.
- Implement OAuth based token authentication for REST API.

Summary

We started this chapter with the intention of building XML-RPC-based and REST-based APIs for web applications. Then, we discussed the usage of the existing XML-RPC API functions while building an API client from scratch.

We looked at the modern way of implementing API features through WordPress REST API. We discussed various aspects of REST API such as custom post type support, creating custom endpoints and creating internal and external API clients.

Complex applications will always exceed the limits of an existing API; hence, we looked at the possibility of creating a custom API with both XML-RPC and REST. User authentication is one of the most important aspects of an API and hence we implemented token based authentication in XML-RPC for preventing unnecessary API access and measuring the API usage. Similarly, we looked at various authentication techniques for REST API and completed the implementation with token based authentication for REST API.

Finally, we looked at the possibility of creating the API documentation through another API function. Having completed the API creation techniques, you should now be able to develop complex APIs to suit any kind of web application.

In the next chapter, we will be restructuring our application plugin to improve consistency of code, while looking at some of the incomplete areas of the forum management application. So, be prepared for an exciting finish to this book!

11
Integrating and Finalizing the Forum Management Application

Building a large web application is a complex task that should be planned and managed with well-defined processes. Typically, we separate large applications into smaller submodules, where each submodule is tested independently from other modules. Finally, we integrated all the modules to complete the application. The integration of modules is one of the most difficult tasks in application development.

The forum management application created throughout this book intended to illustrate the advanced concepts of WordPress web application development. Therefore, we had to use different techniques in different modules to understand the issues and find feasible solutions. In real world, we have to limit the use of different techniques and keep the consistency across all the features of the application. So, we will be fixing some of the inconsistencies of the application while restructuring the necessary components. After the completion of this chapter, developers should be able to build similar or complex applications without any difficulty.

In this chapter, we will cover the following topics:

- Integrating and structuring the forum application
- Integrating the template loader into a user manager
- Creating forum and topic detail pages
- Implementing frontend topic creation and permissions
- Implementing frontend response creation and permissions
- Join users to forums
- Updating the user profile with additional fields
- Scheduling subscriber notifications

- Time for action
- Final thoughts

Let's get started!

Integrating and structuring the forum application

Throughout the first 10 chapters, we implemented the functionality of a forum management system using one main plugin and few other independent plugins. In each chapter, we explained some of the advanced concepts while developing the features related to that concept. So, our application was structured based on modules in WordPress. In the real world, we plan all the features of the application while separating them into sections based on functionality. Here, we have separated them into sections based on WordPress core modules. In the upcoming sections, we are going to fix the inconsistent components in our application and complete the remaining functionality of a basic forum application.

Integrating the template loader into a user manager

In Chapter 2, *Implementing Membership Roles, Permissions, and Features*, we used direct file inclusions to load the necessary templates. A few chapters later, we improved the loading of templates by introducing a common template loader. Now, we can integrate the template loader into the user management functionality to keep the code consistent.

Let's apply the template loader instead of using direct template inclusions. Consider the template loading section of the display_registration_form function, as shown in the following code:

```
include dirname(__FILE__) . '/templates/register-template.php';
exit;
```

Now, we can take a look at the modified version with the support of the template loader object, as shown in the following code:

```
ob_start();
$wpwa_template_loader->get_template_part('register');
echo ob_get_clean();
```

With the implementation of the new process, we can pass the template data through a global variable called $wpwa_template_data. This is the process recommended by WordPress instead of including templates directly. We can replace all the occurrences of manual template file loading in the WPWAF_Login and WPWAF_Registration classes.

WordPress has emerged as a web development framework in recent years. However, it still has a very limited amount of applications compared to generic blogs or websites. So, the best practices and design patterns have not been discussed or implemented for web application development. Here, we have discussed a possible technique for structuring applications. Yet, there is still a lot of scope for improving the current design. On the other hand, you might have a better structuring process for developing web applications with WordPress.

Working with the restructured application

Having resolved the inconsistencies, we now have to understand the process of creating new functionalities from scratch and integrating with the features we created so far. So, in this section, we will build the forum details and topic details pages of or application. In previous chapters, we created the home page of the application to display the list of available forums with topics count using a shortcode. Once, users clicks on the forum link from the list, they will be navigated to the **Forum Details** page. This is the core functionality of the application where the user interacts with other users. Let's identify the requirements of the forum details page.

Building the forum page

This is the page that lists the details of a given forum and the available topics inside the forum. First, we have to identify the possible techniques of implementing such a page and choosing the ideal technique for your application. Let's identify some of the different techniques:

- **Using a shortcode**: Create a shortcode for the forum details page and use it on a WordPress page. This is not the best technique, unless you don't have full control over your site.
- **Using default single post template**: WordPress provides single-post template called single-post.php for displaying post/custom post type details page. We can customize the existing template to add forum and topic details. However, this is used as the common template for individual post display of all post types. Therefore, it's difficult to manage this template for such a requirement.

- **Using single custom post type template**: WordPress allows us to create custom single post type template for each custom post type using `single-post_type.php`. In this technique, we can create different templates for different post types, and hence it is easier to build and manage forum details page. However, this template is theme-dependent and hence we have to use it inside the theme. So, it makes difficult to upgrade or switch the theme and hence is not the best solution, even though it's a highly possible solution.

- **Using post type template**: As discussed earlier, post type templates allows us to create multiple templates for the same custom post type and assign it to different custom posts from the editor. This technique is quite useful when we have multiple forums that require different content and design in the detail page. However, this template is theme-dependent and hence we have to use it inside the theme. So, it makes difficult to upgrade or switch the theme and hence is not the best solution, even though it's a highly possible solution.

- **Using custom templates**: In this technique, we intercept the default template loading process of WordPress and assign our own template to be displayed on frontend. This technique is not theme-dependent, and hence we can add custom templates through plugins. This is the ideal solution, unless you are willing to change the files of the theme or willing to work with less flexible application.

Let's start building the forum details using the custom templates technique with our forum management plugin.

First, we have to intercept the template loading process and load our custom template. So, add the following filter code to the constructor of `WPWAF_Model_Forum` class:

```
add_filter('single_template', array( $this, 'display_forum_template'));
```

This filter will be called every time WordPress tries to load the single post template of a normal post or a custom post type. So, we can check various conditions within this filter implementation and return a custom template based on our requirements. Let's take a look at the implementation of the `display_forum_template` function:

```
public function display_forum_template($single) {
  global $wp_query, $post;
  if ($post->post_type == "wpwaf_forum"){
    if(file_exists(WPWAF_PLUGIN_DIR . 'templates/single-forum.php'))
      return WPWAF_PLUGIN_DIR . 'templates/single-forum.php';
  }
  return $single;
}
```

First, we have to make sure that the correct post type is checked since failing to do so will return the custom template for all post types. Once, we filter the forum post type, we can check the existence of the custom template inside our forum plugin. We can load this template from any location as long as we provide a valid file path. Finally, we return the location of our custom template. Now, WordPress will load the single-forum.php file within our plugin folder on each request to forum details page.

Next task is to create the custom template for forum detail page. Create a new file inside the template folder of forum plugin and save it as single-forum.php. This template file should handle the display of three main sections:

- Forum details
- Topic creation form
- Forum topics list

Let's create the base structure of the forum details page using the following code:

```php
<?php
    global $post,$wpwaf,$wpwaf_single_topic_data;
    get_header();
    // Loading data
?>

<div id="wpwaf_forum_panel">
    <div id="wpwaf_forum_info">
        // Section 1 - Forum details
    </div>
    <div style="clear:both"></div>

    <div id="wpwaf_create_topics">
        // Section 2 - Topic create form
    </div>
    <div style="clear:both"></div>
    <div id="wpwaf_forum_topics">
        // Section 3 - Forum topics
    </div>
</div>
<?php get_footer(); ?>
```

We start the template by adding the necessary global variables needed for the template. Then, we call the get_header function to display the header of the theme.

We are loading the custom template within a plugin and we are using the header and footer functions of existing theme. So, switching the theme doesn't affect the template and the custom template is not dependent on the theme.

Next, we have three sections with HTML containers for displaying forum details, topic creation form, and the list of topics of the forum. We complete the template by calling the default `get_footer` function of the theme to load the footer. In the next few sections, we will be building aforementioned three sections to complete the forum details page.

Displaying forum details

In this section, we display the common information about the forum. We will be using forum title, forum description, and forum administrator information as the information for our application. You may find more forum specific field details in other applications. Let's get started by adding the code for `section 1`:

```
<div id="wpwaf_forum_info_left">
<h3><?php echo $post->post_title; ?></h3>
<div><?php echo $post->post_content; ?></div>
</div>
<div id="wpwaf_forum_info_right">
<h3><?php _e('Administrators','wpwaf'); ?></h3>
<div>
<?php foreach ($administrators as $key => $administrator) { ?>
    <div class="wpwaf_forum_admin_image"><?phpecho get_avatar(
$administrator->ID, 32 );  ?></div>
    <div><?php echo $administrator->data->display_name; ?></div>
<?php }  ?>
</div>
<h3><?php _e('Moderators','wpwaf'); ?></h3>
<div>
<?php  foreach ($moderators as $key => $moderator) { ?>
    <div class="wpwaf_forum_admin_image"><?phpecho get_avatar(
$moderator->ID, 32 );  ?></div>
    <div><?php echo $moderator->data->display_name; ?></div>
<?php  }  ?>
</div>
</div>
```

In the first part, we display the title and the description of the forum using the global `$post` variable we added in initial structuring stage. Then, we need to list the administrators and moderators who will be participating in the forum activities. So, we have two sections that loop through `$administrators` and `$moderators` to display the name and avatar image.

Now, have to generate these two lists by calling the necessary functions from the top section, as shown in the following code:

```php
<?php
    global $post,$wpwaf,$wpwaf_single_topic_data;
    get_header();
    $administrators = $wpwaf->user->get_administrators();
    $moderators     = $wpwaf->user->get_moderators();
?>
```

Finally, we can complete `section 1` by implementing these two functions inside the `WPWAF_User` class, as shown in the following code:

```php
public function get_administrators(){
    $administrators = array();

    $user_query = new WP_User_Query(array('role__in'
=>array('administrator'),'number' => 25, 'orderby' => 'registered', 'order'
=> 'desc'));
    foreach ($user_query->results as $member) {
      $administrators[] = $member;
    }
    return $administrators;
  }

public function get_moderators(){
    $moderators = array();
    $user_query = new WP_User_Query(array('role__in'
=>array('wpwaf_moderator'), 'number' => 25, 'orderby' => 'registered',
'order' => 'desc'));
    foreach ($user_query->results as $member) {
      $moderators[] = $member;
    }
    return $moderators;
  }
```

In both the functions, we use basic `WP_User_Query` with different user role parameters for administrators and moderators. Now, we have the basic information for the forum.

Creating new forum topics

In earlier sections, we added features to let users create forum topics from the backend as well as through the REST API. However, forum details page is the most important location where users normally view and create topics. So, we need to have the topic creation on top of the topics list or at the bottom of the topics list. Here, we are going to add it to the top of the topics list. Let's implement section 2 of the code:

```php
<?php if(current_user_can('edit_wpwaf_topics')) { ?>
<?php if($wpwaf_single_topic_data['msg'] !== ''){ ?>
    <div class="wpwaf_forum_msg_<?php echo
$wpwaf_single_topic_data['msg_status']; ?>"><?php echo
$wpwaf_single_topic_data['msg']; ?></div>
    <?php } ?>

    <div id="wpwaf_create_topics">
    <form action="" method="POST" >
    <div class="wpwaf_create_topics_label"><?php _e('Topic Title','wpwaf');
?></div>
    <div id="wpwaf_create_topics_editor">
        <input type="text" name="wpwaf_topic_title" id="wpwaf_topic_title"
/>
    </div>
    <div class="wpwaf_create_topics_label"><?php _e('Topic
Content','wpwaf'); ?></div>
    <div id="wpwaf_create_topics_editor">
        <textarea name="wpwaf_topic_content"
id="wpwaf_topic_content"></textarea>
    </div>
    <div id="">
        <input type="hidden" name="wpwaf_forum_id" value="<?php echo
$post->ID; ?>" />
        <input type="submit" name="wpwaf_topic_submit"
id="wpwaf_topic_submit" value="<?php _e('Create','wpwaf'); ?>" />
    </div>
    </form>
    </div>
    <?php } ?>
```

We start the template code by checking the permissions for creating forum topics. Only users with the edit_wpwaf_topics capability are able to create topics. Once verified, we check the existence of error or success message for topic creation and display the message with respective CSS classes. Next, we add the HTML form with topic title and topic content fields. The ID of the forum is added as a hidden variable along with the submit button. Now, we have the complete form to create forum topics.

The next task is the handling of topic creation process. We can start by calling a new function on `init` action for handling topic creation:

```
add_action('init',array( $this, 'handle_topic_create') );
```

Implementation of the `handle_topic_create` function is placed in the `WPWAF_Model_Topic,` class as shown in the following code:

```php
public function handle_topic_create(){
    global $wpwaf_single_topic_data,$wpdb,$post;
    $wpwaf_single_topic_data['msg'] = '';

    if(isset($_POST['wpwaf_topic_submit'])){
        if(trim($_POST['wpwaf_topic_title']) == ''){
            $wpwaf_single_topic_data['msg'] = __('Topic title is
requird.','wpwaf');
            $wpwaf_single_topic_data['msg_status'] = 'error';
        }else if(trim($_POST['wpwaf_topic_content']) == ''){
            $wpwaf_single_topic_data['msg'] = __('Topic content is
requird.','wpwaf');
            $wpwaf_single_topic_data['msg_status'] = 'error';
        }else{
            $forum_id =  isset($_POST['wpwaf_forum_id']) ? (int)
$_POST['wpwaf_forum_id'] : '';
            $topic_title = isset($_POST['wpwaf_topic_title']) ?
sanitize_text_field($_POST['wpwaf_topic_title']) : '';
            $topic_content = $_POST['wpwaf_topic_content'];
            $topic_data = array(
                'post_author' => get_current_user_id(),
                'post_content' => $topic_content,
                'post_title' => $topic_title,
                'post_status' => 'publish',
                'post_type' => 'wpwaf_topic'  );

            $topic_id = wp_insert_post($topic_data);
            update_post_meta( $topic_id , '_wpwaf_topic_sticky_status',
'normal' );

            $topic_relations_table = $wpdb->prefix.'p2p';
              $wpdb->insert(
                $topic_relations_table,
array(
                    'p2p_from' => $topic_id,
                    'p2p_to' => $forum_id,
                    'p2p_type' => 'topics_to_forums'  ),
array(
                    '%d',
                    '%d',
```

```
                    '%s' ) );

        $wpwaf_single_topic_data['msg'] = __('Topic created
successfully.','wpwaf');
        $wpwaf_single_topic_data['msg_status'] = 'success';
    }
  }
}
```

We begin the function by defining the necessary global variables and setting the initial message to empty. Next, we go through the required parameter validations for topic title and topic content. If validation fails, we assign the error message and message status to the `$wpwaf_single_topic_data` global variable to be displayed inside the template.

Once validations are successfully completed, we use the `$topic_data` array to assign the basic data needed for topic creation. Here, we used author, content, title, post type, and status parameters. You can add any available parameters for post creation as provided in `https://developer.wordpress.org/reference/functions/wp_insert_post/`.

Then, we use the `wp_insert_post` function to create the new topic and get the return value from this execution as the topic ID. Next, topic sticky status is saved as normal using the `update_post_meta` function.

 In this scenario, we assign the default sticky status as normal to prevent users from spamming the forum. Administrators or moderators can check the topic in backend and assign necessary sticky status after verifying. If you are managing a forum with trusted and responsible members, you can offer members to set the sticky status.

Finally, we need to save the relation between topic and the forum. So, we use the `insert` function of the `$wpdb` object to save the topics to forums relation details in a custom **p2p** table. Then, we add the successful message to complete the process of topic creation from the forum details page.

Displaying forum topics

We have completed the first two sections of the forums detail page, and this will be the final section of the template where we display the topics of the forum. The list of topics of the viewed forum should be ordered to display latest on the top. Also, we need to display additional information about the topic such as started by user, started date, and so on. Let's take a look at the implementation of topics list inside the `single-forum.php` template:

```
<div id="wpwaf_forum_topics">
```

```php
<?php foreach ($forum_topics as $key => $forum_topic) { ?>

<div class="wpwaf_forum_topic">
<div class="wpwaf_topic_sticky_status"><?php echo
$forum_topic['sticky_status']; ?></div>
<div class="wpwaf_topic_author_image" ><?php echo
$forum_topic['topic_author_image'];  ?></div>
<div class="wpwaf_topic_right">
<div class="wpwaf_topic_title" >
    <a href="<?php echo get_permalink($forum_topic['ID']); ?>"><?php
echo $forum_topic['topic_title']; ?></a>
</div>

<div class="wpwaf_topic_started wpwaf_topic_stats" ><span><?php
_e("Started by","wpwaf"); ?> :</span><?php echo
$forum_topic['topic_author_name']; ?></div>

<div class="wpwaf_topic_started_date wpwaf_topic_stats" ><span><?php
_e("Started on","wpwaf"); ?> :</span><?php echo $forum_topic['topic_date'];
?></div>

</div>
<div class="wpwaf_clear"></div>
</div>
<?php    }   ?>
    </div>
```

The implementation of the topics list begins with traversing through the forum topics list retrieved to the template. Inside the loop, we display topic sticky status, gravatar image of the author, topic title, author name, and topic date. We have to link the topic title to the topic details page using the `get_permalink` function.

 We can use the `get_permalink` function to retrieve the single page URL of any post or custom post type.

Next, we can get the list of topics of a forum by calling the `list_forum_topics` function in the top section of the template with the following code:

```php
$forum_topics   = $wpwaf->topic->list_forum_topics($post->ID);
```

Finally, we can add the implementation of the `list_forum_topics` function inside the `WPWAF_Model_Topic` class, as shown in the following code:

```
public function list_forum_topics($forum_id) {
    global $wpdb;
    $topics_to_forums = $wpdb->prefix.'p2p';
    $sql  = $wpdb->prepare( "SELECT wppost.* from $wpdb->posts as wppost
inner join $topics_to_forums as wpp2p on wppost.ID = wpp2p.p2p_from where
wppost.post_type = '%s' and wppost.post_status = 'publish' and p2p_type=
'topics_to_forums' and p2p_to = %d order by wppost.post_date desc",
'wpwaf_topic', $forum_id);

    $result = $wpdb->get_results($sql);
    $topics = array();
    if($result){
      foreach ($result as $key => $value) {

        $topic_author = get_userdata($value->post_author);
        $topic_author_name = $topic_author->data->display_name;
        $topic_author_image = get_avatar( $topic_author->ID, 64 );
        $sticky_status = get_post_meta($value->ID,
'_wpwaf_topic_sticky_status' , true);
        $sticky_labels = array('normal' => __('Normal','wpwaf'), 'sticky'
=> __('Sticky','wpwaf'),       'super_sticky' => __('Super
Sticky','wpwaf'));
        $sticky_status = $sticky_labels[$sticky_status];

        $topics[] = array('ID'=> $value->ID, 'topic_title' =>
$value->post_title,  'topic_content' =>
$value->post_content,'topic_author_name' => $topic_author_name,
'topic_author_image' =>$topic_author_image, 'topic_date' =>
$value->post_date, 'sticky_status' => $sticky_status);
      }
    }
    return $topics;
  }
```

The relationship between topics and forums are stored in a custom **p2p** table. So, we have to join this table with the WordPress posts table to get the list of topics for the given forum. We use custom query to join the two database tables while using the forum ID as a parameter. Once results are retrieved, we use a `foreach` loop to traverse through the results and assign the necessary data to an array called `$topics`.

Author details of the topic are retrieved by passing the `post_author` value of the result object to the `get_userdata` function.

We can use the `get_userdata` function to retrieve a user object for the given ID. If the user doesn't exist, this function returns `false` instead of `WP_User` object.

Next, we retrieve the sticky status of the topic and use an array to replace sticky status key with a user-friendly sticky status label. Once topic details are returned to the template, we will have a completed forum details page with the main features.

Now, you can click on one of the forum links in application home page **Forum List** section and you will get a screen similar to the following screenshot:

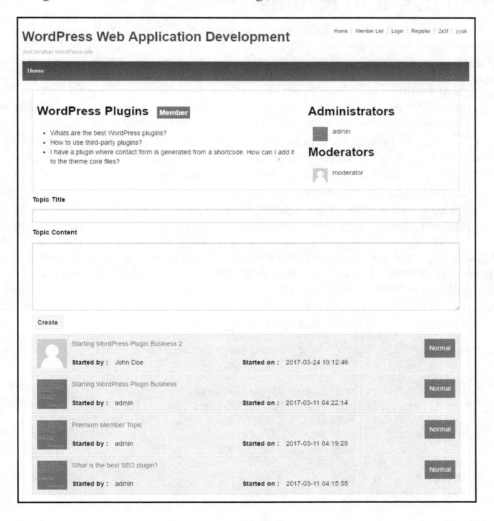

Here, we have only one administrator and one moderator. You will see all the available administrators and moderators in the top section. The topic list currently contains four topics created by an administrator and normal user.

> The topic creation section is only available for the users with `edit_wpwaf_topics` capability. All other user types including guests will see the top and bottom section of this screen without the topic creation form.

Joining users to forums

Generally, some sort of authorization is used to verify the access of users to a forum or group. Allowing users to join to a forum is one way of providing authorization. There are several techniques for implementing the join feature for forums, as listed in the following:

- **Automatic Join**: In this technique, anyone can click on the Join button to join to the forum and the user will be automatically added to the forum. This is useful for public forums where you don't want to keep content private.
- **Request to Join**: This technique requires the user to click on the **Join** button and wait for the approval from administrators of the forum. Until the request is approved, the user won't be able to use the forum.
- **Invite to Join**: In this method, users are not allowed to join or request to join. Instead, administrators send invitations to users and they use the invitation link or code to automatically join the forum. This is ideal for highly private forums.

In this application, we use automatic join feature to keep the implementation simple and apply necessary restrictions based on user permission levels. Before starting the implementation, we need another custom table to keep the data for users of each forum. So, we have to add the following code inside the `create_custom_tables` function of the `WPWAF_Config_Manager` class to include a new custom table:

```
$forum_users_table = $wpdb->prefix.'forum_users';
if($wpdb->get_var("show tables like '$forum_users_table'") !=
$forum_users_table) {
    $sql = "CREATE TABLE $forum_users_table (
id mediumint(9) NOT NULL AUTO_INCREMENT,
join_time datetime DEFAULT '0000-00-00 00:00:00' NOT NULL,
user_id mediumint(9) NOT NULL,
        forum_id  mediumint(9) NOT NULL,
        UNIQUE KEY id (id)  );";
    dbDelta( $sql );
}
```

This table contains forum ID, user ID, and join date and time of the user. We have to deactivate and activate the plugin again to create this custom table.

Now, we are ready to start handling forum user join functionality. Let's start the implementation by adding a new filter to the header section of `single-forum.php` template using the following code:

```
<div id="wpwaf_forum_info_left">
<h3><?php echo $post->post_title; ?><?php echo
apply_filters('wpwaf_forum_header_buttons', '' , $post); ?></h3>
<div><?php echo $post->post_content; ?></div>
</div>
```

This filter will allow us to add any dynamic content to the header section of the template, including the join button for forums. Now, we can add this filter inside the constructer of the `WPWAF_Model_Forum` class with following code:

```
add_filter('wpwaf_forum_header_buttons', array( $this,
'display_forum_join'),10,2);
```

Let's consider the implementation of the `display_forum_join` function inside the same class using the following code:

```
public function display_forum_join($display, $post){
   global $wpdb;
   if(is_user_logged_in()){
     $forum_id = $post->ID;
     $user_id = get_current_user_id();
     if($this->is_forum_member($forum_id,$user_id) ||
current_user_can('manage_options')){
        $display.= "<span id='wpwaf_forum_member' data-forum-
id='".$forum_id."' >". __('Member','wpwaf') . "</span>";
      }else{
        $display.= "<span id='wpwaf_forum_join' data-forum-
id='".$forum_id."' >". __('+ Join','wpwaf') . "</span>";
     }
   }
   return $display;
}
```

First, we check whether the user is logged into the application since guests are not allowed to join forums. Next, we check whether the user is already a member of the forum by passing the current logged in user ID and viewed forum ID to the `is_forum_member` function. Finally, we display the **Join** button or **Member** as label depending on the result returned from the `is_forum_member` function. Before moving into the implementation of **+ Join** button, we can take a look at the `is_forum_member` function:

```
public function is_forum_member($forum_id,$user_id){
   global $wpdb;
   $forum_users = $wpdb->prefix.'forum_users';
   $sql = $wpdb->prepare( "SELECT * from $forum_users where forum_id =
%d and user_id = %d", $forum_id, $user_id);
   $result = $wpdb->get_results($sql);
   if($result){
      return true;
   }else{
      return false;
   }
}
```

In the preceding function, we use a custom query on a newly created `forum_users` table to check the existence of user ID for the given forum. Then, we return whether the user is already a member or not using the Boolean return values.

Now, when nonmember user visits the forum, **+ Join** button will be displayed along with the forum title, as shown in the following screenshot:

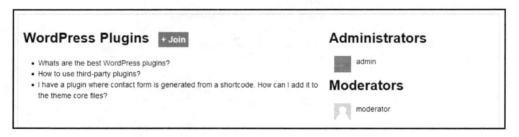

Once the **+ Join** button is clicked, we need to send an AJAX request, verify the user with forum, and save the user as a forum member. So, we need a new JavaScript file to add this functionality. Let's add new file called `wpwaf-front.js` and add it to the plugin using the following code inside the `load_scripts` function:

```
wp_register_script('wpwaf-front', WPWAF_PLUGIN_URL .'js/wpwaf-
front.js', array('jquery'));
   wp_enqueue_script('wpwaf-front');
   $config_array = array(
```

```
            'ajaxUrl' => admin_url('admin-ajax.php'),
            'processing' => __('processing','wpwaf'),
            'member' => __('Member','wpwaf') );
    wp_localize_script('wpwaf-front', 'wpwafFront', $config_array);
```

Here, we include the new script using the `wp_enqueue_script` function and pass the necessary data using the `wp_localize_script` function. Now, we are ready to create the AJAX functions for the forum join feature.

Let's implement the jQuery action for clicking on the **+ Join** button with the following code inside the `wpwaf-front.js` file:

```
jQuery(document).ready(function($){
    $("#wpwaf_forum_join").click(function(){
    var join = $(this);
      $(this).html(wpwafFront.processing);
    var forum_id = $(this).attr('data-forum-id');
    jQuery.post(
            wpwafFront.ajaxUrl, {
            'action': 'wpwaf_forum_join',
            'forum_id':  forum_id },
            function(response){
              if(response.status == 'success'){
                join.attr('id','wpwaf_forum_member');
                join.html(wpwafFront.member);
              }
        },"json");
    });
});
```

First, we create a function for the click event of the Join button. Then, we grab the forum ID from the data attributes of the button. Next, we execute an AJAX request using jQuery post. Finally, we switch the ID of the button and change the label as `Member`.

The next task of this process is to implement the AJAX request inside the `WPWAF_Model_Forum` class with the use of the following code inside the constructer:

```
add_action('wp_ajax_wpwaf_forum_join', array($this, 'forum_join'));
```

Since join functionality is only available to the logged in users, we don't need the AJAX `wp_ajax_nopriv_wpwaf_forum_join` action. Finally, we can look at the implementation of the `forum_join` function using the following code:

```
public function forum_join(){
    global $wpdb;
    $forum_id = isset($_POST['forum_id']) ?(int)$_POST['forum_id']: 0;
    $response = array();

    if(is_user_logged_in()){
      $user_id = get_current_user_id();
      if(!$this->is_forum_member($forum_id,$user_id)){
        $forum_users = $wpdb->prefix.'forum_users';
        $wpdb->insert(
            $forum_users,
array(
            'user_id' => $user_id,
            'forum_id' => $forum_id,
            'join_time' =>date("Y-m-d H:i:s")),
array(
            '%d',
            '%d',
            '%s' )
        );
        $response['status'] = 'success';
      }
    }
    echo json_encode($response);exit;
}
```

We start the function by grabbing the forum ID from the `$_POST` array. Then we call the `is_forum_member` function as earlier to check the forum user status after verifying whether user is already logged in. Next, we use the insert function of the `$wpdb` object to insert the `forum-user` relation into the `forum_users` table. Finally, we return the response as a JSON encoded string.

Now, we have completed the process and the users can join the forums. However, there is no meaning to this user-forum relationship until we add some restrictions. So, let's identify the requirements:

- Users should only see the forum topics and should not have access to topic creation until they join the group.
- Users should not be able to view the details of a forum topic until they join the forum.

At this stage, all logged in users have access to topic viewing, and all users with `edit_wpwaf_topics` capability can create topics. So, let's fix this issue and add meaning to the forum-user relation.

Restricting topic creation to forum members

Topic creation is available inside the `single-forum.php` custom template with basic permission check. Let's update the permission check to validate the members with a forum. Consider the updated code for permission check, as shown in the following:

```php
<?php if(current_user_can('edit_wpwaf_topics')
&&($wpwaf->forum->is_forum_member($post->ID,get_current_user_id() ) ||
current_user_can('manage_options') )) { ?>
```

We have added the `is_forum_member` check and the `manage_options` check along with the `edit_wpwaf_topics` check we used earlier. So, we check whether the user is a member of the given forum or an administrator. Administrators will always have access to topic creation. Now, only forum members will be able to use the forum topic creation form, and other users can only view the summary of topics.

Building forum topic page

We have a list of topics displayed in the forum details page. Now, the user can click on a topic from the forum page to view the complete discussion. Here, we need to build the topic details page with the technique we used for forum details page. The topic details page can be implemented with all the techniques discussed in the *Building the forum page* section. However, we are going to use the same technique of custom template within plugin.

Before we start the implementation, we need to create a new table for keeping the forum reply data. So, let's start by updating the `create_custom_table` function to include the following code:

```php
$topic_replies_table = $wpdb->prefix.'topic_replies';
if($wpdb->get_var("show tables like '$topic_replies_table'") !=
$topic_replies_table) {
    $sql = "CREATE TABLE $topic_replies_table (
    id mediumint(9) NOT NULL AUTO_INCREMENT,
    time datetime DEFAULT '0000-00-00 00:00:00' NOT NULL,
    user_id mediumint(9) NOT NULL,
        topic_id  mediumint(9) NOT NULL,
        topic_content  longtext NOT NULL,
    notify_status  mediumint(9) NOT NULL,
        UNIQUE KEY id (id) );";
```

```
    dbDelta( $sql );
}
```

This table contains basic fields for capturing user ID, topic ID, content of the replies, and the time. We also have a column called `notify_status`, which is used for sending topic notifications in later stages. Now, we come to the main part where we build the topic details page. Let's add the `single_template` filter to the constructer of the `WPWAF_Model_Topic` class as follows:

```
add_filter('single_template', array( $this, 'display_topic_template'));
```

Implementation of the `display_topic_template` function is similar to the `display_forum_template` function, except we change the post type to `wpwaf_topic`. The structure of the template is same as the forum detail page where we have basic topic details, form to reply to topics, and the list of replies for the topic. Since, the code is almost similar, we are going to omit the topic details code. You can find the full source code inside the forum plugin for this chapter.

Creating forum topic replies

We are going to start discussing the topic details page with topic reply creation. Here, we need to place a form between topic details section and replies section to submit responses to topics. Let's take a look at the template code for creating topic responses:

```
<?php if(is_user_logged_in()&&
($wpwaf->forum->is_forum_member($post->ID,get_current_user_id() ) ||
current_user_can('manage_options') )) { ?>
    <?php if($wpwaf_single_reply_data['msg'] !== '' ){ ?>

    <div class="wpwaf_topic_msg_<?php echo
$wpwaf_single_reply_data['msg_status']; ?>"><?php echo
$wpwaf_single_reply_data['msg']; ?></div>
    <?php } ?>

    <div class="wpwaf_create_topics_label"><?php _e('Your
response','wpwaf'); ?></div>
    <div id="wpwaf_create_replies">
    <form action="" method="POST" >
    <div id="wpwaf_create_replies_editor">
    <textarea name="wpwaf_topic_content"
id="wpwaf_topic_content"></textarea>
    </div>
    <div id="">
        <input type="hidden" name="wpwaf_topic_id" value="<?php echo
$post->ID; ?>" />
```

```
          <input type="submit" name="wpwaf_reply_submit"
id="wpwaf_reply_submit" value="<?php _e('Reply','wpwaf'); ?>" />
          </div>
          </form>
          </div>
          <?php } ?>
```

First, we check the permission for displaying the response forum. In this scenario, we don't need to check `edit_wpwaf_topics` capability since any member should be able to submit responses. So, we start with user login check, followed by the verification of the user as a forum member. Once these validations are completed, we display a form with a `textarea` field for creating responses. In the next section, we can look at the process of handling responses.

Handling forum topic replies

Once the user submits the response, we need to validate and save the response to our new custom table. So, we can implement this function on the `init` action similar to the implementation of forum topic creation form. Let's take a look at the function for handling the topic replies:

```php
    public function handle_topic_replies(){
        global $wpwaf_single_reply_data,$wpdb,$post;
        $wpwaf_single_reply_data['msg'] = '';

        if(isset($_POST['wpwaf_reply_submit'])){
            if(trim($_POST['wpwaf_topic_content']) == ''){
                $wpwaf_single_reply_data['msg'] = __('Your response is
requird.','wpwaf');
                $wpwaf_single_reply_data['msg_status'] = 'error';
        }else{
                $topic_id = isset( $_POST['wpwaf_topic_id'] ) ? (int)
$_POST['wpwaf_topic_id']: 0 ;
                $topic_content = $_POST['wpwaf_topic_content'];

                $topic_replies_table = $wpdb->prefix.'topic_replies';
                $wpdb->insert(
                    $topic_replies_table,
        array(
                        'user_id' => get_current_user_id(),
                        'topic_id' => $topic_id,
                        'topic_content' => $topic_content,
        'notify_status' => 0,
                        'time' =>date("Y-m-d H:i:s") ),
        array(
```

```
                        '%d',
                        '%d',
                        '%s',
         '%d',
                        '%s'));

                $wpwaf_single_reply_data['msg'] = __('Response created
         successfully.','wpwaf');
                $wpwaf_single_reply_data['msg_status'] = 'success';
              }
           }
        }
```

As you can see, the implementation is almost similar to the topic handling function. The only difference is that we are saving the data into a custom `topic_replies` table instead of the default posts table. Also we don't use the **postmeta** or **p2p** tables in this scenario.

Now, we have the features for creating both topic and replies in our forum. The final part of the template contains the generation of replies list of a given topic. The code for this implementation is a lot similar to the topic list generation code. Therefore, it's unnecessary to explain the repetitive code. You can find the complete code for this functionality inside the source code folder for this chapter.

Final implementation of the topic details page will look similar to the following screenshot:

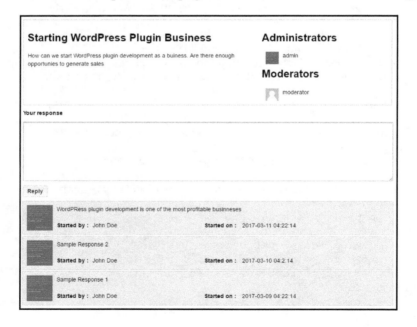

Understanding other forum features

In this chapter, we discussed some of the major and must use features of a forum application. However, there are a large number of other minor features in forum applications. Covering all of such features is not possible as it involves a lot of repetitive and pure PHP code not related to WordPress. So, we are going to identify a set of useful features for forum applications:

- **Private replies**: Usually, forum tickets are private to its members. However, in some situations, we need privacy between the user and the administrator. Assume that we have a support forum and we need the site details of a user to verify the issue. In such case, the user can't add the site details in a reply since it's visible to all other members. In such cases, we have to offer a private reply option for users to make the content visible to admins only.
- **Sticky topic ordering**: We generated the topics list of the forum ordered by the topic creation date. However, we do have different sticky statuses and hence the topics list should be ordered by sticky status. We have to display super sticky topics, followed by sticky topics and finally normal topics. Also, most forum applications highlight these topics in different colors.
- **File attachment support**: We added the support for admins to add file attachments for topics in backend. However, we also need users to attach files in many applications. Most probably, we have to integrate support for image attachments.
- **Topic reply counts**: In the forum topics list, we only have the information about the creator and the create date. We need to display the last user created reply, last updated date, and the reply count to make it easier to identify the topic before going into topic details page.
- **Topic status**: We don't have a topic status at this stage and we can manage forums without statuses. However, it's important to have statuses in most occasions to identify whether a topic is opened, resolved and the criticality.
- **Edit/delete topics**: This is a common requirement in any application for editing mistakes or deleting content when needed.

These are only few of the useful features, and you can find more such features in WordPress forums plugins. I recommended you to try implementing the preceding features and complete the forum application developed throughout this book.

Updating a user profile with additional fields

The forum user profile page was created in Chapter 9, *Enhancing the Power of Open Source Libraries and Plugins*, with the use of Backbone.js and Underscore.js. The **Profile** section of this page was limited to the name of the user as we had very limited information for the users. Here, we will capture more information by using additional fields on the profile screen of the WordPress dashboard. So, let's update the constructor function of the WPWAF_User class to add the necessary actions for editing the profile, as shown in the following code:

```
    add_action('show_user_profile', array($this,
"add_profile_fields"));
    add_action('edit_user_profile', array($this,
"add_profile_fields"));
```

We have defined two actions to be executed on the user profile screen. Both the show_user_profile and edit_user_profile actions are used to add new fields to the end of the user edit form. According to the preceding code, the addition of new fields will be implemented in the add_profile_fields function of the WPWAF_User class. Let's look at the implementation of the add_profile_fields function:

```
    public function add_profile_fields($user) {
        global$wpwa_template_loader,$wpwaf_template_data;
        ob_start();
        $wpwa_template_loader->get_template_part("profile-fields");
        echo ob_get_clean();
    }
```

Inside the add_profile_fields function, we can load a new template using our template loader to contain the HTML code for the new fields. The following code contains the additional fields inside the profile_fields template:

```
    <?php
    global $wpwaf_template_data;
    extract($wpwaf_template_data);
    ?>
    <table class="form-table">
    <tr>
    <th><label for="job_role"><?php _e("Interested Topics","wpwaf");
?></label></th>
    <td><input type="text" class="regular-text" value="<?php echo
$interested_topics; ?>" id="interested_topics"
name="interested_topics"></td>
    </tr>
    <tr>
```

```
    <th><label for="skills"><?php _e("Skills","wpwaf");
?></label></th>
    <td><input type="text" class="regular-text" value="<?php echo
$skills; ?>" id="skills" name="skills"></td>
    </tr>
    <?php
      $countries = array(
        'AF' => 'Afghanistan',
        'AL' => 'Albania',
      );
      ?>
    <tr>
    <th><label for="country"><?php _e("Country","wpwaf");
?></label></th>
    <td>
    <select name="country" id="country">
    <option value="" ><?php _e("Select Country","wpwaf");
?></option>
    <?php foreach($countries as $country_name){ ?>
    <option <?php echo ($country_name == $country)? "selected":
 "";?> value="<?php echo $country_name;?>"><?php echo
$country_name;?></option>
    <?php } ?>
    </select>
    </td>
    </tr>
    </table>
```

Basically, we have three fields for storing the interested topics, skills, and the country name of the forum member. At this stage, the `$wpwaf_template_data` array is empty, and hence these fields won't have default values. It's important to use the CSS class `form-table` for keeping the consistency of design with the existing fields. Now, your profile page on the backend should look something similar to the following screenshot:

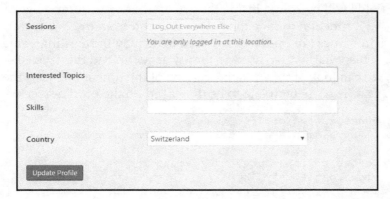

Updating the values of the profile fields

Once a user clicks on the **Update Profile** button, all the custom fields need to be saved automatically into the database. So, we have to define another two actions called `edit_user_profile_update` and `personal_options_update`. We have to add them inside the constructor of the `WPWAF_User` class, as shown in the following code:

```
    add_action('edit_user_profile_update', array($this,
"save_profile_fields"));
    add_action('personal_options_update', array($this,
"save_profile_fields"));
```

Actions hooks defined in the preceding code are generally used to update additional profile fields. So, we will invoke the `save_profile_fields` function of a user model to cater to the persisting tasks. Consider the implementation of the `save_profile_fields` function inside the `WPWAF_User` class, as shown in the following code:

```
    public function save_profile_fields() {
        global $user_ID;

        $interested_topics = isset($_POST['interested_topics']) ?
esc_html(trim($_POST['interested_topics'])) : "";
        $skills = isset($_POST['skills']) ? esc_html(trim(
$_POST['skills']) ) : "";
        $country = isset($_POST['country']) ? esc_html(trim(
$_POST['country'])) : "";

        update_user_meta($user_ID, "_wpwaf_interested_topics",
$interested_topics);
        update_user_meta($user_ID, "_wpwaf_skills", $skills);
        update_user_meta($user_ID, "_wpwaf_country", $country);
    }
```

Custom profile fields will be stored inside the `wp_usermeta` table, and hence we use the `update_user_meta` function to save the values grabbed from the `$_POST` array. Once the custom profile field values are updated, we need to display the existing values on the frontend profile screen. Earlier, we used an empty array to load the `profile-fields` template. Now, we can look at the updated version of the function to pass the necessary data to the `profile-fields` template to be displayed on the profile screen:

```
    public function add_profile_fields($user) {
        global $wpwa_template_loader,$wpwaf_template_data;

        $interested_topics = esc_html(get_user_meta($user->ID,
"_wpwaf_interested_topics", TRUE));
        $skills = esc_html(get_user_meta($user->ID, "_wpwaf_skills", TRUE));
```

```
    $country = esc_html(get_user_meta($user->ID, "_wpwaf_country",
TRUE));

    $wpwaf_template_data['interested_topics'] = $interested_topics;
    $wpwaf_template_data['skills'] = $skills;
    $wpwaf_template_data['country'] = $country;
    ob_start();
    $wpwa_template_loader->get_template_part("profile-fields");
    echo ob_get_clean();
}
```

With the new implementation, we can access the template variables inside the template using the $wpwaf_template_data array. Having completed the profile field creation, we can now move onto our main goal of displaying the profile details inside the forum member profile screen in the frontend. We can easily use the get_user_meta function to retrieve the necessary profile details. Let's look at the updated version of the create_forum_member_profile function inside the WPWAF_User class:

```
    public function create_forum_member_profile($forum_member_id) {
        global $wpwaf, $wpwaf_topics_data, $wpwa_template_loader;

        $user_query = new WP_User_Query(array('include' =>
array($forum_member_id)));

        $wpwaf_topics_data = array();
        foreach ($user_query->results as $forum_member) {
            $wpwaf_topics_data['display_name'] =
$forum_member->data->display_name;
            $wpwaf_topics_data['interested_topics'] =
get_user_meta($forum_member->ID, "_wpwaf_interested_topics", TRUE);
            $wpwaf_topics_data['skills'] = get_user_meta($forum_member->ID,
"_wpwaf_skills", TRUE);
            $wpwaf_topics_data['country'] = get_user_meta($forum_member->ID,
"_wpwaf_country", TRUE);
        }

        $current_user = wp_get_current_user();

        $wpwaf_topics_data['forum_member_status'] = ($current_user->ID ==
$forum_member_id);
        $wpwaf_topics_data['forum_member_id'] = $forum_member_id;
        $wpwaf_topics_data['forum_list'] = $wpwaf->forum->get_forum_list();

        $wpwa_template_loader->get_template_part("forum-member");
        exit;
    }
```

Here, we have retrieved all the custom profile fields to be passed as template variables. Finally, the process will be completed by updating the `forum-member-template.php` template to include the profile field data, as shown in the following code:

```
<div class='forum_member_profile_panel'>
<h2><?php echo __('Personal Information','wpwaf'); ?></h2>
<div class='field_label'><?php echo __('Full Name','wpwaf'); ?></div>
<div class='field_value'><?php echo esc_html(
$wpwaf_topics_data['display_name']); ?></div>
<div class='field_label'><?php echo __('Interested Topics','wpwaf');
?></div>
<div class='field_value'><?php echo esc_html(
$wpwaf_topics_data['interested_topics']); ?></div>
<div class='field_label'><?php echo __('Skills','wpwaf'); ?></div>
<div class='field_value'><?php echo esc_html(
$wpwaf_topics_data['skills']); ?></div>
<div class='field_label'><?php echo __('Country','wpwaf'); ?></div>
<div class='field_value'><?php echo esc_html(
$wpwaf_topics_data['country']); ?></div>
</div>
```

Now, go to the browser and access `/user/profile/{user id}` and you will get a screenshot similar to the following one:

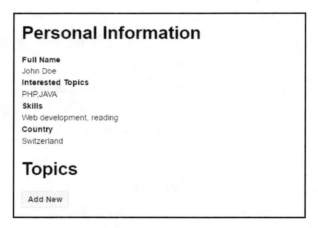

So, we have completed the process of adding and displaying custom profile fields. In the next section, we will be completing the implementations of this book by developing the topic subscriber notification scheduling.

Scheduling subscriber notifications

Sending notifications is a common task in any web application. In this scenario, we have subscribers who want to receive e-mail updates about forum activities. In Chapter 9, *Enhancing the Power of Open Source Libraries and Plugins,* we created a simple e-mail notification system on post publish for sending e-mail notifications for topic creators and administrators. Using the same technique used for sending forum topic updates can become impossible due to the large number of subscribers. Therefore, we will take a look at the scheduling features of WordPress for automating the notification sending process.

As a developer, you might be familiar with cron, which executes certain tasks in a time-based manner. WordPress scheduling functions offer the same functionality with less flexibility. In WordPress, this action will be triggered only when someone visits the site after the scheduled time has passed. In a normal cron job, the action will be triggered without any interaction from users. Let's see how to schedule subscriber notifications for predefined time intervals using the wp_schedule_event function of WordPress:

```
wp_schedule_event($timestamp, $recurrence, $hook, $args);
```

The preceding code illustrates the basic implementation of the wp_schedule_event function. The first parameter defines the starting time of the cron job. The next parameter defines the time interval between the executions of cron. WordPress provides built-in time intervals called hourly, twice daily, and daily. Also, we can add custom time intervals to the existing list of values. The third parameter defines the hook to be executed to provide the results of the cron. You should use a unique name as the hook. The last parameter defines the arguments to the hook, which we can keep blank in most cases.

 The wp_schedule_event function initializes recurred function executions and hence should be avoided inside a hook such as init, which gets executed on every request. Ideally, scheduling events should be done inside the plugin activation handler.

First, we have to update the activation_handler function to call the scheduling function on plugin activation. Consider the following code for an updated activation_handler function:

```
public function activation_handler(){
  $this->add_application_user_roles();
  $this->remove_application_user_roles();
  $this->add_application_user_capabilities();
  $this->flush_application_rewrite_rules();
  $this->create_custom_tables();
  $this->create_event_schedule();
}
```

Let's schedule subscriber notifications by implementing the `create_event_schedule` function inside the main plugin file as follows:

```
public function create_event_schedule() {
    wp_schedule_event(time(), 'everytenminutes',
'notification_sender');
    }
```

Inside the activation hook, we have initialized the scheduled event using the `wp_schedule_event` function. The activation time of the plugin is used as the starting time of the scheduled event. We have used a custom interval called `everytenminutes` to execute the task at 10-minute intervals. Since this is a custom interval, we have to add it to the existing schedules before using it. Finally, we have the hook called `notification_sender` for executing a custom functionality. Next, we need to add the custom time interval into the existing schedules list.

This notification-related functionality is common to all parts of an application, and hence we cannot specify a model for the implementation. Generally, we use these kinds of functionalities in the utility class or in a file. Here, we will include it inside the `wpwaf-actions-filters.php` file. Let's begin with the implementation of a custom interval:

```
function everytenminutes($schedules) {
  $schedules['everytenminutes'] = array(
    'interval' => 60*10,
    'display' => __('Once Ten Minutes','wpwaf')
  );
return $schedules;
}
add_filter('cron_schedules', 'everytenminutes');
```

WordPress allows the customization of schedules using the `cron_schedules` filter with the preceding syntax. We have added a 10-minute schedule using 600 seconds as the time interval. Now, the schedules list will have four values including the 10-minute interval. Next, we have to implement the `notification_sender` hook for sending notifications to subscribers.

Notifying subscribers through e-mails

The process of notifying subscribers through e-mails is far more complex compared to the notification procedure used earlier with the publishing of topics. Here, we need to cater to the following list of tasks to automate the notification sending:

- Add a notify status on new topic replies to identify new topics.

- Grab the new replies within the time interval using a notify status for replies.
- Get the list of subscribers for each topic.
- Send notifications to filtered subscribers.

First, we need a way to track the topics that have been already notified and those that are yet to be notified. Therefore, we will use the `notify_status` column value of the `topic_replies` table. We already assigned default value as 0 while creating replies. The `notify_status` parameter of 0 means the reply is new and subscribers haven't been notified.

Next, we will look at the implementation of the `notification_sender` hook inside the `wpwa-actions-filters.php` file:

```php
add_action("notification_sender", "notification_send");
function notification_send() {
global $wpdb;
require_once ABSPATH . WPINC . '/class-phpmailer.php';
require_once ABSPATH . WPINC . '/class-smtp.php';
  $phpmailer = new PHPMailer(true);
  $phpmailer->From = "example@gmail.com";
  $phpmailer->FromName = __("Forum Application","wpwaf");
  $phpmailer->SMTPAuth = true;
  $phpmailer->IsSMTP();
  $phpmailer->Host = "ssl://smtp.gmail.com";
  $phpmailer->Username = "example@gmail.com";
  $phpmailer->Password = "password";
  $phpmailer->Port = 465;
  $phpmailer->IsHTML(true);
  $phpmailer->Subject = __("New Forum Updates ","wpwaf");
  // Remaining code
}
```

We have defined the `notification_sender` action with a function called `notification_send`. The first part of the function contains the necessary code for initializing the `PHPMailer` class for sending e-mails. Afterward, we have to grab the replies with the `notify_status` parameter of 0 for sending e-mails to subscribers. Consider the next part of the code for retrieving posts based on `notify_status`:

```php
function notification_send() {
  // Initial code
  $topic_replies = $wpdb->prefix.'topic_replies';
  $sql = $wpdb->prepare( "SELECT * from $topic_replies where
notify_status = %d ", 0 );
  $result = $wpdb->get_results($sql);
  $topics = array();
```

```
    $message = "";
  if($result){
  foreach ($result as $key => $value) {
        $topic_id = $value->topic_id;
        $message.= "<a href='" . get_permalink($topic_id) . "'>" .
get_the_title($topic_id) . "</a>";

        $topic_subscriptions_table = $wpdb->prefix.'topic_subscriptions';
        $sql_sub  = $wpdb->prepare( "SELECT
tsr.*,usr.user_nicename,usr.user_email FROM $wpdb->users as usr inner join
$topic_subscriptions_table as tsr on usr.ID = tsr.id  WHERE
topic_id = %d ", $topic_id );
        $result_sub = $wpdb->get_results($sql_sub);

  if($result_sub){
  foreach ($result_sub as $key => $subs_data) {
          $phpmailer->AddBcc($subs_data->user_email,
$subs_data->user_nicename);
        }
      }
        $phpmailer->Body = __("New Updates from your favorite
topics","wpwaf"). '<br/><br/><br/>'  . $message;
  $phpmailer->Send();

        $wpdb->update(
          $topic_replies,
  array( 'notify_status' => 1 ),
  array( 'topic_id' => $topic_id ),
  array( '%d' ),
  array( '%d' ) );
      }
    }
  }
```

After the initial `PHPMailer` configurations, we start querying the `topic_replies` table for replies with `notify_status` set as 0. Next, we traverse through the replies and execute a subquery to get the subscribers of each topic of the reply. Once subscribers are retrieved from the `topic_subscriptions` table, we traverse through the sub `foreach` loop and add subscriber e-mails as Bcc to the `PHPMailer` object.

Next, we add content of the e-mail `PHPMailer` object body and call the `Send` function to send the notification to each subscriber.

This process will be continued for each and every post with a `notify_status` parameter of 0. Once the email is sent, we update the `notify_status` parameter to 1 to prevent duplicate notification in the next schedule.

WordPress scheduling works in a similar way to the cron jobs in Linux-based systems. However, we have a limitation compared to the normal cron jobs. WordPress scheduling is initialized based on user activities. Once a user accesses the application, WordPress will check for the available schedules. If the next scheduled time has already passed, WordPress will execute the hook. If there are no user actions within the application, schedules will not be executed until someone interacts with the application.

Currently, we have the call to the activation handler inside `WPWAF_Forum` class. However, our cron schedule will not be registered and executed properly with the current code due the action loading process. So, we have to remove the activation handler call from the `WPWAF_Forum` class as well as remove the inclusion of the `wpwaf-actions-filters.php` file from the `includes` function. Then, we have to add these code to the main `wpwaf-forum.php` file, as shown in the following code:

```
require_once plugin_dir_path( __FILE__ ) . 'wpwaf-actions-filters.php';
register_activation_hook( __FILE__, 'activation_handler' );
function activation_handler(){
    require_once plugin_dir_path( __FILE__ ) . 'classes/class-wpwaf-
config-manager.php';
    $config_manager  = new WPWAF_Config_Manager();
    $config_manager->activation_handler();
}
```

Finally, we have completed the process of building a basic foundation of the forum application. We looked at various different techniques in building a web application-specific functionality.

Time for action

Throughout this book, we have developed various practical scenarios to learn the art of web application development. Here, we have the final set of actions before we complete the forum application for this book. By now, you should have all the knowledge to get started with WordPress web development. After reading this chapter, you need to try the following set of actions for getting experienced with the process:

- Find out different ways of structuring WordPress for web applications.
- Add forum-user permission checks to backend topic creation.
- Link users, moderator, and administrators in topic and forum details pages to their respective profile pages.

- Display the files attached to the forum by administrators from the backend.
- Implement topic statuses to identify open and resolved topics.

Final thoughts

WordPress is slowly but surely approaching as a framework for web application development. Developers are getting started on building larger applications by customizing existing modules and features. However, there are a lot of limitations and a lack of resources for web development-related tasks. So, the best practices and design patterns are yet to be defined for building applications with WordPress.

In this book, we developed an application structure, considering the best practices of a general web application development. The WordPress architecture is different from the typical PHP frameworks, and hence this structure might not be the best solution. As developers, we want to drive WordPress into a fully featured web application framework.

In this chapter, we completed the development of the demo forum application for this book. So, feel free to innovate your own application structures and the techniques.

Summary

We began this chapter by looking at the issues of the application plugins developed throughout the first 10 chapters of the book. Once the inconsistencies were fixed, we implemented a few new requirements, such as subscriber notifications, forum details page, topic details page, topic creation, join to forums, and additional user profile fields in order to understand how to add new features into existing applications and integrate all parts.

Here, we are completing the demo application for this book with the basic foundation of the forum application. You can improve and complete the remaining functionality of forum application with the code provided in book website.

You can now take a look at the next chapter for supplementary modules for WordPress applications. This will be a theoretical chapter explaining the concepts to improve your application with utility features.

12
Supplementary Modules for Web Development

In web application development, we mainly focus and plan our business logic. Throughout the first 11 chapters of this book, we developed features that are directly related to the forum management application. However, there are supplementary features that are not related to the business requirements of the application and yet play a vital part in the success of a project.

Multilanguage support, caching, performance, and security are important features of any web application. WordPress provides built-in features to support these types of non-application-related tasks. Apart from this, WordPress also offers some features that can be used to improve the flexibility and user experience of applications. Throughout this chapter, we will give a brief introduction to these supplementary modules so that you can use them when the opportunity arises.

In this chapter, we will cover the following topics:

- Internationalization
- Working with the media grid and image editor
- Introduction to the post editor
- Lesser-known WordPress features
- Managing application scripts and styles
- Version control
- E-commerce
- Importing and exporting data
- Migrating WordPress applications
- Introduction to multisite

- Time for action
- Final thoughts

Let's get started.

Internationalization

Internationalization is the process of making your application ready for translating to other languages. WordPress itself provides translation for its core by default. In most cases, we will be developing web applications using plugins or themes. So, it's essential to make the theme and plugins translatable for an improved flexibility. We can develop web applications as standalone projects for a specific client or as projects for any client that you wish to use. Internationalization is more important in the latter as a product is used by many clients compared to a project. Even with projects, it's an important aspect of development, when your client wants a non-English application.

In this section, we will look at internationalization support in WordPress and how to translate and manage plugins.

Introduction to WordPress translation support

WordPress allows translation support for plugins using the **GetText Portable Object**. We need to have three things to enable translation support in WordPress:

- Defining the text domain
- Enabling translations on strings using WordPress functions
- Loading the text domain

WordPress uses the text domain to define all the text strings that belong to a certain plugin. In our scenario, we choose wpwaf as the text domain for all our plugins. This should be a unique identifier for your plugin and can have alphanumeric characters and dashes. This text domain needs to be placed in all translation functions, just as we did throughout the last 11 chapters.

Then, we need to enable translations by using the WordPress translate functions. We have to enable translations on every string that gets displayed on the site. The following code contains a sample translation function extracted from our main plugin:

```
$wpwaf_single_topic_data['msg'] = __('Topic created
successfully.','wpwaf');
```

As you can see, we have enabled translation using the __() function and we have used wpwaf as the text domain. Let's consider the translation functions in WordPress.

The translation functions in WordPress

WordPress provides a lot of translation functions for different scenarios. Among those functions, __ and _e are the most frequently used functions. Both these functions retrieve translated strings using the WordPress translate function. The difference between the two functions is that the first one returns the translated string, while the latter directly displays the translated string. Generally, we can use __() for variables and business logic, while _e() is used for templates. Apart from these two functions, there are many other functions such as _n(), _x(), esc_attr__(), and so on. These functions will be used in advanced use cases. You can learn more about these functions inside the codex using http://codex.wordpress.org/Function_Reference/translate.

Creating plugin translations

Most popular plugins are translation-ready, which means you can use the built-in translation files or create translation files for any language. However, this feature seems to be lacking in many less popular plugins, as well as in application plugins that were built for a specific website. So, as a developer, it's important to understand how to add support for translation files and create translation files from scratch. Let's see how we can build a fully translatable plugin. Create a new plugin in a file called wpwaf-lang.php. Then, add a shortcode with a translatable string, as shown in the following code:

```php
<?php
// Plugin information
add_shortcode('wpwaf_lang_checker','wpwaf_lang_checker');
functionwpwaf_lang_checker(){
  $app_name = "<h1>" . __('My Application','wpwaflang') .
"</h1>";
  return $app_name;
}
```

Here, we have a basic shortcode that displays the text My Application inside a header tag. We have enabled translation using the __() function and we have used wpwaflang as the plugin text domain. Now, we need to create translation files for this plugin.

Creating the POT file using Eazy Po

First, we have to create the **Portable Object Template** (**POT**) file for the plugin. This file is considered as the base for translations. If you want to create a translation for a new language, you have to use this file and generate the translation file. Apart from the .pot file, we also have the .mo and .po files. The **Portable Object** (**PO**) file is what we get as the result by translating the .pot file. The **Machine Object** (**MO**) file contains a compiled version of the .po file and is used to apply the translations. Having gotten a basic introduction to these file types, now we can move into creating those fields.

We can use the *Eazy Po* software to generate the .pot file for our application. You can download Eazy Po from http://www.eazypo.ca/download.html/. This is a portable application that doesn't require an installation. We have chosen this software since it's easier to create a .pot file with this tool. We can click on the EazyPo.exe file to open the tool. Once Eazy Po is opened, you can click on **File** | **New from source code files** to create a .pot file for our plugin. You will get a screenshot similar to following:

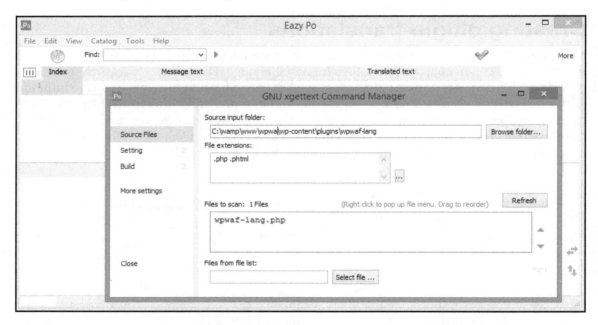

We have to provide the path for the source code folder and it will detect the files to scan in our plugin. Since we are using a sample plugin, we only have one file in this scenario. Next, you can click on the **Build** tab and define the output location for the .pot file, as shown in the following screenshot:

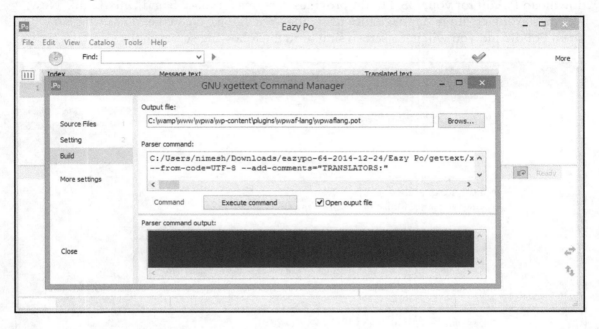

Finally, you can click on the **Execute command** button and the .pot file will be generated on the specified location. It will also load the .pot file with available translations.

We can use this tool to create, edit, and translate files using the .pot file. However, we are going to explain these features with *PoEdit* software since it's the most popular tool and it support multiple operating systems.

Creating and editing translations with PoEdit

We can use the PoEdit software to generate and manage translations. You can download *PoEdit* from `https://poedit.net/`. I have downloaded the version for Windows. You can download PoEdit for your OS. PoEdit provides versions for macOS and Unix/Linux. Now, we can starting creating language files using the `.pot` file we created earlier using Eazy Po. Open PoEdit and you will get a screen similar to the following screenshot:

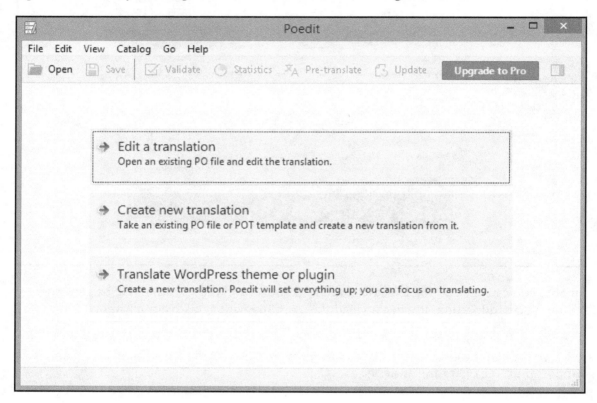

We can click on the **Create new translation** option and it will ask you to specify the location of the POT file. Once location is provided, it will load the POT file with available translations, as shown in the following screen:

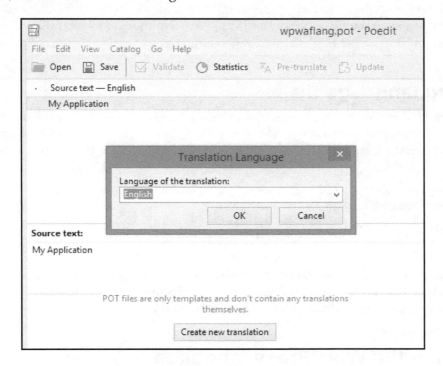

Now, we have to click on the **Create new translation** button and it will ask you to specify the language for the translation. First, we define English since it's the most commonly used language. Then you can add your translations in the **Translation** field in front of the available strings in the POT file.

Once translations are added, we can click on the **Save** button on the top menu to save the translation file. We have to save the translation file using the combination of translation slug for the plugin and the language code. So, our English file should be saved as wpwalang-en_US.po in the lang folder of our plugin. In here, we use wpwalang as the text domain and then en_US as the language. Once the .po file is saved, it will automatically create the compiled .mo file.

Now, let's create another file for the French language. We have to open the POT file again and follow the same process. This time we need to select French as the language. In this case, we have to add translations. So, get the translated text for **My Application** and add it to the **Translation** section. We have to repeat this task for all other translations. Then, choose **Save** and save the file as wpwalang-fr_FR.po in the lang folder. Now, we have two translation files for the English and French languages.

Loading language files

Now, we have to let WordPress know that there are translation files available for this plugin. WordPress provides a function called load_plugin_textdomain to define the translation file path. Let's add the following code to our plugin for the loading plugin text domain:

```
add_action('init', 'wpwaf_lang_textdomain');
functionwpwaf_lang_textdomain() {
  load_plugin_textdomain('wpwaflang', false, dirname(
 plugin_basename( __FILE__ ) ) . '/lang');
}
```

We have added the path to our language files folder with the plugin text domain. Now, WordPress will look for translation files with the prefix wpwaflang followed by the language code. Now, everything is set up for the translation support for our new plugin.

Changing the WordPress language

WordPress version 4.0 and later allows us to change the site language from the admin section. Once the language is changed, the text in our plugin will be displayed in their respective language. Let's change the language to French using **Site Language** in the WordPress **Settings** | **General** section, as shown in the following screenshot:

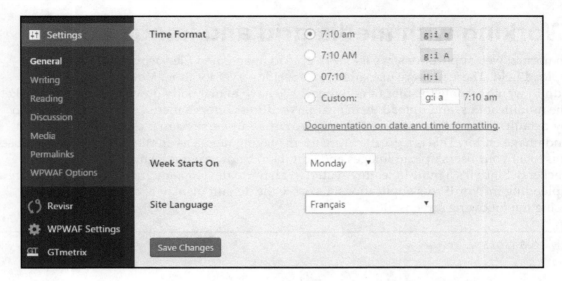

Once the language is changed, you will see the French version of the WordPress admin section. Now, create a new page/post and add our shortcode. You will see that My Application is converted to French as defined in our translation file.

The next thing we need to know is how to update translation files. Assume that we have added new functionality to the plugin with new strings. Then, we need to update our translation files to include the new strings. So, first, we open the .pot file using *Eazy Po* and recreate it with the new strings and save in the same location. Then we can load the language files using *PoEdit* and click on the **Update from POT file** option from the **Catalog** menu. It will ask you for the location of the POT file. Once the location is added, new translation strings will appear on the file with existing translations. Then you have to add translations for new strings and save the file as usual.

By following this process, you can make the plugins ready for translation to any language you want.

Working with media grid and image editor

In normal web applications, we let users upload images and files using the HTML file upload field. These files are uploaded to a specific server location. However, what if the admin wants to view the files or edit them? We have to manually download the files, make the modifications, and upload them again. WordPress offers a media management section by default. This section is improved in WordPress 4.0+ versions to include the media grid and image editor. This is a great feature for managing media as administrators. You can use this to let your users upload images and edit them before saving them in the WordPress backend. Since it's a built-in feature, you don't have to develop any functionality for image uploading in WordPress applications. Let's see the default display of the new media grid using the following screenshot:

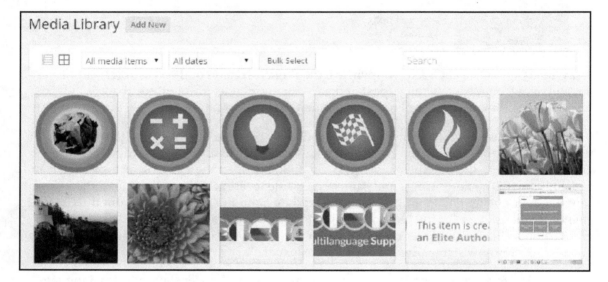

Once you click on a single item, all the details will be displayed in a pop-up menu with the ability to navigate between the other media items. Also it lets us edit images instantly without needing any tools. The following screenshot previews the media item information screen:

As a developer, you have to get the support of the WordPress media uploader and image editor to let users upload and manage images, especially in the admin section.

Introduction to the post editor

The WordPress post editor provides amazing features to edit the content of your site. It's improving with every version, and now we have come to a stage where we are considering frontend direct content editing. The default post editor provides lots of built-in items to format your content using HTML tags. Also, we use the post editor for adding shortcodes to content through buttons.

Using the WordPress editor

In web applications, we usually need to use text areas to get descriptive information from the user. In such scenarios, we just put the default HTML text area field or use a comprehensive editor such as *TinyMCE*. Adding and configuring these types of editors usually takes a lot of time. In WordPress, we have the ability to use a built-in editor anywhere you wish. Normally, we see it as the post/page editor. However, we can use it on both the frontend and backend of the application by just including the `wp_editor` function. This will create a nice content editor similar to the WordPress post editor. The following code shows the syntax of the `wp_editor` function:

```
wp_editor( $content, $editor_id, $settings = array() );
```

Once this line is used, you will get a great looking content editor, as shown in the following screenshot:

Once it's enabled, users can edit and format the content without any issues. Also, it offers the **Add Media** button, allowing users to upload images instantly and place them inside the content. In a normal application, we have to upload the file separately, get the URL manually, and add it to the content. So, developers should use `wp_editor` whenever possible instead of default text areas or manually adding editors such as TinyMCE.

Recent WordPress versions have also included some useful and time-saving features into the WordPress editor. Let's get a brief introduction to some of the new features in content editor.

Keyboard shortcuts

Now, we have the ability to use keyboard shortcuts for the items in WordPress visual editor. We can see the keyboard shortcut of each item by hovering over the icon. The following screenshot previews editor items with keyboard shortcuts:

Editor item locations

In recent versions, you can see a change in item locations. Some of the buttons are removed and some items have changed locations. Now, the paragraph drop-down appears on the top section of the menu instead of the bottom since it is used frequently.

Highlighting broken links

We can invalid broken or invalid links in the post editor by mistake. Once the post is published, users have major issues since the link is broken and there is no way to identify the correct link. This feature highlights the broken links, and hence we can fix these links before we publish the post. The following screenshot shows the content editor with a broken link:

These are some of the new features in WordPress editor. WordPress keeps improving the editor with new features and we will see many more time saving features in the near future.

Video embedding

Video embedding is also quite a useful feature in developing applications. These days, most applications use videos to provide content. The WordPress editor allows you to just paste the URL as text and get the embedded video as the output. Without this feature, we need to upload videos or get the link, find the embedded code, and display the video manually. In an application where you need to embed videos, this feature becomes handy.

This feature doesn't work with any URL. WordPress provides a list of predefined providers that support URL embedding. The following are some of the popular providers that are supported through this feature:

- Vimeo
- YouTube
- Twitter
- Flickr
- Instagram
- SlideShare

You can find the complete providers list at `http://codex.wordpress.org/Embeds`.

Lesser-known WordPress features

Throughout this book, we have looked at the major components related to web application development. WordPress also offers some additional features that are rarely noticed among the developer community. Let's get a brief introduction to the following lesser-known features of WordPress:

- Caching
- Transients
- Testing
- Security
- Performance

Caching

In complex web applications, performance becomes a critical task. There are various ways of improving the performance from the application level as well as the database level. Caching is one of the major features of the performance-improving process, where you keep the result of complex logic or larger files in the memory or database for quick retrievals. WordPress offers a set of functions for managing caching within applications. Caching is provided through a class called WP_Object_Cache, which can be used effectively to manage a non-persistent cache.

We can cache the data using the built-in wp_cache_add function, as defined in the following code:

```
wp_cache_add( $key, $data, $group, $expire );
```

The cached data is added using a specific key as the first parameter. The $group parameter defines the group name of the cached data. It's somewhat similar to namespacing, where we are allowed to create the same class inside multiple namespaces. By defining the $group parameter, we allow the possibility of creating duplicate cache keys in different groups. The fourth and final parameter defines the expiration time for the cached data.

The cached data can be accessed using the wp_cache_get function, as shown in the following code:

```
wp_cache_get( $key, $group );
```

The existing functions allow you to manage caching functionality for simple use cases. However, this might not be the best solution for larger web applications.

 The non-persistent nature of WordPress cache is a limitation where you lose all the cached data on page refresh.

More information about WordPress caching can be accessed from the codex at http://codex.wordpress.org/Class_Reference/WP_Object_Cache.

Generally, developers prefer the automation of caching tasks using existing plugins. So, let's look at some of the most popular plugins for providing caching inside WordPress:

- W3 Total Cache: http://wordpress.org/plugins/w3-total-cache/
- WP Super Cache: http://wordpress.org/plugins/wp-super-cache/

These are the most popular caching plugins, exceeding over seven million downloads in combination inside the WordPress plugin directory. Developers have to get used to these plugins to cater to the performance of complex applications.

Transients

A WordPress transient API caters to the limitations of the caching functions by providing a database-level cache for temporary time intervals. Compared to caching, transients are used by many developers for working with large web applications. Transient functions work in a manner similar to caching functions, where we have functions for settings and getting transient values. An example usage of transients is illustrated in the following code:

```
set_transient( $transient, $value, $expiration );
get_transient( $transient );
```

The syntax of the transient functions is similar to the caching function with the exception of the `group` parameter. Each and every transient value will be stored in the `wp_options` table as a single row. The following screenshot shows a typical database result set with transient values:

option_id	option_name ▾	option_value	autoload
1572	_transient_timeout_project_error_message_95	1370667651	no
1597	_transient_timeout_project_error_message_119	1370675035	no
1593	_transient_timeout_project_error_message_116	1370674749	no
1591	_transient_timeout_project_error_message_115	1370674729	no
1587	_transient_timeout_project_error_message_114	1370674466	no
1589	_transient_timeout_project_error_message_113	1370674509	no
1585	_transient_timeout_project_error_message_110	1370674260	no
1583	_transient_timeout_project_error_message_109	1370674061	no
2768	_transient_timeout_plugin_slugs	1375832527	no
1098	_transient_timeout_gform_update_info	1368776863	no

If you are using external plugins, you will see a large number of existing transient values within your database. In situations where you need persistent cache, make sure that you use transients instead of caching functions.

Testing

Application testing is another critical task that is used to identify potential defects before releasing to the live environment. Testing is mainly separated into two areas called **unit testing** and **integration testing**. Unit testing is used to test each small component independent from others, while integration testing is used to test the application in combination with all the modules.

Compared to other popular frameworks, WordPress code is not the easiest to test. However, we can use PHPUnit for testing themes as well as plugins in WordPress. You can find a guide for working with PHPUnit at
`http://make.wordpress.org/core/handbook/automated-testing/`.

WordPress provides a set of test cases for testing major features. Many developers have a limited knowledge about existing test cases as it's not available inside the core. You can access a complete list of test cases at
`http://unit-tests.svn.wordpress.org/trunk/tests/`. Make sure that you gain knowledge about testing WordPress by going through the existing test cases. Then, you can write test cases for your own plugins and themes for unit testing purposes.

Security

In WordPress web applications, security is considered to be one of the major threats. Most people believe that WordPress is insecure as a large number of WordPress websites are hacked every day. However, not many people know that the reason behind the hacking of most WordPress sites is due to the lack of knowledge of the site administrators. Once the necessary security policies are implemented, we can use WordPress applications without major issues.

The WordPress codex provides a separate section called *Hardening WordPress* for defining the necessary security constraints. You can read this guide at
`http://codex.wordpress.org/Hardening_WordPress`. The following are some of the common and most basic guidelines for securing WordPress applications:

- Update the core plugins and themes to the latest version and remove the unused plugins and themes.
- Check third-party plugins for malicious code before usage.
- Move the `wp-config.php` file from the default directory.

- Restrict the access to WordPress core folders using the necessary permission levels (the BulletProof Security plugin can be used to restrict permissions).
- Use unique and strong usernames and passwords.
- Limit admin access via SSH and/or whitelisted IPs.

There can be unlimited ways of breaking web applications and it's hard to imagine and plan for every possibility. Apart from the basic guidelines, we can also use popular and stable WordPress plugins for securing our applications. Here is a list of most popular security plugins provided in the WordPress plugin directory:

- iThemes Security: http://wordpress.org/plugins/better-wp-security/
- BulletProof Security: http://wordpress.org/plugins/bulletproof-security/

Performance

As we discussed in the Caching section, application performance is a very important factor in web development. We might build the best application with a wide range of quality features. But, if the performance is low, users will have to spend a long time to achieve the desired results from the application. If application performance becomes critical, users may even look for alternative applications instead of using a low-performance application. So, it's important to consider every possible action that improves the performance of the application.

In general, improving performance means we have to reduce the time of loading an application feature or executing an application feature, while reducing the bandwidth used for the request. So, we want the application to deliver the results as fast as possible while using the minimum amount of data, especially for mobile-based users.

Let's find out the possible ways of improving performance of an application:

- **Caching application data**: We already discussed this in the Caching section on how caching improves the performance of the applications.
- **Compressing and minimizing files**: Generally, the size of data sent in a response impacts the loading or execution time. As the size gets lower, applications can provide the results faster. Compressing and minimizing files like CSS, JavaScript, and images considerably reduces the size of the response. You can find many plugins for compressing and minimizing files of your application.

- **Loading third-party files from fast CDNs**: Generally, we use at least a few open source libraries when developing applications. jQuery is one of the most common among such libraries. We load the jQuery within the WordPress files to keep the consistency and prevent duplication. However, loading such files through a **Content Delivery Network** (**CDN**) can be used to improve the loading time of such files.

- **Removing low-quality plugins**: We tend to use many plugins in application development, and sometimes we can't check the code quality of each plugin we use due to time constraints. So, some of the plugins with low-quality code or a lack of proper implementation can create major performance issues in our applications. Therefore, we need to check how each plugin affects the performance of the site and replace low-quality plugins with alternative ones.

- **Limiting the number of database queries**: We use many plugins in web development, and each plugin uses numerous database queries. In most occasions, these queries might be slowing down the application without our knowledge. Also, there can be many duplicate queries that can be converted into single queries with proper coding. So, it's important to check the database query usage of the application and limit it as much as possible.

- **Optimizing existing queries**: Sometimes, developers tend to use their own queries when those features are available through optimized WordPress functions. Also, developers may add unnecessary complexity to queries due to the lack of knowledge. So, it's important to identify the database queries that mostly impact the performance and optimize them.

These are some of the main criteria that affect the performance of an application. There are many other such criteria improving the performance of an application. Now, developing plugins or custom code to check these performance issues is not part of the application development and hence should not be considered unless performance is a major part of your application and the existing resources are not capable of providing solutions.

So, we use existing plugins/services to measure the performance in application development and identify the possible improvements. There is a wide range of existing plugins in the WordPress plugins directory for measuring performance of applications. We are going to look at the most popular solutions that cover the discussed aspects.

P3 - Plugin Performance Profiler plugin

This is a highly popular plugin in the WordPress plugin directory allowing you to check the performance of each plugin separately. By using this plugin, we can measure the impact of each activated plugin in any given page. You can download and install the plugin from `https://wordpress.org/plugins/p3-profiler`. Once the plugin is activated, you can click on the **P3 Plugin Profiler** menu item in the **Tools** menu to load the scanning features. Then, you can click on the **Start Scan** button and you will get a screen similar to the following screenshot:

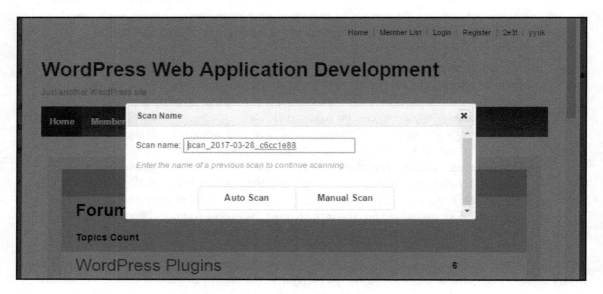

We can use the **Auto Scan** or **Manual Scan** option to start scanning the site. The Auto Scan option scans different content of your site randomly and generates the reports. On the other hand, manual scan allows us to only visit the content based on our preference by clicking the links on the application. Once results are generated, you will have a screen similar to the following with various details:

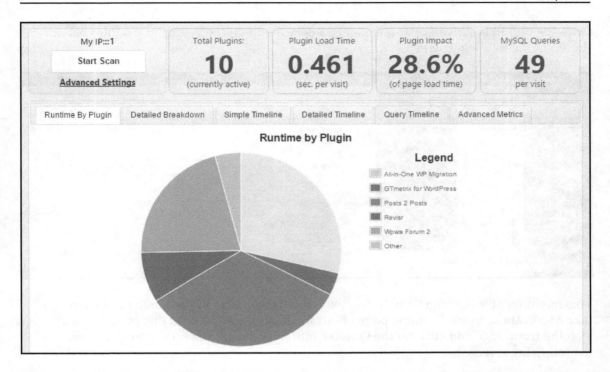

We can see the plugin loading time, plugin impact, and the database queries per visit along with various charts in the available tabs. This allows us to directly see the plugins with most impact. In this scenario, *Posts to Posts* plugin has the highest impact, and it is surprising since it's a simple plugin with minimum features. So, we can look at the code and use other tools to check and identify if there is an issue in the plugin that creates a major impact on performance. After such verifications, we can keep the plugins or replace them with alternative plugins to reduce the plugin impact on our application.

Query monitor plugin

This plugin allows you to debug your database queries including the AJAX and REST API requests. Database queries have a major impact on the performance and, unless properly optimized, they could create major issues in applications. This plugin is the best solution for identifying potential bottlenecks in your database usage. You can download this plugin at `https://wordpress.org/plugins/query-monitor/`. Let's take a look at the functionality of this plugin.

Once the plugin is activated, you will get a query menu on the WordPress admin bar, as shown in the following screenshot:

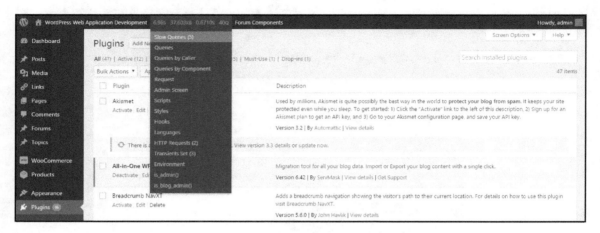

This menu will be available in both frontend and backend for the administrators. Now, let's take a look at the frontend home page of our forum application with this plugin. We can visit the front page and click on the **Queries** button get to get the sample screen similar to the following screenshot:

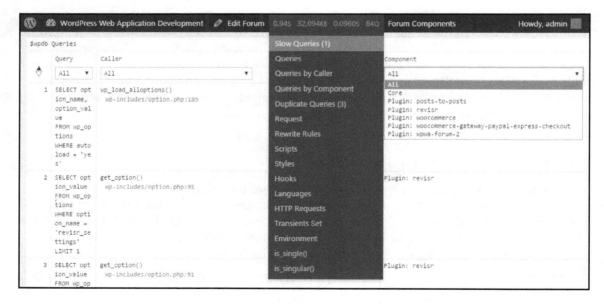

The results show the query execution times, number of queries, slow queries, and many other details. So, we can check the slow queries and find ways of optimizing them. Also, the most important feature is that we can check all the queries executed within the request and the plugin responsible for executing these queries. We can filter the queries executed by each plugin by using the **Component** drop-down box on the right-hand side. This feature is very useful in identifying the plugins that execute most queries and has the most impact on the performance. Apart from these main features, we also get the following useful features with this plugin:

- Shows affected rows and time for all queries
- Notifications for slow queries, duplicate queries, and queries with errors
- Filter queries by query type (SELECT, UPDATE, DELETE, and so on)
- Shows all hooks fired on the current request, along with hooked actions, their priorities, and their components
- Shows the template filename for the current request

So, make sure to use this plugin for your application and fix any issues with database queries.

GTmetrix for WordPress

This is another awesome plugin that allows us to test our application pages with services like *Google Page Speed* and *YSlow*. In the earlier two plugins, we checked and improved the performance of plugins and database queries. This plugin will help us identify and resolve issues and data caching, minimizing, compression, image sizes, scripts, styles, and many other aspects of the application. You can download the plugin at https://wordpress.org/plugins/gtmetrix-for-wordpress/.

Compared to the other two plugins we discussed, this plugin requires an API Key from http://www.gtmetrix.com. You can create a free account at this site and get your API key from https://gtmetrix.com/api/. Next, you have to add your e-mail and API Key in the **Settings** section of this plugin. This account gives you free credits to check your site. You may need to purchase credits when you have large amount of API requests.

Once the plugin is activated, you will get a screen similar to the following for creating tests:

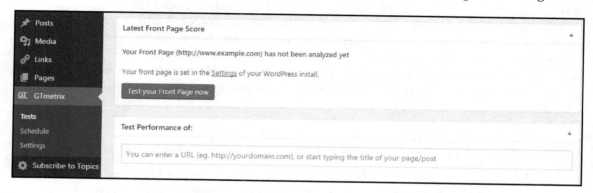

Here, we can test the front page of our application or add any URL we want to test in the second form. Once the test is executed, you will get a summarized results page on the same screen. We can click on the **Detailed Report** link and we will be redirected to gtmetrix.com with the full report. The following screenshot shows a sample report of a website:

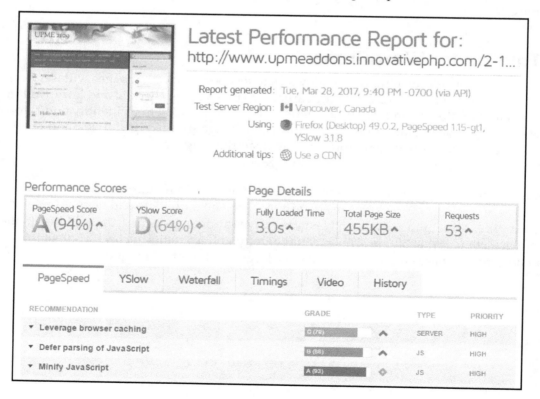

We can view the *Page Speed* and *YSlow* scores along with the scores of different categories and list of recommendations for improving the site performance. We should try to implement all the recommendations, even though it might not be possible to implement some of them in your applications.

In this section, we discussed three plugins that check various aspects of an application and provide suggestions to improve the performance. I think it's a must to use such plugins in application development for simplifying the performance testing process. There are many such plugins available for more features, and you can check each of them from the WordPress plugin directory.

Managing application scripts and styles

In application development, we use scripts and style files from third-party open source libraries, WordPress core, and the files created from scratch for our own application requirements. So, it very important to understand how to load and work with these files properly. When scripts and styles are not used properly, we have to face some issues as listed:

- Scripts and styles of one plugin could create conflicts with scripts and styles of another plugin.
- Possibility of duplicate file inclusion.
- Application might try to use the scripts before they are included.

We can use the WordPress recommended techniques for loading of scripts and styles to avoid such issues. WordPress recommends developers use `wp_enqueue_scripts` for the frontend, and the `admin_enqueue_scripts` function for the backend loading of scripts and styles. So, we have to use following syntax to add the files correctly into WordPress:

```
functionwpwa_enqueue_scripts(){
  wp_register_script( 'wpwa-questions', plugins_url(
'js/questions.js', __FILE__ ), array('jquery'), '1.0', TRUE );
  wp_enqueue_script( 'wpwa-questions' );

  wp_register_style( 'wpwa-questions-css', plugins_url(
'css/questions.css', __FILE__ ) );
  wp_enqueue_style( 'wpwa-questions-css' );
}
add_action( 'wp_enqueue_scripts', 'wpwa_enqueue_scripts' );
```

First, we register the files with WordPress using the `wp_register_script` and `wp_register_style` functions. This technique prevents duplication of files. We can register and enqueue the scripts multiple times in multiple locations and WordPress will only load the script once per request.

Conditionally loading script and styles

This is one of the important aspects of script and styles loading, which is not properly handled in many plugins. We also added all the scripts and styles in the main class without considering any conditions. Including every script and style within the main function is recommended when your application is small and these scripts and styles are needed for most of your functions.

As we discussed earlier, loading of unnecessary files affects the performance of your application and may create conflicts with other scripts as well. So, it's important to identify when scripts and styles are needed and enqueue it on features that only need these files. We can use the existing WordPress tags to check the basic conditions before loading. Consider the following code:

```
functionwpwa_enqueue_scripts(){
  if ( is_front_page() ) {
    wp_enqueue_script( 'wpwa-questions' );
  }
  if ( is_single() ) {
    wp_enqueue_script( 'wpwa-forum' );
  }
}
add_action( 'wp_enqueue_scripts', 'wpwa_enqueue_scripts' );
```

In the first part, we check if the front page of the application is loaded and includes the `wpwa-questions.js` file. In the next part, we check if we are on a post single or custom post type single page before loading the `wpwa-forum.js` file. So, both files are loaded only when needed and not available at the same time.

These conditional files are useful in basic applications. However, we need advanced conditional check functions in the web application since we have many custom features beyond the default WordPress functions. Let's consider the following code taken from the popular WooCommerce plugin:

```
    if ( is_cart() ) {
        self::enqueue_script( 'wc-cart', $frontend_script_path . 'cart' .
$suffix . '.js', array( 'jquery', 'wc-country-select', 'wc-address-
i18n' ) );
```

```
        }
    if ( is_checkout() || is_account_page() ) {
        self::enqueue_script( 'select2' );
        self::enqueue_style( 'select2',$assets_path . 'css/select2.css'
    );
);
```

As we can see, there are three condition checks called `is_cart`, `is_checkout`, and `is_account_page`. The loading of different script and style files are done based on these condition checks. These are not functions provided by WordPress. WooCommerce has built their own conditional functions to cover plugin specific features. Similarly, we should create our own functions that check whether we are on a specific page of the application or whether we are executing a specific function of the application.

Conditional loading of scripts and styles creates a huge performance boost and minimizes the conflicts with other plugins and themes. Therefore, it's a must to use this technique in large web applications.

Inline script loading

This technique is introduced in WordPress version 4.5 for adding additional scripts to an already registered script in your application. This is another way of conditionally adding scripts to your application files. Consider the following code:

```
wp_enqueue_script( 'wpwa-forum' );
$inline_js = 'jQuery(function($){
    $("body").on("dblclick", ".wpwaf_img_prev" , function() {
    $(this).remove();      });
});';
wp_add_inline_script('wpwaf-forum', $inline_js);
```

In this scenario, we have already registered and enqueued the `wpwa-forum` script. Then, we add custom jQuery script into this file using the `wp_add_inline_script` function. The important thing is that we can register the script in one location and dynamically add other scripts to this file from different locations.

If this technique is used properly, we need only one script file for all the features of our application and it will be populated with dynamic script sections when needed. So, the size of the script file is reduced at any given point, creating a performance boost. You have to make sure that you use these two techniques wisely in applications.

Version control

Version control is the process of managing changes to your source code files. Generally, this is not critical in applications with a single developer. However, this is a *must use* aspect in application development with large teams. In such applications, many developers need to work on the same file, and it's impossible to wait till the other developer completes working on the file. In such scenarios, version control becomes a must use feature. Even in a single developer application, it's useful to track the changes. So, let's identify the important features we get with version control:

- **Managing versions**: We release applications or plugins several times with new features. We need the capability to track previous versions and use them instantly. Version controlling allows us to keep different versions using the concept, branches. So, it's very easy to access any version of your application without needing to keep backups manually.

- **Reduce code conflicts**: If multiple people are working on the same code file, we can't prevent creating conflicts and loosing codes. Version control allows us to get an updated version of the file each time and submit the changes to the server without affecting the code of other people.

- **Reverting changes**: Sometimes, we have to try different techniques to implement a specific feature. When the selected technique is not providing the solution, we need to go to the starting point and try another technique. Version control allows us to revert changes instantly and get back to a previous state. The most important thing is that we can define multiple commit points while developing and revert back to any point.

- **Keep track of the team**: If version control is not used, all the team members will be adding code to the same file and it will be impossible to know who made the changes and what changes were made. Version control lets users add their changes, and anyone can view who made specific changes, changed the date and the previous state of the file making it so easy to track.

- **Compare files**: As developers, we don't remember every change we make to the application code. So, sometimes it's important to compare our code files with a previous version or file of another user. In such scenarios, we have to find comparing tools, get the backups, and do the comparison. Version controlling allows you to track the differences between two files without additional tools and manual backups.

WordPress allows version control access for `wordpress.org` hosted plugins. These days, entire applications are built from a single plugin. BuddyPress is a great example of such plugin a that allows us to create a fully-features social network or community site. So, if you are developing applications through your own such plugins, you can consider hosting it on `wordpress.org` and using the existing version control system. Also, it allows you to track how different versions of your plugin are used.

If you are developing applications for different clients and don't want to release the features as a free plugin, you can create your own version control system using the features of your hosting account or use third-party services like GitHub or Bitbucket.

I recommend you to use GitHub or Bitbucket as these services provide a wide range of additional features and SVN client software for different operating systems. Both these services provide unlimited projects for public access. However, if you need to keep your application version controlling private, you can use free private repositories of Bitbucket or premium private repositories of GitHub.

E-commerce

The transaction of buying and selling online using Internet is known as e-commerce. The main components of an e-commerce application consist of product management, order management, stock management, shopping cart, and payment handling. In general, building an e-commerce based site with other frameworks is a highly costly process and hence everyone can't afford it. However, building an e-commerce application with WordPress is a very easy task, even without any development knowledge. Since this is a zero-cost solution, anyone can build his/her own product stores within few hours and start selling.

WordPress offers advanced free and premium e-commerce plugins, and all we have to do is install and use them or customize them according to our needs. Before choosing an e-commerce plugin, we need to identify what we are selling and what the best solution is. We can categorize different types of products used in online selling as following:

- Physical products such as books, CDs, and shirts
- Digital products such as e-books, plugins, and presentations
- Services such as hiring a developer or designer
- Subscriptions or memberships that provide content on a recurring basis

There are a few plugins that offer all the product types mentioned here. However, many plugins will support only a few of the product types and hence you have to choose the plugin based on the types of product you plan to sell.

The next, most important thing is to identify the features of the e-commerce solution based on the following categories:

- **Types of supported products**: We already discussed the main product types in the previous section and it's important to check the availability of these product types.

- **Availability of payment gateways**: Most of the e-commerce solutions provide one or two payment gateways for free and charges for other payment gateways. So, it's important to check whether your preferred payment gateway is supported by the plugin and whether you can afford its cost.

- **Ease of use in product purchase and shopping cart**: The process of making a purchase should be simple for the user. So, your solution should allow the user to search products, add products to shopping cart, check more products, and make the purchase using a limited number of steps without using unnecessary redirections. AJAX-based solutions are the best choice for simplifying the process.

- **Design or theme of the product store**: Design plays a huge part in attracting the user and making a sale. Most solutions work with your existing theme design. However, if the primary function of your application is an e-commerce store, you should consider using a plugin that supports specific shop-based themes with eye-catching and easy-to-use designs.

- **Supplementary features**: Some applications may require additional features such as dynamic pricing, discount codes, and loyalty programs. Such features are not available in all solutions, and hence it's important to check the availability of such minor features.

Now, we can do the selection based on the preceding criteria. *WooCommerce* is the top WordPress solution for e-commerce based applications as it provides all the features we identified in the previous two sections. Apart from WooCommerce, there are other quality solutions such as *Easy Digital Downloads* and *WP eCommerce*. In this section, we are going to look at WooCommerce as it is the most popular solution. You can download WooCommerce from `https://wordpress.org/plugins/woocommerce/`.

Creating products with WooCommerce

The basic setup of WooCommerce can be completed in a few minutes with the step-by-step setup wizard. Then you can start creating the products immediately. WooCommerce uses custom post types to handle products and their details. Let's take a look at the product creation screen using the following screenshot:

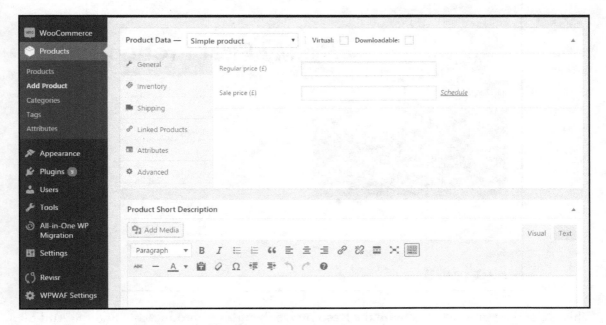

The top part of the screen is omitted and contains the product title and the WordPress default editor field. As you can see, WooCommerce offers various settings for creating a product such as configure pricing, product type, inventory, shipping details, and other additional attributes. So, we can easily manage an advanced store with WooCommerce.

Once a product is created, we can view it on the frontend similar to the following screenshot:

This is a simple product page with the **Responsive** theme with product info and the **Add to cart** button. This design depends on your theme, and there are themes specially designed for online stores. You can get better and eye-catching design by using such themes.

Now, the user can add products to the cart and complete the payment using the users, preferred payment method. WooCommerce is the ideal plugin for setting up an online store and start selling quickly. You can research more about the features of e-commerce sites using the other options of WooCommerce and dozens of free and premium extensions.

Migrating WordPress applications

Generally, we develop applications on a local server or testing server before they are migrated to a live server, after proper testing. This is one of the tedious tasks as a developer or site owner, unless we use the proper tools. When developing web applications with other frameworks, we don't have modules called plugins. So, we have to manually back up the database, files, and uploaded media, and upload to another server via FTP. Instead, we can use WordPress existing tools to completely or partially migrate the application without much effort from our end. There are plugins that allow you to back up the database, files, and media separately, and then import them manually to the live server. We are going to look at a plugin that offers all these features within the same plugin, making migration a super simple task.

You can find a plugin called *All-in-One WP Migration*. This plugin is available at `https://wordpress.org/plugins/all-in-one-wp-migration/`. Once activated, you can click on the **Export** item from the **All-In-One WP Migration** menu item on the left menu. You will get a screen similar to following:

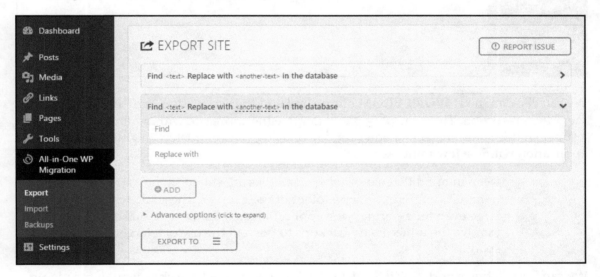

The exporting feature starts with the database replace feature. We can use this feature to find and replace anything in the database. This is quite useful for changing the URLs of custom data to match the live site URL. Next, we can select the **File** option from the **EXPORT TO** setting, and the plugin will generate the backup of your site to be downloaded as a single file with `wpress` as the extension. We can download the backup to our local machine.

Export to file is the only free option in this plugin. However, it offers a lot more features through export to FTP, Google Drive, Dropbox, Box, Amazon premium extensions, and so on.

Now, we have to go to the live site and install the same plugin. This time, we have to use the **Import** section, as shown in the following screenshot:

We can click on the **IMPORT FROM** button and add the exported `wpress` file generated in the previous section. Then, the plugin will migrate the entire site within minutes, making it a super simple solution. Unlike other frameworks, we can completely migrate a WordPress application within a few minutes.

 Keep in mind that exported `wpress` files are stored in the `/wp-content/ai1wm-backups` folder of your server. These files can be very large even for a normal web application. So, you have to make sure to remove the unnecessary backups to prevent the use of a large server space.

We can find all the exported and available backup files in the **Backups** menu of the plugin. So, we can easily restore a site to its previous point using a single click. This is the best plugin available for site migration and you can find many other site migration plugins and tools for WordPress.

Importing and exporting application content

In the previous section, we looked at how to migrate an entire site with all its content. Importing and exporting content is similar, where we back up the database and import it to another site. As usual, we can find many existing plugins for the import/export process. However, most of these plugins import/export entire database tables and it's not the ideal solution in some scenarios.

Assume we want to export all the users with custom profile data in our forum application. Since most existing plugins export the entire database table, it's not possible to export only the necessary content. Export with a plugin will add all usermeta details, instead of only exporting the custom fields we created. In such scenarios, we need to build our own import and exporting features. So, in our application, we might need different sections to:

- Import/export users with custom fields
- Import/export topics of a given forum

Also, we will be using many plugins in web development instead of developing everything from scratch. So, we should check the import/export features of each plugin we use. Most of the quality plugins provide import/export features to the plugin specific data instead of using entire database tables.

Introduction to multisite

WordPress provides a module called multisite where you can create multiple networks of WordPress sites using a single installation. All the sites in the network share the same files. These sites can be installed as subfolders of the main site or subdomains. We need to know how WordPress multisite is used and how it can support web application development.

Let's identify the common usages of WordPress multisite:

- It lets users create their own blog, website, or product-selling website within your site. This is a widely used technique where you let your users purchase a membership to manage their site within your network.
- It manages multiple products. WordPress theme and plugin developers use this technique to create demo sites for their plugins and themes using a single installation.

- It manages the branches of a large-scale organization. Many large organizations have branches in multiple countries. So, multisite allows them to manage a separate site for each country within the network. Since all branches have similar features, multisite makes it very easy to manage.

Having looked at the practical use cases of WordPress multisite, now we have to know why multisite should be preferred over several single sites. Let's consider the advantages of using multisite:

- WordPress themes and plugins are shared across multiple sites.
- You can manage multiple sites within one hosting account.
- You can add/upgrade/delete plugins and themes once without duplicating these tasks for all sites.
- You can control all the sites and users as a single super admin.
- Upgrading and customizing the site is less time-consuming and effective.
- You can dynamically create a new site any time within minutes, rather than wasting time on installing separate sites.

Based on the practical scenarios and advantages, we can clearly see that we need to have multiple sites that use similar sets of features to get the most out of multisite features. Consider the following screenshot for the superadmin section of a multisite network:

As you might notice, this screen is completely different to the normal admin section of WordPress. Here, we have a menu item called **Sites**, which is used to add/edit/delete new sites inside the network. The superadmin of the network can manage these sites, while an admin can manage a single site within the network.

Also, there are important sections called **Themes**, **Plugins**, **Settings**, and so on. These sections are used globally across all plugins. A plugin or theme activated from this section will act as a network-activated theme or plugin. If you deactivate them, it will affect all the sites within the network.

Managing WordPress multisite is an advanced topic that is beyond the scope of this book. What we need to know is how and when to use multisite in web application development. In general, WordPress web applications will be developed for direct clients, and hence multisite may not play a vital role. However, if you are developing an application that provides a service to the user, then multisite could be an awesome option.

Time for action

Throughout this book, we developed various practical scenarios to learn the art of web application development. Here, we have the final set of actions before we complete this book. By now, you should have all the knowledge of getting started with WordPress web development. After reading this chapter, you need to try the following set of actions for getting experienced with the process:

- Translate the Forum Manager plugin using the technique discussed in this chapter.
- Implement conditional scripts and styles loading in the forum plugin.
- Figure out practical scenarios for implementing Cache and Transients.

Summary

Generally, other PHP frameworks don't provide advanced built-in features for supplementary modules we discussed in this chapter. So, we have to find or develop them from scratch. However, WordPress comes with a powerful plugin directory with close to 50,000 plugins. It keeps increasing every day at a speed beyond the imagination. So, we can find an existing plugin for almost all the features we need. All the supplementary modules discussed in this chapter are covered by a large number of plugins and hence we can quickly work on nonfunctional tasks of our application compared to other PHP frameworks.

WordPress is slowly but surely becoming a trend in web application development. Developers are getting started on building larger applications by customizing existing modules and features. However, there are a lot of limitations and a lack of resources for web development-related tasks. So, the best practices and design patterns are yet to be defined for building applications with WordPress.

We started this book by discussing how WordPress can be adapted to web applications and developed a simple question-answer interface using existing features. Then, we looked at user and database management capabilities while initiating the development of our forum management plugin. We learned the techniques of content restriction in WordPress and how to apply them in practical applications. Also, we looked at the possibilities of extending core features as well as techniques for developing extensible plugins.

Then, we looked at customizing the backend features as well as the frontend features with the use of widgets and themes. The use of open source plugins and libraries is a key component in web application development, and hence we had an in-depth look at the integration of open source libraries. We developed a simple API to understand the importance of APIs in web development. Finally, we integrated all the developed components into our application and looked at the possibilities of securing and improving the performance of web applications.

In this book, we developed an application structure considering the best practices of general web application development. The WordPress architecture is different from typical PHP frameworks, and hence this structure might not be the best solution. As developers, we want to drive WordPress into a fully-featured web application framework. So, feel free to innovate your own application structures and techniques that can be used for WordPress application development.

Configurations, Tools, and Resources

In this appendix, we will set up and configure WordPress and necessary tools to follow the demo application in this book. You will also find a list of resources and tutorials on libraries and plugins used in this book. Let's start by configuring and setting up WordPress.

Configuring and setting up WordPress

WordPress is a CMS that can be installed in a few minutes with an easy setup guide. Throughout this book, we are implementing a forum management application with advanced users. This short guide is intended to help you set up your WordPress installation with necessary configurations to be compatible with the features of our application. Let's get started!

Step 1– downloading WordPress

We are using WordPress 4.7.2 as the latest version available at the time of writing this book, so we have to download version 4.7.2 from the official website at
`http://wordpress.org/download/`.

Step 2 – creating the application folder

First, we need to create a folder for our application inside the web root directory. Then extract the contents of the downloaded zip file into the application folder. Finally, we have to provide the necessary permissions to create files inside the `application` folder. Make sure that you provide write permission for the `wp-config.php` file before starting the installation. Generally, we can use 755 permissions for directories and 644 permissions for files. You can learn more about WordPress file permissions at `http://codex.wordpress.org/Hardening_WordPress#File_Permissions`.

Step 3 – configuring the application URL

Initially, our application will be running on a local machine with the local web server. There are ways of working in the local environment:

1. Create a virtual host for running the application.
2. Use a localhost for running the application.

Creating a virtual host

Virtual hosts, often referred to as **vhosts,** allow us to configure multiple websites inside a single web server. Also, we can match a custom URL to refer to our application. This method is preferred in web application development as the migration from local to real server becomes less complex.

Let's say we want to run the forum application as `www.forummanager.com`. All we have to do is configure a virtual host to point the application folder to `www.forummanager.com`. Once set up, this will call the local application folder instead of an actual online website.

By using an actual server URL for a virtual host, we can directly export the local database into the server without changes.

The following resources will help you to set up virtual hosts on different operating systems:

- **Windows (Wamp):**
    - `https://john-dugan.com/wamp-vhost-setup/`
    - `https://www.youtube.com/watch?v=fcvQUwD4lg8`
- **Mac:**
    - `http://goo.gl/mZfVCi`

- **Fedora**:
    - http://www.techchorus.net/setting-apache-virtual-hosts-fedora
- **Ubuntu**:
    - https://tecadmin.net/create-virtual-hosts-in-apache-on-ubuntu/

Using a localhost

The second and commonly used method is to use a localhost as the URL to access the web application. Once the application folder is created inside the web root, we can use http://localhost/application_folder_name to access the application.

Step 4 – installing WordPress

Open a web browser and enter your preceding application URL to get the initial screen of the WordPress installation process, as illustrated in the following screenshot:

We have to select the language for the site as the initial step from WordPress Version 4.7.2. Select the language as **English (United States)** for this installation and click on the **Continue** button. Then we have to manually create the database before starting this installation process. So, create a new database from your favorite database editor and create a database user with the necessary permission to access the database.

Next, click on the **Create a Configuration File** button to load the screen shown in the following:

The preceding screenshot displays all the information needed to continue with the installation. Click on the **Let's go!** button after reading the contents to get the next screen, as shown in the following screenshot:

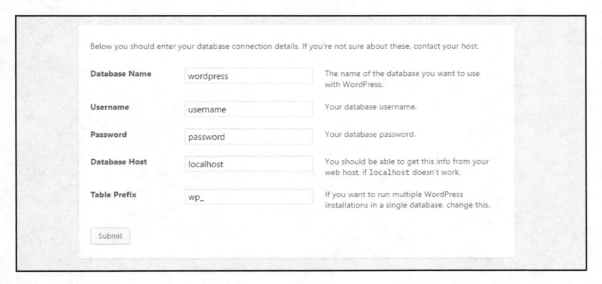

Here, we have to enter the details for connecting to the database. Use the details in the database creation process for defining the database name, user, password, and database host. Finally, we have to enter the table prefix. By default, WordPress uses wp_ as the prefix. It's ideal to set a custom prefix, such as a random string, for your tables to improve the security of your application. Once all the details are entered, hit the **Submit** button to get the next screen, as shown in the following screenshot:

Click on the **Run the install** button to get the next screen, as shown in the following screenshot:

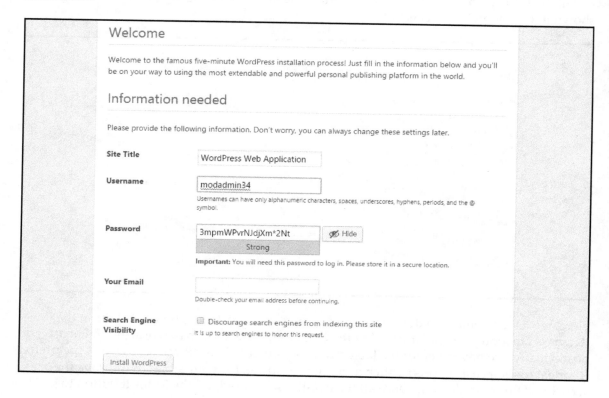

Fill the form with the requested details. By default, WordPress provides a blank field for the username. Ideally, you should be using a custom username as the admin role, instead of admin as the username, to improve the security of the application. Once all the details are filled, submit the form to complete the installation and get the following screen:

Details of your admin account will be displayed in this screen. Click on the **Log In** button to get the login form and log into the admin area. Now, we are ready to go!

Step 5 – setting up permalinks

Permalinks allow you to define the custom URL structure for your posts, pages, and custom URLs using mod_rewrite.

Your Apache installation must have `mod_rewrite` installed and turned on for permalinks to work.

By default, WordPress uses query parameters to load posts and pages through the ID. Usually, we change the existing URL structure to provide a pretty URL. So, navigate to the **Settings | Permalinks** section on the admin menu and you will find different URL structures. Select the **Post name** option for the URL and click on the **Save** button. Your screen should look something like the following:

Permalink Settings

WordPress offers you the ability to create a custom URL structure for your permalinks and archives. Custom URL structures can improve the aesthetics, A number of tags are available, and here are some examples to get you started.

Common Settings

○ Plain   `http://localhost/wp-web-application/?p=123`

○ Day and name   `http://localhost/wp-web-application/2017/03/30/sample-post/`

○ Month and name   `http://localhost/wp-web-application/2017/03/sample-post/`

○ Numeric   `http://localhost/wp-cookbook/archives/123`

● Post name   `http://localhost/wp-web-application/sample-post/`

○ Custom Structure   `http://localhost/wp-web-application` `/%postname%/`

Step 6 – downloading the Responsive theme

We are using a free theme called **Responsive** for the developer portfolio management application of this book. We can download the Responsive theme from the official WordPress themes directory at `http://wordpress.org/themes/responsive`. Then we have to copy the extracted `theme` folder into the `/wp-content/themes` directory of our application.

Step 7– activating the Responsive theme

Now we have to activate the theme from the WordPress admin panel. Choose **Appearance | Themes** from the left menu and click on the **Activate** link under the Responsive theme.

Step 8 – activating the plugin

Now copy the `wpwa-forum` plugin into the `/wp-content/plugins` folder. Use the **Plugins** section on the admin menu to activate the plugin for this book.

Step 9 – using the application

Now we have completed the process of configuring WordPress for our forum management application. Open the browser and visit `http://www.yoursite.com/user/register` or `http://localhost/application_folder/user/register`, based on your URL structure, to load the registration page of the application. You can use the menu and forms to navigate through the site and check all the features built throughout this book.

Open source libraries and plugins

We used a number of open source libraries and plugins throughout the book. The following list illustrates all the libraries and plugins used with the respective URLs to get more information:

- **The Responsive theme**: This theme is developed by CyberChimps. You can find this at `http://goo.gl/Uf9Mp1`
- **The Members plugin**: This plugin is developed by Justin Tadlock. This can be found at `http://goo.gl/HuhDax`
- **The Rewrite Rules Inspector plugin**: This plugin is developed by Daniel Bachhuber and Automattic. You can find this at `http://goo.gl/oBVJmL`
- **The Posts 2 Posts plugin**: This plugin is developed by Alex Ciobica and scribu. This is available at `http://goo.gl/8pQGmT`
- **Pods-Custom Content Types and Fields**: You can find this framework at `http://goo.gl/ixMspf`
- **The Custom List Table Example plugin**: This plugin is developed by Matt Van Andel. You can find this at `http://goo.gl/3tnfmf`
- **Backbone.js**: This library can be found at `http://goo.gl/VyhEDl`

- **Underscore.js**: This library is available at `http://goo.gl/aZ42YD`
- **PHPMailer**: This library can be found at `http://goo.gl/VX90ym`
- **Postman extension**: This extension for chrome is available at `https://www.getpostman.com/`
- **JSON Basic Authentication**: This plugin is available at `https://github.com/WP-API/Basic-Auth`

Online resources and tutorials

Web application development with WordPress has still not matured, so you will find various perspectives from various people about using WordPress as an application development framework. This section provides various tutorials and articles for understanding various perspectives on using WordPress for web application development:

- *Wordpress As An Application Platform, Tom McFarlin* (`http://goo.gl/gONP3i`)
- *WordPress For Application Development, Tom McFarlin* (`http://goo.gl/ubDasf`)
- *My Thoughts on Building Web Applications with WordPress, Tom McFarlin* (`http://goo.gl/fTUqQf`)
- *Why WordPress Isn't Viewed as an Application Framework, Tom McFarlin* (`http://goo.gl/Ophmak`)
- *Using WordPress as a Web Application Framework, Harish Chouhan* (`http://goo.gl/BFHqVB`)
- *8 Awesome WordPress Web Apps Paving the Way for WordPress as a SaaS Platform* (`https://goo.gl/uKdI6Z`)
- *Build an App With WordPress - The compulsory todo list, Harley Alexander* (`http://goo.gl/rwMB6c`)

Index

A

action hooks
  home page template, extending 322
  planning, for layouts 325
  widgets, customizing to enable extendable
    location 323
actions, WordPress 15
admin dashboard
  about 15, 18, 236
  appearance 19
  pages 18
  posts 18
  responsive nature 279, 280
  role 18
  settings 19
  supplementary features 280
  users 18
admin list tables
  content restrictions, adding 272
  default admin list tables, working 253
  extended lists, building 262
  subscribe status, managing 271
  unsubscribe status, managing 271
  using 252
  using, for forum topics 263
admin screens
  admin theme, creating 276, 277
  existing themes, using 273, 274
  plugin-based third-party admin themes, using
    274, 275, 276
  visual presentation 273
admin theme
  creating 276, 277
admin toolbar
  customizing 236, 237
  items, managing 238, 240

removing 237
Advanced Custom Fields
  about 376
  reference link 376
All-in-One WP Migration
  reference link 485
Amazon Product Advertising API
  reference link 383
answers
  star rating 46
API client
  about 384
  building 384
API server 384
application content
  exporting 487
  importing 487
application data tables 110
application folder
  creating 492
application frontend menu
  generating 309
  navigation menu, creating 309
  user-specific menus, displaying 314
application frontend
  about 286
  template execution hierarchy 287
  theme, file structure 286
  web application frameworks, template execution
    process 290
application layout
  customizing 17
  widgetizing 299
application options panel
  building 247, 249
Application Programming Interface (API)
  about 382

access tokens, integrating 392
  advantages 382
  documentation, providing 398
  user authentication, integrating 390
application scripts
  inline scripts, loading 479
  loading 478
  managing 477
application styles
  loading 478
  managing 477
application URL
  configuring 492
  localhost, using 493
  virtual host, creating 492
application-specific theme
  creating 295
application
  migrating 485
  using 499
archives
  restrictions 195
attachment protection 197
autosaving 122

B

Backbone.js
  about 334
  and Underscore.js, integrating 336
  forum user profile page, creating with 337
  reference link 342, 499
bbPress 22
Blue Admin
  about 275
  reference link 275
BuddyPress plugin
  about 92
  features 93
built-in features, WordPress
  actions 15
  admin dashboard 15
  caching 14
  database management 13
  filters 15
  media management 13
  plugins 15
  REST API 14
  routing 13
  scheduling 14
  template management 13
  themes 15
  user management 13
  widgets 15
  XML-RPC API 14
BulletProof Security
  reference link 470

C

caching
  about 14, 467
  nonpersistent cache 14
  persistent cache 14
  reference link 467
CakePHP 11, 50
capabilities
  about 58
  creating 59
  default capabilities 59
  reference link 143
code structuring
  importance 335
CodeIgniter 11, 50
comment-related tables 104, 105, 108
comments template
  customizing 33, 34, 35
components
  admin dashboard 18
  application layout, customizing 17
  plugins 19
  widgets 20, 21
  WordPress page layout, structure 17
  WordPress themes 16
Content Management System (CMS)
  about 10
  WordPress, used as 10
content restrictions
  about 176
  adding, to admin list tables 272
  benefits 177
  implementing, in pages 180

implementing, in posts 180
membership, role 177
plugins 199
post/page restrictions 183
shortcode-based restrictions 180
site lockdown 190
usage 176
content types
  pages 180
  posts 180
  restrictions 180
controller classes
  reference link 406
Create, Read, Update, Delete (CRUD) 114
custom API
  creating 388
custom content types
  about 126
  Pods framework 166
  with REST API 404
custom CSS
  managing, with live preview 327
custom e-mail
  sending. PHPMailer used 354
custom field data
  custom post type, messages customizing 158
  saving 154
custom fields
  with meta boxes 144
custom generated content
  restrictions 197
Custom List Table Example plugin
  about 499
  reference link 499
custom list table
  reference link 262
custom menu pages
  about 243
  and options pages, differences between 245
custom options
  adding, to theme customizer 317
custom pages
  custom menu pages 243
  features, adding 243
  options pages 243

Custom Post Type UI
  about 172
  reference link 172
custom post types plugin
  reference link 28
custom post types
  about 126
  classes 130
  custom fields, with meta boxes 144
  custom taxonomies, creating for topic categories 138
  custom taxonomies, creating for topic tags 138
  features, implementing with plugins 172
  forum class, creating 131
  forums 127
  implementing, for forum application 129
  messages, customizing 158
  planning, for forum application 127
  reference link 163
  relationship between 163
  roles, in web applications 126
  settings, implementation 131
  topic 128
  topic class, creating 131
custom profile fields 90
custom routes
  creating, for custom table data 409
  creating, for forum topics 407
  managing 406
custom routing
  custom template 292
custom tables
  creating 111, 113
  database, extending 109
  querying 115, 116
custom taxonomies
  creating, for topic categories 138
  creating, for topic tags 138
custom template loader
  building 148
custom templates
  creating 71
  direct template inclusion 293
  implementing 64
  PHP templates, using 292

theme templates, versus plugin-based templates 294

using, in WordPress 293

with custom routing 292

customizer

custom options, adding to theme customizer 317

options, managing 316

widgets, handling in theme customizer 319

widgets, managing 316

D

dashboard widgets 281

database management 13

database

autosaving 122

custom tables, querying 115, 116

existing tables, querying 114

extending, with custom tables 109

features 120

limitations 120

meta tables, using 122

post revisions 121

posts, working 116

querying 113

transaction support 121

WordPress query classes 118

default admin list tables

comment list 261

post list 253

user list 260

working 253

default capabilities 59

default roles

and custom roles, selecting between 57

and custom roles, selecting between scenario 1 57

and custom roles, selecting between scenario 2 57

of WordPress 56

dependent plugins

status, verifying 212

development plan

for forum management application 22

Drupal 204, 236

E

e-commerce

about 481

features 482

WooCommerce, products creating 483

e-mail subscription 198

e-mails

subscriber, notifying 448

Easy Digital Downloads

about 377

reference link 377

Eazy Po

URL, for downloading 456

editor

broken links 465

item locations 465

keyboard shortcuts 465

using 464, 465

endpoints

creating, for custom table data 409

creating, for forum topics 407

managing 406

entity relationship diagram

reference link 105

event-driven architecture

versus MVC 12

existing tables

adapting, in web applications 105

comment-related tables 104, 105, 108

post-related tables 102, 106

querying 114

records, deleting 115

records, inserting 114

records, selecting 115

records, updating 114

roles 100, 101

term-related tables 103, 108

user-related tables 101, 106

existing themes

using 273, 274

Exploit Scanner

reference link 377

extendable plugins

developing, tips 232

extended lists
  building 262
extensible file uploader plugin
  creating 214

F

Facebook Graph API
  reference link 383
Facebook login
  implementing 375
file fields
  converting, with jQuery 216
file types
  customizing 220, 221, 222
file uploader plugin
  extending 220
filter
  about 15
  reference link 118, 221
forum application
  application layouts, widgetizing 299
  custom post types, implementing 129
  custom post types, planning 127
  custom tables, creating 111, 113
  forum list, building shortcodes used 296
  home page template, designing 307
  home page, building 295
  home page, widgetizing 298
  tables, planning 110
  tables, types in web applications 110
forum class
  creating 131
  permissions, assigning to 137
forum details
  displaying 424
forum list
  building, shortcodes used 296
forum management application
  application goals 22
  development plan 22
  features, planning 24
  functions, planning 24
  implementing 451
  integrating 420
  planning 23

structuring 420
target audience 22
user roles 23
forum page
  building 421
forum topics
  admin list tables, using 263
  checkbox displaying for records 265
  column default handlers, implementing 265
  creating 426
  custom class, defining 263
  custom column handlers, implementing 264
  custom columns, listing 266
  custom list, adding as menu page 268
  displaying 428
  generated list, displaying 268, 269, 270, 271
  initial configurations, creating 264
  instance variables, defining 263
  list data, retrieving 267
  list, creating of bulk actions 267
  sortable columns, defining of list 266
forum user profile page
  creating, with Backbone.js 337
  events, integrating to Backbone.js views 349
  models, creating for server 350, 351
  models, validating for server 350
  new topics, creating from frontend 347
  structuring, with Backbone.js 341
  structuring, with Underscore.js 341
  topics list, displaying on page load 343
forum, features
  delete topics 441
  edit topics 441
  file attachment support 441
  private replies 441
  sticky topic ordering 441
  topic reply counts 441
  topic status 441
forums, join feature
  automatic join 432
  invite to join 432
  request to join 432
forums
  about 22, 127, 240
  topic page, building 437

topic replies, creating 438
topic replies, handling 439
users, joining to 432
frontend login 90
frontend profile 91
frontend registration
about 90
custom template, implementing 64
custom templates, creating 71
form submission, handling 74
functions, access controlling 68
implementing 62
page template, implementing 63
registration form, designing 71
registration process, planning 73
router, building for user module 64
shortcodes, implementing 62
system users, activating 82
users, logging automatically 81
functions, forum management application
forum topic permissions, managing 24
forum user profile management 24
forum, joining 24
forums management 24
frontend login 24
notification service 25
panel, setting 24
registration 24
responsive design 25
REST API 25
third-party libraries 25
topics management 24
functions
access, controlling 68
do_action function, using advantages 69

G

GetText Portable Object 454
Google Maps API
reference link 383
GTmetrix for WordPress
about 475
reference link 475
GTmetrix
references 475

H

Help menu
about 281
reference link 281
home page
template, designing 307
template, extending with action hooks 322
widgetizing 298

I

image editor
working with 462, 463
inline scripts
loading 479
InnoDB 121
input/output streams
reference link 345
integrationtesting 469
internationalization
about 454
plugin translations, creating 455
translation support 454
iThemes Security
reference link 470

J

Joomla 204, 236
jQuery
file fields, converting 216
JSON Basic Authentication
reference link 500

L

Laravel 50
library
initializing 369
LinkedIn API
reference link 362, 364
LinkedIn app
building 366
LinkedIn
reference link 366
login form
creating, in frontend 83

process, implementation verifying 88
submission, handling 86
login strategies
    configuring 361
    LinkedIn account authentication, implementing 363
    LinkedIn account, verifying 364
    response, generating 364

M

Machine Object (MO) 456
main navigation menu
    customizing 241, 243
    items, creating 243
Mark as Correct button 46
master tables 110
media grid
    working with 462, 463
media management 13
media uploader
    integrating, to buttons 218
member list 91
Members plugin
    about 499
    reference link 499
Membership 2
    about 200
    reference link 201
membership plans-based restrictions 179
menus
    restrictions 194
meta boxes
    custom fields 144
    reference link 146
meta tables
    using 122
Meteor.js 126
multisite
    about 487
    usage 487
Mustache 147
MVC
    versus event-driven architecture 12

N

navigation menu
    creating 309
    menu item restrictions, saving 313
Ninja Forms
    about 376
    reference link 376
nonce value 152

O

OAuth 359
OnTheGoSystems 172
open source JavaScript libraries
    Backbone.js 334
    Backbone.js, and Underscore.js integrating 336
    Backbone.js, forum user profile page creating 337
    code structuring, importance 335
    in WordPress core 333
open source libraries
    about 499
    selecting 332
    using, in WordPress core 332
open source plugins
    Advanced Custom Fields 376
    Easy Digital Downloads 377
    Ninja Forms 376
    using, for web development 376
open-closed principle
    reference link 204
OpenAuth
    about 359
    user authentication, implementing 359
options pages
    about 243
    application options panel, building 247, 249
    building 244
    creating, for plugins 244
    custom layout, creating 245
    WordPress options API, using 250, 251, 252
options
    managing, with customizer 316

P

p2p table 410, 428, 430, 440
page template
  about 63, 291
  implementation 63
  pros and cons 63
performance
  GTmetrix for WordPress 475
  improving, of application 470
  Plugin Performance Profiler plugin (P3) 472
  query monitor plugin 473
permalinks
  setting up 497
PHPMailer
  custom functions, creating 356
  custom version, creating of pluggable wp_mail
    function 355
  loading, in plugins 356
  reference link 354, 500
  usage, within WordPress core 355
  used, for sending custom e-mail 354
pluggable plugins
  pluggable functions, using 231
  using, with functions 227, 228
pluggable templates
  creating 321
Plugin Performance Profiler plugin (P3)
  about 472
  reference link 472
Plugin Security Scanner
  reference link 377
plugin translations
  creating 455
  language files, loading 460
  POT file, creating Eazy Po used 456, 457
  translations, creating with PoEdit 458
  translations, editing with PoEdit 458
  WordPress language, modifying 460
plugin-based third-party admin themes
  using 274, 275, 276
plugins
  about 15, 19, 499
  activating 499
  Custom Post Type UI 172
  custom post types, features implementing 172
  for content restrictions 199
  Membership 2 200
  preparing 50
  reference link 60, 164, 165
  restrict content 200
  Toolset Types 172
  used, for verifying security 377
  using 376
  WP Private Content Plus 200
Pods framework
  about 113, 166
  for custom content types 166
  reference link 113, 167, 170
  selecting, for web development 170
Pods-Custom Content Types and Fields
  reference link 499
PoEdit
  URL, for downloading 458
Portable Object (PO) 456
Portable Object Template (POT) file
  about 456
  creating, Eazy Po used 456
post editor
  about 463
  editor, using 464, 465
  video embedding 466
post list
  about 253
  custom actions, creating for custom posts 254,
    255
  custom filters, creating for custom post types
    255, 256
  custom list columns, displaying 259
  custom post status links, creating 257
post revisions
  about 121
  disabling 121
  enabling 121
post status
  reference link 258
post type templates
  about 161
  creating 162
  using 162

post-related tables
  about 102, 106
  hotel reservation system 107
  online shopping cart 107
  project management application 107
post/page restrictions
  about 183
  meta box, creating for topic restrictions 184
  topic restriction, settings saved 187
  verifying 188
Postman extension
  reference link 401, 500
postmeta table 440
Posts 2 Posts plugin
  about 499
  reference link 499
posts
  restrictions 193
  working 116
private data 90
private page 199
profile fields
  values, updating 444

Q

query monitor plugin
  about 473
  features 475
  reference link 473
question-answer interface
  answers, status modifying 35, 37, 38, 39
  answers, status saving 40, 41, 42
  building 27
  building, prerequisites 27, 28
  comments template, customizing 33, 34, 35
  question list, generating 42
  questions, creating 28, 30
questions
  approving 46
  categorizing 46
  design, customizing 45
  plugins, features enhancing 45
  rejecting 46

R

register post type
  about 33
  reference link 32
registration form submission
  handling 74
  success path, exploring 78
registration form
  designing 71
registration process
  planning 73
Representational State Transfer (REST)
  about 334
  reference link 334
responsive previews
  in theme customizer 328
Responsive theme
  about 244, 498, 499
  activating 499
  downloading 498
  reference link 244, 498, 499
REST 381
REST API
  about 14
  access tokens 415
  authentication 415
  client, building 411
  client, from external site 414
  client, in same site 411
  custom content types 404
  custom routes, managing 406
  disabling 404
  endpoints 400
  endpoints, managing 406
  for web applications 399
  GET requests, testing 402
  POST requests, testing 402
  reference link 400
restrict content
  about 200
  reference link 200
restriction levels
  about 178
  membership plans-based restrictions 179

unique password-based restrictions 179
  user groups-based restrictions 178
  user roles-based restrictions 178
restructured application
  forum details, displaying 424
  forum page, building 421
  forum topic page, building 437
  forum topic replies, creating 438
  forum topic replies, handling 439
  forum topics, creating 426
  forum topics, displaying 428
  forum, features 441
  users, joining to forums 432
  working with 421
reusable libraries
  creating, with WordPress plugins 206
Rewrite Rules Inspector plugin
  about 499
  reference link 499
rewrite rules
  reference link 67
roles, WordPress
  reference link 143
router
  building, requisites 64
routing
  about 13, 64
  query variables, adding 65
  rewrite rules, flushing 66
  rules, creating 64
Ruby on Rails 126

S

scheduling 14
Screen Options menu 281
search list 91
searches
  restrictions 193
security
  about 469
  reference link 469
serialized array 109
shortcode-based restrictions 180
shortcodes
  about 62, 291

implementing 62
  used, for building forum list 296
  using, pros and cons 63
Simple Mail Transfer Protocol (SMTP) 356
singleton pattern 52
site lockdown 190
Slate Admin theme
  about 275
  reference link 275
Smarty 147
Social Locker
  about 198
  reference link 198
star rating feature 46
Sticky Status 407
subscribe status
  managing 271
subscriber
  notifications, scheduling 447
  notifying, through e-mails 448
supplementary content restriction
  attachment protection 197
  custom generated content, restrictions 197
  e-mail subscription 198
  private page 199
  Social Locker 198
  techniques 196
  types 196
supplementary features, admin dashboard
  about 280
  dashboard widgets 281
  Help menu 281
  Screen Options menu 281
  user language control 282, 283

T

tables
  application data tables 110
  master tables 110
  transaction tables 110
  types, in web applications 110
  URL, for creating 112
template engine
  about 147
  creating 150

custom template loader, building 148
   versus template loader 153
template execution hierarchy
   about 287
   reference link 287
template execution process
   web application frameworks 290
template files, functionality
   archive pages 288
   single pages 288
   single posts 288
template loader plugins
   using 209
template loader
   integrating, into user manager 420
   versus template engine 153
template management 13
template name
   defining 149
term-related tables 103, 108
testing
   about 469
   references 469
Theme Authenticity Checker (TAC)
   about 377
   reference link 377
Theme Check
   reference link 377
theme customizer
   custom options, adding 317
   responsive previews 328
   widgets, handling 319
themes
   about 15, 286
   file structure 286
third-party libraries
   using 376
Timber plugin
   reference link 148
Toolset Package 173
Toolset Types
   about 172
   reference link 173
topic 128
topic categories

custom taxonomies, creating 138
topic class
   creating 131
   permission, assigning to 137
topic creation
   restricting, to forum members 437
topic files
   loading 223, 224
   saving 223, 224
topic tags
   custom taxonomies, creating 138
   permissions, assigning 142
transaction management 121
transaction support 121
transaction tables 110
transient 157, 468
translation functions
   about 455
   reference link 455
translation support
   about 454
   translation functions 455
Twig 147
Twig templates engine
   about 147
   reference link 147
Twitter login
   implementing 375
Twitter REST API
   reference link 383

U

Underscore.js
   and Backbone.js, integrating 336
   reference link 500
unique password-based restrictions 179
unittesting 469
unsubscribe status
   managing 271
user authentication
   implementing, with OpenAuth 359
   library, initializing 369
   LinkedIn app, building 366
   login strategies, configuring 361
   of application 371

strategies, requesting process 369
user groups-based restrictions 178
user language control 282, 283
user management features
  BuddyPress plugin 92
  custom profile fields 90
  for web applications 89
  frontend login 90
  frontend profile 91
  frontend registration 90
  implementing, with plugins 92
  member list 91
  private data 90
  search list 91
  User Profiles Made Easy plugin 94
  User Role Editor plugin 96
user management
  about 13, 50, 89
  plugin, preparing 50
user manager
  template loader, integrating 420
user profile
  fields, values updating of fields 444
  updating, with additional fields 442
User Profiles Made Easy plugin
  about 94
  features 94
User Role Editor plugin
  about 96
  features 96
user roles, forum management application
  about 23
  admin 23
  free members 24
  moderator 23
  premium members 24
user roles-based restrictions 178
user roles
  about 53
  adding 54
  application installation 54
  creating, for application 53
  default roles, of WordPress 56
  plugin actvation 54
  reference link 53

removing 58
user-related tables 101, 106
user-specific menus
  displaying 314
users
  joining, to forums 432

V

version control
  about 480
  features 480
vhosts 492
video embedding
  about 466
  reference link 466
virtual host
  references, for setting up 492

W

W3 Total Cache
  reference link 467
web application development
  simplifying, with WordPress built-in features 12
web application frameworks
  template execution process 290
web application layout
  creation techniques 291
  custom template, with custom routing 292
  page templates 291
  shortcodes 291
Web applications, categories
  products 17
  projects 17
web applications
  custom post types 126
  existing tables, adapting 105
  REST API 399
  table, types 110
  user management features 89
  users, registering 61
  XML-RPC API 383
web development
  open source plugins, using 376
  Pods framework, selecting 170
  WordPress plugins 205

WebDevStudios 172
widget 298
widgetizing
  about 298
  application layouts 299
  home page 298
widgets
  about 15, 20, 21
  creating 301
  customizing, to enable extendable locations 323
  handling, in theme customizer 319
  managing, with customizer 316
  restrictions 195
WooCommerce
  about 482
  products, creating 483
  reference link 482
WordPress core
  open source JavaScript libraries 333
  open source libraries, using 332
  PHPMailer, usage 355
WordPress file permissions
  reference link 492
WordPress options API
  reference link 250
  using 250, 251, 252
WordPress page layout
  structure 17
WordPress plugins
  about 204
  architecture 204, 205
  dependencies, handling 210, 211, 212
  extending, with actions 213, 214
  extending, with custom actions 224, 225
  extending, with custom filters 224, 225
  extending, with filters 213, 214
  extensible plugins 213
  for web development 205
  pluggable plugins, using with functions 227, 228
  reusable libraries, creating 206
  template loader plugin, planning 206, 207
  template loader plugin, using 208
WordPress query classes
  about 118
  WP_Comment_Query class 119

WP_Date_Query 120
WP_Meta_Query 120
WP_Tax_Query 120
WP_User_Query class 119
WordPress themes 16
WordPress, features
  about 466
  caching 467
  performance 470
  security 469
  testing 469
  transients 468
WordPress
  about 9, 331
  application folder, creating 492
  application URL, configuring 492
  application, using 499
  archives, restrictions 195
  built-in features, for simplifying web application
    development 12
  components, identifying 16
  configuring 491
  database 100
  downloading 491
  features, restrictions enabling 193
  installing 493, 494, 497
  limitations 25, 26, 27
  menus, restrictions 194
  MVC, versus event-driven architecture 12
  permalinks, setting up 497
  plugin, activating 499
  posts, restrictions 193
  reference link 12, 25
  Responsive theme, activating 499
  Responsive theme, downloading 498
  searches, restrictions 193
  selecting, guidelines 25, 26, 27
  setting up 491
  URL, for downloading 491
  used, as CMS 10
  used, as web application framework 11
  widgets, restrictions 195
WP MVC 12
WP Private Content Plus plugin
  about 200

reference link 199, 200
WP Super Cache
   reference link 467
WP_Comment_Query class
   reference link 120
WP_Customize_Color_Control class
   reference link 318
wp_enqueue_script function
   reference link 337
wp_insert_post function
   reference link 428
WP_Query class
   extending, for application 117
   extending, for applications 117
   reference link 116
WP_User_Query class
   reference link 119

wpdb class
   about 113
   reference link 113, 116

X

XML-RPC 381
XML-RPC API
   about 14
   for web applications 383
   reference link 384

Y

YouTube API
   reference link 383

Z

Zend 11, 50